MEDIUM ÆVUM MONOGRAPHS

EDITORIAL COMMITTEE

K. P. CLARKE, A. J. LAPPIN, S. MOSSMAN

N. F. PALMER, P. RUSSELL, C. SAUNDERS

EDITOR FOR THIS VOLUME

N. F. PALMER

MEDIUM ÆVUM MONOGRAPHS

XXXVII

HELLISH IMAGINATIONS FROM AUGUSTINE TO DANTE

An Essay in Metaphor and Materiality

ALASTAIR MINNIS

The Society for the Study of Medieval Languages and Literature

OXFORD MMXX

THE SOCIETY FOR THE STUDY OF

MEDIEVAL LANGUAGES AND LITERATURE

OXFORD, 2020

http://aevum.space/monographs

© Alastair Minnis, 2020

British Library Cataloguing in Publication Data

A catalogue record for this book is available from the British Library

ISBN-13:
978-0-907570-51-6 (pb)
978-0-907570-67-7 (hb)
978-0-907570-38-7 (pdf)
978-0-907570-48-6 (epub)

CONTENTS

Abbreviations vii

Acknowledgements ix

Introducing hellish imaginations xii

1. Augustinian foundations, I:
De Genesi ad litteram on the soul's *similitudo corporis* 1

2. Augustinian foundations, II:
De civitate Dei on the body-fire composite 8

3. Feeling the burn:
Gregory the Great and Hugh of St Victor
on imagination after death 18

4. Accommodating Aristotle:
new encounters with image and spirit 26

5. Imaginations *as* hell?
William of Auvergne's thought experiment 38

6. Hellish imaginations professionalized:
William of Auvergne, Avicenna, Albert the Great 49

7. Metaphor confronted, the imagination contained:
Aquinas and Bonaventure 60

8. Scholastic solutions: fire entraps the soul,
spiritual pain overflows the body 74

9. Towards a scholastic theory of metaphor 84

10. Negotiations of metaphor and materiality:
from Latin to vernacular, and back again 92

11. Likening spiritual to corporeal forms:
vernacular theology's hellish imaginations 102

12. Images of air: *Purgatorio* XXV
and the Cistercian *similitudo corporis* 117

13. Dante, poet of material perfection 134

14. Metaphor and the limits of language 156

15. Hellish imaginations from the midwives of purgatory 168

16. The death of purgatory and Protestant debate
on hell-fire – metaphorical or material? 188

17. Conscience: the worm-metaphor's greatest tenor 202

Coda: final judgments 221

Bibliography 228
    Primary sources 228
    Secondary literature 237

General Index 260

ABBREVIATIONS

Alberti opera Albert the Great, *Opera omnia*, 38 vols, ed. A. Borgnet (Paris, 1890-9)

Aquinas, *Summa theologiae* Thomas Aquinas, *Summa theologiae*, Blackfriars edn, 61 vols (London and New York, 1964-81)

Aquinatis opera Thomas Aquinas, *Opera omnia* (Parma, 1852-72), at http://www.corpusthomisticum.org/snp2016.html

Augustine, *De civitate Dei* Augustine, *De civitate Dei*, ed. Emanuel Hoffman, CSEL, 40.1-2, 2 vols (Vienna, 1899-1900). Trans. R. W. Dyson (Cambridge, 1998)

Augustine, *De Genesi ad litteram* Augustine, *De Genesi ad litteram*, ed. Joseph Zycha, CSEL, 28.1 (Vienna, 1894). Trans. Edmund Hill, *The Works of Saint Augustine: A Translation for the 21st Century*, 1.13: *On Genesis* (New York, 2002)

Bonaventurae opera Bonaventure, *Opera omnia*, 11 vols (Quaracchi, 1882-1902)

CCCM Corpus Christianorum continuatio medievalis

CSEL Corpus scriptorum ecclesiasticorum Latinorum

EETS os	Early English Text Society, Original Series
Lombard, *Lib. sent.*	Peter Lombard, *Sententiae in IV libris distinctae*, Spicilegium Bonaventurianum, 4-5, 2 vols (Grottaferrata, 1971-81). Trans. Giulio Silano, 4 vols (Toronto, 2007-10)
MED	*Middle English Dictionary*, ed. Hans Kurath, Sherman M. Kuhn *et al.*, in the *Middle English Compendium* (Ann Arbor, MI), at http://ets.umdl.umich.edu/m/med/
OED	*Oxford English Dictionary*, at https://www.oed.com/
PG	*Patrologia Graeca*, ed. Jacques-Paul Migne, 161 vols (Paris, 1857-66)
PL	*Patrologia Latina*, ed. Jacques-Paul Migne, 221 vols (Paris, 1841-65)

The Latin Vulgate Bible is cited from the edition by R. Weber (revised by R. Gryson) published by the Deutsche Bibelgesellschaft (1994). My translations of Biblical quotations by medieval authors generally follow Challoner's revision of the Douay Bible, as being close to the Vulgate.

ACKNOWLEDGEMENTS

Having written a book about medieval paradises it seemed a logical move to proceed to hell, and its hopeful avatar, purgatory. This is a shorter book, not because there is less to say about medieval hells (*au contraire...*) but because here I am focusing on a specific aspect of scholastic literary discourse on which hell cast its reeky light, namely the theory of metaphor: specifically, on the anxious relationship between hellish metaphor and its material tenor. When we read of the grotesque torments (punitive in hell, redemptive in purgatory) meted out to the unhappy dead, are we dealing with metaphor or materiality? Can fire and worms (as invoked in Old Testament prophecy) torment a soul which has left its body? The worm was judged a metaphor with relative ease albeit with some academic sophistication (while legions of worms gnawed on damned souls in the popular imagination), but fire – being an element which, albeit material, had something of the spiritual about it – was a tougher proposition for the intellectuals. The possibility was voiced that the human imagination did not merely make stuff up about hell but itself is an instrument of hellish torment. Aristotelian faculty psychology, so beloved by the schoolmen, posed huge difficulties for that theory, a version of which was contained in St Augustine's doctrine of the soul having a likeness of the body which it carried with it in dreams and beyond death, all ready to experience mental suffering (and pleasure, in the case of the blessed). According to Aristotle, the imagination cannot function without a material organ. But then, that pagan philosopher did not hold the doctrine of the immortality of the soul (though his Christian interpreters cleverly argued otherwise), and his Peripatetic followers did not believe in the existence of demons (as Thomas Aquinas once admitted).

In the pages below, I shall attempt to chronicle some of the clashes between those two doctrines, culminating in a fresh reading of *Purgatorio* XXV. My discussion does not end with Dante, however, since I have offered some accounts from Reformation and seventeenth-century thinkers which, I hope, help to provide a context for our understanding of the significance of the medieval debates. Furthermore, I have drawn on the testimony of several medieval holy women concerning hellish imaginations, not least because it problematizes any attempt to draw neat distinctions between 'academic' and 'popular' and/or 'vernacular' theologies, distinctions which this study has resisted.

Looking back, Augustine's doctrine seems to have some life left in it, given recent neuropsychiatric study concerning the brain-body relationship, particularly the phenomenon of 'phantom limb pain': is the perception of that pain 'all in the mind'? Placing this within an Augustinian perspective (maybe for the first time in history?): if the entire body is deemed a phantom limb, and the mind (soul, psyche, whatever) survives death, could it be the source of pain which is perceived as bodily – though it does not emanate from a direct physical stimulus? (If so, Aristotle was wrong...) This is, inevitably, a highly controversial topic in contemporary medical research, and much is to be done; the Cambridge neuroscientist Horace Barlow has likened the situation in his subject today as analogous to an asexual 'Martian zoologist spending five decades studying the structure and function of the human testicles while not knowing anything about sex'.[1]

Moving quickly on to consider the current situation of hell: Pope John Paul II, speaking in 1999, defined it as 'the state of those who definitively reject the Father's mercy'. To describe this reality, he continued, 'Sacred Scripture uses a symbolical language' which, correctly interpreted, shows 'the complete frustration and emptiness of life without God. Rather than a place, hell indicates the state of those who freely and definitively separate themselves from God, the source of all life and joy'.[2] On reading those words, it is hard to resist the conclusion that metaphor has won out. But that does not mean that the pain in question is any the less. To quote a modern Catholic poet who suffered acutely from hellish imaginations, Gerard Manley Hopkins,

---

[1] V. S. Ramachandran and William Hirstein, 'The perception of phantom limbs: the D. O. Hebb Lecture', *Brain*, 121 (1998), 1603-30 (p. 1626).
[2] See below, Chapter 17.

ACKNOWLEDGEMENTS

mind has mountains; cliffs of fall
Frightful, sheer, no-man-fathomed.

My attempt to fathom some of the shallows of medieval hells has benefitted from comments by Piero Boitani, K. P. Clarke, Vincent Gillespie, Bruce Gordon, Richard Firth Green, Ian Johnson, Andrew Kraebel, David Lummus, Tim William Machan, and Barbara Newman. I am grateful to Gina Hurley and Clara Wild for assistance in acquiring elusive materials. The bibliography on hell is as extensive as hell itself was supposed to be. Consideration of all the relevant literature would require an eternity, and I have not attempted such a foolhardy enterprise. Suffice it to say that I have been particularly inspired by D. P. Walker's absorbingly trenchant *The Decline of Hell: Seventeenth-Century Discussions of Eternal Torment* (1964); Piero Camporesi's rhetorically supercharged *La casa dell' eternità* (1987; translated, not always felicitously, into English as *The Fear of Hell: Images of Damnation and Salvation in Early Modern Europe*); and John Casey's calmly incisive *After Lives: A Guide to Heaven, Hell, and Purgatory* (2009). Discovering the work of Tiziana Suarez-Nani on angelology was an unalloyed pleasure.

Special thanks are due to the *Medium Ævum* editorial team, Stephen Pink, Nigel Palmer and an anonymous reader, for their diligence and careful attention, which I deeply appreciate.

Without the support of my family, particularly my wife Florence, not a word of this would have been written.

ALASTAIR MINNIS
alastair.minnis@yale.edu

St Boswells
Melrose
March 2020
in tempore pestilentiae

Introducing hellish imaginations

> 'I wish you all joy of the worm'
> Shakespeare, *Antony and Cleopatra*, act 5, scene 2

Sawles Warde, a lively Middle English translation of a sermon once attributed to St Anselm, paints a graphic picture of the postmortem punishments in store for those who do not guard their souls well during their lives:

> Hell is wide without measure and deep without bottom, full of an incomparable fire — for no earthly fire may compare with it — full of unbearable stench — for no living thing on earth can tolerate it — full of indescribable sorrow — for no mouth may, for wretchedness or for woe, describe it or tell it. So thick is the darkness therein that one could grasp it, for that fire gives no light but blinds the eyes of them who are there with a smothering smoke, a smell most loathsome. And even so in that same black darkness they perceive black things, such as devils that beat them and afflict them always and harass them with all kinds of tortures, and dragons with tails, grisly as devils, which swallow them whole and spew them out after before and behind, or tear them up and chew them up every piece, and they afterward become whole as they were before for such a suffering without remedy. And full well they see (a horror and a terror for them, and to increase their pain) the loathsome Hell-worms, toads and frogs which gnaw out the eyes and the nose-gristles. ... That fire burns them up all to cold coals; that pitch boils them up until they are completely melted and again resurrects them at once to suffer all the same (and a

great deal worse) forever without end. And this same despair is the greatest pain to them, that they will not ever more have hope of any recovery but are certain of every evil to last in woe, from world into world, forever into eternity.¹

And so on and so forth – there is much more to come in this rhetorically adept pious rant. Which is uttered by Fear, identified as Death's messenger and remembrance of Death. The above passage is designed to strike fear into its readers and hearers, and one can easily envisage it doing just that.² But it also raises troubling issues. How could all that burning,

---

¹ *Sawles Warde*, in *The Katherine Group: MS Bodley 34*, ed. Emily Rebekah Huber and Elizabeth Robertson (Kalamazoo, MI, 2016), accessed at https://d.lib.rochester.edu/teams/text/sawles-warde. Here I follow their translation. The original Early Middle English (as per their edition) proceeds as follows: Helle is wid withute met ant deop withute grunde, ful of brune unevenlich, for ne mei nan eorthlich fur evenin thertowart; ful of stench untholelich, for ne mahte in eorthe na cwic thing hit tholien; ful of sorhe untalelich, for ne mei na muth, for wrecchedom ne for wa, rikenin hit ne tellen. So thicke is thrinne the theosternesse thet me hire mei grapin, for thet fur ne yeveth na liht ah blent ham the ehnen the ther beoth with a smorthrinde smoke, smeche forcuthest. Ant tah i thet ilke swarte theosternesse swarte thinges ha iseoth, as deoflen thet ham meallith ant derveth áá ant dreccheth with alles cunnes pinen, ant iteilede draken, grisliche ase deoflen, the forswolheth ham ihal ant speoweth ham | eft ut bivoren ant bihinden, otherhwile torendeth ham ant tocheoweth ham euch greot, ant heo eft iwurtheth hal to a swuch bale bute bote as ha ear weren. Ant ful wel ha iseoth (ham to grisle ant to grure, ant to echen hare pine) the lathe Helle-wurmes, tadden ant froggen the freoteth ham ut te ehnen ant te nease-gristles. … Thet fur ham forbearneth al to colen calde; thet pich ham forwalleth athet ha beon formealte ant eft acwikieth anan to drehen al thet ilke (ant muche deale wurse) áá withuten ende. Ant tis ilke unhope is ham meast pine, thet nan naveth neaver mare hope of nan acoverunge, ah aren sikere of euch uvel to thurhleasten i wa, from world into worlde, áá on echnesse.
² Hellish narratives like the one in *Sawles Warde* may be classified among those didactic discourses which, as Daniel McCann has described, stimulate and manipulate the most difficult and dangerous of passions for therapeutic purposes, evoking emotions which are powerful enough to enable *salus animae*, the health of the soul. Reading a text generates memory phantasms,

tearing and gnawing, that constant beating, swallowing and regurgitation, possibly have any effect on separated souls, souls which lack their bodies? Obviously, if we are talking of the hell which will come into being after the General Resurrection, when souls are reunited with their reconstituted bodies, material bodies all ready and able to suffer every extreme of physical abuse, that would make some kind of sense, though the putative existence in the post-resurrection world of such animal life as dragons, worms, toads, and frogs would require adroit explanation. But what about hell and purgatory as they are believed to exist at present, the abodes of souls separated from their bodies and therefore incapable, it would appear, of feeling physical pain? Does this mean that our *Sawles Warde* passage is replete with imaginations of hell which, however vivid, function as a sort of metaphorical discourse relative to what hell is really like? How does the imagery of venomous creatures conjured up here, and which also features prominently in such hugely popular other-worldly adventures as the visions of St Paul (in the apocryphal *Visio Pauli*), Tundale, Thurkill, and The Monk of Eynsham, together with tales of St Patrick's Purgatory and the purgatorial spirit Gy

verbal simulations recreated imaginatively through the work of memory, which generate emotions; this is true of all texts, but a particularly intense version occurs in those which seek to 'heal the souls of their readers' and help prepare them for ultimate salvation. *Soul-Health: Therapeutic Reading in Later Medieval England* (Cardiff, 2018), pp. 1-3, 12, 18; see also his article, 'Dreadful health: fear and "sowle-hele" in *The Prickynge of Love*', in *Fear in the Medical and Literary Imagination, Medieval to Modern: Dreadful Passions*, ed. Daniel McCann and Claire McKechnie-Mason (Basingstoke and London, 2018), pp. 17-36. Here McCann builds on Mary Carruthers' insistence that 'recollection was understood to be a re-enactment of experience, which involves cogitation and judgment, imagination, and emotion'. 'Memorial *phantasia* are both representations of things ... and "re-presentations" of experience no longer present'. *The Book of Memory: A Study of Memory in Medieval Culture* (Cambridge, 1990), pp. 57-8. Further, the imagination can compose images of things not present (or, not normally present) in everyday life, the better to provoke potentially dangerous but spiritually beneficial emotions in thought about the afterlife.

(of the *De spiritu Guidonis*),³ stand up to the microscopic analysis of the late-medieval schoolmen, who brought to bear on the subject the best science available to them, allied with theological rigour? Further still: this passage asserts that despair is the greatest pain which damned souls suffer. That may be read as a local rhetorical overstatement, but it might also suggest that mental anguish is worse than physical pain as inflicted on the body, of however intense a kind.

The following study will consider the answers to such questions which were offered by some of the most creative minds of the Middle Ages. Given that 'Hell ... is arguably the most powerful and persuasive construct of the human imagination in the Western tradition',⁴ and therefore a topic of vast proportions, I have focused on two interrelated questions: the psychological, ontological and literary implications of the imagination of hell (particularly its pains and punishments), and the issue of whether the images or phantasms produced by the human imagination and stored in the memory themselves play any part in the infliction of punitive suffering on the soul. Hence the deliberate ambiguity of the phrase in my title, 'hellish imaginations' – for my concern is with both the imagination *of* hell and imagination *in* hell (and in purgatory, that temporary and temporal clearing-house for redeemable souls which will have no cause to exist after the Resurrection, when only hell and the paradise of the blessed – the so-called *patria* – shall stand).

---

[3] For editions see: *Die Visio Pauli: Wege und Wandlungen einer orientalischen Apokryphe im lateinischen Mittelalter unter Einschluss der alttschechischen und deutschsprachigen Textzeugen*, ed. L. Jiroušková, Mittellateinische Studien und Texte 34 (Leiden, 2006); *Visio Tnugdali: Lateinisch und Altdeutsch*, ed. Albrecht Wagner (Erlangen, 1882); *Visio Thurkilli relatore, ut videtur, Radulpho de Coggeshall*, ed. P. G. Schmidt (Leipzig, 1978); *The Revelation of The Monk of Eynsham*, ed. Robert Easting, EETS os 318 (Oxford, 2008); *St. Patrick's Purgatory: Two Versions of 'Owayne Miles' and the 'Vision of William of Stranton'*, together with the long text of the *'Tractatus de purgatorio Sancti Patricii'*, ed. Robert Easting, EETS os 298 (Oxford, 1991); *Three Purgatory Poems: 'The Gast of Gy', 'Sir Owain', 'The Vision of Tundale'*, ed. Edward E. Foster (Kalamazoo, MI, 2004), at https://d.lib.rochester.edu/teams/publication/foster-three-purgatory-poems.

[4] *The Penguin Book of Hell*, ed. Scott G. Bruce (New York, 2018), p. xiii.

At the centre of this inquiry is, as it conceptually insists on being, the role of metaphor – understood as a form of 'transferred' or 'transumptive' language. That definition, which goes back to Aristotle, was perpetuated in medieval poetic theory, and (despite centuries of challenge and critique) maintains an influence on the *OED*'s denotation of 'a name or descriptive word or phrase' being 'transferred to an object or action different from, but analogous to, that to which it is literally applicable'.[5] The question, then, is whether medieval descriptions in material terms of hellish pains and punishments are to be understood as examples of such 'transference', representations of spiritual entities and situations which are analogous to, but different from, what is being described in literal speech. If they are to be understood as the 'vehicles' of metaphoric signification, then identification of their related 'tenors' becomes a pressing issue (to apply I. A. Richards' widely-used distinction).[6] In other words (the words being Paul Ricoeur's), what is 'the conceptual import' behind the 'pictorial envelope'?[7] In a religion which has as its central tenet the Incarnation, at which momentous historical moment the word became flesh, and spirit accommodated itself to matter, theologians who studied the metaphorical meanings embedded in sacred Scripture were

---

[5] Aristotle, *Poetics*, 22 (1457b), trans. Ingram Bywater in *The Complete Works of Aristotle: The Revised Oxford Translation*, ed. Jonathan Barnes (Princeton, 1995), II, 2332; *Three Medieval Rhetorical Arts*, ed. James J. Murphy (Berkeley, CA, 1971), pp. 61-2 (Geoffrey of Vinsauf, *Poetria nova*); *OED*, s.v. metaphor, 1, accessed at https://www.oed.com/. Jacques Derrida has challenged Aristotle's formulation by declaring that, in his original discussion, every word is a metaphor, while Paul Ricoeur believes 'It is impossible to talk about metaphor non-metaphorically...There is no non-metaphorical standpoint from which one could look upon metaphor'. Ricoeur, *Rule of Metaphor: Multi-disciplinary Studies of the Creation of Meaning in Language*, trans. Robert Czerny, with Kathleen McLaughlin and John Costello (Toronto, 1977), p. 18, cf. p. 339. See also Ricoeur's essay, 'The metaphorical process as cognition, imagination, and feeling', in *On Metaphor*, ed. Sheldon Sacks (Chicago, 1970), pp. 141-57.

[6] Richards explains his distinction between tenor and vehicle in *The Philosophy of Rhetoric* (London and New York, 1936), pp. 96-8.

[7] Ricoeur, 'The metaphorical process', p. 147.

INTRODUCTION

compelled, as an unavoidable imperative, to address 'the borderline between the verbal and the nonverbal'.[8]

It has been well said, by Averil Cameron, that 'metaphor is at the heart of Christian language',[9] and from the 'pervasive metaphor in Christian language' it 'was a small step ... to the symbolic repertoire of early Christian art – the Good Shepherd, the vine, and so on. For Christian language, like Christian art, was trying to express mysteries that were essentially inexpressible except through symbol'.[10] And yet: the

---

[8] Again drawing on Ricoeur; 'The metaphorical process', p. 149.

[9] Averil Cameron, *Christianity and the Rhetoric of Empire: The Development of Christian Discourse* (Berkeley, CA, 1991), pp. 58, 59. Cameron gives the example of Ephesians v.30-2: 'we are members of his body, of his flesh, and of his bones. ...This a great sacrament; but I speak in Christ and in the church'. She proceeds to claim that 'the body' is 'the most characteristic of Christian metaphors'; 'The theme of the Incarnation of Christ imposed the language of the body, and with it bodily symbolism, on Christian writing. All the central elements in orthodox Christianity – the Incarnation, the Resurrection, the Trinity, the Virgin Birth, and the Eucharist – focus on the body as symbolic of higher truth' (p. 68, cf. p. 175). However, religious metaphor must negotiate a relationship with materiality, as is brought out impressively by Elizabeth A. Clark, 'The celibate bridegroom and his virginal brides: metaphor and the marriage of Jesus in Early Christian ascetic exegesis', *Church History*, 77/1 (2008), 1-25. She finds that in the Church Fathers' attempts to construct Jesus as the 'celibate bridegroom', metaphorical language rendered present 'the literal body and its sexual passions' rather than erasing it. 'Perhaps', she concludes, the Fathers 'understood metaphor all too well: sexual associations continued to "hover over" the metaphor of the "celibate bridegroom," keeping sexual renunciation as an object of erotic desire, while prompting patristic writers to keep on theologizing' (p. 25). In other words, here the verbal fails to do what, in theory, it purports to do – to suppress the nonverbal. But (to push Clark's argument a little further) this failure seems part of the implicit design, because of the rhetorical and affective power wielded by the metaphoric discourse. See especially Clark's fine account of 'metaphor theory', pp. 2-7.

[10] Cameron, *Christianity and the Rhetoric of Empire*, p. 59. Here Cameron finds a major reason for the eventual, yet extraordinary, success of fledgling Christianity in being adopted and developed as the state religion. 'A large part of Christianity's effectiveness in the Roman Empire lay in its capacity to create its own intellectual and imaginative universe' (p. 6).

'nonverbal' pushes powerfully against the 'verbal'. For Christianity's doctrines and devotions 'teleologically tend toward physical realization',[11] a fact manifest by the mystery of Eucharistic confection which presents the body and blood of Christ on every altar, the somatic nature of so many iterations of mystical experience, the physical integrity of the Virgin Mary, the communication between earth and heaven offered by relic veneration, the imprint of the stigmata ... and of course the General Resurrection, when 'the dust of bodies long dead will return, with an ease and swiftness that we cannot understand, to members which are thereafter to live a life without end'.[12] At which point will metaphors be drawn down to earth,[13] the distinction between vehicle and tenor having been dissolved, as their words have been made flesh? Or will at least some metaphors remain as metaphors, their pictorial envelopes being revealed as transitory, transitional, and ultimately redundant in the 'new heaven and new earth'[14] (together with the new hell) which will then come into existence?

An even more speculative thought also demands attention. Metaphor may play a crucial role in how we think about *any* world – not only the other world but also the present one. Cognitive linguistics currently argues that, far beyond serving as a device for making singular and individual comparisons (however highly valued that function may be), metaphorical thought is a fundamental, indeed indispensable, means of organizing and comprehending our total experience – this being a constitutive feature of many, if not all, human languages. 'Our bodily experience and the way we use imaginative mechanisms are central to how we construct categories to make sense of experience', writes George

---

[11] Dyan Elliott, *The Bride of Christ Goes to Hell: Metaphor and Embodiment in the Lives of Pious Women*, 200-1500 (Philadelphia, 2012), p. 7.

[12] Thus Augustine, drawing on I Corinthians xv.52, 'In a moment, in the twinkling of an eye, at the last trumpet: for the trumpet shall sound and the dead shall rise again incorruptible. And we shall be changed'. *De civitate Dei*, xx, 20 (ed. Hoffman, II, 477; trans. Dyson, p. 1013. This passage is cited by Peter Lombard, *IV Sent.*, dist. xliii, 6 (249), 2 (*Lib. Sent.*, II, 514; trans. Silano, IV, 237).

[13] Cf. Elliott, *The Bride of Christ*, p. 265.

[14] Cf. Apocalypse xxi.1.

Lakoff.[15] This theory he pits against the 'traditional' philosophical view (described as having enjoyed 'over two thousand years' of hegemony) which regards reason as 'abstract and disembodied, since it is independent of any limitations of the human body, the human perceptual system, and the human nervous system'.[16] Instead, for Lakoff,

> - Thought is embodied, that is, the structures used to put together our conceptual systems grow out of bodily experience and make sense in terms of it ...
> - Thought is imaginative, in that those concepts which are not directly grounded in experience employ metaphor, metonymy, and mental imagery-all of which go beyond the literal mirroring, or *representation*, of external reality. It is this imaginative capacity that allows for 'abstract' thought and takes the mind beyond what we can see and feel.[17]

---

[15] *Women, Fire, and Dangerous Things: What Categories Reveal about the Mind* (Chicago, 1987), p. xii.

[16] Ibid., p. xiii. Lakoff credits the 'traditional view' with seeing 'reason as literal, as primarily about propositions that can be objectively true or false. The new view takes imaginative aspects of reason – metaphor, metonymy, and mental imagery – as central to reason, rather than as a peripheral and inconsequential adjunct to the literal' (p. xi). He has in mind the occasional tendency to see metaphor as an unnecessary add-on to literal, precise speech, as a gratuitous, occluding, merely pleasant or frivolous extra. As Raymond W. Gibbs says, metaphor is now recognized as 'not simply an ornamental aspect of language, but a fundamental scheme by which people conceptualize the world and their own activities'; a 'natural outcome of human minds'. Hence, 'theories of metaphor are now, more than ever, linked to detailed theoretical frameworks that aim to describe the underlying nature of language, thought, and communication'. Gibbs goes on to speak of the 'paradox of metaphor', whereby 'metaphor is creative, novel, culturally sensitive, and allows us to transcend the mundane while also being rooted in pervasive patterns of bodily experience common to all people'. 'Metaphor and thought: the state of the art', in *The Cambridge Handbook of Metaphor and Thought*, ed. Raymond W. Gibbs (Cambridge, 2008), pp. 3-13 (pp. 3-5).

[17] Ibid., p. xiv.

Stirring stuff. Yet, despite being relegated to the dark two thousand years of 'objectivist' philosophy, the late-medieval schoolmen discussed below would have gone along with much of it. But definitely not with all of it. Thought cannot always be embodied: if that were the case, it could not survive the grave, and no medieval theologian could possibly advocate such an extinction. Reason would not be reason if it were unable to function independently of the body. Thought may well be imaginative: but is that the case only when the bodily organs which enable it are united with the mind, soul or psyche? There were more things in the medieval heaven, hell and earth than are dreamed of in Lakoff's secular philosophy. The following pages shall consider some of them.

CHAPTER 1

Augustinian foundations, I:
De Genesi ad litteram on the soul's *similitudo corporis*

We must begin with the words of St Augustine of Hippo (354-430), since he, in this regard as in so many others, did much to establish the intellectual discourse and the analytical framework in which pressing doctrinal issues were discussed for centuries. Some (but not all) of his most important statements concerning the pains of hell were included in the fourth book of Peter Lombard's *Libri sententiarum* (compiled *c.* 1154-58 with a second edition appearing in 1158), which during the 1220s came to be established as *the* major theological textbook, a work pored over by generation after generation of trainee theologians, who therefore were obliged to respond in one way or another to Augustine's remarks. Inevitably, therefore, we shall be drawing on some of their commentaries, seeing how they sought to make sense of (often provisional and exploratory) statements by the saint which raised more questions than they answered. Special reference shall be made to the *Sentences* commentaries of Albert the Great, OP (completed in 1249), Bonaventure of Bagnoregio, OFM (1248-53, subsequently revised) and Thomas Aquinas, OP (1252-56). Death intervened before Aquinas could get to the part of his vast *Summa theologiae* which would have expressed his mature views on many of the subjects under consideration here, though in what is extant we find much important material, which shall be drawn on below. Also of crucial importance to the following discussion are the contributions of the Austin canon Hugh of St Victor (d. 1142), whose influence on Aquinas's exegetical theory was considerable,[1] and William of Auvergne (*c.* 1180-1249, elected Bishop of

---

[1] A particularly cogent account of this has been provided by Marcus Paul Elder, '*Eruditio sacri eloquii*: the integration of scriptural hermeneutics and theological system in Hugh of St Victor' (unpub. D.Phil. diss., Yale University, 2010).

Paris in 1228), who produced his *De universo* shortly before the production-mill of *Sentences* commentaries began to grind.

The first of Augustine's major contributions comes in the twelfth book of his massive commentary on Genesis, *De Genesi ad litteram*.² Significantly (as the following discussion will make clear) it follows on from one of the passages from this treatise which has been much quoted in modern scholarship, where a distinction is made between three types of sight or vision (*tria genera visionum*).³ 'Corporeal' vision refers to normal sight, when we see the material things in front of us. 'Intellectual' vision occurs when God is seen in His own nature, inasmuch as the rational and intellectual part of man is able to conceive of Him. This vision, which never errs, is not seen through the body, but rather is beyond all likeness (*similitudo*) and every image (*imago*). 'Spiritual' (for which here read, non-corporeal) vision combines aspects of both these types, given that we are looking with the spirit (*anima*) at images of bodies (*corporales imagines*) which are not before us (*absentia*). For the 'image of an absent body, though like a body, is of course not itself a body': 'non est corpus, quamuis corpori similis sit, imago absentis corporis'.⁴ The mental images in question can either be true (*veras*),

---

² The crucial discussion is at *De Genesi ad litteram*, xii, 32, 60-33 and 62 (ed. Zycha, pp. 426-8; trans. Hill, pp. 499-502).

³ On the considerable cultural significance of this specific excursus see especially Barbara Newman, 'What did it mean to say "I saw"? The clash between theory and practice in medieval visionary culture', *Speculum*, 80/1 (2005), 1-43. Studies of aspects of the key concepts include: Dallas Denery, *Seeing and Being Seen in the Later Medieval World: Optics, Theology and Religious Life* (Cambridge, 2005), and Katherine Tachau, *Vision and Certitude in the Age of Ockham: Optics, Epistemology and the Foundations of Semantics 1250–1340* (Leiden, 1988).

⁴ *De Genesi ad litteram*, xii, 7,16 (ed. Zycha, p. 388; trans. Hill, p. 471). As M. D. Barbezat puts it in his cogent summary, 'Through spiritual vision, a soul separate from the body can experience phenomena like those that arise through regular sense perception even though the soul lacks the requisite sensory organs. Importantly, spiritual vision carries sensations drawn from the other senses within it, such as touch, taste, and smell. ... [A]ll of these sensations are experienced through the category of spiritual vision, when they occur in the imagination, the memory, dreams, or visions'. 'Since this vision

representing actual bodies that we have seen and retain in our memory, or fictitious (*fictas*), as fashioned by the power of thought. In the first case we can think of a city that we know well, like Carthage; in the second, we can think of one we do not know, like Alexandria.[5] Seeking clarifications of these types of vision in the Bible, Augustine offers as a clear example of *visio intellectualis* what St Paul saw when he was caught up to the third heaven (II Corinthians xii.2-3).[6] In contrast, Pharaoh experienced a merely 'spiritual' vision when he dreamed about seven ears of corn and seven oxen (Genesis xli.1-32), these being likenesses of bodily things which were not accompanied with understanding, since the prophet Joseph had to interpret what Pharaoh had imagined.[7] Augustine affirms the superiority of the former type of vision over the latter, given that the likenesses of things can cause potentially deceptive illusions in the soul, when it is not using its intelligence. Indeed, even the corporeal sight can easily be deceived, as when one gazing at the stars thinks they are stationary. And in spiritual vision the soul often mistakes the images of material things (whether of existing things or fictitious ones) for the material things themselves, which may result in confusion. All of this, quite logically, brings Augustine to consider what degree of confidence we may have, what application of intelligence we can or should bring to bear, in respect of visions of the pleasures of heaven and the pains of hell. For him this application is a tentative process, involving the posing of questions and the provision of analogies rather than the assertion of conclusions.

An analogy with dream-experience readily presents itself. Initially, it may seem quite surprising to see Augustine pursue this line of argument, given that so many features of his heavily Neoplatonic world-view

---

is independent of material bodies', the inference may be drawn that separated souls – whether in sleep or following death – 'can utilize it as well'. 'In a corporeal flame: the materiality of hellfire before the Resurrection in six Latin authors', *Viator*, 44 (2013), 1-20 (p. 5).

[5] *De Genesi ad litteram*, xii, 6,15 (ed. Zycha, p. 387; trans. Hill, p. 470).
[6] *De Genesi ad litteram*, xii, 5,13 (ed. Zycha, p. 385-6; trans. Hill, pp. 469-70).
[7] *De Genesi ad litteram*, xii, 9,20 (ed. Zycha, p. 391; trans. Hill, p. 473).

promoted a distrust of the imagination, particularly when it operates without the firm guidance of reason.[8] And yet, 'the argument from imagination' constitutes one of his proofs for the immateriality of the human soul, as Bruno Niederbacher has made admirably clear.[9] Hence in the present discussion he takes a quite positive approach to imaginative data. Sometimes we regret waking up from dreams in which we were 'set among things we had always longed to have, while at other times, on waking up terrified out of our wits and subjected to frightful tortures, we have been afraid to go to sleep again in case we should be fetched back into the same horrors'.[10] Even more telling, he continues, is the testimony of those who have had temporary out-of-body experiences, albeit not as profound as St Paul's rapture. People 'who have been detached from the senses of the body, less totally indeed than if they had actually died, but still more profoundly than if they were just asleep', have 'described much more vivid sights and experiences than if they had been describing dreams'. Having been 'carried away from the body's senses' and 'lain there as if they were dead', they have witnessed the pains of hell. These visions, Augustine assures us, are not deceptive, for there is no intent to

---

[8] Negative attitudes to dreams in early Christianity are well summarized by Charles Stewart, 'Dreams and desires in ancient and early Christian thought', in *Dreams and History: The Interpretation of Dreams from Ancient Greece to Modern Psychoanalysis*, ed. Daniel Pick and Lyndal Roper (Hove, East Sussex, 2004), pp. 37-56 (pp. 48-9). 'Within ascetic "anthropology" – as patristic theories of human psychology are known – dreams were the ultimate diagnostic of the condition of the self. How much passion still lurked inside one? How strong or weak was one's will, even in sleep, to resist demonic incursions and manipulations?' The most useful overview of medieval attitudes to dream-experience and dream-interpretation remains Steven F. Kruger, *Dreaming in the Middle Ages* (Cambridge, 1992).

[9] Bruno Niederbacher, 'The human soul: Augustine's case for soul-body dualism', in *The Cambridge Companion to Augustine*, 2nd edn, ed. David Vincent Meconi and Eleonore Stump (Cambridge, 2014), pp. 125-41 (esp. pp. 130-31). 'Imaginations are incorporeal', and the faculty that enables us to perform them 'with immaterial content must itself be immaterial'; Augustine 'identifies this faculty with the human soul, which is a rational soul'.

[10] *De Genesi ad litteram*, xii, 32,61 (ed. Zycha, p. 427; trans. Hill, pp. 501-2).

deceive. 'Although it is not bodily sights but sights resembling bodily ones that souls divested of their bodies are affected with, for better or worse, what they see is both real joy and real affliction, made from spiritual substance (*facta de substantia spirituali*)'.[11] It is the soul and not the body that is being affected, which experiences pleasure or pain.

How is this possible? Because, Augustine suggests, the souls in question 'have borne in themselves some likeness to their own bodies (*similitudinem corporis sui*), by means of which it was possible for them to be carried away to those places and to experience such things with something like their senses'.[12] Not, then, with the bodily senses – but with *something like* them, *talia similibus*. And those souls have not experienced actual 'bodily sights but sights *resembling* bodily ones'. Which raises the crucial question: what do these temporary severances of body and soul portend for life after death? If the soul can see such things when its body is lying 'senseless but still not totally dead', why cannot it also have such vision 'when death overtakes it and it quits the body for good'? It may well bear that above-mentioned *similitudo corporis*, 'which is not bodily but like a body, even in the nether world (*apud inferos*)', and 'in places that are not bodily but like bodily places, whether places of ease and rest or of punishment and pain'.

The soul is most certainly not corporeal, Augustine declares. But one cannot 'deny that it can have a resemblance to the body (*similitudinem corporis*) with all its parts' without also denying 'that it is the soul which in dreams sees itself walking or sitting to being carried hither and thither on foot or even in flight'.[13] There is quite a leap in Augustine's argument here, as he shifts from the world of dreams to the nether world. To deny that it is the soul which, in dreams, sees itself waking, sitting etc. is here being put on a par with denying that the soul is acutely aware of what it perceives as bodily pain. But Augustine needs to establish the presence of a *similitudo corporis* in the soul so that he can speculate about how the pains of hell may actually be suffered, following the departure of the soul from the body in death. Flipping this argument over may clarify the issue:

---

[11] *De Genesi ad litteram*, xii, 32,61 (ed. Zycha, p. 427; tr. Hill, p. 500).
[12] *De Genesi ad litteram*, xii, 32,60 (ed. Zycha, p. 426; tr. Hill, pp. 499-500).
[13] *De Genesi ad litteram*, xii, 33,62 (ed. Zycha, p. 428; tr. Hill, p. 501).

knowing how in dreams we perceive ourselves to be sitting, walking etc. even though our bodies are not actually engaged in those actions, helps us to understand how, in the afterlife, we shall perceive bodily pain and suffer on account of it – not corporeally but spiritually. Hell does indeed have a 'substantial reality' (*substantia*), and its pains are real, but Augustine judges it to be 'of a spiritual, not a bodily nature': 'sed eam spiritualem arbitror esse, non corporalem'.[14]

What Augustine means by 'spiritual' here is quite a shift from the sense intended when he spoke of *visio spiritualis* in contrast with *visio intellectualis*. (Indeed, the sheer slipperiness of the term *spiritualis* and *spiritualiter* – in Augustine's discourse certainly, but even more palpably in later scholastic thought – complicate any inquiry like the one undertaken here.) He has moved from prophetic vision (which is 'spiritual' inasmuch as corporeal likenesses are involved rather than actual bodies) concerning the pains of hell and the pleasures of heaven to the actual abodes of the dead, in an effort to at once establish and bridge the gap between the physical sensations characteristic of present-day life and the spiritual adventures of the soul when it is separated from the body. Concomitantly, the corporeal *similitudo* which Augustine postulates in the soul is of a different order from the *imagines* based on everyday experiencing of the world, or simply invented by the mind. The formation of such imagery is a normal part of the human thought-process, yet may be exploited by God as when, for example, He willed that Pharaoh should dream about ears of corn and oxen. But, far from being an *imago*, a product of the imagination, Augustine's *similitudo corporis* has a much more elevated, and indeed a significantly ontological, status. It is, so to speak, a proxy for the sentient body within the soul which enables it to suffer pain and enjoy pleasure. Hence it is of crucial importance for the divine economy of punishment and reward: without it the damned could not suffer and the blessed could not enjoy the pleasures of heaven. But what implications does this theory have for those 'places that are not bodily but like bodily places, whether places of ease and rest or of punishment and pain'? By confining the scene of activity

---

[14] *De Genesi ad litteram*, xii, 32,61 (ed. Zycha, p. 427; tr. Hill, p. 501).

to the soul itself, Augustine has obviated the need for hell or heaven to have any specific, or any material, location. The suffering (or enjoyment) undertaken by the soul's *similitudo corporis* seems to involve only the likenesses of bodily places – not physical places as such.

So, then, it might be said that, for the Augustine of *De Genesi ad litteram*, it's 'all in the head'. But nonetheless painful (or pleasurable) for that. He has identified a spectacular instance of metaphorical language expressing the immaterial through the material. And if, following Aristotle, a good metaphor involves an acute perception 'of the similarity in dissimilars',[15] then hellish pain palpably marks the similarity between the dissimilars of the corporeal and the spiritual. The significance of this theory for human attempts to understand hell can hardly be exaggerated. Augustine bequeathed a compelling and controversial legacy to his readers, both past and present, who have tended to see here a denial (albeit qualified), or at least a radical diminution, of materiality: the means of punishment and the location of hell are not actually corporeal, but rather the images of corporeal realities which the soul carries with it following separation from its body.[16] As we shall see, his scholastic successors could not allow the force of this metaphorical reading to remain unmuted, believing that Augustine's words had at least the appearance of being contrary to the testimony of holy Scripture and indeed the opinions of other saints.

---

[15] *Poetics*, 22 (1459a); trans. Bywater in *The Complete Works of Aristotle*, ed. Barnes, II, 2334-5. Ricoeur characterizes Aristotle as believing that 'the gift of making good metaphors relies on the capacity to contemplate similarities'; 'to make good metaphors is to contemplate similarities or (according to some other translations) to have an insight into likeness'. 'The metaphorical process', p. 143. On the crucial role of similarity in the formation of metaphor see further Andrew Ortony, 'The role of similarity in similes and metaphors', in *Metaphor and Thought*, ed. Andrew Ortony (Cambridge, 1993), pp. 186-201.

[16] For succinct statements to this effect see Alan E. Bernstein, *The Formation of Hell: Death and Retribution in the Ancient and Early Christian Worlds* (Ithaca, NY, 1993), p. 329, and Donald Mowbray, *Pain and Suffering in Medieval Theology: Academic Debates at the University of Paris in the Thirteenth Century* (Woodbridge, 2009), p. 135.

CHAPTER 2

Augustinian foundations, II: *De civitate Dei* on the body-fire composite

Augustine's other major discussion of the dynamics of infernal suffering occurs in the twenty-first book of *De civitate Dei*, where the context is very different. Rather than emerging from a discussion of the different kinds of vision possible in this life and into the next, here Augustine's initial concern is to prove that the human body can experience intense pain indefinitely, with no fixed end. Bodies can be burned without being consumed – a fact which, however strange it may seem, may be proved with reference to the marvels of nature, and which supports Augustine's assertion that the torments of hell are everlasting.[1] That makes good sense if read with reference to the world following the General Resurrection, when bodies return to their souls, thereby presenting obvious opportunities for physical punishment or pleasure. Phrase after phrase throughout the first ten chapters of this penultimate book make it quite clear that Augustine is primary investigating the suffering to be experienced by re-embodied souls in the hell which will exist after the Last Judgment – in a future time when body and soul will be connected indissolubly, in a way that no pain, however extreme, can sever.[2] The matter of what happens in the hell or the heaven of disembodied souls, pending the Last Judgment, is curiously marginalized – all the more curious given its prominence in the treatment provided in *De Genesi ad litteram*.

The objective defined here in *De civitate Dei* is to provide arguments supporting the view 'that human bodies, animate and living, can not only survive death, but can also endure the torments of everlasting fire'. Quite clearly, Augustine has resurrected bodies in mind here. His initial point

---

[1] *De civitate Dei*, xxi, 2-8 (ed. Hoffman, II, 512-34; trans. Dyson, pp. 1045-64).
[2] *De civitate Dei*, xxi, 3 (ed. Hoffman, II, 514-15; trans. Dyson, p. 1046).

is that 'there are animals which are certainly corruptible, because mortal, yet which live in the midst of flames'.³ Although Augustine freely admits that the equivalence is problematic, because such 'animals do not live for ever, and, moreover, they live in great heat without pain', nevertheless he warms to the argument, offering a long series of marvellous but natural phenomena, drawn mainly from Pliny and slightly qualified by the rider that he himself does not necessarily believe in all of them, just those that he has verified by personal experience. The salamander lives in fire, yet survives.⁴ Certain mountains in Sicily have been 'fiercely ablaze from time immemorial down to the present day, yet still remain whole'. So, then, 'not everything which burns is consumed' – a fact that renders much more plausible the proposition that the bodies of the damned 'may burn without being consumed, and may suffer without perishing'. Augustine proceeds to describe an abundance of 'wondrous works of God' which defeat 'our weak and moral powers of reasoning'.⁵ The flesh of the peacock does not rot after death; frozen chaff preserves snow buried under it; charcoal is so brittle that it can easily be broken, yet so strong that it cannot be corrupted by moisture or overcome with age; quicklime becomes white in fire, and can store fire within itself, while being cold to the touch; a diamond cannot be destroyed by either iron or fire or any other force whatever (except, allegedly, the blood of a goat); the lodestone

---

3   *De civitate Dei*, xxi, 2 (ed. Hoffman, II, 513-14; trans. Dyson, p. 1045).
4   *De civitate Dei*, xxi, 4 (ed. Hoffman, II, 517; trans. Dyson, p. 1048).
5   *De civitate Dei*, xxi, 5 (ed. Hoffman, II, 523; trans. Dyson, p. 1054). The receptivity of the mature Augustine to 'unique and surprising happenings' in the natural world has been evoked memorably by Peter Brown, who notes the capacity for 'sudden amazement' that the saint had developed, together with (and related to) a greater respect for miracles. The martyrs had died for an 'impossible belief' which was not susceptible of rational explanation. 'This is the attitude which Augustine had reached when, in the twenty-second book of the *City of God*, he attempted, by an unwieldy and picturesque catalogue of strange occurrences in Hippo, Carthage, Calama, Uzalis, Fussala and little churches in the countryside, to persuade men reared on ancient physics, that the pure, uncontaminated Empyrean of their imagination might yet find room for the substance of their human flesh ...'. *Augustine of Hippo: A Biography*, new edn with an Epilogue (London, 2000), pp. 419-22.

has the wondrous power of attracting iron.[6] And so on and so forth; Augustine has a lot more to say. He sums up with the stirring declaration that 'God has made a world full of innumerable miracles, in sky, earth, air and waters, while the earth itself is beyond doubt a miracle greater and more excellent than all the wonders with which it is filled'. Why, then, can God 'not bring it about both that the bodies of the dead shall rise, and that the bodies of the damned shall be tormented in everlasting fire'?[7]

The nature of that torment is adumbrated in the tantalizing scriptural statement that 'their worm shall not die, and their fire shall not be quenched' (Isaiah lxvi.24; cf. Judith xvi.21, 'he will give fire, and worms into their flesh, that they may burn, and may feel for ever', and Sirach vii.19, 'the vengeance on the flesh of the ungodly is fire and worm').[8] Here the issue of whether literal or figurative discourse is being used is to the fore; are we dealing with metaphor or with materiality? Fire, being an element, arguably had a certain affinity with spiritual entities, but the worm, that biting and gnawing *vermis*, presented an unavoidable problem, due to its association with gross physicality. Was that creature material or metaphorical, the 'vehicle' to a 'tenor' denoting spiritual pain – that being the 'conceptual import' underlying the 'pictorial envelope'?

Augustine launches into an extensive (though ultimately inconclusive) exegesis of those troubling terms.[9] Some say that they pertain to the punishment of the soul, not the body. For the word 'fire' is not inappropriately (*non incongrue*) used to express the searing pain of a soul whose repentance came too late, and fruitlessly. They understand the word 'worm' in the same way, in accord with the words of Proverbs xxv.20, 'so the sadness of a man consumeth the heart'. On this reading, then, neither material fire nor gnawing worm is actually involved in inflicting pain; they serve as metaphors for suffering within the soul,

[6] *De civitate Dei*, xxi, 4 (ed. Hoffman, II, 517-21; trans. Dyson, pp. 1049-52).
[7] *De civitate Dei*, xxi, 7 (ed. Hoffman, II, 526-7; trans. Dyson, p. 1057).
[8] On the intricate relationship that developed between the fire and the worm in Christian theology see the general discussion in Alan E. Bernstein, *Hell and its Rivals: Death and Retribution among Christians, Jews and Muslims in the Early Middle Ages* (Ithaca, NY, 2017), pp. 67-98.
[9] *De civitate Dei*, xxi, 9 (ed. Hoffman, II, 534-7; trans. Dyson, pp. 1064-6).

which takes the form of regret for missed opportunities. But in sharp contrast, 'others' are in no doubt that 'both body and soul will suffer pain in that future punishment; and these affirm that the body will be burned with fire, while the soul is to be, in a certain manner (*quodammodo*), gnawed by the worm of anguish (*verme moeroris*)'. That is to say, the word 'fire' literally relates to corporeal suffering, while the word 'worm' must be understood spiritually (i.e. metaphorically), as relating to mental grief. Augustine finds merit in this suggestion, because clearly it would be 'absurd' to suppose that in hell either body or soul would be free from pain. But, for his own part, he finds it 'easier to say that "fire" and "worm" both pertain to the body than to suppose that neither does'.[10] So, then: at one moment he is distinguishing between material fire and metaphorical worm; at another, he is acceding to the argument that both these terms denote material entities. A quite extraordinary hedging of bets.

The implications of that opaque and indecisive statement are not drawn out. Instead Augustine wonders why Holy Scripture is silent about the pain which the soul will suffer, preferring to refer to corporeal suffering. Perhaps because, while not actually said, it is understood that in a suffering body 'the soul will also be tormented by fruitless repentance'? An emphatic reference to corporeal suffering is made in Sirach vii.19, where 'the vengeance on the flesh of the ungodly' is said to be 'fire and worms'. Why didn't the author just speak of 'the vengeance of the ungodly'? Why bring 'flesh' into it? Because both fire and worms are to be the punishments of the flesh?[11] 'Let each one choose as he wishes', Augustine declares; 'let him ascribe the fire to the body and the worm to the soul, the former literally (*proprie*) and the latter figuratively (*tropice*); or let him attribute both, literally (*proprie*), to the body'.[12] He himself has sufficiently discussed the question of whether it is possible for a living creature to remain alive in fire – and confirmed that, by a miracle

---

[10] *De civitate Dei*, xxi, 9 (ed. Hoffman, II, 536; trans. Dyson, p. 1065).
[11] Augustine adds that the author may have in mind the fact that those who live according to the flesh are heading for a second death (adopting the idiom of Romans viii.13).
[12] *De civitate Dei*, xxi, 9 (ed. Hoffman, II, 536; trans. Dyson, p. 1066).

of our Creator, creatures can burn without being consumed, and suffer without dying. For God Himself has created all the wonders of the world that he celebrated above.

At this point Augustine seems to be losing patience with the form of analysis he is pursuing, and inclining to refer the whole thing back to the mysteries of divine omnipotence – that being the most effective argument-stopper for any theologian. If God wants to make something work, it will; He will devise ways of inflicting pain on the bodies and souls of the damned, no matter how the process is inscribed in Scripture, whether literally or metaphorically. Why agonize about the matter? The exegetical decision is up to the individual. A person may believe that the worm refers literally (*proprie*) to the punishment of the body, or that here incorporeal things are being represented by corporeal ones, in which case the worm refers to the punishment of the soul. The truth will be made clear in the next life – and the knowledge of the blessed will be so complete that they will need no experience (*experientia*) to teach them the nature of the pains in question. Wisdom alone will suffice. For what we now know in part, they will know perfectly (cf. I Corinthians xiii.9).[13]

But Augustine does not give up looking for answers in the here and now. He offers two disquisitions that bring him within touching distance of the abovementioned *De Genesi ad litteram* account, though he never attains the (relative) precision which characterizes that earlier discussion. First comes the argument that since the soul, which is eternal, can suffer yet not die, it seems reasonable to envisage a situation in which the body can suffer and not die.[14] The characteristic of being able to suffer is 'present in the souls of all men now', and will 'also be present in the bodies of the damned' – a neat soundbite which was deployed in Peter Lombard's *Sentences* in support of the proposition that 'the bodies which will burn then will not be consumed'.[15] An inanimate body cannot suffer any pain; it 'is the soul, not the body, which feels pain, even when the pain arises in the body'. From that Augustine concludes that the human

---

[13] *De civitate Dei*, xxi, 9 (ed. Hoffman, II, 536-7; trans. Dyson, p. 1066).
[14] *De civitate Dei*, xxi, 3 (ed. Hoffman, II, 514-17; trans. Dyson, pp. 1045-8).
[15] *De civitate Dei*, xxi, 3 (ed. Hoffman, II, 515; trans. Dyson, pp. 1046-7); cf. Peter Lombard, *IV Sent.*, dist. 44, 5(254) (II, 519; tr. Silano, IV, 241).

body cannot experience suffering except through the soul, which is 'either the only or the principal sufferer of pain'.[16] Thus it can feel pain even when unconnected to a body, 'for the rich man was certainly suffering in hell when he said, "I am tormented in this flame"', though (so the implication goes) he was not suffering from real flame.[17] The allusion is to Luke xvi.24, often referred to as the episode of Dives and Lazarus. Here the rich man who is 'buried in hell' begs that Lazarus, the poor beggar whom he ignored in life, might briefly assuage his pain by dipping 'the tip of his finger in water, to cool my tongue (*linguam meam*)'. This scriptural passage raises troubling questions about the pain which may be experienced by a disembodied soul in hell as it currently exists, and hence is of considerable importance for the schoolmen's investigations (as we shall see). Yet Augustine does not go there, remaining silent on such matters. Instead he embarks on the abovementioned litany of the wonders of nature.[18]

Where he does address the issue of the pain felt by non-corporeal entities is in the course of an affirmation of the belief that 'the pool of fire and brimstone' will torment both devils and damned humans (Apocalypse xx.9; cf. Matthew xxv.41, at which point Christ refers to the 'everlasting fire which was prepared for the devil and his angels').[19] If it is supposed that devils have some sort of a body, composed of dense and humid air, the matter is easy to resolve. But what if they do not?

[16] On the significance and longevity of this idea see especially Esther Cohen, 'The animated pain of the body', *The American Historical Review*, 105/1 (2000), 36-68, which goes on to consider medieval efforts to translate the sensation of pain into language and imagery which can be shared by people other than the sufferer. This is the focus of her subsequent monograph, *The Modulated Scream: Pain in Late Medieval Culture* (Chicago, 2010), which is remarkable for the extent to which it considers medical and juridical discussions in addition to material from mystics and professional theologians.

[17] To cite once again Barbezat's cogent summary of Augustine's thinking, everything described here 'existed incorporeally like the stuff of dreams. It follows that the flames "were incorporeal" along with everything else, but that Dives could not tell the difference'. 'In a corporeal flame', p. 6.

[18] I.e. the discussion ranging from *De civitate Dei*, xxi, 4 through xxi, 7.

[19] *De civitate Dei*, xxi, 10 (ed. Hoffman, II, 537; trans. Dyson, pp. 1066-7).

Following a tactically dismissive statement that this is 'not a question which requires to be investigated with laborious care or contentiously debated' (heavily ironic in retrospect, given the amount of debate the question did provoke), Augustine asks,

> Quur enim non dicamus, quamuis miris, tamen ueris modis etiam spiritus incorporeos posse poena corporalis ignis adfligi, si spiritus hominum, etiam ipsi profecto incorporei, et nunc potuerunt includi corporalibus membris et tunc poterunt corporum suorum uinculis insolubiliter adligari?
> [Why should we not say that there is some marvellous yet true way in which even incorporeal spirits may be afflicted by the pain of material fire? After all, the spirits of men are certainly incorporeal, yet now they are enclosed within the material members of the body and then, in the world to come [following the General Resurrection], they will again be indissolubly joined to their own bodies.][20]

Unprepossessing and innocuous this passage may seem, but its importance for the schoolmen can scarcely be exaggerated. Time and time again, it would be enlisted in arguments which saw in the conjunction of the spiritual soul and the material body a basis for comprehending and rationalizing the conjunction of spiritual soul and material flame.

In the original discussion, however, Augustine is primarily interested in the capacity of demons to feel pain. Even if they are incorporeal, he declares, they will 'nonetheless be tormented by the touch of material fire', without in any way feeding those flames. Whilst initially affirming that this is 'beyond the understanding of man', Augustine returns to Luke xvi.24, to pose the question of how a human disembodied soul seems to

---

[20] *De civitate Dei*, xxi, 10 (ed. Hoffman, II, 537-8; trans. Dyson, p. 1067). Augustine did much to establish the term *spiritus*, in theological and philosophical contexts like this, as referring to the immaterial, spiritual part of a human being, mind, soul (especially as distinct from body). Foundationally it designated a breathing or gentle blowing of air, a breath, breeze, particularly the breath of life.

be burning in hell (since it has obvious implications for the issue of demonic suffering; one and the same fire will torment all the recipients of divine justice). The flame described here is akin to the other apparently corporeal references in this scriptural passage – the 'eyes' the rich man lifted up to behold Lazarus, the 'tongue' on which he begged that a little 'water' might be dropped, the 'finger' of Lazarus with which he asked this might be done. All of these terms, then, seem to have material referents. But in fact, Augustine says, they all designate incorporeal things – and may be compared to what is seen by those who are asleep or in an ecstasy, 'to whom incorporeal things appear in corporeal likeness (*similitudinem corporum*)'. Even when a man is in such a disembodied state, 'he still sees himself in a form so like his bodily appearance (*similem suo corpori uidet*) that he cannot perceive any difference at all'.[21]

This is beginning to sound very like what Augustine said in *De Genesi ad litteram* about the *similitudo corporis* which enables the soul to suffer pain and enjoy pleasure – a statement which, as noted above, can easily be read as a denial of the materiality of the fires and the location of hell. But there Augustine had primarily the separated soul in mind, whereas here he is prioritizing the post-resurrection hell and the pain the reconstituted human body will feel in it. 'Hell ... will be a place of material fire, and will torment the bodies of the damned, whether men or demons: the solid bodies of men, and the aerial bodies of the demons (*corpora damnatorum, aut et hominum et daemonum, solida hominum, aeria daemonum*)'.[22] What about the possibility that demons may not

---

[21] *De civitate Dei*, xxi, 10 (ed. Hoffman, II, 538; trans. Dyson, p. 1068).
[22] *De civitate Dei*, xxi, 10 (ed. Hoffman, II, 538-9; trans. Dyson, p. 1068). On Augustine's demonology and its predecessors, see especially Gregory A. Smith, 'How thin is a demon?', *Journal of Early Christian Studies*, 16/4 (2008), 479-512, and Seamus O'Neill, 'The demonic body: demonic ontology and the domicile of the demons in Apuleius and Augustine', in *Philosophical Approaches to Demonology*, ed. Benjamin W. McCraw and Robert Arp (New York, 2017), pp. 39-58. Smith has nicely affirmed that 'Being invisible ... is not the same as being immaterial', and 'Being invisible is also not the same as being a metaphor' (pp. 481-2), the key point being that early Christian traditions often affirm the materiality of the aerial bodies of demons. Therefore attempts to reduce demonic temptations to

have bodies, aerial or whatever? In that case, 'they will nonetheless be in contact with the material flames in such a way as to receive pain from them' – a claim made without any substantiation. Those 'solid bodies of men' must refer to resurrected bodies; what the disembodied souls of the damned endure in the meantime is not discussed. At this point Augustine is concerned to establish that the 'everlasting fire' of hell will torment demons, whatever their corporeal status. And he has done precisely that, though relying on declaration rather than explanation. Little wonder that Peter Lombard places material from this chapter of *De civitate Dei* (here misattributed to *De Genesi ad litteram*) in his section on 'whether demons are burned by a corporeal fire' (IV, dist. 44, vi [256]) rather than in the section which immediately follows, on 'whether souls without bodies feel incorporeal fire' (IV, dist. 44, vii [257]).[23]

The passage from Augustine that the Lombard *does* include in that latter section is what the saint said about the *similitudo corporis* in *De Genesi ad litteram*: 'Augustine teaches that the human soul has a likeness to the body', intimations of which are experienced in dreams, when the soul sees itself walking or sitting, and the like. It may well bear that *similitudo*, 'which is not bodily but like a body, even in the nether world', and if that is the case then it would also 'seem to be in places that are not bodily but like bodily places, whether places of ease and rest or of punishment and pain'. The Lombard bolsters that brief account with

    psychological phenomena, 'extensions of the self', should be resisted. 'When it comes to demons in Roman and later antiquity, or indeed to the human soul, tidy material divisions between mind and body are best checked at the door', Smith declares (p. 512), pushing back against the argument that, between the second and fourth centuries, demons became increasingly internalized and 'spiritual'. Turning to the later Middle Ages, the argument has convincingly been made (though something of Smith's cautious expansiveness is in order here also) that within scholasticism demons and angels in effect 'lost their bodies', with Bonaventure attempting 'to uphold an unalloyed incorporeality for the angelic host', and Aquinas 'severing angelic nature from any vestige of corporeality', establishing angels as 'pure form', 'pure intellectuality'. Dyan Elliott, *Fallen Bodies: Pollution, Sexuality, and Demonology in the Middle Ages* (Philadelphia, 1999), pp. 132, 133-4.

[23] Lombard, *IV Sent.* (II, 520-1; trans. Silano, IV, 241-3).

material from the *Prognosticon futuri saeculi* of St Julian of Toledo (*c.* 644-90).²⁴ If the incorporeal soul of a living human is held in the body, why would it not also be held by a corporeal fire after death? One bodily form is merely being replaced by another. Julian is adamant – more so than Augustine was – that being held by the fire means that a soul will suffer the torment of fire, not only by seeing it but also by experiencing it (*non solum videndo sed etiam experiendo*). Yet again, Luke xvi.24 (where the rich man's soul is described as burning in hell) is cited in support. Julian's conclusion is that the dead are not deprived of their senses, and do not lack the affections (*affectiones*) of hope, sadness, joy and fear: 'they already begin to have some foretaste of what is reserved for them at that general judgment'.²⁵

---

[24] *Prognosticon futuri saeculi*, ii, 17, in *PL*, XCVI, cols 482B-C. On Julian's later medieval reception see J. N. Hillgarth, 'St. Julian of Toledo in the Middle Ages', *Journal of the Warburg and Courtauld Institutes*, 21, no. 1/2 (1958), 7-26.

[25] Lombard, *IV Sent.*, dist. 44, 7 (257), 3 (II, 521, trans. Silano, IV, 243). As Barbezat notes, 'Julian's account of hellfire acknowledges that a separate soul's experience consists essentially of images or likenesses, but that hellfire itself is more than an image or spiritual likeness' – an essentially Gregorian position ('In a corporeal flame', p. 11).

CHAPTER 3

Feeling the burn:
Gregory the Great and Hugh of St Victor
on imagination after death

Those brief and bald statements in IV, dist. 44, vii (257) of the *Libri sententiarum* require some contextualization. First, it should be realised that Julian of Toledo's initial comparison of the actual combination of incorporeal soul and corporeal body with the potential combination of incorporeal soul and corporeal fire is fundamentally an extrapolation of the passage from *De civitate Dei*, xxi, 10 quoted on p. 14 above.[1] So then, here we do not seem to be too far from Augustine. But the influence of Gregory the Great (d. 604), saint and pope, permeates what Peter Lombard has quoted from Julian; the Lombard correctly notes that Julian is dependent on 'the authority of some statements of Gregory'. In a crucially important chapter of his *Dialogues* Gregory had provided a sharpened-up version of Augustine's comparison of the body-soul composite with the fire-soul composite.[2] Which Julian here follows. And his claim that souls will not just look at, but also be afflicted by, fire is a verbatim quotation from that same chapter of Gregory's. But justice is not done by the Lombard to Gregory's treatment (at this point in the *Sentences* the authorities are confusingly blurred together), which, if read

---

[1] *Prognosticon futuri saeculi*, ii, 16 (*PL*, XCVI, cols 482A-B). Further, in the chapter immediately preceding the one included in the *Sentences*, Julian explicitly cites Augustine's *similitudo corporis* disquisition from *De Genesi ad litteram* – which the Lombard does not include in his citation of Julian, presumably because it would closely replicate what he himself is quoting from *De Genesi ad litteram*. *Prognosticon futuri saeculi*, ii, 16 (*PL*, XCVI, col. 482A-B).

[2] 'If the incorporeal spirit can be held in the body of a living man, why should it not be held in corporeal fire?' *Dialogi*, iv, 29 (*PL*, LXXVII, col. 365C-D). I have followed the Migne chapter-enumeration. For a recent translation (from which I have diverged occasionally) see Odo John Zimmerman, *Saint Gregory the Great: Dialogues* (Washington, DC, 2002).

at full length, looks very much like a direct response to Augustine's ideas, though Gregory himself does not acknowledge that.

The soul is 'burned' inasmuch it sees itself to be burned, Gregory argues. 'An invisible burn and an invisible pain are received from visible fire'.[3] In other words, vision generates acute mental pain; the separated soul suffers from and through imaginations. This is how we may credit the idea of a corporeal thing, the fire, burning that which has no body; this explains how 'the incorporeal mind is tortured with an incorporeal fire that causes pain'. That burning, that spiritual flame, are metaphors for spiritual suffering, not literal claims that the soul is being burned just like wood can be. Gregory recounts the otherworld vision of 'a prominent man named Reparatus', who saw an 'immense pyre of wood' burning – this occurred not that we should think that 'wood is actually burned in hell', but in order to teach us to fear hell-fire through our current experience of that pain-inducing element.[4] There may be no wood in hell, but fire – as we know and feel it – is certainly present, and awaiting sinners.

So, then: Gregory's thinking is close to Augustine's in that sensations of extreme heat are believed to be caused by mental images of fire rather than by real fire. To see the burn, it would seem, is to feel the burn. Yet the fire itself is real, and materially comparable with the type we encounter in our present life. And here Gregory parts company with Augustine. As M. D. Barbezat nicely puts it, 'Gregory's fire is not spiritual or imaginary, even if it is experienced that way'.[5]

The Canon Regular Hugh of St Victor, praised by his contemporaries as 'a second Augustine',[6] was indebted to the original Augustine, as well as Gregory the Great, in treating of how hellish suffering is effected. However, in the final analysis Gregory seems to be the determining influence. Having mentioned the experiences of visionaries who have had

---

[3] *PL*, LXXVII, col. 368A; trans. Zimmerman, p. 226.
[4] *Dialogi*, iv, 31 (*PL*, LXXVII, cols 369C-72A; trans. Zimmerman, pp. 229-30).
[5] Barbezat, 'In a corporeal flame', p. 9.
[6] Beryl Smalley, *The Study of the Bible in the Middle Ages*, 3rd edn (Oxford, 1984), p. 85.

corporeal likenesses (*signa quaedam corporalibus similia*) of spiritual things presented to them, Hugh asks the (by now inevitable) question, what may be inferred from this concerning the state of permanently separated souls?[7] (At least, 'permanently separated' until the General Resurrection.) Whether those souls 'which depart from here, never more to return, [will] see or fully perceive (*videant aut sentiant*)' in the afterlife things in the manner characteristic of visionary experience, 'is entirely doubtful', warns Hugh, thus entering a caveat concerning the appropriateness of the comparison between what has been seen by temporarily absent souls and what will be seen by those souls which do not return to their bodies. However, he continues, it may be deemed 'more probable' to suppose that, because certain souls which, 'when living in bodies' were 'affected by corporeal images (*corporalibus imaginibus*) through the delight of visible things', they will suffer torments in those very same images when they depart from their bodies. That is to say, death does not entirely remove the 'corporeal capacity' (*corporalem passibilitatem*) of souls to suffer. Certain imaginations of corporeal things (*corporalium imaginationibus delectationis*) having been impressed upon them by experiences of wicked delight during their lives, sinners will carry those images with them into their afterlives, there to become instruments of torture.[8] Leaving behind the body does not mean leaving behind bodily suffering. Hugh actually manages to find something positive here (though he does not put it in so many words), inasmuch as we can do something to help our postmortem prospects – good moral behaviour now will obviate punishment later. If souls which, 'while remaining here', manage 'to cleanse and deprive themselves' of thoughts involving sinful 'delights and fantasies (*delectationibus et*

---

[7] *De sacramentis christiane fidei*, II.16.2, in *PL*, CLXXVI, col. 584B-C; trans. Roy J. Deferrari, *Hugh of Saint Victor on the Sacraments of the Christian Faith* (Cambridge, MA, 1951), pp. 437-8.

[8] A little later Hugh makes the comparable point that, though they lack bodies, it is appropriate that souls be punished through corporeal elements, since they took perverse delight in those same corporeal elements while joined to the body. *De sacramentis*, II.16.3 (*PL*, CLXXVI, col. 586A; trans. Deferrari, p. 439).

cogitationum phantasiis)', subsequently they will 'not perceive (*non sentient*)' any related pains and torments in a corporeal way. To the extent that their souls have been cleansed they are 'impassible', unable to suffer, because 'they bring with themselves nothing worthy of punishment'.

In other words, the fewer hurtful images we store up for use in our later suffering, the better. And Hugh seems to believe that such later suffering has a corporeal aspect, though he does not explain the dynamics; indeed, he asserts that it is impossible to do so. If we are asked, 'how can souls without bodies suffer from corporeal things?', the reply must be, 'We do not know how this can be done'.[9] But our ignorance does not affect the truth of the matter, since 'it is most truly proven by testimony on the authority of the Sacred Scripture and Catholic faith that souls even before the reception of bodies [at the General Resurrection] are tortured by corporeal and material fire (*corporali et materiali igne*)'.[10] Here Hugh rejects the metaphorical explanation of hell-fire, the belief of 'certain men' that 'souls freed from bodies sustain only those punishments' which are inflicted by conscience, 'the accuser within' (*conscientia intus accusatrix*).

Saint Gregory is emphatically quoted as being in support:

> Beatus Gregorius dicit quod in eo ardent quod se ardentes vident. Quid sibi vult putatis hoc quod dicit, quod animae in eo ipso ardent quod ardorem suum vident? In rebus aliis corporalibus non est ita ut ardorem sentiat quicunque ignem conspicatur. Quae est ergo visio illa animae qua sentit omne quod videt, vel si non omne hoc certe quod ad poenam videt?
> [Blessed Gregory says that they burn inasmuch as they see themselves burning. What else do you want? Do you think as he says, that souls burn inasmuch as they see their own burning? In other corporeal

---

[9] *De sacramentis*, II.16.3 (*PL*, CLXXVI, col. 585A; trans. Deferrari, p. 438).

[10] *De sacramentis*, II.16.3 (*PL*, CLXXVI, col. 584D; trans. Deferrari, p. 438). Hugh proceeds to affirm that 'we must not seek everywhere to try to believe by reason what we are commanded to believe. Sacred Scripture, the teacher of our faith, tells us this. What more do we seek? Let us accept, let us not contradict.'

things is it not the case that whoever sees fire feels the heat? What, then, is [to be said concerning] that vision of the soul by which it feels all that it sees – or, if not all, certainly that which appertains to [its] punishment?][11]

Is Hugh simply seeking to explain what he thought Gregory meant, or quietly correcting (or clarifying, as Hugh probably would have seen it) what Gregory said? As noted above, Gregory believed in the materiality of hell-fire, thereby parting company with Augustine, whilst supposing that the separated soul's suffering was spiritual or imaginary. Hugh seems to be simplifying the issue, by declaring that what can be seen must also be felt, and so the separated soul feels what it sees – or, if not everything it sees, at least that part of its vision which effects its punishment. This argument is strengthened with the suggestion that, in the separated soul, all the senses will be equal, and heightened to achieve that status: 'it would be the same there to see as to touch, to touch as to feel pain'.[12] Hugh melds this with his thought that whatever mental baggage is borne into the next world will determine one's suffering: 'on going out from here in the corruption of vices', sinners 'take with them the capacity for suffering (*passibilitas*)'.

Besides, Hugh proceeds to ask robustly, does it really matter if we cannot understand how disembodied souls have sensory feelings? What does matter is that they do have them. 'What they suffer *from* is of no consequence but rather *how much* they suffer'.[13] And they suffer a lot. The force of pain (*vis doloris*) consists 'not in the torment but in the sense of the sufferer (*in sensu patientis*)'. Therefore Hugh invites us to consider the possibility that, even if the material of the tormenting elements was absent externally, the internal pain of the sufferers would be no less. Material elements are not necessary in order for that pain to be suffered: God is 'able even without material elements (*sine elementis etiam*

---

[11] *De sacramentis*, II.16.3 (*PL*, CLXXVI, col. 585A-B; trans. Deferrari, p. 438 [with several changes]).
[12] *De sacramentis*, II.16.3 (*PL*, CLXXVI, col. 585C; trans. Deferrari, p. 439).
[13] *De sacramentis*, II.16.3 (*PL*, CLXXVI, col. 585D; trans. Deferrari, p. 439. My italics).

materialibus) to give the sense of pain to souls which were to be tortured'. This explains how separated souls can suffer pain of a kind which, were they in the body, they would experience as physical. Here Hugh seems to have arrived at a profoundly Gregorian understanding of hellish imaginations.

When Hugh addresses the characteristic imagery of hell, he seems to have Augustine's approach in *De civitate Dei* (xxi, 9) in mind, though his treatment is remarkable for the way it highlights the interpretive problems attendant on the ambiguities surrounding the term *spiritualiter* and its related word-forms. If one wants to understand the worm purely and simply as referring to the remorse of the sinner's conscience, and therefore thinks that that corporeal fire should be understood in the same way, i.e. spiritually and not corporeally, then a major problem is presented by the clear reference to the flesh at Sirach vii.19, 'the vengeance on the flesh of the ungodly is fire and worms'.[14] Does this mean, then, that both images, of worm and fire, must be interpreted corporeally? 'Because of considerations of this kind no one thing can be defined lightly,' says Hugh with ostentatious understatement. But he ventures a plausible explanation: anyone who 'lived evilly in the flesh' will 'also be tortured in the flesh through fire and in the spirit through the worm of conscience (*conscientiae vermis*)'. A distinction seems to be in play here, in relation to the two images: between the corporeal fire which acts on the flesh and the spiritual worm (of conscience) which acts on the soul.

And yet, Hugh feels the pressure of the fact that Scripture often talks about hell and its torments as being spiritual in nature, which seems to support a spiritual understanding of the crucial images. But he firmly resists such pressure, by distinguishing between the singularity of truth and the plurality of expression.

> Multa sunt alia quae vel ambigue dicta sunt, vel ambigue dici possunt. Sed aliud est rerum veritas, aliud verborum varietas. Neque nos oportet propter multitudinem dicendi a simplicitate deviare credendi.

---

[14] *De sacramentis*, II.16.5 (*PL*, CLXXVI, col. 588A-B; trans. Deferrari, p. 442).

[There are many other things which either have been said ambiguously or can be said ambiguously. But the truth of things is one thing, the variety of words another. We should not on account of the multitude of ways of speaking deviate from the simplicity of believing.][15]

For Hugh the materiality of hell-fire is an aspect of 'the simplicity of believing'; thus he rejects a metaphorical explanation in this case. The rest seems to involve 'the variety of words'. At the heart of this problem is the prodigious ambiguity of the term 'spiritual'. References to gnashing of teeth and weeping (cf. Matthew viii.12) are, on Hugh's analysis, to be understood 'spiritually' in the sense of 'non-corporeally', presumably because disembodied souls have neither teeth to gnash nor eyes to weep with, and a similar explanation may be afforded for the worm of conscience. And indeed for another passage cited by Hugh, Job xxiv.19, where it is said concerning the tortures of the wicked, 'they pass from the snow waters to excessive heat'. Hugh suggests that this may mean: at present the impious are tormented in spirit, but they will progress to the highest punishment of all on the final day of judgment.[16] Such spiritual interpretations are, in his view, supported by the spiritual substance of infernal things, including wicked spirits and disembodied souls. So, then, spiritual natures and spiritual interpretations are mutually reinforcing, although obviously different inasmuch as one pertains to ontology and the other pertains to exegesis. So far, so clear. Yet Hugh's successors continued to struggle with this issue, to some extent entrapped by their own technical vocabulary.

Hugh died shortly before Peter Lombard began teaching in the Cathedral School at Paris (1143-44); his influence on the *Libri sententiarum* is writ large. However, Hugh's innovative treatment of postmortem punishment does not influence the Lombard's compilation of materials in Book IV, dist. 44, vii (257). Julian of Toledo is the major force there, if 'force' is the right word – rather the *Prognosticon* serves as

---

[15] *De sacramentis*, II.16.5 (*PL* CLXXVI, col. 589A; trans. Deferrari, p. 443).
[16] *De sacramentis*, II.16.5 (*PL* CLXXVI, col. 588B; trans. Deferrari, p. 442).

a filter through which the views of Augustine and Gregory on hellish imaginations were consolidated (or blurred together). That was the form in which generation after generation of *Sentences* commentators were presented with the questions of how the damned could experience pain, and how the expression in Sacred Scripture of that pain should be interpreted. The Lombard's collage of *auctoritates* raises issues rather than provides answers. Some of the answers contributed by his thirteenth-century readers may now be considered.

CHAPTER 4

Accommodating Aristotle:
new encounters with image and spirit

Here we enter a very different ideological landscape from those familiar to Augustine and Gregory, in respect of the issue of postmortem suffering. Yet many of the old problems remained and continued to perplex theologians – particularly those caused by the apparent existence of two versions of hell, one wherein the disembodied souls of the damned are currently being punished and the other which will follow the General Resurrection and Last Judgment. As if that was not complicated enough, a firm distinction was now being made between hell and purgatory – a place of temporary torment, where not-too-bad sinners paid the penalty for their misdeeds and were rendered fit to enter heaven. (That being the heaven of disembodied souls, for the time being; a paradise offering joys far in excess of those associated with Eden awaited the re-embodied souls of the blessed.)

The elaboration of this distinction precipitated fresh topics for debate, such as: are the fires of hell and those of purgatory of equal intensity and do they inflict equal pain? does hope exist in purgatory whereas it is absent in hell? do demons torment souls in purgatory as well as in hell?[1] Bonaventure and Aquinas believed that demons were not involved in purgatorial punishment, an idea which was assimilated in Dante's *Purgatorio*, which is free of devils, and exists 'uniquivocally' as 'a place of hope and a means of ascent towards heaven', to quote Eamon Duffy.[2] At

---

[1] For discussion of these issues see Jacques Le Goff. *The Birth of Purgatory*, trans. Arthur Goldhammer (Chicago, 1984), pp. 251-2, 262, 273 [part 3, ch. 8], and Robert Easting, 'Purgatory and the Earthly Paradise in the *Purgatorio sancti Patricii*', *Cîteaux: commentarii cistercienses*, 37 (1986), 23-48 (esp. pp. 40-1).

[2] *The Stripping of the Altars: Traditional Religion in England, c. 1400 - c.1580*, 2nd edn (New Haven, Conn., 2005), p. 343. In similar vein, Le Goff declares that, for Dante, purgatory is actually 'a place of hope, of initiation into joy, of gradual emergence into the light', and also notes that both

least part of that claim might have surprised the legions of visionary women who frequently visualized demons practicing their sensational tortures in that very place – women who, in Barbara Newman's brilliant phrase, 'served as midwives at the birth of purgatory'.³ But many of them seem to have shared the common academic opinion that purgatory was a place of hope. Catherine of Genoa (1447-1510) summed up the doctrine with admirable precision: 'the souls in purgatory enjoy the greatest happiness and endure the greatest pain; the one does not hinder the other'. In brief, 'there is in purgatory as much pain as in hell'.⁴ A temporary hell remains a hell, for the duration of anyone's stay within it. Quite how the balance of pain and joy is meant to be achieved, is left unresolved. John Casey has spoken well of Catherine's belief in

> Bonaventure and Aquinas supposed that hope existed in purgatory, a marked improvement on hell. *Birth of Purgatory*, pp. 251, 273, 346 [part 3, chs. 8 and 10].

3   Barbara Newman, 'On the threshold of the dead: Purgatory, Hell, and religious women', in her *From Virile Woman to WomanChrist: Studies in Medieval Religion and Literature* (Philadelphia, 1995), pp. 108-36 (p. 111). 'While not the exclusive preserve of women', Newman avers, 'purgatorial piety ... occupied a privileged place and took on a distinctive character in their religious lives'. Indeed, their purgatorial witness was well under way (she has Hildegard of Bingen and Elisabeth of Schönau in mind) before the period – the final third of the twelfth century – that Le Goff proposes as crucial for its 'birth'.

4   *Trattato del purgatorio*, chs 8 and 12, in *Dialogo spirituale tra anima e corpo; Trattato del purgatorio*, ed. Palmina Trovato (Casale Monferrato, 1999), pp. 132, 137. With this may be compared Takami Matsuda's examination of Middle English didactic poetry and homiletic treatises, where 'purgatorial punishment' is generally presented as being 'little different from hell in terms of severity'. *Death and Purgatory in Middle English Didactic Poetry* (Cambridge, 1997), p. 93. Here purgatory 'was received into the dualism of heaven and hell as a useful addition which could provide a practical and apparently wider path to salvation for sinners, without seriously disturbing the existing dichotomy, rather than as a third region requiring a complete restructuring of the geography of the afterlife' (p. 112). Matsuda also highlights the 'non-development of an original iconography of Purgatory', with visual artists not being scrupulous about differentiating between purgatory and hell; demonic figures regularly appear in both places (pp. 103-7).

'unspeakably pleasant torments', bringing out the irresolvable nature of her paradox.[5]

Simultaneously, the meanings of *spiritualiter* and its cognates multiplied even more. Roger Bacon, OFM (d. *c.* 1292) blamed Aristotle along with his Muslim commentators, whose eagerly-studied writings inaugurated an ideological revolution, for uses of the term *spiritualis* which are 'not in accordance with its proper and primary signification, from "spirit", as we say that God and angel and soul are spiritual things'.[6] Here Bacon seems to hark back to a time when the terminology was simpler – but it had never been simple, as any investigation of the history of the term *spiritualis* and its cognates in scriptural exegesis quickly makes clear. We are dealing with a large and complicated picture, as complexity was heaped upon complexity. Hugh of St Victor's worry about the semantic ambiguities caused by confusion between *rerum veritas* and *verborum varietas* was addressed by the most influential theologians of the thirteenth century. The responses offered by Thomas Aquinas at the beginning of his *Summa theologiae* are precise, cogent, and memorable. In the science of theology not only words but also things can signify. In the former case, we have the literal or historical sense. In the latter, the spiritual sense, which is divided into three: the allegorical, tropological and anagogic senses, respectively concerned with Old Testament prefigurations of the New, recommendations for moral behaviour, and intimations of the Last Things. A neat classification. Too neat, for it elides many of the complexities any exegete encountered in blow-by-blow commentary on complex scriptural texts. But as an attempt at theoretical abstraction it was an attractive and influential one.

Should Holy Scripture employ metaphors? Yes, says Aquinas. 'It is natural for man to reach intellectual things by means of sensible things, because all our knowledge originates in sensation', and therefore 'it is

---

[5] John Casey, *After Lives: A Guide to Heaven, Hell, and Purgatory* (Oxford, 2009), pp. 231-4.

[6] *Opus majus*, pars V, perspectivae pars prima, dist. vi, cap. 4; in *Opus maius*, ed. J. H. Bridges, 3 vols (London, 1900), I, 43. For discussion see Alastair Minnis, *From Eden to Eternity: Creations of Paradise in the Later Middle Ages* (Philadelphia, 2016), pp. 200, 313n.

quite appropriate that in Holy Scripture spiritual things are imparted to us under the guise of metaphors taken from corporeal things'.[7] There is a remarkable shift in the argument at this point, as Aquinas moves from his foundational Aristotelianism to Pseudo-Dionysius's Neoplatonism, and the proposition that 'the divine ray cannot shine upon us in any other way except wrapped up in a large number of sacred veils'. Divine truths in Scripture are best imparted to us in the guise of figures drawn from base, inferior bodies, because that way there is less chance of us being led astray, by thinking that the divine is really like that: thus Aquinas enlists Neoplatonic doctrine relating to the unknowability of God in defence of metaphorical expression. Which, he explains in the following article, is located within the literal sense, for sometimes that *sensus* deploys figurative meanings, as when 'the arm of God' is used to signify the effective power of God, who of course does not have a physical limb of this kind.[8] Similarly, the secular master Henry of Ghent, who taught in the Parisian faculty of theology *c*. 1275-92, states that 'all metaphor and parable (*metaphora et parabola*) pertains to the historical sense',[9] which sometimes uses 'language that is figurative and employs "transferred" speech' (*sermo translatus*).[10] The ambition of this classification of the senses of Scripture is impressive, a fine example of the systematizing zeal characteristic of scholasticism. It provided a fresh impetus for consideration of the *sermo translatus* of hellish imaginations.

All such inquiry was now conducted within thought-systems which were heavily influenced, if not dominated, by the 'new' Aristotle with his accompanying Muslim commentators, one of the major consequences

---

[7] *Summa theologiae,* Ia qu. 1, art. 9, resp.; trans. in *Medieval Literary Theory and Criticism c. 1100 - c. 1375: The Commentary Tradition,* ed. Alastair Minnis and A. B. Scott with David Wallace, rev. edn (Oxford, 1991), p. 239.
[8] *Summa theologiae,* Ia qu. 1, art. 10, resp., 1 and 3; trans. in *Medieval Literary Theory and Criticism,* ed. Minnis and Scott, pp. 242-3.
[9] *Summa quaestionum ordinariarum,* art. 16, qu. 3, 11; trans. in *Medieval Literary Theory and Criticism,* ed. Minnis and Scott, p. 261.
[10] *Summa quaestionum ordinariarum,* art. 16, qu. 3, 13; trans. in *Medieval Literary Theory and Criticism,* ed. Minnis and Scott, p. 262.

being a reconsideration of the relationship between body and soul.[11] Here we may witness, as Magdalena Bieniak and Raffaella Roncarati say, 'the evolution of anthropology from the dualist perspective' characteristic of Neoplatonism 'towards a unitary conception of man'.[12] A consequence of this seismic cultural shift was the allocation of a more crucial role to the human imagination, a mental power which Neoplatonism had generally mistrusted.[13] However, Augustine did give it its due in his formulation of the *similitudo corporis*, that facsimile of the collective

---

[11] The literature on this subject is, of course, substantial. I have found particularly helpful John Haldane, 'Body and soul', in *The Cambridge History of Medieval Philosophy*, ed. Robert Pasnau, 2 vols (Cambridge, 2009-10), I, 293-304; Robert Pasnau, *Theories of Cognition in the Later Middle Ages* (Cambridge, 1997), together with his article 'The mind-soul problem', in *Mind, Cognition and Representation: The Tradition of Commentaries on Aristotle's 'De anima'*, ed. Paul J. J. M. Bakker and Johannes M. M. H. Thijssen (Aldershot, 2007), pp. 3-19; R. C. Dales, *The Problem of the Rational Soul in the Thirteenth Century* (Leiden, 1995); and Martin Stone, 'The soul's relation to the body: Thomas Aquinas, Siger of Brabant and the Parisian debate on monopsychism', in *History of the Mind-Body Problem*, ed. Tim Crane and Sarah Patterson (London, 2000), pp. 34-69. A useful introduction to medieval perception-theory has been provided by A. Mark Smith, 'Perception', in *Cambridge History of Medieval Philosophy*, ed. Pasnau, I, 334-45. On the study of Aristotle's *De anima* see especially Sander W. de Boer, *The Science of the Soul: The Commentary Tradition on Aristotle's 'De anima', c. 1260 - c. 1360* (Leuven, 2012). See further, Antonia Fitzpatrick's recent contribution (on the extent to which, for Aquinas, the body was crucial to human identity), *Thomas Aquinas on Bodily Identity* (Oxford, 2017).

[12] Magdalena Bieniak and Raffaella Roncarati, *The Soul-Body Problem at Paris ca. 1200-1250: Hugh of St-Cher and His Contemporaries* (Leuven, 2010), p. 3.

[13] On the literary-theoretical aspects of this shift See Alastair Minnis, 'Literary imagination and memory', in *The Cambridge History of Literary Criticism, vol. 2: The Middle Ages*, ed. Alastair Minnis and Ian Johnson (Cambridge, 2005), pp. 239-74. See further Carruthers' monumental *The Book of Memory*, together with *Intellect et imagination dans la philosophie médiévale*, ed. M. C. Pacheco and J. F. Meirinhos, 3 vols (Turnhout, 2006), and Michelle Karnes, *Imagination, Meditation, and Cognition in the Middle Ages* (Chicago, 2011).

sentient powers of the human body which (he believed) exists in the soul. This *similitudo* makes use of images, as it perceives and suffers pain or pleasure. An important clarification: the term *imago* was generally used as 'shorthand for immaterial sensory impressions involving all the senses'; *all* 'the sensory attributes of a material thing encountered in regular life, touch, taste, smell, and appearance, can ... be referred to as an image, or more precisely as part of the image' of some bodily thing.[14] Imagery in this broad sense is what Augustine supposed the *similitudo corporis* would retain, reproduce and deploy in the separated soul. The notion that those powers survive death is quite contrary to Aristotle's insistence that they perish with the body;[15] indeed, it may be said that Aristotelianism

---

[14] Barbezat, 'In a corporeal flame', p. 19. While the imagination plays a crucial role in the functioning of the *similitudo corporis*, it does so in association with multiple sensations of the kind experienced in dreams and out-of-body experiences, which are independent of material bodies and therefore (on Augustine's thinking) can be experienced by separated souls as well.

[15] The 'elephant in the room' here is, of course, Aristotle's apparent belief that, when a human body ceases to perform its normal life functions, its functional form (the soul) no longer exists; in short, the soul dies with the body. But he complicated the issue by stating that the intellect is not the form of anything bodily – which Aquinas appropriated to mean that 'the human soul survives death as a "subsisting thing"'. The crucial texts are *De anima*, 408b18-24 and 413a3-7; cf. Gareth B. Matthews, 'Death in Socrates, Plato and Aristotle', in *The Oxford Handbook of Philosophy of Death*, ed. Ben Bradley and Fred Feldman (Oxford, 2015), pp. 186-99 (pp. 194-9). At *Nicomachean Ethics*, 1111b20-23 Aristotle says that, for a human being, immortal life is simply an impossibility, and no amount of wishing can alter that fact. However, Aquinas (inevitably) interprets this passage as meaning that 'a man can wish to be immortal, an impossible thing according to the condition of this perishable life': i.e. it is impossible for a man to live forever in his present, mortal body. A quite different point. *St Thomas Aquinas, Commentary on the Nicomachean Ethics*, trans. C. I. Litzinger, 2 vols (Chicago, 1964), I, 196 (Book III, lect.5; 1111b20-23). However, Aquinas at least admitted that Aristotle's 'Peripatetic followers' did not believe in the existence of demons, though he goes on to claim that 'still other philosophers' set the matter right, by being 'forced to admit that demons exist'. Here I quote from Aquinas's *De malo* (perhaps completed *c*. 1270-2), qu. xvi, art. 1, resp.; *The De malo of Thomas Aquinas*, ed. Richard Regan and Brian Davies (Oxford, 2001), pp. 812-13.

empowered the imagination only when it functioned within the body-soul composite.

Further, Augustine recognizes the role which certain metaphorical or imaginative forms of speech have in scriptural discourse relating to postmortem pain, as is indicated by his nuanced treatment of the terms 'fire' and 'worm'. But the corporeal (or, quasi-corporeal) sufferings of the damned are experienced as such, although all of this takes place within the soul. This is subtle stuff, and tentatively expressed – a modus operandi which allowed his scholastic successors to either use it selectively or dismiss it as falling short of firm assertion. But it is clear that Augustine believed that images of hell-fire and pain could not simply be reduced to metaphors for the mental grief of fruitless repentance, however important it was to value that grief and however important it was to respect the divinely-inspired imaginative discourse of certain passages of sacred Scripture.

What is at stake here is well illustrated by Thomas Aquinas's reaction to passages in Augustine's treatise *De diversis quaestionibus lxxxiii*, where Augustine affirms his belief that true knowledge proceeds from divine illumination (a clear reflex of his Neoplatonism)[16] by asserting that whatever a corporeal sense attains is in flux, and if something is constantly changing it cannot be a source of true knowledge. Augustine adds that 'everything that we sense by means of the body we also receive in images (*imagines*), even when the things are not present to the senses', as for instance in sleep or in a frenzy (*furor*), and yet our senses cannot tell us 'whether we are receiving the sensible images themselves or false images'. In such a case, 'nothing can be perceived which is indistinguishable from what is false'.[17] That statement reads as a rather more negative, and

---

[16] This being the belief that 'knowing eternal truths is a result of an inner illumination', things being seen immediately within a 'sort of incorporeal' light. Gareth B. Matthews, 'Augustinianism', in *The Cambridge History of Medieval Philosophy*, ed. Pasnau, I, 86-98 (p. 88). On Augustine's rejection of a theory of recollection in favour of a theory of illumination, see Peter King, 'Augustine on knowledge', in *The Cambridge Companion to Augustine*, 2nd edn, ed. Meconi and Stump, pp. 142-65 (pp. 147-52).

[17] *De diversis quaestionibus lxxxiii*, qu. 9, in *PL*, XL, col. 13.

indeed suspicious, formulation of what, in *De Genesi ad litteram*, Augustine had recognized as the phenomenon that likenesses of material things can create in the soul mental images which can be either true or fictitious, either representing actual bodies or being creations of the power of thought itself (cf. Chapter 1 above). So, then, the things to which the senses react, and the operations of the senses themselves, are quite unreliable, and Augustine cannot conceive of them as functioning within the soul in a way which helps bring about true understanding. Such a dependency is set in opposition to the divinely-sent light of the intellect, which determines the truth in and from things.

In the first part of his *Summa theologiae*, written between 1266 and 1268, Aquinas deftly agrees with Augustine's statement that a mere impression made by sensible bodies is not enough to lead to an intellectual activity. But, Aquinas continues, this does not imply that we need a top-down 'impression' from above to enable our intellection, as Plato held. He prefers to follow an Aristotelian *via media* in treating of the relationship between intellect and sense by invoking the agent intellect,[18] which 'by a process of abstraction makes images received from the senses actually intelligible'.[19] Thus Augustine's worries may be laid to rest: 'the agent intellect is required for us to know the truth found in changeable things in an unchanging way, and to distinguish real things from likenesses of things'. Aquinas sees his predecessor's concern about the superior being led by the inferior as being assuaged by the fact that the agent intellect is immaterial and thus superior to the imagination, which deals in bodily things.

This entire discussion by Aquinas reads as a ground-clearing exercise for his next *quaestio* (article 7), which has been described as 'the

---

[18] On which see especially the impressive summary explanation by Z. Kuksewicz, 'The potential and the agent intellect', in *The Cambridge History of Later Medieval Philosophy: From the Rediscovery of Aristotle to the Disintegration of Scholasticism, 1100-1600*, ed. Norman Kretzmann, Anthony Kenny, Jan Pinborg, and Eleonore Stump (Cambridge, 1982), pp. 593-601.

[19] *Summa theologiae*, 1a, qu. 84, art. 6 (XII, 32-9).

touchstone of Aristotelian-Thomistic realism',[20] on whether the intellect can understand without turning to sense-images. Aquinas's definitive *responsio* features an arresting soundbite from Aristotle's *De anima*: the soul never thinks without an image.[21] At least, while it is joined to the body (a crucial qualification – on which, much more later). In the present state of life, 'for the intellect actually to understand (not only in acquiring new knowledge but also in using knowledge already acquired), acts of the imagination and the other faculties are necessary'.[22] Furthermore, as Aquinas had said in article 6, the imagination has an active capacity whereby, 'by separating and joining', it 'forms different images of things', including 'things not received from the senses'.[23] Elsewhere, in his commentary on Aristotle's *De anima*, Aquinas notes how 'images can arise in us at will, for it is in our power to make things appear, as it were, before our eyes – golden mountains, for instance, or anything else we please, as people do when they recall past experiences and form them at will into imaginary pictures'.[24] At this point imagination is being seen as compositive[25] and associational. To take the (oft-cited) example of the golden mountain, our imagination can combine the image of gold with the image of a mountain to produce the composite image of a golden

[20] By Paul T. Durbin, in a note to his translation of this part of the *Summa* (XII, 38).
[21] *Summa theologiae*, 1a, qu. 84, art. 7 (XII, 40-1).
[22] On the mental mechanisms involved here, and for similar appropriations of Aristotelian thought, see the succinct discussion by Pasnau, *Theories of Cognition*, esp. pp. 11-19.
[23] *Summa theologiae*, 1a, qu. 84, art. 6, ad 2 (XII, 38-9).
[24] *In librum de Anima commentarium*, iii. 3, 633 [lect. 4], ed. Angelo M. Pirotta, 2nd edn (Turin, 1936), p. 214; trans. Kenelm Foster and Silvester Humphries, *Aristotle's 'De Anima' in the Version of William of Moerbeke and the Commentary of St Thomas Aquinas* (New Haven, CT, 1951), p. 383.
[25] On the notion of 'compositive' imagination, see especially Harry Wolfson, 'The internal senses in Latin, Arabic and Hebrew philosophic texts', *Harvard Theological Review*, 28/2 (1935), 70-133, and Deborah L. Black, 'Imagination and estimation: Arabic paradigms and Western transformations', *Topoi*, 19 (2000), 59-60. As Black says, 'it is impossible to isolate any universal features that are common to all medieval exponents of the philosophical doctrine of internal senses' (p. 68).

mountain – a mental creation which cannot be perceived by the senses, since it has no referent in the real world. Hence, the compositive imagination is capable of acts of creativity which transcend empirical boundaries – making things seem to appear 'before our eyes' even though they do not appear before our actual eyes. This explains why (to return to article 7) we may gain some knowledge of 'incorporeal realities, which have no sense images, by analogy with sensible bodies, which do have images'. Here, quite intriguingly in this supposed apogee of 'Aristotelian-Thomistic realism', Aquinas has turned from Aristotle to the Neoplatonist Pseudo-Dionysius. The tensions between Aristotelian theories of abstractive cognition and Augustinian/Neoplatonic illuminationist models are rife in Aquinas's treatment of how the soul works with the body to acquire and use knowledge, but synthesis and synergy are being sought – a fact which is being recognized in recent scholarship on scholastic epistemology, in contrast with a previous tendency to regard Aristotelian faculty psychology as having swept the board.[26]

Other readers of Aristotle and the large deposit of commentary attached to his writings went much farther in their claims for the powers of the imagination. Some of the Stagirite's Muslim interpreters claimed that, if someone manages to achieve a strong enough imagination, this can have a direct impact on another person or some other creature. In his *Errores philosophorum* (*c.* 1270) Giles of Rome criticized Algazel (Al-Ghazālī) for the erroneous belief that the imagination can act on other bodies, 'and that the influence of the soul passes over to other bodies in such a way that by its thinking it destroys a spirit or kills a man'. This is

---

[26] See for instance Joseph Owens' discussion, which highlights the survival of Augustinian illuminationism in the thought of Bonaventure (and other Franciscan theologians) together with the secular master Henry of Ghent. 'Faith, ideas, illumination, and experience', in *The Cambridge History of Later Medieval Philosophy*, ed. Kretzmann, Kenny, Pinborg and Stump, pp. 440-59. See further Z. Kuksewicz, 'Criticisms of Aristotelian psychology and the Augustinian-Aristotelian synthesis', ibid. pp. 623-28; and José Filipe Silva and Juhana Toivanen, 'The active nature of the soul in sense perception: Robert Kilwardby and Peter Olivi', *Vivarium*, 48/3-4 (2010), 245-78, who emphasize the debt of these thinkers to Augustine.

denounced as *fascinatio* (hostile enchantment), by which means 'the eye' can cast 'a man into the ditch' and cast 'a camel into a hot pool'.[27] The longevity of this idea, and the ongoing need to refute it, may be illustrated by the fact that, writing approximately a century later, Nicole Oresme (d. 1382) felt obliged to counter a similar claim made by Avicenna (Ibn-Sīnā), the Persian polymath whose ideas will occupy us considerably in the following discussion. Avicenna held that by the power of his imagination a man can make 'a mule fall down', says Oresme. But the idea that 'your imagining would move me, when I am unwilling, or would move a stone', is insupportable.[28] The notion that an enchanter could by sight alone make a camel fall into a pit became one of the articles (no. 112) condemned at Paris in 1277.[29] Also prohibited, in both 1270 and 1277, was the denial that the separated soul can suffer the pains of corporeal fire.[30]

These issues were crucially interwoven. If the imagination could move stones, mules and camels, could it not also function as a major instrument of mental torture? If one man's imaginings can have a debilitating effect on another's body, why can it not have a debilitating effect on that same man's soul? Avicenna had troublingly relevant things to say on this subject as well. Scholasticism, it would seem, was right to be wary when it addressed the fearsome powers of the imagination – particularly if those powers were believed to induce spiritual pain in the separated soul, by

---

[27] *Errores philosophorum*, ed. Joseph Koch and English trans. John O. Riedl (Milwaukee, WI, 1944), pp. 44-5. I follow Robert Bartlett's definition of *fascinatio* as 'hostile enchantment', the result of a 'desire to do harm'; *The Natural and the Supernatural in the Middle Ages* (Cambridge, 2008), pp. 141-5.

[28] *De causis mirabilium*, ed. Bert Hansen, in *Nicole Oresme and the Marvels of Nature: A Study of his De causis mirabilium with Critical Edition, Translation, and Commentary* (Toronto, 1985), p. 346.

[29] Condemned proposition 112 (1277), in *Chartularium Universitatis Parisiensis*, ed. Henricus Denifle and Aemilio Chatelain, 4 vols (Paris, 1889-97), I, 549.

[30] Condemned proposition 8 (1270) and 19 (1277), in *Chartularium Universitatis Parisiensis*, ed. Denifle and Chatelain, IV, 487, 544.

deploying images of fire in the absence of the real thing. But the Paris condemnations affirmed that the real thing had to be present.

The significance of those condemnations has been debated vigorously by modern scholars, some arguing that they changed the course of scholastic thought, while others believe that well-established ongoing processes of intellectual inquiry continued with little hindrance.[31] According to a standard if simplistic explanation, this was an attempt by the Bishop of Paris, Stephen Tempier, to restrict and control some of the teachings of Aristotle and his Muslim commentators (particularly in relation to natural philosophy), which had found favour among masters in the arts faculty of the University of Paris, much to the annoyance of masters in the theology faculty. However one may wish to represent the matter, it seems quite clear that the attempt was both clumsy and ineffective; the genius was already out of the bottle (to rewrite the idiomatic phrase). Many influential theologians had been assimilating and debating Aristotle's works for several generations. As far as hellish imaginations were concerned, the intellectual trajectory had firmly been set in motion by the 1240s – perhaps earlier, depending on how much influence one affords to the precocious and provocative work of William of Auvergne, one of Tempier's predecessors as bishop of Paris (serving from 1228 until his death in 1249), and the subject of our next chapter.

---

[31] For a useful summary of the opposing viewpoints see Ian P. Wei, *Intellectual Culture in Medieval Paris: Theologians and the University, c. 1100 - 1330* (Cambridge, 2012), pp. 167-8, and further, J. F. Wippel, 'The Condemnations of 1270 and 1277 at Paris', *Journal of Medieval and Renaissance Studies*, 7 (1977), 169-201; Luca Bianchi, '1277: A Turning Point in Medieval Philosophy?', in *Was ist Philosophie im Mittelalter? = Qu'est-ce que la philosophie au Moyen Âge? = What is philosophy in the Middle Ages?: Akten des X. Internationalen Kongresses für mittelalterliche Philosophie der Société Internationale pour l'Étude de la Philosophie Médiévale, 25. bis 30. August 1997 im Erfurt*, ed. Jan A. Aertsen and Andreas Speer (Berlin and New York, 1998), pp. 90-110.

CHAPTER 5

Imaginations *as* hell? William of Auvergne's thought experiment

One of the earliest, and most ambitious, scholastic treatments of the nexus between imaginative power and hellish punishment is to be found in the *De universo* which William of Auvergne wrote between 1231 and 1236, or perhaps as late as 1240. Here he robustly explores the argument that because the soul is a spiritual substance, lacking any material form, any pain which it suffers must be spiritual. William's argument proceeds from the premise that the impressions (*impressiones*) of all material things that the soul receives through the body are themselves spiritual. In the case of heat, 'the spiritual form impressed by the fire through the body upon the soul, although it is neither fire nor heat, nonetheless scorches the soul and causes it to burn' – according to the soul's own testimony (*se ipsa teste*). In other words, the soul believes it is burning even though no physical heat is involved.

> Quid ergo mirum, si sola imaginatione ignis ardere sibi videatur, et ardere se judicet, cum ipsa imaginatio substantiae animae vicinior sit, quam sensus, et solummodo spirituale sit?
> [What surprise is there, then, if the soul appears to itself to burn and judges itself to be burning by the imagination of fire alone, since this very imagination is closer to the substance of the soul than the senses, and is purely spiritual?][1]

This sounds like a reformulation of Gregory the Great's statement that the soul is 'burned' inasmuch it sees itself to be burned, with the role of imagination being emphasized. William draws the (inevitable, it now seems) analogy with dream experience:

---

[1] *De universo*, I.i.65, in *Guillelmi Alverni opera omnia*, 2 vols (Paris, 1674; repr. Frankfurt, 1963), II, 681. Here I follow the translation provided by Alan E. Bernstein, 'Esoteric theology: William of Auvergne on the fires of Hell and Purgatory', *Speculum*, 57/3 (1982), 509-31 (p. 514).

> Interdum somniant se ardere, et esse in igne, et cruciantur intolerabiliter, tanquam in veritate ardeant; quare quoniam veritas, et substantia ignis apud eos non est, sed sola species ignis, vel in fantasia, vel imaginatione eorum est, manifestum est eos cruciatum hujusmodi ardoris a sola specie ignis pati.
>
> [Sometimes [people] dream that they are burning and are in fire and are being tormented intolerably, as if they were truly burning. And therefore, since the truth and substance of fire are not in them, but only the appearance of fire is in either their fantasy or their imagination, it is manifest that they suffer the torment of this type of fire merely from the appearance of fire.][2]

A strong appearance is quite sufficient to cause pleasure or pain in the soul, and the appearance of fire, a frightening thing indeed, creates an intense experience of suffering. Therefore it would seem that, in order to effect postmortem punishment, God simply needs to apply his omnipotent strength to the imaginative faculty (*vis imaginativa*), which, given its spiritual nature, will remain in the separated soul, ensuring it depicts 'very strong appearances of all types of torments', working with images that the imagination had formed when it was hosted in a living human body. God certainly need not restrict himself to flames – other horrendous appearances may be produced, 'by means of the imagination or the intellect alone'. Thereby spiritual faculties produce spiritual pain, as is fitting for the soul to suffer.

So, then, it might seem that William has resolved the problem of the separated soul's pain by what looks like a version of the suffering-enabling *similitudo corporis* postulated in Augustine's *De Genesi ad litteram*: fearsome *imagines* derived from empirical experiences in this life carry over into the next, to cause unbearable grief. Gregory the Great agreed with at least that part of Augustine's treatment of the subject, as indeed did Hugh of St Victor. However, that is definitely *not* the case with William. For at this point his argument takes a sharp turn:

---

[2] *De universo*, I.i.65 (II, 682); trans. Bernstein, 'Esoteric theology', p. 514.

> Quod si quis inferat: ergo supervacue creatus est ignis huiusmodi: Respondeo, quia multae sunt utilitates ipsius, quarum una est, ut & corporaliter, et vere torqueat corpora animarum hujusmodi, et etiam animas ipsas. Amplius. Cum ipse sit Deus veritatis, et veritas, non decet magnificentiam gloriae ipsius, ut utatur mendaciis somniorum. [What if someone were to say: therefore fire of this kind had been created superfluously. I respond: [it was created] because its utilities are many, of which one is, that corporeally and really it torments the bodies of such people and their souls too. Further: since this is the God of truth and is truth, it does not suit the magnificence of his glory to use the lies of dreams.][3]

This statement reveals that William *does* believe in the actual existence of fire in hell[4] – and that it was not created superfluously, rendered redundant by hellish imaginations. 'Such people' as are punished in the afterlife are not free from corporeal torment, no matter what part the imagination may also play in that punishment.

William proceeds to ask if fire is the only corporeal force existing in hell, recalling that the poets speak of the rivers Lethe, Cocytus, and Styx. Here we may be dealing with Platonic metaphors (*metaphoras platonicas*), he opines, presumably recalling the doctrine (a commonplace of twelfth-century literary theory and exegesis) that under poetic integuments profound truths may be found.[5] He adds that 'Saracens', i.e. Muslims, believe that in hell is a tree with most bitter fruit, which its inhabitants are forced to eat. However, to dispute all the available fables, delusions and foolish figments is not as much laborious as it is unnecessary,

---

[3] *De universo*, I.i.65 (II, 682). Le Goff quotes part of this passage out of context; *Birth of Purgatory*, p. 245 [part 3, ch. 8].

[4] However, at this point William does not seek to resolve the issue of how such fire could actually cause the separated soul pain. Perhaps he felt he had said enough already, in recounting the natural marvels relating to fire, which help to render plausible God's deployment of it in enacting his justice. *De universo*, I.i.63-4 (ii.680-1). Cf. the persuasive analysis by Wei, *Intellectual Culture in Medieval Paris*, pp. 208, 211.

[5] On which see especially Peter Dronke, *Fabula: Explorations into the Uses of Myth in Medieval Platonism* (Leiden, 1974).

gratuitous (*supervacuus*): here, it seems, is where actual superfluity is to be found, certainly not in respect of the doctrine of material hell-fire. That said, William admits that true Christian doctrine, which in this respect accords with 'the doctrine of the Hebrews', holds that in hell exceedingly cold water does actually exist. So, then, this discussion seems to centre on what is materially present in hell as opposed to what has been said metaphorically about its conditions.

The argument is difficult to follow here.[6] However, in the first instance it should be noted that the argument in favour of infernal pain being spiritual rather than material is not presented as coming from his own mind; rather he is representing the thought of an 'exceedingly wise Christian doctor'.[7] This person is not named, but the parallels with Augustine's *De Genesi ad litteram* are quite obvious,[8] and he seems to be the most plausible identification. But it must be emphasized that William

---

[6] Furthermore, Bernstein's discussion of this problematic passage ('Esoteric theology', p. 515) is insufficiently clear. Wei is confident that Bernstein took 'fire of this kind' (*ignis huiusmodi*) to refer to the incorporeal species of fire that William had just discussed, and hence was surprised when William abruptly seemed to dismiss this species in favour of a fire which burns corporeally and is unlike what is experienced in dreams, however enhanced by divine action. 'There is no contradiction to explain', Wei argues, if 'fire of this kind' is 'taken to refer to the special kind of corporeal fire that can nevertheless burn separated souls in purgatory and hell'. Wei, *Intellectual Culture in Medieval Paris*, p. 211. I totally accept Wei's understanding of *ignis huiusmodi*; that was how I myself initially read the passage. But this does not, I believe, fundamentally compromise the challenge of Bernstein's presentation of how William explores the doctrine of punishment through hellish imagination, a doctrine which surfaces again and again in the long-running medieval debate on how the separated soul can suffer pain.

[7] Et quoniam aliquis ex sapientibus christianorum atque doctoribus dixit ...; Non est igitur mirum, si vir ille sapientissimus dixit ... *De universo*, I.i.65 (II, 681, 682).

[8] They are noted by Bernstein, 'Esoteric theology', pp. 517-19, who also points out parallels with Origen and Ambrose, pp. 516-17.

has pushed the saint's thinking far beyond anything he actually said.[9] Arguably, William has engaged in a radical thought-experiment of the kind which scholastic disputation permitted, before the master was obliged to return from his high-flying speculation to the certainties and restraints of Christian dogma.[10] Though in the final analysis William does not seek to banish actual fire from hell, the notion of imaginations as hellish torment has been allowed a remarkably full and positive formulation. It is not the case that, in following through this argument, William suggested that damned souls are merely tormented by dreams or imaginations as we know them, staple features of our existence in this life. Rather he sought to offer an analogy between ordinary, present-day nightmares and the far more terrifying images that can be produced when God Almighty gets to work on the human *vis imaginativa*, creating intensely horrifying appearances which provoke genuine horror in the soul.

That having been said, William feels obliged to affirm the view that 'it does not suit the magnificence' of the 'glory' of the God of Truth 'to use the lies of dreams'. Besides, 'dreaming of fires would not sufficiently deter men from vices and sins, since very few would be able to understand that souls can be tormented either by dreams or by imagining tortures'.[11]

---

[9] One wonders if William's 'Augustine' encompassed him as the author of *De spiritu et anima* – if so, that would help account for some of the intellectual moves he makes here. This Pseudo-Augustinian treatise will be discussed below.

[10] In using the term 'thought experiment' I have been influenced by Dominik Perler's procedure in 'Thought experiments: the methodological function of angels in Late Medieval epistemology', in *Angels in Medieval Philosophical Inquiry*, ed. Isabel Iribarren and Martin Lenz (London and New York, 2008), pp. 143-53, together with the excellent collection of essays *Medieval Thought Experiments: Poetry, Hypothesis, and Experience in the European Middle Ages*, ed. Philip Knox, Jonathan Morton, and Daniel Reeve (Turnhout, 2018). Despite the scepticism occasionally expressed in the latter volume concerning the viability of the term, particularly in certain specialized and technical philosophical contexts, I am convinced of its value in the analysis of scholastic disputational technique. See further my review of this collection, in *Speculum*, 95/1 (2020), 270-2.

[11] Cf. Bernstein, 'Esoteric theology', p. 515.

What William seems to be getting at here is that it is easy to reduce, to misread, the theory he has been propounding concerning divinely-enhanced hellish imaginations as a claim that infernal horrors are no worse than dreams of torment. Assertion of the actual presence of material fire in hell puts paid to that comforting illusion. And here is one of the ways in which the doctrine of material hell-fire is 'useful'. On top of its obvious and primarily 'useful' function in the enactment of divine justice, it has a major deterrent value, which runs the risk of being weakened by simplistic comparison of infernal fire with mere dreams of fire. Men must be deterred from vices and sins; nothing should interfere with that.[12] Indeed, and here we go far beyond William of Auvergne for a moment, it may be argued that a 'fundamental reason for the long triumph of hell was the firm and almost universal belief in its value as a deterrent in this life'.[13]

Returning to William: he may be making a distinction between what professional theologians can understand and may be allowed to debate, and what may be disseminated more widely, beyond the privileged intellectual confines of the schools. This interpretation, which has been suggested by Alan Bernstein,[14] has much to commend it. One may

[12] Elsewhere Bernstein brings out well how how hell was frequently used by preachers as 'a goad to confession'; 'The invocation of hell in thirteenth-century Paris', *Supplementum festivum: Studies in Honor of Paul Oskar Kristeller*, ed. James Hankins, John Monfasani, and Frederick Purnell, Jr. (Binghamton, NY, 1987), pp. 13-54 (p. 42). For example, in the section 'On the fear of hell' which forms part of his *Tractatus de diversis materiis predicabilibus*, the Dominican Stephen of Bourbon (d. 1261) lists no fewer than '91 characteristics of hell, each representing a detail in a vision of eternal horror' (pp. 13-14). The major deterrent value of such material is obvious and that is why Stephen has taken such pains (so to speak) to compile it; speculation about how that horror is actually produced is inappropriate in such a context.

[13] Thus D. P. Walker, *The Decline of Hell: Seventeenth-Century Discussions of Eternal Torment* (London, 1964), p. 4.

[14] Bernstein makes a 'distinction between esoteric and exoteric knowledge, between what may be taught to theology students and what may be preached publicly'. 'Esoteric theology', p. 515. See also Bernstein, 'The invocation of Hell', pp. 13-54 (pp. 13-14). Wei believes the deployment of this distinction

compare the way in which Henry of Ghent explicitly contrasted the *provectos* and the *simplices*, the more advanced students and the elementary learners.[15] Sacred Scripture should not be expounded indiscriminately to everyone, Henry declares. Lesser mortals, who are incapable of understanding subtle and difficult doctrine, need be taught only what is sufficient for their salvation, as in preaching. A broad (*grossus*) and common exposition of Scripture is, in general, appropriate to the *simplices*, while more profound teaching should be offered to the

> is unnecessary, since there is no actual 'contradiction' in William's text to resolve; cf. p. 41, n. 6 above. 'God had chosen' as his 'means of punishment' a 'special kind of corporeal fire, and it was this decision on God's part that William then tried to explain. God had already chosen to work in a way that would deter people from sin, so there was no reason for theologians to decide to preach something they knew to be untrue'. Wei, *Intellectual Culture in Medieval Paris*, p. 211. This is powerfully said, but to my mind Bernstein's approach has much life in it. While there is no doctrinal 'contradiction' here (as Wei has brought out well) there nevertheless remains a distinction between speculative, specialist thought and the teaching of essential salvific doctrine, of which I believe William shows his awareness. D. P. Walker's highly opinionated study *The Decline of Hell* takes the discussion to a whole new (and radically controversial) level by postulating that his chosen seventeenth-century authors reveal 'The peculiar dangers attached to any discussion of the eternity of hell': 'they produced a theory of double truth: there is a private, esoteric doctrine, which must be confined to a few intellectuals, because its effect on the mass of people will be morally and socially disastrous, and a public, exoteric doctrine, which these same intellectuals must preach, although they do not believe it. The second kind of truth is not, of course, a truth at all, but a useful, pragmatically justifiable lie' (p. 5). In light of this, Walker concludes that 'nearly all discussions of hell until well into the 18th century are veiled by a mist of secrecy and dishonesty' (p. 5). Strong words! But in defence of William of Auvergne *cum suis* it may be noted that rationalization and justification of their pedagogic praxis reached back as far as the Church Fathers, among whom Augustine may be cited as a preeminent example. The charge of 'dishonesty', in the sense of *knowing* perpetuation of 'double truth' that shades into untruth, in the preaching of doctrine they did not believe in, does not stick in their case.

[15] Cf. Alastair Minnis, 'Medium and message: Henry of Ghent on scriptural style', in *Literature and Religion in the Later Middle Ages: Philological Studies in Honor of Siegfried Wenzel*, ed. R. Newhauser and John Alford (Binghamton, NY, 1994), pp. 209-35 (pp. 225, 228-30).

provectos, and to them alone, for to others it may be useless and even dangerous. Henry finds support in Augustine's statement that 'there are some things which with their full implications are not understood or are hardly understood ... And these things should never, or only rarely in account of some necessity be set before a popular audience'.[16] In sum, a teacher is perfectly justified in withholding material which he knows could be harmful. It seems that William of Auvergne believed that, in respect of hellish suffering, his attempt to investigate matters which are 'not understood or are hardly understood' should not be set before a popular audience.[17]

This scenario, as intimated by Bernstein, has provoked a sharp rebuke by Jacques Le Goff, who has defended William of Auvergne against what he regards as a charge of 'duplicitous teaching'.[18] Despite this, Le Goff

---

[16] *De doctrina christiana*, IV.ix,23; trans. D. W. Robertson, *Saint Augustine: On Christian Doctrine* (Indianapolis, IN, 1958; repr. 1980), p. 133.

[17] A particularly striking assertion of the importance of withholding potentially dangerous information occurs in the context of a refutation of the doctrines of the Welsh Lollard Walter Brut, which was compiled by a team of theologians recruited by John Trefnant, Bishop of Hereford, who tried Brut for heresy in 1391-3. According to the 'absolute power' of God (a principle of extreme logical possibility) a woman can confect the Eucharist, just as women can contract matrimony with their fathers and their own sons, and a nun can marry a professed religious; further, women can make the sun and moon, lift up the highest mountain and throw it in the sea, and any woman can conceive and give birth to God, destroy the world, make the blind see and the mute speak. But anyone who preaches such things deserves to have his tongue cut out, exclaims Brut's adversary. It seems clear that such sensational and disturbing, though logically possible, propositions are best kept away from the general public. See Alastair Minnis, '*Respondet Walterus Bryth* ...Walter Brut in debate on women priests', in *Text and Controversy from Wyclif to Bale: Essays in Honour of Anne Hudson*, ed. Helen Barr and Ann M. Hutchinson, Medieval Church Studies 4 (Turnhout, 2005), pp. 229-49 (pp. 241-2). Here I argue that Brut's opponents were amplifying the heretic's views the better to oppose them; hence they wrote him into a debate which featured much of their own casuistry, and which upped the intellectual ante far beyond what Brut himself seems actually to have said (insofar as we can infer that from the trial records).

[18] Le Goff, *Birth of Purgatory*, pp. 241-2 [part 3, ch. 8]. Cf. Wei's reaction; *Intellectual Culture in Medieval Paris*, p. 211 (cited in p. 43-4, n. 14 above).

offers the critique that 'however great a theologian he may have been', William 'remained closer to the concerns and mental habits of this flock than the new academic intellectuals, who outstripped him in scholastic theology at the price of becoming somewhat shut up in the Latin Quarter ghetto just then coming into existence'. One might concur with the notion that William was acutely aware of what the 'mental habits' of his 'flock' could and could not cope with – and, in opposition to Le Goff's outrage, find here a very good reason for his desire to be discriminating with the truth, an attitude which was by no means unique to him and which certainly did not undermine his credentials either as a pastor or as a scholastic theologian. The Christian teacher is not in the business of making things up concerning postmortem punishments and rewards; that would be 'duplicitous' indeed. His job is rather to disseminate different aspects of the truth, various kinds of truth, in light of the make-up of a given audience. 'Corporaliter et vere torqueat corpora animarum hujusmodi, et etiam animas ipsas'...[19] That claim has much support in the Bible and in the writings of many saints, and therefore it may be said to express a definite truth (however one might wish to gloss or contextualize it). Furthermore, this truth is of such a transparent quality that it can be set before a popular audience in a direct and unmediated way: what is difficult to understand about a vivid account of the visceral punishments characteristic of purgatory and hell? Such eminent thinkers as Augustine, Gregory the Great and Hugh of St Victor may have taken very seriously the idea that punitive fire may not actually burn the soul but rather trigger an acutely painful imaginative reaction. But such speculation is best confined to the professional theologians. After all, it does not in any way detract or compromise the truth involved here, concerning the materiality of hell-fire. That is fundamental. Quite *how* it hurts the separated soul remains controversial – and there is a considerable lacuna in William's treatment, inasmuch he does not address Gregory's proposition that the soul is not 'burned' directly by that fire. A proposition which (as noted above) Gregory had been able to

---

[19] *De universo*, I.i.65 (II, 682).

hold in his head alongside the proposition that material fire exists in the afterlife.

The passages quoted above regarding hellish imaginations are read by Le Goff as follows: 'what [William] wants to say, I think, is that since fire is efficacious when it exists only in man's imagination, in dreams, for example, it is even more efficacious when it is real'.[20] William is indeed saying that. But he is saying *more* than that. His contention is that the imaginations of dreams may give us some genuine intimation of how horrible the spiritual torments of hell will be, when once again (to follow through the thought experiment) the imagination may play a vital role – after death, as in life. Le Goff's phrase '*only* in man's imagination' underestimates and demeans the uses to which the imagination can be put, under divine direction, as an instrument of suffering – an idea well understood by William.[21] Le Goff notes that William 'sketches a typology and phenomenology of fire', identifying animals like the salamander

---

[20] Le Goff, *Birth of Purgatory*, p. 245 [part 3, ch. 8].

[21] My critique of Le Goff here focuses on his interpretation of William of Auvergne. As is obvious to any medievalist, elsewhere he displays a highly sophisticated understanding of imagination, as proclaimed in his *L'imaginaire médiéval: Essais* (Paris, 1985), trans. by Arthur Goldhammer as *Medieval Imagination* (Chicago, 1988). Goldhammer has, quite fairly I believe, been criticized for translating *imaginaire* as 'imagination'. *L'imaginaire* denotes the shared mental outlook which characterizes a society, as revealed by the rites and images that shape it; here the rationalizations and accommodations of the powerful elite, both secular and religious, are refused heremony. Collective imagination plays a major part in the creation of an *imaginaire*, but certainly is not coterminous with it. That said, Le Goff does not address significantly the issue of the medieval compositive imagination, being concerned with what was possible to think rather than with the actual mechanism of thought. An eloquent affirmation of the potential of the compositive imagination for contemporary cultural interpretation has been offered by Nicholas Watson 'The phantasmal past: time, history, and the recombinative imagination', *Studies in the Age of Chaucer*, 32 (2010), 1-37, who proposes the recognition, and exploitation, of 'complex analogies' between medieval 'deployments of the idea of imagination and our own activities as historians summoning past forms into the present as we inventively recombine the information surviving in our collective *memoria*, the archive' (p. 31).

which are impervious to it, and finding in Sicily a kind of fire with curious properties.[22] All of this shows that God is capable of creating a fire which burns without consuming the object on which it feeds. From which it may be inferred that in hell a certain kind of fire will torture the damned for all eternity, while purgatorial fire will purify sinners for limited periods of time, rendering them fit for heaven. In this particular account of 'the universe of creatures' William is in fact following in the footsteps of St Augustine, as quoted in Chapter 2 above – who also was intrigued by the salamander and the mysterious fire of Sicily (precedents which Le Goff does not note here). Of course, William is seeking to comprehend the idea of fire which burns perpetually without consuming. Augustine had done so before him, and those denizens of 'the Latin Quarter ghetto' would do so after him.

---

[22] Le Goff, *Birth of Purgatory*, p. 245 [part 3, ch. 8].

CHAPTER 6

Hellish imaginations professionalized: William of Auvergne, Avicenna, Albert the Great

Le Goff's thinking here seems driven by the view that the scholastic systematization of postmortem justice and retribution was a consequence of concern that the belief was in danger of 'being swamped by vulgar and superstitious piety', fear 'of an other world so close to popular folklore and to the popular sensibility, an other world defined more by the imagination than by theory, more by the senses than by the spirit'.[1] Le Goff has purgatory specifically in mind here, but his postulation of a major professionalizing movement obviously reaches farther than that. A little later, when discussing what he sees as the remarkable achievement by the Dominican polymath Albert the Great (d. 1280) in rationalizing belief concerning purgatory which 'arose as much from imagery as from reasoning, as much from fantastic tales as from authorities', Le Goff remarks that 'though he may have wished to purify the imagination, it was not a question of principled hostility but one of determining when the imagination stood in contradiction to logic, truth, or the deeper meaning of the belief'.[2] Here the imagination is being relegated to the world of 'popular folklore' and 'popular sensibility', the domain of 'fantastic tales' – tales such as, one may infer, the visions of Tundale, Thurkill, Owein Miles and The Monk of Eynsham. When it enters the realm of scholastic disputation there is a need to 'purify' it, Le Goff claims, or at least to render null and void its supposed resistance to logic, truth, and deeper meaning. He is using 'imagination' in the broad sense of the word which is common in both English and French parlance, rather than addressing its significance when understood historically in its complex late-medieval sense, as a compositive and associational power which could create similitudes, including images that had no direct

---

[1] Le Goff, *Birth of Purgatory*, p. 240 [part 3, ch. 8].
[2] Ibid., p. 259 [part 3, ch. 8].

referents in the material world, all of which were stored for future use in the mental treasury of the memory. Thus understood, the imagination often featured crucially in scholastic disputation, with the possible role of imagery in the afterlife being treated with the utmost intellectual seriousness.

Which brings us back to William of Auvergne. Where did he get his ideas about the power of hellish imaginations, ideas which soar far beyond anything in Augustine or Gregory? Perhaps from one of those radical Muslim Aristotelians who (*inter alia*) had dared to suggest that the human imagination can physically move stones, men and camels. Bernstein detects the influence of Avicenna,[3] who (he claims) believed the torments of hell are wholly spiritual, and based on certain images (*formae*) which the soul acquired whilst joined to its body; once acquired, the soul independently performs its own internal operations involving them, without any external cause.[4] Those forms came from two sources – the usual processes of sense perception, of course, but also through the agency of higher powers; here Avicenna's Neoplatonic legacy comes into view. In particular, the pains endured by damned souls are caused by the heightened visualization of physical punishments which they thought about while still joined to the body: since the soul perceives more clearly when it is separated from the body (because then it is free from corporeal interference) those forms are likely to be stronger and clearer, and hence more horrific, than anything experienced either in waking reality or in

---

[3] Roland J. Teske, the doyen of William of Auvergne scholars, has concluded that 'William is an heir of Avicenna to a much greater extent than has, I believe, commonly been recognized, even though William is certainly a rather ungracious heir who far too seldom shows any, much less a sufficient, acknowledgment of his debt to Avicenna'. *Studies in the Philosophy of William of Auvergne, Bishop of Paris (1228-1249)* (Milwaukee, WI, 2006). pp. 217-37 (p. 237).

[4] Bernstein, 'Esoteric theology', pp. 527-8. It should be noted that Bernstein is reliant on the Latin version of Avicenna's *Metaphysica* (as of course William of Auvergne was), which somewhat obscures the Muslim author's presentation of this crucial issue.

dreams. Here, then, is substantiation of what Bernstein calls the metaphorical reading of the pains of hell.[5]

Thus far I have been following Bernstein's characterization of Avicenna's intellectual position, which is generally supported by Jean R. Michot's major study of the Persian's ideas about the destiny of man.[6] But the matter is rather more complicated. In the first instance, it is quite true that, as Peter Heath notes, Avicenna mentions 'the possibility of an "imagined" version of a Qur'anic heaven and hell in the case of souls who have so imprinted in their imaginations similitudes … of the delights of heaven or the torments of hell as described in the Qur'an that they are unable to conceive of an afterlife assuming any other form'.[7] That is to say, when 'simpleminded souls' have 'been indoctrinated in a "belief concerning the hereafter"', they will 'carry the belief with them into the afterlife', experiencing in their compositive imaginations whatever they had expected to occur in the life to come.[8] Herbert A. Davidson, whom I have been quoting here, explains further that the disembodied souls of such people will experience things in a way that mirrors what they had experienced, through their sensory faculties, in the present world. The absence of the body will not hinder that operation. Indeed, Avicenna articulates the theory that 'experiences generated by the imaginative faculty can be "of greater potency and directness" than those tied to sense

---

[5] Bernstein, 'Esoteric theology', consistently uses the discourse of metaphor at pp. 510, 513, 517, 521, 522, 523, 524, 526, and 530-31, to describe how the language of physical pain affords metaphors for immaterial pain, the latter being 'the conceptual import' behind the 'pictorial envelope' (Ricoeur's words again), with pain being the connecting element between the two.

[6] *La destinée de l'homme selon Avicenne* (Louvain, 1986), pp. 18-56 (esp. pp. 18-19, 23-30).

[7] Peter Heath, *Allegory and Philosophy in Avicenna (Ibn Sina): With a Translation of the Book of the Prophet Muhammad's Ascent to Heaven* (Philadelphia, 1992), p. 69.

[8] Herbert A. Davidson, *Alfarabi, Avicenna, and Averroes, on Intellect: Their Cosmologies, Theories of the Active Intellect, and Theories of Human Intellect* (Oxford, 1992), pp. 112-13.

perception, just as "what is dreamed is more vivid ... than what is sensed"'.

However, the claim that Avicenna himself thought like that has been challenged. It should be emphasized that he attributes the controversial view to another, unnamed, scholar, without saying whether he believes it or not. 'Given Avicenna's explicit statements that the imagination passes away with the body', Heath deems 'unconvincing' Michot's argument that 'Avicenna came to accept the idea of imaginative apperceptions of heaven and hell'.[9] In similar vein, Davidson concludes that he 'could not, with consistency, have himself accepted that rationalization'.[10] Unconvincing and inconsistent it may be, but perhaps Avicenna 'recorded the rationalization of promised physical pleasures in the hereafter in order to protect himself against any charge that he was wholly rejecting Islamic accounts of the life to come'.[11] What, then, of the obvious challenge to that rationalization, the fact that the compositive imagination operates through a physical organ, a ventricle of the brain, which will cease to function at death? Avicenna comes up with the notion that the disembodied soul will, in some mysterious way, attach itself to one of the celestial spheres, and that something therein will serve as 'the organ through which the soul exercises its compositive imaginative function'. In other words (the words being Davidson's), 'a celestial sphere or an aspect of one of the spheres serves as a surrogate brain for the disembodied compositive imagination'.[12] This is bizarre for several reasons, not least because there is no evidence whatever (in Avicenna's worldview) that a celestial sphere is disposed to receive, or capable of

---

[9] Heath, *Allegory and Philosophy in Avicenna*, p. 78 note 72. Bieniak and Roncarati agree with Heath, attributing to Averroes the belief that the cognitive faculties which make use of corporeal images (imagination, *vis aestimativa* and memory) cannot continue to operate 'when the corporeal substratum is lacking'. 'The disappearance of sensible images implies the loss of all the powers which make use of them'; 'none of these faculties can survive after a man's death'. *The Soul-Body Problem*, pp. 140, 153.

[10] Davidson, *Alfarabi, Avicenna, and Averroes*, p. 116.

[11] Ibid., p. 115

[12] Ibid., p. 114.

receiving in terms of its composition, a disembodied soul in this way.[13] But perhaps the imperative of respecting Islamic accounts of postmortem reward and punishment led him into offering a theory he would normally have rejected, as a professional philosopher – who had to argue that philosophy was permissible in Islam.

Thomas Aquinas seems to have had no hesitation in addressing these arguments in their own terms, and assuming they represented the authentic thought of Avicenna (as we shall see). As far as William of Auxerre is concerned, they may be deemed a boost and reinforcement of the views of certain traditional authorities. It may be restated that William's disquisition owes much to Gregory the Great, and Augustine before him. And we need not travel further than Hugh of St Victor for the theory that the separated soul will be blessed with some sort of heightened sensory perception, enabling it to feel and therefore suffer all the more acutely (cf. Chapter 3 above). So, to some extent, William was putting old wine in new bottles: to claim that he engaged in an 'act of individual eclecticism' by espousing a 'largely obscured Christian tradition' of metaphorical reading 'dating back to Origen' is going too far.[14] That said, there is a fresh impetus here, for which Avicenna deserves due credit; the fit of the ideas in question is compelling.

Those ideas have been seen (most insistently by Bernstein) as driving an intellectual movement whereby the possibly corporeal aspects of hell were downplayed, with metaphorical explanations being offered and a strong emphasis placed on the 'spiritual effects of its torments on the damned'.[15] Against this Donald Mowbray has argued that, during the thirteenth century, theologians devoted 'greater and more sophisticated attention' to the issue of 'the corporeality of suffering in hell'.[16] I concur

---

[13] Davidson adds, 'Since the compositive imaginative faculty could not operate without a brain, and since Avicenna's earlier reasoning [wherein he rejects the theory of the transmigration of souls] would exclude the celestial sphere's serving as a surrogate brain, disembodied souls should not, in his system, be able to experience the hereafter through their imaginative faculties'. *Alfarabi, Avicenna, and Averroes*, p. 114.

[14] Bernstein, 'Esoteric theology', p. 531.

[15] Bernstein, 'The invocation of Hell', p. 22.

[16] Mowbray, *Pain and Suffering*, p. 133.

with that latter argument; anyone with doubts on the matter would be well advised to read the forceful refutation of Augustine's speculations in *De Genesi ad litteram* which are contained in the *Sentences* commentary of Albert the Great (which originated from lectures delivered in Paris during the period 1243-5). Hell's fires are corporeal and so is its location, which, Albert declares, is under the earth, as is intimated by Isaiah xiv.9, 'Hell below was in an uproar to meet thee at thy coming'.[17] The relative ease with which the schoolmen accepted the doctrine of hell's physical location – as a geographical fact about the present, pre-Resurrection, universe – is remarkable.[18] As Tiziana Suarez-Nani has cogently said, 'for

---

[17] *In IV. Sent.*, dist. 44, F, art. 38, resp. (*Alberti opera*, XXX, 594). Cf. Mowbray, *Pain and Suffering*, p. 134. Aquinas agrees, pointing out that, in his *Retractationes* (ii.9), Augustine declares that he should have simply said that hell is beneath the earth, rather than merely giving the reason why it is stated or believed to be under the earth. *In IV Sent.*, dist. 44, qu. 3, art. 2, qc. 3, co., in *Aquinatis opera* (Parma edn). All references to Aquinas's *Sentences* commentary are to this edition, which was consulted online. On the relevant views of William of Auvergne and Bonaventure see Le Goff, *Birth of Purgatory*, pp. 244, 252-4 [part 3, ch. 8]. Belief in the material locations of hell and purgatory made belief in the materiality of punitive fire a lot easier.

[18] The matter has been discussed usefully by Diana Walsh Pasulka, who brings the debate right up to the present day; *Heaven Can Wait: Purgatory in Catholic Devotional and Popular Culture* (Oxford, 2014). A particularly interesting contribution has been made by Margaret Burrell, who looks at geological features of the locations of hell and purgatory as described in two Anglo-French texts, Benedeit's *Le Voyage de Saint Brendan* and Marie de France's *L'Espurgatoire seint Patriz*. In the case of the former, an Icelandic volcano eruption might have influenced its description of a fiery island, populated by thousands of demons and the damned. In the case of the latter, the Burren (in northwestern County Clare, Ireland) has a subterranean cave system of considerable complexity which 'might well have been a source for the account of the demonical location of purgatory's pit'; this is offered as an alternative to the usual association of St Patrick's purgatory (on which more below) with Station Island on Lough Derg, Co. Donegal. 'Hell as a geological construct', *Florilegium*, 24 (2007), 37-54. Pasulka's chapter 'When Purgatory was a place on earth' (*Heaven Can Wait*, pp. 30-58) focuses on the Lough Derg site, noting that, despite the controversy surrounding it and several attempts to shut it down, 'Pilgrims continued to visit the location

medieval thinkers, there was no doubt that immaterial substances were related to and located in physical space'; 'biblical passages ... told of many angelic movements from the sky to the earth', while a comprehensive picture of 'the created world required the inclusion of all creatures (even spiritual creatures) in a spatio-temporal framework'.[19] This affirmation of materiality strongly militated against any purely metaphorical readings of hell, together with purgatory, as distinct places of punishment. Further, it lent weight to the doctrine that hell-fire was also material; Albert's combination of the two issues is symptomatic of a major thought-trend. But let us return to his strained engagement with

throughout the eighteenth century, and clerics continued debating the terrestrial location of purgatory until 1860' (p. 33). Such literalizing enterprises have roots in ancient and medieval cosmological thought.

[19] Tiziana Suarez-Nani, 'Space and movement in medieval thought: the angelological shift', in *Space, Imagination and the Cosmos from Antiquity to the Early Modern Period*, ed. Frederik A. Bakker, Delphine Bellis and Carla Rita Palmerino (Cham, Switzerland, 2018, corrected publication 2019), pp. 69-89 (p. 73). Peter Lombard (*Sentences*, I, dist. 37, ch. 6[270]) formulated three possible modalities of localisation: through the circumscription of bodies (*circumscriptio*, i.e. containment by dimensions, which require materiality); by divine ubiquity (*ubiquitas*, ruled out because only God can be everywhere at once), and – the generally accepted theory – through definition or delimitation (*definitio*). *Definitio* could be explained in terms of the localisation which results when an angel enters into contact with some body (including a human body), which bears the implication that angels inactive in this regard are 'not localized in the space of the material world'. (True, they may be said to be in the Empyrean Heaven – but that is not a material place, and therefore, from this perspective, can be regarded as nowhere.) A second explanation of *definitio* regarded localisation as 'based in the being of created spirits themselves', which led to abstruse discussion based on space seen as a mathematical quantity or dimension rather than as a physical property. For example, John Duns Scotus, OFM (d. 1308) held that, 'strictly speaking, the angel is "indifferent" to all spatial configurations, and can therefore occupy any place' (Suarez-Nani, pp. 73-7). However (it may be added), that does not mean that angels can occupy the same space simultaneously. The question of whether a million angels may fit upon a needle's point was never debated as such, and belongs in the realm of parody and anti-Catholic satire. Cf. Peter Harrison, 'Angels on pinheads and needles' points', *Notes and Queries*, 63 (2016), 45-7.

Augustine. When Augustine spoke of the matter maybe he was merely stating a view rather than affirming it (*non asserendo*), Albert suggests. Or indeed, in this matter he may not have had the plain revelation of the truth which was enjoyed by other saints – a quite outspoken remark, given the deference routinely afforded to Augustine, and the extraordinary manoeuvres the schoolmen usually engaged in to enlist his support.[20]

Albert's affirmation of the materiality of hell, in terms of its fire and its location, goes hand in glove with a robust affirmation of the immateriality of the soul.[21] His rebuttal of what Augustine speculated in *De Genesi ad litteram* concerning a *similitudo corporis* which enables the soul to see bodily experiences in sleep, and which may be carried with it into the nether world, is perhaps one of the most oblique offered by any of the *Sentences* commentators, but certainly one of the most effective. Having started off by quoting the Lombard's iteration of Augustine's doctrine, Albert responds not directly to it but instead cites the controversial view of one of Augustine's predecessors, Tertullian (*c.* 155-*c.* 240), that the soul is a copy (*effigia*) of the body, with the human interior being shaped in the likeness of its exterior. Tertullian says this expressly, Albert avers – and it is a heresy. By contrast, Augustine does not, in truth, assert this, but raises it as a debatable matter, which 'more greatly appears to be absurd and false rather than true'. Albert seeks to reduce the idea *ad absurdum* by claiming that, in dreams, it is not the soul that is seeing bodily activities taking place but a man living in his body, and this is hardly surprising since he is corporeal. If the embodied soul were indeed to see such things, then the separated soul would engage in dreaming – a ridiculous thing to say. Albert throws in the suggestion that, when Augustine referred to what the soul might carry with it into the next world, he had in mind the taints and merits that were contracted in this world. A gracious way of saving the appearances.

[20] *In IV Sent.*, dist. 44, F, art. 38 (*Alberti opera*, XXX, 594). Albert aggressively asserts that 'in this question nothing beyond the statements of the saints is to be said' – with the exception of what Augustine said in *De Genesi ad litteram*, it would seem!
[21] *In IV Sent.*, dist. 44, G, art. 41 (*Alberti opera*, XXX, 598-9).

Albert's knowledge of Tertullian's assertion of the corporeality of the human soul seems to derive from the Carthaginian author's treatise *De anima*,[22] where St Luke's tale of Dives and Lazarus is cited as proof positive of the truth of that doctrine. (Here I am quoting more of Tertullian's text than Albert does.) If the soul did not possess some sort of facsimile body, how could it possibly be kept in a particular location, and punished with fire or refreshed there?[23] As Petr Kitzler succinctly puts it in his summary of Tertullian's discussion, 'Only that which has a body can feel something and if it feels something it must have a body'. Thus Tertullian affirms the literal sense of Luke xvi.24, refusing to believe that it can be read metaphorically. Although Albert does not specifically address this radical exegesis in his *Sentences* commentary, he tacitly gainsays Tertullian by reading the scriptural passage metaphorically (though he does not use that term), thereby denying that it provides evidence for the postmortem continuation of corporeal agency. How could the rich man buried in hell have a bodily tongue? And why should he want this member cooled, rather than any other? What exactly is meant by the tip of Lazarus's finger (*extremum digiti sui*), and the drop of liquid for which Dives begged? Albert reels off the following explanations. The reference to the tongue may be said to indicate the power of the soul which enables the tongue to taste and produce speech. According to St Gregory (Albert claims) the rich man's sin was greed, and talkativeness, which is the companion of gluttony; therefore it is appropriate that his tongue should feel pain over and above what is endured by the other body parts. The possibility that Lazarus might extend his finger signifies the potential proffering of pity, which in this case cannot be bestowed; Albert plays on the connection between the 'extremity' or tip of that finger and the extreme depravity in which the sinner had lived. And the little drop of water signifies cooling, which is not possible for the damned, since they are cast into a lake (of fire) in

---

[22] On which see Petr Kitzler, 'Tertullian's concept of the soul and his corporealistic ontology', in *Tertullianus Afer. Tertullien et la littérature chrétienne d'Afrique*, ed. J. Lagouanere and S. Fialon, Instrumenta Patristica et Mediaevalia 70 (Turnhout, 2015), pp. 43-62.

[23] 'Tertullian's concept of the soul', p. 54.

which there is no water (cf. Apocalypse xx.14); little wonder that Dives should long for that particular refreshment.

The contrast with Augustine's interpretation of Luke xvi.24 is striking. Both theologians agree that Luke's images designate incorporeal things, but where Augustine instantly reaches for the comparison with what is seen by those who are asleep or in an ecstasy[24] – an analogy which Albert roundly rejects, in light of its profound ontological and psychological implications – Albert provides a moralizing or tropological exegesis, reading the text as a warning against the sins of greed and garrulity. The category of the 'spiritual' reading of Scripture is broad indeed, as already noted; here it accommodates an understanding of the spiritual nature of the soul along with a spiritual or allegorical reading of hellish suffering which, while not disturbing belief in the materiality of hell (but rather assuming it), can see the imagery of Luke xvi.24 as having moral significance. But the deconstruction of metaphor constitutes a common and clear procedural basis for all such exegetical manoeuvres.

In light of this complexity, I would wish to challenge the view that theologians sought to dematerialise the pains of hell in a professionalizing effort 'to prevent popular religion from confusing or contaminating the rational expression of doctrine'.[25] William of Auvergne's relevant remarks cannot be enlisted to make that case. Of course, it was devotionally expedient and useful for the *simplices* to be frightened by the thought of intense physical suffering; the crucial position afforded to the figure of Fear, Death's messenger, in *Sawles Warde*, was well conceived. The disturbing thought that those dragons, worms, toads and frogs described in that text, and so many others, were metaphors of mental anguish was best kept between the *provectos*, who understood just how terrible mental anguish could, and would, be. That is a perfectly fair point to make, since it is consonant with scholastic attitudes to the selective dissemination of knowledge. However, the gap between the needs of the experts and those of 'the non-theological classes' (to borrow a phrase from Alexander

---

[24] Cf. Chapter 2 above.
[25] Bernstein, 'The invocation of Hell', p. 22.

Murray)[26] was not as wide as Bernstein implies and Le Goff fears. We are some distance away from the slippery slope which leads to Spinoza's declaration that the Bible consists 'almost wholly of lies useful to the vulgar', the 'few useful truths it contains' being 'superfluous for intellectuals in whom the natural light of reason shines clearly'.[27] Equally fundamental is the fact that, within late-medieval thought, the role of imagination and metaphor in the hermeneutics of hell is more complicated than sometimes has been supposed.

---

[26] Alexander Murray, 'Demons as psychological abstractions', in *Angels in Medieval Philosophical Inquiry*, ed. Iribarren and Lenz, pp. 171-84 (p. 173).
[27] Walker, *The Decline of Hell*, p. 7, citing Spinoza's *Tractatus theologico-politicus* (1670).

CHAPTER 7

Metaphor confronted, the imagination contained: Aquinas and Bonaventure

The intellectual stakes are made clear by Thomas Aquinas's direct attack on the Avicennan ideas cited above, which occurs in his commentary on the fourth book of the Lombard's *Sentences*, where he poses the question, is the infernal fire by which the bodies of the damned are punished, a corporeal fire?[1] Having initially noted that philosophers like Avicenna did not believe in the Resurrection, thereby effectively undermining anything 'they' may have to say on the matter under debate, Aquinas explains that this is why Avicenna *cum suis* believed that only the soul could be subjected to punishment after death. Since the soul is incorporeal, it cannot be punished by a corporeal fire, they say; hence whatever is stated concerning the future punishment of souls after death is stated metaphorically (*metaphorice dicatur*). In their opinion, the torments of the wicked will be purely spiritual, inasmuch as they will be prevented from achieving ultimate joy and happiness, which they naturally desire. Aquinas continues to expound this unacceptable theory, as a prelude to refuting it, as follows:

> Unde sicut omnia quae de delectatione animarum post mortem dicuntur, quae videntur ad delectationem corporalem pertinere, sicut quod reficiantur, quod rideant, et hujusmodi; ita etiam quidquid de harum afflictione dicitur quod in corporalem punitionem sonare videtur, per similitudinem debet intelligi; sicut quod igne ardeant, vel foetoribus affligantur, et cetera hujusmodi.
> [Wherefore, just as all descriptions of the pleasure of souls after death that seem to denote bodily pleasure – for instance, that they are refreshed, that they laugh, and so forth – must be taken by way of similitude, so also in respect of whatever is said concerning the

---

[1] *In IV Sent.*, dist. 44, qu. 3, art. 2, qc. 1, co. (*Aquinatis opera*).

suffering of souls which seems to imply bodily punishment; for instance, that they burn in fire, or suffer foul smells, and so forth.]²

Since difficult ideas concerning spiritual pleasure and pain are unknown to the populace at large (*ignota multitudini*), to them such matters need to be expressed figuratively (*figuraliter*) in terms of corporeal pleasures and pains, so that men may be greatly moved to the desire or the fear thereof.

Aquinas then goes much further, directly crediting Avicenna by name with a doctrine which, as modern Avicenna scholars have emphasized, is actually attributed to somebody else, an unnamed scholar, in the philosopher's presentation of the issue (cf. p. 52 above). At any rate, what is in question here is not merely imagination *about* hell but imagination *in* hell, the role imagination plays in the infliction of pain.

> ... animae malorum post mortem non per corpora, sed per corporum similitudines punientur, sicut in somnis propter similitudines praedictas in imaginatione existentes videtur homini quod torqueatur poenis diversis ...
> [.... the souls of the wicked are punished after death not by actual bodies but by the likenesses of bodies, just as in a dream, on account of those aforesaid likenesses existing in his imagination, it seems to a man that he is suffering various pains ...]³

Here, then, is a succinct summary of the very ideas which William of Auvergne had explored in his thought-experiment (could Aquinas have been responding directly to him?), even including the notion that the common people should be kept in fear by the thought of corporeal pain, although it may be doubted if this can be experienced in hell, at least in a way they can understand. The degree of attention Aquinas affords those ideas is proof positive of the challenge they presented, and the interest they held for William becomes all the more clear.

---

² Ibid.
³ Ibid.

That said, there is an obvious difference. As we have seen, Avicenna presented the view that when 'simpleminded souls' have been taught in this world about the pains of hell and the pleasures of heaven they will bear those same views with them into the next world, where their compositive imaginations will function to produce the very imagery they were expecting. But this, according to that same view, only applies to the simpleminded; souls that enjoy a high degree of intellectual perfection have no need of such devices. In attempting to explain this doctrine of hellish imaginations, which he associated directly with Avicenna, Aquinas (like William of Auvergne before him) makes no such distinction. He does not separate out souls in terms of the amount of compositive imagination they will need to practice to make sense of the hereafter. Aquinas works on the supposition that, although at present simple souls benefit from instruction through the use of metaphor, their simplicity shall not be reflected in the types of torture in store for them; their current intellectual deficiencies and incapacities will not determine the nature of their postmortem suffering. No-one will be punished for *simplicitas*. Other standards of divine justice shall apply, which are free of considerations of intellectual formation (and of class, one may add).

Aquinas focuses on the idea that hellish torments will be caused not by actual bodies but by the likenesses of bodies. Which leads him to make an obvious and challenging connection: the esteemed Saint Augustine himself seems to have held something like this position, as expressed in *De Genesi ad litteram*, Book XII, where he offers the opinion that after death the soul is carried away to a place which is spiritual and not corporeal, this being supported (to expand Aquinas's statement a little) by the analogy with the experience of people whose souls have temporarily left the body, whether in sleep or in more traumatic occurrences.[4] Aquinas proceeds to refute this argument, as being inappropriate (*inconveniens*), not a fit way to resolve the problem.[5] His intellectual mission here is to impose restraining limits, containing parameters, on what Augustine had said. The imagination is a power that

---

[4] *De Genesi ad litteram*, xii, 32,60 (ed. Zycha, p. 426; tr. Hill, pp. 499-500).
[5] *In IV Sent.*, dist. 44, qu. 3, art. 2, qc. 1, co.

makes use of a bodily organ, Aquinas emphasizes, and since such a material thing does not exist in a separated soul, it has no means of producing *visiones imaginativae* like those experienced in the soul of a dreamer. (The dreamer's soul still resides in his body, and therefore his imagination can still function; given that a separated soul has no body to enable it to imagine, the comparison between the dreamer's experience and what may be experienced by a separated soul simply does not hold up). Recognizing the problem (Aquinas continues), in his *Metaphysics* Avicenna claimed that the separated soul uses as a sort of substitute organ (*quasi pro organo*) some part of a heavenly body, which will enable the posthumous imagination of pain and pleasure.

Here, then, Aquinas addresses that aspect of Avicenna's text which has caused his modern readers so much consternation: the notion that a disembodied soul can somehow attach itself to one of the celestial spheres, and something in such a sphere will enable it to exercise its compositive imagination – as if such a link could possibly be forged 'not only to a different "bit" of sensible or sublunary matter but to some different kind of matter, celestial matter'.[6]

In trying to make sense of this (and his attempt is quite impressive) Aquinas suggests that Avicenna was somewhat indebted to the opinion of certain 'philosophers of old' who held that souls return to the stars who are their companions. Aquinas must have in mind the discourse of Plato's *Timaeus* (41d-e), where the Demiurge is credited with having assigned each soul to a star (as like a chariot), from which they would descend when forced to join with bodies, and to which they could return to enjoy a blessed existence if they had lived a righteous life on earth.[7]

---

[6] This phrase is taken from Thérèse-Anne Druart, 'The human soul's individuation and its survival after the body's death: Avicenna on the causal relation between body and soul', *Arabic Sciences and Philosophy*, 10 (2000), 259-73 (p. 266 note 18).

[7] *In IV Sent.*, dist. 44, qu. 3, art. 2, qc. 1 co. These ideas were influentially echoed by Boethius in that most controversial part of his *De consolatione Philosophiae*, namely book III, metre 9 (for which the *Timaeus* is a direct source). For a summary account of medieval commentaries on this work with special reference to this metre, see Lodi Nauta, 'The *Consolation*: the Latin commentary tradition, 800-1700', in *The Cambridge Companion to Boethius*,

But this, Aquinas declares robustly, is quite absurd, according to the teaching of Aristotle, who refuted the idea of Pythagoras that the soul can pass from one body to another (i.e. the doctrine of the transmigration of souls). Here Aquinas is drawing on Aristotle's *De anima*, where the notion that any soul could be clothed with any body was rejected, since each body-soul composite has its own special configuration.[8] Each soul must use its body just as each art must use its special tools or instruments. A soul cannot pass from one body to another, and (though Aquinas does not spell this out) a heavenly body cannot supply something which a soul lacks following its separation from its unique earthly body. Imaginative visions, therefore, cannot occur in separated souls, and they cannot be the means whereby hellish torments are inflicted.

It is somewhat ironic that Aquinas, in seeking to refute Avicenna, has formulated a doctrine which contemporary Avicenna scholars regard as actually in keeping with the Muslim philosopher's substantive thought. And, for the record, Avicenna rejected the theory of the transmigration of souls, which makes all the more strange his attempt to find a substitute organ in some heavenly sphere to enable the functioning of compositive imagination in disembodied souls.[9]

What, then, of Augustine's view that after death the soul is not carried away to a corporeal place?[10] He may have meant, Aquinas suggests, that the place is not corporeal because the soul exists there not corporeally (like a body exists in a place) but spiritually (just like angels exist in a place). I read this as a rather roundabout way of saying that a spiritual entity can exist in a corporeal place without itself being corporeal – which Augustine certainly had not meant! Rather he had envisaged an

---

ed. John Marenbon (Cambridge, 2009), pp. 255-78 (at pp. 264-73). See further Stephen McCluskey's fine synopsis of the larger intellectual context, 'Boethius's astronomy and cosmology', in *A Companion to Boethius in the Middle Ages*, ed. Noel Harold Kaylor and Philip Edward Phillips (Leiden, 2012), pp. 47-73. On the subsequent decline of the constitutive ideas see Richard C. Dales, 'The de-animation of the heavens in the Middle Ages', *Journal of the History of Ideas*, 41/4 (1980), 531-50.

[8] *De anima*, 1 (407b). Here the idea is dismissed as a Pythagorean fabrication.
[9] Davidson, *Alfarabi, Avicenna, and Averroes on Intellect*, p. 114.
[10] *In IV Sent.*, dist. 44, qu. 3, art. 2, qc. 1, ad 2.

incorporeal entity, the soul, proceeding after the body's death to an incorporeal world (whether heaven or hell) in which it would experience not actual 'bodily sights but sights *resembling* bodily ones' (cf. Chapter 1 above). Here Aquinas is doing quite a bit of argument-stretching (or, 'reverent interpretation' as it was then called) to get the saint on-side. He also resorts to the explanation, as his teacher Albert the Great had done before him, that perhaps Augustine may have been venturing a mere opinion rather than speaking definitively (*opinando, et non determinando*), 'as he does frequently in that book'. As indeed he does in *De Genesi ad litteram*. But the challenge of the views Aquinas is citing here was very real, and deeply troubling to schoolmen heavily invested in Aristotelian epistemology and psychology.

Then Aquinas executes a sharp argument-move by declaring that, whatever may be said about the fire which torments separated souls, it must be affirmed that the fire which torments the bodies of the damned after the Resurrection is definitely corporeal, because a body cannot fittingly have a punishment applied to it which is in itself not corporeal.[11] Another passage of Augustine is easily brought into play here – his affirmation of the materiality of punitive fire (*De civitate Dei*, xxi, 10, as extracted in the Lombard's text), which was made in a context where post-resurrection bodies are clearly referenced. For further discussion Aquinas refers us to another *quaestio*, on whether sensitive powers remain in the separated soul,[12] to which we may now turn.

His discussion of whether the separated soul can be punished by corporeal fire begins with Augustine's statement in *De Genesi ad litteram* (as reiterated by Peter Lombard) that the things that affect the soul for good or ill after its separation from the body are not actually corporeal but resemble corporeal things.[13] Augustine had gone on to say that what is seen in such visions is both real joy and real affliction, made from spiritual substance; the soul suffers pain, because it bears in itself a likeness to its own body (*similitudo corporis*; cf. Chapter 1 above). But here Aquinas is not interested in what Augustine had gone on to say. He

---

[11] *In IV Sent.*, dist. 44, qu. 3, art. 2, qc. 1, co.
[12] *In IV Sent.*, dist. 44, qu. 3, art. 3, qc. 3.
[13] *In IV Sent.*, dist. 44, qu. 3, art. 3, qc. 3, arg. 1.

simply attributes to Augustine the belief that the separated soul is not punished with a bodily fire, and proclaims a close parallel to this in the passage in Gregory the Great's *Dialogues* where the possibility is raised that the soul is punished merely by the sight of the fire.[14] (Indeed, Aquinas's entire treatment is heavily indebted to all the possibilities concerning the materiality of hellish punishments which were raised briefly in book iv, chapter 29 of the *Dialogues*. Gregory's analysis, however, is presented in a piecemeal fashion, with finicky *divisio textus* being undertaken, and Gregory's conclusive statement withheld until much later in Aquinas's discussion.) Aquinas opines that punishment through sight of fire cannot be the answer, since the only way the soul could experience this is by intellectual vision, because it lacks the corporeal organs necessary for sensitive or imaginative vision (*sensitiva vel imaginaria*). Generally speaking, intellectual vision cannot be the cause of sorrow, because (according to Aristotle) 'there is no sorrow contrary to the pleasure of considering',[15] and so the soul cannot be punished by that type of vision. Against such arguments is set the point that, since both demons and the damned will suffer alike from the same corporeal fire which will flourish after the General Resurrection, separated souls also must suffer from that same fire.[16] Quite a non-sequitur.

However, the matter is made clear in Aquinas's rigorous *responsio*.[17] When we speak of the fire of hell this is not said metaphorically

---

[14] *In IV Sent.*, dist. 44, qu. 3, art. 3, qc. 3, arg. 5. Cf. *Dialogi*, iv, 29; *PL*, LXXVII, col. 368A (as cited above).

[15] A rather distant iteration of statements made in Aristotle's *Topics*, i, 13 and *Nicomachean Ethics*, x, 3.

[16] *In IV Sent.*, dist. 44, qu. 3, art. 3, qc. 3, s. c. 1. Bonaventure adds an interesting twist by saying that, while he cannot be sure, it seems more probable that the punishment of demons by fire will not take place until after the General Resurrection – whereas the punishment of damned souls is not deferred. *In II Sent.*, dist. 6, art, 2, qu. 1 (*Bonaventurae opera*, II, 164-5). But what about the *Glossa ordinaria*'s explanation of James iii.6, 'a tongue inflamed by Gehenna', Gehenna being the devil, who is always burning, bearing with him the torments of flame wherever he is? Bonaventure reads this metaphorically: we are dealing not with material fire but the flames of anger and envy, which cause incessant torment.

[17] *In IV Sent.*, dist. 44, qu. 3, art. 3, qc. 3, co.

(*metaphorice*), he asserts, and neither is it an imaginary fire, but rather a real corporeal fire (*nec ignis imaginarius, sed verus ignis corporeus*). At Matthew xxv.41 Christ says that this fire was prepared for the devil and his angels, who are incorporeal, just like the human soul.[18] Therefore the human soul can suffer from corporeal fire. Here, then, is a robust rejection of the metaphorical reading of the torments of hell together with the role of imagination in those very torments.

But how can the incorporeal soul possibly suffer from corporeal fire? Some argue that the mere seeing of the fire makes the soul suffer: here Aquinas returns to his drip-feed of material from Gregory's *Dialogues*, iv, 29, this time to develop the proposition that, in itself, the act of seeing does not cause pain, but pain may be caused inasmuch as something with the power to hurt is being seen. Which leads into the argument that, although corporeal fire cannot burn the disembodied soul, the soul nevertheless apprehends that fire as being hurtful to itself, and as a result of that *apprehensio* (mental grasping, seizure) is filled with fear and sorrow. As Psalm xiii.5 puts it, 'there have they trembled for fear, where there was no fear', and Gregory says that 'the soul burns through seeing itself aflame'.[19] But Aquinas still feels that this is insufficient as an explanation. For the soul would be suffering not from real fire but from the mere apprehension of fire – which, Aquinas seems to think, would be insufficiently painful. He admits that a genuine feeling of sorrow or pain may result from a 'false imagination' (*ex aliqua falsa imaginatio*), citing Augustine's relevant discussion in *De Genesi ad litteram* in support. But there, as we have seen (in Chapter 1 above), Augustine had explored what the imagination can come up with in dreams or in traumatic out-of-body

---

[18] The issue of whether angels, and hence demons, were pure form (Aquinas's view) or in some way included matter in their composition (Bonaventure's) was a major bone of contention. For discussion see David Keck, *Angels and Angelology in the Middle Ages* (Oxford, 1998), pp. 94-99, 111-12; Armand Maurer, *The Philosophy of William of Ockham in the Light of its Principles* (Toronto, 1999), Chapter 8: On angels, pp. 339-74; and John F. Wippel, 'Metaphysical composition of angels in Bonaventure, Aquinas, and Godfrey of Fontaines', in *A Companion to Angels in Medieval Philosophy*, ed. Tobias Hoffmann (Leiden, 2012), pp. 45-78.

[19] *PL*, LXXVII, col. 368A.

experiences as a means of understanding how the pains of hell can be 'of a spiritual, not a bodily nature'. Rather than denigrating the imagination's creations as 'false' he was making positive use of them in his speculation. In contrast, Aquinas's purpose is to distinguish between suffering from the thing itself and suffering from the likeness (*similitudo*) of the thing as conceived in the mind; the mere image of hell-fire is, he supposes, at a far remove from actual fire.

Aquinas's downplaying of the kind of pain caused by such imagery extends to the extraordinarily dismissive claim that it would be even less than the suffering which can be caused by imaginary visions (*per imaginarias visiones*) experienced during life, since the latter result from real images of things (*veras imagines rerum*), which the soul carries about with it, whereas the former result from false conceptions feigned by the erring soul (*falsas conceptiones quas anima errans fingit*).[20] Furthermore, it is highly unlikely that separated souls, or demons who (given their origin as angels) are endowed with subtle intelligence, would think it possible for a corporeal fire to hurt them, unless they were actually distressed by it. In other words, demons do not scare easily, being far too clever to be frightened by mere imaginations of fire. Separated souls, it may be inferred, will be similarly unconcerned.

This is a far cry from the Aquinas who heralded the imagination's ability to form images of things not perceived by the senses (such as golden mountains – or, one may add, hellish punishments), and granted, in a Pseudo-Dionysian moment, that we can know something of 'incorporeal realities, which have no sense images, by analogy with sensible bodies, which do have images' (cf. p. 35 above). In the separated soul, the *vis imaginativa* cannot perform its normal actions of forming

---

[20] *In IV Sent.*, dist. 44, qu. 3, art. 3, qc. 3, co. The notion that images formed by the compositive imagination of things that have no basis in reality – and which therefore can be dismissed as fictions – are somehow less affecting than those with direct referents in the present world, seems quite extraordinary. Not to mention the fact that, if hell-fire is judged to be materially real, then imaginings concerning it can hardly be dismissed as false conceptions of the erring soul – rather they are fundamentally accurate conceptions of the well-informed soul.

images derived from sensory contact with our present world. *Virtus imaginativa non est absque organo corporali*: 'there is no power of imagination without a bodily organ'.[21]

A major rider is that the memory will have at its disposal an inalienable store of images gained whilst joined to the body. Elsewhere in his commentary on the *Sentences*, IV, dist. 44, when considering whether the acts of the sensitive powers remain in the separated soul, Aquinas admits as much. He starts out by referencing the connection Augustine had made, in *De Genesi ad litteram*, between the way we see bodies when asleep or during more traumatic experiences, and the way the separated soul may see images of bodies.[22] Yet again, Aquinas notes that frequently in this book Augustine speaks 'as one inquiring and not deciding' (*inquirendo loquitur, non determinando*), thereby excusing him from the rash claim (as Aquinas sees it) that a viable comparison may be made between the soul of a sleeper and the separated soul.[23] This cannot be done, Aquinas asserts, because the soul of the sleeper uses the corporeal organ of imagination whereby corporeal similitudes are imprinted, following sensory perception of the outside world, which cannot be said of the separated soul, since it is deprived of such contact.[24] As he puts it succinctly in his *Quaestiones disputatae de anima*, 'the powers of the sentient part of the soul, of which one is the imaginative power itself, do not remain in the soul when it is separated from the body'.[25] However, it may be noted that likenesses of things are present in the soul in respect of not only the sensitive and imaginative power but also the intellective power, depending on the extent of abstraction from matter and material conditions.[26] Wherefore Augustine's comparison holds in this respect, Aquinas concedes: just as the images of corporeal things are imaginatively

---

[21] Here I intersperse a quotation from Aquinas's *De malo*, qu. xvi, art. 1, 16, ed. Regan and Davies, pp. 806-9.
[22] *In IV Sent.*, dist. 44, qu. 3, art. 3, qc. 2, arg. 3.
[23] *In IV Sent.*, dist. 44, qu. 3, art. 3, qc. 2, ad 3.
[24] Ibid.
[25] *Quaestiones disputatae de anima*, art. 21, resp.; trans. John Patrick Rowan (St Louis, MO and London, 1949); html edition by Joseph Kenny, at https://isidore.co/aquinas/QDdeAnima.htm.
[26] *In IV Sent.*, dist. 44, qu. 3, art. 3, qc. 2, ad 3.

(*imaginaliter*) held in the soul of the dreamer or of one who is enduring a temporary but intense disembodied experience, so in the separated soul they are intellectively (*intellectualiter*) but not imaginatively present. But present they are, and (to expand Aquinas's discussion) ready for whatever use to which God may put them.

Further, while *memoria* can designate a power of the sensitive part of the soul, which functions only when it is joined to the body, Aquinas recognizes that it can also designate that part of the imagination which pertains to the intellective faculty; *that* shall remain in the separated soul.[27] So, then, it could be inferred that, when God gets to work on that repository, all kinds of frightening images can be produced, which will cause great hurt to the soul: spiritual pain is not a soft option. Here, inspired by the material from William of Auvergne discussed above, I am offering a counter-argument to the (radically different) one being pursued by Aquinas. But this argument goes very much against the grain of Aquinas's thinking, because he held that *imagines* are not needed to enable the separated soul to understand; whatever is needed is supplied directly by God, through infusion.[28] Indeed, the separated soul thinks in much the same way as an angel thinks – an angel's intellect, which ever

---

[27] *In IV Sent.*, dist. 44, qu. 3, art. 3, qc. 2, ad 4.
[28] *In III Sent.*, dist. 31, qu.2, art.4. See further, A. C. Pegis, 'The separated soul and its nature in St. Thomas', in *St. Thomas Aquinas, 1274-1974: Commemorative Studies*, ed. É. Gilson (Toronto, 1974), pp. 131-58 (p. 139). This article consolidates and develops relevant discussion in Pegis's book, *St. Thomas and the Problem of the Soul in the Thirteenth Century* (Toronto, 1934). Elsewhere Pegis eulogizes Aquinas as a thinker who ardently believed that 'to know by dependence on the imagination is natural to the soul – as natural as to be joined to the body'; hence '[t]he disembodied soul is outside its natural place, resulting from some violence. .... [D]eath and disembodiment are against the nature of the human soul'. How, then, should one account for the knowledge which is possible to a disembodied soul? Pegis responds with fideistic affirmation: whilst Aristotle taught Aquinas that 'Embodiment is the natural condition of the human soul', Aquinas transcended such teaching by refusing to 'enclose the soul in the body and in the world of bodies'. 'Between immortality and death: Some further reflections on the *Summa Contra Gentiles*', *The Monist*, 58/1 (1974), 1-15 (pp. 13, 14).

and always is totally separate from corporeal reality, 'has as its proper object intelligible substances'.[29] The obvious rejoinder to this argument (and something not pursued by Aquinas here) is that the thought-process of an angel, a creature having neither awareness nor understanding of corporeal pain, can hardly serve as an analogue of what happens in the human mind, whether embodied or disembodied, when it has to process the fact of hellish punishment.

Bonaventure treats the matter rather differently, and allows much more continuity of thought-process from the embodied soul to the separated soul. In his question on whether the separated soul has the use of sensitive powers he pays respectful attention to Augustine's opinion in *De Genesi ad litteram* that the soul carries with it certain images of things

---

[29] Here I apply phrasing from Aquinas's *Summa theologiae*, 1a, qu. 84, art. 7, resp. (XII, 41). In sum, the separated soul 'can understand without turning to phantasms, perfectly understand itself, and intuit the existence of things. In many ways the separated soul's cognition is diminished, but in other ways it is enhanced. Though the soul is naturally in the body, in some respects the separated state is better for it.' Thus Mark K. Spencer summarizes a reading of Aquinas's thinking on the separated soul which he attributes to the formidable Thomists, Francis Sylvester of Ferrara (d. 1528), Thomas Cajetan (d. 1534), and Francisco Suárez (d. 1617). 'The personhood of the separated soul', *Nova et Vetera*, 12/3 (2014), 863-912 (p. 899). Spencer goes on to argue that a Thomist can hold the position that separated souls constitute persons. This 'survivalist' position is a response to the 'corruptionist' viewpoint exemplified by Patrick Toner's essay, 'St. Thomas Aquinas on death and the separated soul', *Pacific Philosophical Quarterly*, 91/4 (2010), 587-99. Two recent highly nuanced contributions (which, however, reach opposing conclusions) are: Jeffrey Brower, *Aquinas's Ontology of the Material World: Change, Hylomorphism, and Material Objects* (Oxford, 2014), and Melissa Eitenmiller, 'On the separated soul according to St. Thomas Aquinas', *Nova et Vetera*, 17/1 (2019), 57-91. Such inquiry must take account of the fact that, if full personhood/personal identity/humanness is denied to the separated soul, this raises a major problem in relation to postmortem punishment and reward, since the soul can hardly await the return of its body before fully participating in pain or bliss. Aquinas and his contemporaries wrestled with this issue, and *Benedictus Deus* (1336), Pope Benedict XII's constitution on the Beatific Vision, was to make very clear that no such waiting period may be postulated. Cf. Minnis, *From Eden to Eternity*, pp. 209-14, 225-7.

that it formed whilst in the body, with which it is able to imagine and know, by use of an interior *potentia sensitiva* (in contrast with the external one, which functioned before the experience of disembodiment).[30] It is most consonant with reason, and neither contrary to the faith nor to the authority of the saints, to hold that the separated soul is able to make use of the intellect, to imagine, and to sense (though they will function as modes rather than as separate powers, functioning in a way akin to the thought-processes of angels).[31] As far as the imagination is concerned, Bonaventure proceeds to emphasize, it does not need a bodily organ to function, because of what it holds in the memory.[32] Hence his explanation of Luke xvi.24, where the rich man pleads that his tongue (*lingua*) might be cooled by a drop of water applied by Lazarus: that tongue has only an imaginative existence ('non erat nisi lingua imaginativa'), thanks to the *imagines* which the soul has retained.[33] The implication seems to be that Dives is deploying imaginations deriving from his life whilst in the body.

But this does not mean that Bonaventure is endorsing the radical ideas of William of Auvergne's thought experiment, or indeed elaborating on

[30] *In IV Sent.*, dist. 50, pars II, art. 1, qu. 1 (*Bonaventurae opera*, IV, 1044-7).

[31] [I]deo recte dicitur anima separata sentire, imaginari et intelligere, non per diversas potentias, sed per unam, quae potest omnibus his modis cognoscere, sicut ponere est in Angelo ... Cf. the statement: anima per potentiam intellectivam intelligat et cognoscat his tribus modis, ... et illud dicitur intelligere, imaginari et sentire, secundum quod Sancti dicunt. *In IV Sent.*, dist. 50, pars II, art. 1, qu.1, resp. (*Bonaventurae opera*, IV, 1046). The matter of angelic epistemology, the mechanisms through which those superior creatures can acquire and process knowledge, was hotly debated. See Keck, *Angels and Angelology*, pp. 101-5, 113; Martin Lenz, 'Why can't angels think properly? Ockham against Chatton and Aquinas', in *Angels in Medieval Philosophical Inquiry*, ed. Iribarren and Lenz, pp. 155-67; and Harm Goris, 'Angelic knowledge in Aquinas and Bonaventure', in *A Companion to Angels in Medieval Philosophy*, ed. Hoffmann, pp. 149-85.

[32] On Bonaventuran theory of imagination (and much else besides) see especially the work of Michelle Karnes: 'Nicholas Love and medieval meditations on Christ', *Speculum*, 82/2 (2007), 380-408; 'Marvels in the medieval imagination', *Speculum*, 90/2 (2015), 327-65; and her book *Imagination, Meditation, and Cognition in the Middle Ages*.

[33] *In IV Sent.*, dist. 50, pars II, art. 1, qu.1, ad 1 (*Bonaventurae opera*, IV, 1046).

Hugh of St Victor at this point. On the contrary, he is quite resistant to Augustine's idea that, if in dreams and traumatic experiences we can suffer in the body whilst going beyond the body, so we might suffer in a similar way (though more intensely) when the soul is separated from the body. This does not suffice as an explanation, Bonaventure asserts, because we believe that angelic spirits (i.e. demons), who do not possess images and affections drawn from the body, suffer corporeally from fire. It is to be believed that infernal pain results from the real action of fire (*ignis actio*), and not from the operation of the imagination: 'poena illa infernalis sit per veram ignis actionem, non per phantasticam imaginationem'.[34] Yet again, we encounter the belief that imagination on its own is insufficient to produce the requisite pain. The materiality of hell-fire must be maintained (and metaphorical explanation eschewed), even if the question of exactly how it can harm a separated soul is difficult to explain. So, what answers, then, *did* the schoolmen manage to come up with?

---

[34] *In IV Sent.*, dist. 44, pars II, art. 3, qu. 2, resp. (*Bonaventurae opera*, IV, 934).

CHAPTER 8

Scholastic solutions: fire entraps the soul, spiritual pain overflows the body

The desire to preserve and affirm some crucial aspect of 'the corporeality of suffering in hell' (to echo one of Mowbray's phrasings)[1] is the crucial driving-force behind the investigations conducted by Bonaventure and Aquinas into the question of whether the separated soul can suffer from corporeal fire. So, in his discussion, Aquinas returns yet again to Gregory's *Dialogues*, iv, 29,[2] this time to quote his predecessor as saying that we can infer from the Gospel that the soul suffers from the fire not only by seeing it but also by experiencing it (*non solum videndo, sed etiam experiendo*).[3] There are two ways to consider the idea of corporeal fire, Aquinas opines. First, as a corporeal thing, which therefore has no power to act on the soul. Second, as the instrument of divine justice: because the soul by sinning subjected itself to corporeal things, it should be subjected to them in its punishment. Maybe fire acts on the spirit of a man or demon in the way in which the sacraments sanctify the soul – though obviously that procedure would have nothing to do with sanctification![4] But, yet again, this does not seem to suffice, since in addition to performing its ultimate designated purpose every instrument has its own natural action – which indeed is necessary for the achievement of that higher purpose. For example, in baptism it is by laving the body, thereby carrying out its usual material function, that water confers grace. But how can fire perform its natural action, of burning and thereby

---

[1] Mowbray, *Pain and Suffering*, p. 133.
[2] *In IV Sent.*, dist. 44, qu. 3, art. 3, qc. 3, co.
[3] In fact, Gregory's conclusive view is that material fire is involved (here he differs from Augustine), but the suffering is caused by the soul's perception that it is surrounded by fire rather than by material fire hurting the separated soul in some mysteriously physical way (here he resembles Augustine). Cf. Barbezat, 'In a corporeal flame', pp. 8-9.
[4] *In IV Sent.*, dist. 44, qu. 3, art. 3, qc. 3, co.

causing corporeal pain, in the course of achieving its ultimate purpose, the punishment of the damned soul? A body is needed to enable contact between the fire and the soul, just as a body is needed in order that the rite of baptism may be performed, whereby the soul is sanctified.

Two ways whereby a spirit may be united to a body are then identified by Aquinas.[5] One is the way in which form is joined to matter; in this case the spirit gives the body life whilst being somewhat burdened by it. Obviously, this is not the manner in which the spirit of a man or a demon can be united to corporeal fire. Another manner relates to the way in which an incorporeal spirit is related to a particular place. Of course, in the normal course of events a corporeal thing is not able to detain an incorporeal spirit in a particular place, to tie it to that place so that it is unable to seek another: by its nature a spirit is not subject to place in this way. But, as the instrument of just divine vengeance, corporeal fire is indeed enabled to detain a spirit, thus punishing it by stopping it from doing what it wants, hindering it 'from acting where it will and as it will'. Gregory's *Dialogues* are drawn on yet again, this time for its posing of the question, since the rich sinner is condemned to fire (Luke xvi.24), will any wise man deny that the souls of the wicked are imprisoned in flames?[6] Julian of Toledo, as quoted by the Lombard, says basically the same thing: if the incorporeal spirit of a living man is held by the body, why cannot it be held after death by a corporeal fire?[7] Naturally enough, in Aquinas's treatment this segues into Augustine's original version of this same argument; in *De civitate Dei* the saint had wondered if the fact that the incorporeal spirits of men are 'now enclosed within the material members of the body' might provide a basis for understanding how 'even incorporeal spirits' might be afflicted by 'the pain of material fire' (cf. Chapter 2 above).[8] Fed through Aquinas's ideas machine, this emerges as follows: just as the soul is united to the body which gives it life, and therefore it conceives a great love for its body, so in hell the soul is chained

---

[5] Continuing with *In IV Sent.*, dist. 44, qu. 3, art. 3, qc. 3, co.
[6] *PL*, LXXVII, col. 368A-B.
[7] Lombard, *IV Sent.*, 7(257), 2 (II, 520-1; trans. Silano, IV, 242). Cf. p. 17 above.
[8] *De civitate Dei*, xxi, 10 (ed. Hoffman, II, 537-8; trans. Dyson, p. 1067).

to fire, but from this union it 'conceives a loathing (*horror*)' rather than great love. Of course, 'corporeal fire does not make the soul hot', but it is capable of inflicting extreme pain on it, nevertheless.[9]

Here Aquinas is developing what Bonaventure had said at the same stage of his *Sentences* commentary. Bonaventure too had enlisted Augustine's authority to argue that, in view of the union of the spiritual and the corporeal as exemplified by the union of soul and body in the human being, in hell the loving conjunction of body and soul is replaced with the loathsome conjunction of fire and soul.[10] In these statements the schoolmen are creating 'a new form of suffering for the soul',[11] a rationalization of how the material can cause pain in the immaterial, the corporeal can impact on the spiritual. The soul is surrounded – 'enchained, in a manner of speaking (*quodammodo retineat alligatum*)'[12] – by the fire, prevented from performing its natural functions, and thus it endures acute distress. As Aquinas puts it when he turns to the issue in his *Compendium theologiae ad fratrem Raynaldum*,[13] spiritual substances

---

[9] *Quaestiones disputatae de anima*, art. 21, ad 14. In this same text Aquinas remarks that 'in the magic arts (*artes magicas*)' certain 'spirits are bound to certain things by the power of superior demons, either by rings (=amulets?) or images (*vel anulis vel imaginibus*) or other such things', and 'it is in this way, through the divine power, that the souls and the demons are confined in their punishment by corporeal fire'. *Quaestiones disputatae de anima*, art. 21, resp. How curious that Aquinas should venture here into the sphere of *fascinatio* (hostile enchantment), by offering a high-risk comparison with a dubious magical practice – wherein, it would seem, images (in this case, presumably occult symbols, strange and secret markings) are allowed a power that Aquinas denies mental images in relation to the workings of the separated soul. True, he affirms that any supposedly magical bonding by demons can occur only with divine permission. But here, again, is evidence of the fact that (*pace* Le Goff) 'popular folklore and … the popular sensibility' can be far closer to, and more interactive with, arcane scholastic disputation than his binaristic approach allows.

[10] *In IV Sent.*, dist. 44, pars. II, art. 3, qu. 2 (*Bonaventurae opera*, IV, 934).

[11] Mowbray, *Pain and Suffering*, pp. 119-20.

[12] Aquinas, *In IV Sent.*, dist. 44, qu. 3, art. 3, qc. 3, co.

[13] *Compendium theologiae*, cap. 180; Latin text accessed on the Corpus Thomisticum website, https://www.corpusthomisticum.org/ott101.html. The date of this treatise is difficult to determine, but it is reasonable to

can be tied or bound (*alligentur*) to certain bodies, such as hell-fire: 'not in the sense that they animate the body in question (*non ita quod ipsum vivificent*)' but inasmuch as 'they are in some way fettered to it (*adstringantur*)'.[14] The fact that a spiritual substance is 'subjected to the dominion' of a lowly created thing, incarcerated by corporeal fire, 'is grievous to it (*ei est afflictivum*)'. The soul is in agony not only because it sees but also because it actually experiences (*experiendo*) the fire. To sum up the matter (albeit somewhat reductively): the schoolmen are following Gregory's belief that the fire is indeed real (here breaking away from Augustine) but not the belief, which Augustine and Gregory shared in large measure (and was developed by Hugh of St Victor), that distressing mental images are the primary means whereby the separated soul suffers. That spiritual entity cannot be burned. Neither is the horror at the thought of being burned a major cause of its suffering (though it certainly

---

    suppose that Aquinas began writing it during the period 1265-7 and resumed work on it later, leaving it incomplete at the time of his death. For the English translation here I have drawn on *The Compendium of Theology by Thomas Aquinas*, trans. Cyril Vollert (St Louis, MO and London, 1952), pp. 195-8.

[14] In explaining how spiritual substances can be tied down to, detained by (*alligentur*), certain bodies, Aquinas once again cites the body-soul composite and the power of the magic arts to imprison a spirit 'in images or amulets [literally, 'rings'] or other such objects' (trans. Vollert, p. 195). The rich connotations of the verb *adligo* / *alligo*, including its metaphorical valence, in such a context, should be noted; cf. *De civitate Dei*, xxi, 10, on the junction of body and soul, quoted in Chapter 2 above. Its meanings range from: to tie, bind, fasten; to secure, tie up (also, put a noose around); to hold together physically, establish firmly, have an astringent effect upon; to keep in chains, fetter; to tie for purposes of restraint; to grip firmly; to impede the activity or movement of, immobilize, pin down; to restrict the movements of, confine locally; to enclose in a constricting manner, envelop; to restrict the scope or freedom of; etc. Cf. *The Oxford Latin Dictionary*, ed. P. G. W. Glare, 2nd edn, 2 vols (Oxford, 2012), I, 115. Thus the term is used to express unions which may be desired (or at least regarded neutrally) but which often are not, rather being seen as at best dubious and at worst as enforced, demeaning entrapment.

is present).¹⁵ Rather, pain is inflicted by the entrapping and confining envelope of flame, against which the soul reacts with ongoing horror, as an ignominious, debasing form of imprisonment which, for the damned, will never end.

That doctrine became a major scholastic consensus, the standard solution to a deeply troubling question. Its propagation meant that great weight was placed on the passage in *De civitate Dei* where the saint hypothesized that the well-known combination of body and soul might provide a model for the mysterious combination of fire and soul required for the infliction of hellish torment (cf. Chapter 2 above). From this passage Bonaventure and Aquinas deduced their explanations of how the separated soul could be punished by bodily fire. Maybe in the Genesis commentary Augustine had been speaking merely 'as one inquiring' (*inquirendo*), Aquinas manipulatively suggests, with his definitive position (*determinando*) being expressed in *De civitate Dei*.¹⁶ Here Aquinas is seeking to put some distance between the two treatises, with *De civitate Dei* given priority and the problematic theory of the *similitudo corporis* in *De Genesi ad litteram* being left behind, in order to bolster his desired solution to the problem of how an immaterial soul can be punished by material fire: the answer being that the soul is enveloped in fire throughout eternity, while not actually being burned. It suffers immeasurably – but from incarceration rather than incineration.¹⁷

But what should be said about Isaiah's incessantly gnawing *vermis*? Whereas issues relating to the separated soul were paramount in the discussions about fire, when the ontological status of the worm of hell

---

[15] In Aquinas's *Compendium theologiae*, cap. 180, the emphasis is placed on the apprehension (*apprehensio*) of the fire as causing imprisonment rather than as specifically burning, this awareness (*consideratio*) being distressing to the spiritual substance (trans. Vollert, p. 196).

[16] *In IV Sent.*, dist. 44, qu. 3, art. 3, qc. 3, ad 1.

[17] As Bonaventure puts it nicely in his *Breviloquium*, here speaking of conditions following the Resurrection: 'the purpose of this fire is not to increase itself, but to destroy the peace of the soul within its body, and the peace of the incorporeal spirit within itself'. *Breviloquium*, pars vii, cap. 6. *Bonaventurae opera*, V, 28; trans. Dominic Monti, Works of St Bonaventure, IX (St Bonaventure, NY, 2005), p. 290.

arose, the issue of whether it is metaphorical or material, the schoolmen thought primarily in terms of the conditions which will come into existence following the Last Judgment. In his treatment Bonaventure cites the two opinions provided by Augustine: some say, following the words of Scripture, that the worm is material, whereas others, following reason, wish to say that the worm is spiritual.[18] And Augustine said that the second view is more pleasing to him – Bonaventure adds that it is more pleasing to him also. (Bonaventure conveniently ignores the fact that Augustine had gone on to remark that he finds it 'easier to suppose that both 'fire' and 'worm' pertain to the body than to suppose that neither does'.)[19] At Isaiah xiv.11 it is said of the devil, 'and worms shall be thy covering': but the devil does not have a material worm, so therefore damned souls cannot either.[20] Then again, the worm is a material creature and not immortal, but the worm referred to in Isaiah lxvi.24 cannot die.[21] There will be a more intense fire in hell than we experience now, and a worm cannot live in such intense heat. If you say it will survive, by some miracle, then it follows that, because it cannot suffer from fire, it must have an incorruptible body – that is to say, a body of the kind with which the blessed will be honoured (a gloriously shining, crystalline, thing of beauty). Which, obviously, is absurd. Besides, how can a worm possibly resurrect?[22] Putrefaction is needed for it to generate, and that will not be possible in the post-resurrection world, where no change, and hence no decay, is possible.

Bonaventure goes on to ask, since a worm is born from decay and gnaws, how can the worm of conscience be metaphorically spoken of thus (*qua metaphora dicitur...*) since conscience does not decay?[23] Here he

---

[18] *In IV Sent.*, dist. 50, pars II, art. 2, qu. 1, resp. (*Bonaventurae opera*, IV, 1051).

[19] *De civitate Dei*, xxi, 9 (ed. Hoffman, II, 536; trans. Dyson, p. 1065).

[20] *In IV Sent.*, dist. 50, pars II, art. 2, qu. 1, con., 1 (*Bonaventurae opera*, IV, 1050).

[21] *In IV Sent.*, dist. 50, pars II, art. 2, qu. 1, con., 2 (*Bonaventurae opera*, IV, 1050).

[22] *In IV Sent.*, dist. 50, pars II, art. 2, qu. 1, con., 4 (*Bonaventurae opera*, IV, 1050).

[23] *In IV Sent.*, dist. 50, pars II, art. 2, qu. 2, 4 (*Bonaventrae opera*, IV, 1052).

seeks the connecting element, the analogy, between the vehicle and the tenor of the metaphor. His answer is to reject the suggestion that a material worm is involved, and so the difficulty of making decay a crucial aspect of the analogy disappears. Bonaventure's conclusion is that the fire may be material but the worm is definitely spiritual.

Aquinas is in substantial agreement.[24] Judith xvi.21 and Sirach vii.19 seem to indicate that the worm will be corporeal, but Augustine, in *De civitate Dei*, labels as probable the opinion that, as far as the soul is concerned, the worm should be understood metaphorically (*topice*; cf. Chapter 2 above).[25] And that is Aquinas's view also. He refers to the commonplace scholastic doctrine that, after the General Resurrection, following the cessation of the heavenly movements by which all animal and plant life is currently maintained in existence, no such life-forms will remain in the renewed world.[26] Nothing corruptible can exist then, and therefore the worm which afflicts the damned must be understood to be of a spiritual rather than a corporeal nature. (It should be recalled that the notion that the cessation of heavenly movements would stop fire from functioning was ruled out by one of the 1277 Parisian condemnations. So then, fire can survive in the renewed universe. But worms cannot.)[27] Aquinas identifies his spiritual worm as the remorse of conscience (*remorsus conscientiae*), so-called because it originates from the corruption of sin just as a corporeal worm originates from material corruption, and remorse torments the soul in a way akin to the gnawing of a corporeal worm. The connection between metaphorical tenor and vehicle is thus strong and clear. At the General Resurrection the bodies of men will be restored to their souls, and the physical pain inflicted on them will easily be comprehensible (well, *relatively* easily). However, an actual worm cannot be an agent of such torment, because it, together with all its fellow-creatures, will have passed into oblivion. Its only existence, therefore, can be metaphorical.

---

[24] *In IV Sent.*, dist. 50, qu. 2, art. 3, qc. 2, arg. 1.
[25] *In IV Sent.*, dist. 50, qu. 2, art. 3, qc. 2, s. c. 1.
[26] *In IV Sent.*, dist. 50, qu. 2, art. 3, qc. 2, co.
[27] Mowbray, *Pain and Suffering*, p. 155.

But that is not the end of the matter. What about the testimony of scriptural passages such as Judith xvi.21 and Sirach vii.19, which assert that worms will exact vengeance on the flesh of the ungodly? First, Aquinas reaches for a metaphorical explanation: the souls of the damned are called their 'flesh' inasmuch as they were subject to the flesh. But he goes beyond that, with the solution that the spiritual worm may be understood as inflicting torment on the body, 'according as the afflictions of the soul overflow into the body, both here and hereafter'.[28] Here Aquinas appeals to the widely-held scholastic doctrine of *redundantia*, which the schoolmen had developed in order to affirm that the bodies of the blessed will enjoy happiness together with the souls which have rejoined them, thereby refuting the invidious suggestion (a legacy from Neoplatonism) that the soul could be truly happy only when separated from its encumbering body. This is achieved 'from the overflow (*redundantia*) of the soul's glory onto the body', Aquinas explains.[29] The senses of the blessed deserve their reward also, and therefore at the Resurrection 'happiness of soul' will overflow onto the body (*fiet redundantia ad corpus*), 'which drinks of the fullness of soul'.[30] Bonaventure similarly argues that, for the blessed, happiness exists in the soul inherently and substantially, and in the body (when joined to the soul) through a certain *redundantia* (overflow) and *comparticipatio* (co-participation).[31] Correspondingly, in the case of the damned, the spiritual pain suffered by their souls will overflow onto their bodies, causing great physical suffering.

---

[28] *In IV Sent.*, dist. 50, qu. 2, art. 3, qc. 2, ad 1.
[29] *In IV Sent.*, dist. 44, qu. 2, art. 4, co.
[30] *Summa theologiae*, 1a 2ae, qu. 4, art. 6, resp. (XVI, 108-9); cf. Augustine, *Epistola 118, ad Dioscurum*, 3 (*PL*, XXXIII, col. 439).
[31] *In IV Sent.*, dist. 49, pars I, art. unicus, qu. 2 (*Bonaventurae opera*, IV, 1004-6). Cf. Caroline Walker Bynum, *The Resurrection of the Body in Western Christianity, 200-1336*, expanded edition (New York, 2017), pp. 252-3. This edition adds a new introduction and appends Bynum's 1995 essay, 'Why all the fuss about the body? A medievalist's perspective'.

Bonaventure spells out that connection in his own discussion of the problematic worm.³² Just as material fire by touching the body affects it and punishes the soul joined to it, so vehement sorrow and remorse, or the sadness of the soul, will spill over (*redundat*) onto the body, because 'a sorrowful spirit drieth up the bones' (Proverbs xvii.22). Since therefore there will be in the damned great remorse of conscience and sorrow, that grief will overflow (*redundet*) the flesh. This is what God means by the statement that He will give 'worms into their flesh' (Judith xvi.21), a declaration greatly expressive of bodily fear, because the people here addressed abhor the pain of the body rather than that of the soul. Alternatively, the 'flesh' here refers to carnal work, i.e. the work of sin, from which the spiritual worm is generated. In sum, the senses of the damned cannot be spared from unhappiness when they rejoin their bodies.³³ Their sorrows are as comprehensive and inclusive as the joys of the blessed.

But which are more distressing, the sorrows inflicted by the worm or those related to the fire? During the 1270s and 1280s a succession of schoolmen lined up to pronounce the worm of conscience the more distressing agent of torture, including several of Bonaventure's Franciscan successors: Matthew of Aquasparta (d. 1302), Gauthier of Bruges (d. 1307), Richard of Middleton (d. *c.* 1308), and Gervase of Mont-Saint-

---

³² *In IV Sent.*, dist. 50, pars II, art. 2, qu. 2, ad 1 (*Bonaventurae opera*, IV, 1051).

³³ But what about Augustine's statement in *De civitate Dei* regarding the possibly metaphorical nature of the worm? Aquinas points out, quite rightly, that a chief concern of Augustine in that particular passage was to challenge the suggestion that the damned would suffer no bodily pain. The saint did 'not wish to assert absolutely that this worm is material'; his point was rather that it is 'better to say that both are to be understood materially, than that both should be understood only in a spiritual sense' – because then it could easily be concluded that 'the damned would suffer no bodily pain'. *In IV Sent.*, dist. 50, qu. 2, art. 3, qc. 2, ad 2.

Eloi (d. 1314).[34] Various reasons are given: the worm (understood *metaphorice* as conscience) is more intimate in its operations; its contrariety with the soul is the more acute, the repugnance the greater; just as the pleasure which arises from the spiritual and the interior is of greater magnitude than what results from the corporeal and the exterior, so too the pain induced by such causes is the more intense. There is much more in the same vein. Thus the theologians categorized and calibrated the types and methods of infernal punishment with rigorous, and indeed ruthless, exactitude.

---

[34] The relevant views of Matthew of Aquasparta, Gauthier of Bruges and Gervase of Mont-Saint-Eloi are summarized by Mowbray, *Pain and Suffering*, pp. 139-44. For Middleton's relevant *quaestio* (labeled *utrum in inferno sit maior pena vermis quam ignis*) see *In IV Sent.*, dist. 50, art. 5, qu. 2, in *Magistri Ricardi de Mediavilla super quatuor sententiarum*, 4 vols (Brescia, 1591), IV, 707-8.

CHAPTER 9

Towards a scholastic theory of metaphor

Time to take stock, in terms of the literary-theoretical implications of all this. As far as the separated soul is concerned, the best academic explanation for the infliction of pain was the proposition that the desired and loving conjunction of body and soul will be replaced with the forced, repugnant and horrific embrace of fire and soul, which will last throughout all eternity. Presumably such a situation will continue following the General Resurrection (though the theologians quoted above do not spell that out). Fire will exist then in the same species as now; indeed, it constitutes a major point of contact and continuity between this world and the 'new heaven and new earth'. That point may be better understood if it is recalled that, within a tradition that goes back to Graeco-Roman philosophy and science, the element of fire was afforded a special and superior status. The hugely popular *De proprietatibus rerum* of Bartholomew the Englishman (1240) describes fire as a sensible body which is yet more excellent than all other bodily things, and closest to spiritual nature; it naturally moves upwards and rises above all the other elements.[1] Indeed, the empyrean or highest

---

[1] *De proprietatibus rerum*, x, 3 (Nuremberg, 1519), unfol. Here Bartholomew draws on the long list of the excellent properties of fire which had been used by Pseudo-Dionysius to justify the fact that the Bible honours the depiction of fire above all others. Indeed, it seemed to this eloquent Christian Platonist that the 'imagery of fire best expresses the way in which the intelligent beings of heaven are like the deity' – and he notes that the highest order of angels, those closest to God, are named 'seraphim', meaning 'fire-makers', i.e. carriers of warmth who bear overflowing heat. *The Celestial Hierarchy*, chs 7 and 15; trans. Colm Luibheid in *Pseudo-Dionysius: The Complete Works* (New York and Mahwah, NJ, 1987), pp. 161-2, 183-4; see also *Angelic Spirituality: Medieval Perspectives on the Ways of Angels*, ed. and trans. Steven Chase (New York and Mahwah, NJ, 2002), pp. 49-50, 53, 58-9, 74, 100, 102-3, 122, 124, 127-8, 152, 163, 167, 168-73, 209-10. There is, of course, a transition here from the material properties of fire to the metaphorical deployment of those same properties as vehicles for spiritual truths: seraphim

heaven, nearest the throne of God, was generally supposed to be occupied by the element of fire.² So, then, there was little difficulty in envisaging fire to transition from the present life to the next, where it could encircle and torment the separated soul. But the action of material fire is a lot easier to account for when it is making contact with a material body, even though an explanation is needed of why that body can be burned without being consumed.

Such an explanation can be supplied with relative ease, drawing on the miracles of nature which may be cited by way of comparison – those abundant and 'wondrous works of God' which defeat 'our weak and mortal powers of reasoning', to return to Augustine's joyous statement. (Though Aquinas was unimpressed by Augustine's example of the salamander: 'it cannot remain in the fire without being at last consumed'.)³ In the post-resurrection hell there will, however, be no literal worm, for such a creature (or indeed any other animal) will not exist in that universe, because, as a creature lacking a soul, it will have been rendered extinct as part of a divine plan which involves giving the blessed as much pleasure as possible and causing the damned as much pain as possible. Therefore it must be understood spiritually – or, to be more precise, metaphorically.

The implications which such doctrine had for the theory of metaphorical and figurative and imaginative language as deployed in

---

are not actually fiery creatures but their spiritual properties, their fiery passion for doing God's work, can be described in those terms. And yet: seraphim are supposed to dwell in the empyrean or highest heaven, which is occupied by the element of fire. A stunning concatenation of metaphor and materiality.

2   In ancient cosmologies, aspects of which medieval learning inherited, the empyrean was designated the realm of pure fire, with the emphasis being placed on light-giving rather than burning. Cf. Bartholomew the Englishman, *De proprietatibus rerum*, viii, 4; Vincent of Beauvais, *Speculum naturale*, iii, 87, in *Speculum maius*, 4 vols (Douai, 1624), I, 219. Since Peter Lombard had raised the issue of where the angels were located following their creation, at *Sentences*, II, dist. 2, ch. 4(10), his commentators were obliged to discuss the empyrean.

3   *In IV Sent.*, dist. 44, qu. 3, art. 1, qc. 3, ad 3.

scriptural exegesis and related textual commentary, are well summarized by Aquinas in an analysis provided in the last book of his *Summa contra gentiles*.[4] When Scripture refers to the bodily rewards of the blessed following the General Resurrection, they are to be understood spiritually (*spiritualiter*), as when Proverbs (ix.2, 4-5) says of wisdom, 'She hath mingled her wine, and set forth her table', and has her say to the unwise, 'Come, eat my bread, and drink the wine I have mingled for you'. Or when Sirach (xv.3) states, 'With the bread of life and understanding, she shall feed him, and give him the water of wholesome wisdom to drink'. The risen will have no use of food, since their bodies will be complete and unchangeable. Christ may have partaken of food when he arose from the dead (cf. Luke xxiv.43, Acts x.40-1), but that was to show that he had truly resurrected, being present in a genuine physical body. The food then taken did not become part of his flesh,[5] but returned to its prior material state. Here we see how Scripture lays before us certain intelligible things in the likeness of sensible things (*sub similitudine sensibilium*), so 'from what our soul knows it may learn to love the things it knows not'.[6] Granted this, Aquinas continues, when Scripture threatens sinners with specific bodily punishments, these should be understood in a bodily fashion and in their literal meaning (*corporaliter sunt intelligenda, et quasi proprie dicta*).[7] 'A superior nature is suitably punished by being turned

[4] *Summa contra gentiles*, iv, 83, n. 19. I have used the Parma edition at http://www.corpusthomisticum.org/scg4079.html, and here drawn on the translation of Book IV by Charles J. O'Neil, at https://isidore.co/aquinas/english/ContraGentiles4.htm.
[5] Such changing attitudes are comprehensively tracked by P. L. Reynolds, *Food and the Body: Some Peculiar Questions in High Medieval Theology* (Leiden, 1999). Cf. esp. p. 19: 'The body is the agent of digestion, for it converts food into itself. The body turns food, which is potential flesh, into actual flesh'.
[6] *Summa contra gentiles*, iv, 83, n. 19. The quotation is from one of Saint Gregory's homilies on the Gospels; *Homiliae in Evangelia*, I, hom. 11, 1 (*PL*, LXXVI, col. 1114), with which (obviously) may be compared Romans i.20: 'the invisible things of him from the creation of the world are clearly seen, being understood by the things that are made'. Cf. Aquinas's use of this Romans passage at *In IV Sent.*, dist. 48, qu. 2, art. 1, co.
[7] *Summa contra gentiles*, iv, 90, n. 8. Cf. the similar statement in Aquinas's *Compendium theologiae*, cap. 179: 'if Sacred Scripture is found to promise a

over to its inferiors' – by which I presume Aquinas means that the superior soul, having been re-embodied, is suitably disciplined by having lowly corporeal punishments inflicted upon it.

Then Aquinas goes on to say:

> Nihil tamen prohibet quaedam etiam quae de damnatorum poenis in Scripturis dicta corporaliter leguntur, spiritualiter accipi, et velut per similitudinem dicta: sicut quod dicitur Isaiae ult.: *vermis eorum non morietur*: potest enim per vermem intelligi conscientiae remorsus, quo etiam impii torquebuntur; non enim est possibile quod corporeus vermis spiritualem corrodat substantiam, neque etiam corpora damnatorum quae incorruptibilia erunt. *Fletus etiam et stridor dentium* in spiritualibus substantiis non nisi metaphorice intelligi possunt: quamvis in corporibus damnatorum, post resurrectionem, nihil prohibeat corporaliter ea intelligi ....
> [For all that, there is no reason why even some of the things we read in Scripture about the punishments of the damned expressed in bodily terms should not be understood in spiritual terms, and, as it were, figuratively. Such is the saying of Isaiah [lxvi.24]: 'Their worm shall not die': by 'worm' can be understood that remorse of conscience by which the impious will also be tortured, for a bodily worm cannot eat away a spiritual substance, nor even the bodies of the damned, which will then be incorruptible. Then, too, the 'weeping' and 'gnashing of teeth' [Matthew viii.12] cannot be understood of spiritual substances except metaphorically, although there is no reason not to accept them in a bodily sense in the bodies of the damned after the Resurrection.][8]

---

reward of material goods to the souls of the saints, such passages are to be interpreted in a mystical sense (*mystice sunt exponenda*); for spiritual things (*spiritualia*) are often described in Scripture in terms of their likeness to material things (*sub corporalium similitudine*). But texts that portend the corporal punishments of the souls of the damned, specifying that they will be tormented by the fires of hell, are to be understood literally' (trans. Vollert, p. 195).

[8] *Summa contra gentiles*, iv, 90, n. 9.

This remarkable statement is of considerable consequence for an understanding of the literary theory which scholastic commentary generated in such abundance. Reading *spiritualiter* certain passages that describe material things and actions means reading them figuratively, *per similitudinem*; thus Isaiah's *vermis* becomes the remorse of conscience. But in that scriptural passage, the worm's characteristic physical activity cannot be read *corporaliter*, because it is impossible for a corporeal creature to degrade a spiritual substance in this way. Similarly, the 'weeping' and 'gnashing of teeth' (Matthew viii.12) can only be read metaphorically (*nisi metaphorice*), since spiritual substances are again concerned. But – and here comes the challenging rider – following the Resurrection, at least some statements regarding hellish punishments can be understood *corporaliter*, because the dead have had their bodies restored to them, and are able to suffer corporeal punishments. When bodies rematerialise, metaphors materialise. Well, at least some of them. The worm must remain figurative. But weeping and gnashing of teeth may confidently be anticipated in the post-resurrection hell.

Aquinas instantly nuances that last statement by explaining that, since the damned body has to remain stable in order to endure its punishments perpetually, it cannot lose moisture in the form of tears; nevertheless there will be 'the sorrow of the heart and the perturbation of the eyes and head which usually accompany weeping'.[9] The resurrected body is capable of carrying out those physical convolutions without any loss or change. It may be added that the damned are now open to the pain of hell-fire, the schoolmen having concluded that, in their case, the *impassibilitas* of the resurrected body does not preclude the experience of physical pain; only the bodies of the blessed enjoy that privilege. This is in addition to the pain inflicted by the overflow (*redundantia*) of the soul's suffering onto the body. And, even when the body-soul composite is back in place, presumably there will remain some version of the 'soul-fire composite' which so hurtfully thwarted the disembodied soul from performing its proper operations.

[9] Ibid.

That soul-fire composite may, following Mowbray, be deemed the creation of 'a new form of suffering for the soul',[10] whereas the *redundantia* approach to sourcing and rationalizing suffering may be deemed an adjunct of (or perhaps a symmetrical parallel to) the doctrine of the overflow of joy from soul to body which the blessed will enjoy in superabundant measure. To cap it all, when the body returns so will the fear and pain of natural burning, albeit in this case not accompanied by consumption. Even *visio* and *apprehensio* have a role to play in this superabundance of suffering. *Pace* the Augustine of *De Genesi ad litteram*, and certain later negotiations of that doctrine, images derived from past experience are not the actual instrument of the infliction of pain. However, in the post-resurrection hell the soul will see the fire as a present threat, something actually hurtful to itself ('sic anima ignem ut noxium sibi videns'), thereby adding to its distress.[11]

But if it is dark in hell, how can anything be seen? The answer is that nothing can be seen clearly, and only such things will be dimly seen as are able to afflict the heart. By careful divine planning, Aquinas explains, 'there is a certain amount of light, as much as suffices for seeing those things which are capable of tormenting the soul. The natural situation of the place is enough for this, since in the centre of the earth, where hell is said to be, fire cannot be otherwise than thick and cloudy, and, as it were, reeky (*faeculentus et turbidus, et quasi fumosus*)'.[12] Or, to follow *Sawles*

---

[10] Mowbray, *Pain and Suffering*, pp. 119-20, as quoted above.

[11] *In IV Sent.*, dist. 44, qu. 3 art. 3, qc. 3, co.

[12] *In IV Sent.*, dist. 50, qu. 2, art. 3, qc. 4, co. Bonaventure reaches the same conclusion: *In IV Sent.*, dist. 50, pars 1, art. 2, qu. 1, co. (*Bonaventurae opera*, IV, 1041). See also the brief statement in Hugh Ripelin of Strasbourg's *Compendium theologicae veritatis*, vii, 22, in *Alberti Magni opera omnia*, 21 vols, ed. Pierre Jammy (Lyon, 1651), XIII, text C, 142. Aquinas offers the opinion that 'this darkness is caused by the massing together of the bodies of the damned, which will so fill the place of hell with their numbers, that no air will remain, so that there will be no translucid body that can be the subject of light and darkness, except the eyes of the damned, which will be darkened utterly'. Richard of Middleton similarly notes that, while *per se* light is delectable, *per accidens* it can lead to sorrow, as is the case in hell, given the horrors visible there. Besides, we are not dealing with pure light (of the kind

Warde, one may conceive of a fire that gives no proper light but blinds the eyes of those who are there with a smothering smoke. Quite a potent amalgam of means and methods of suffering. All justified as being in accord with divine justice, with extreme punishments fitting extreme crimes against God and man. The pains of hell-fire will be endured both *corporaliter* and *spiritualiter*, resulting in anguish far beyond what anyone can imagine at present.[13] Here metaphor has been rendered redundant, with tenor dispensing with vehicle and the nonverbal overwhelming the verbal.

But – to return to the epistemological needs of the present world – Aquinas nevertheless affirmed that 'some of the things we read in Scripture about the punishments of the damned expressed in bodily terms' may well be understood 'in spiritual terms, and, as it were, figuratively (*per similitudinem*)',[14] that similitude being identifiable with the analogous comparison which is essential to metaphor. The 'worm of conscience' was his primary example – indeed, this is the ubiquitous primary example in much late-medieval exegesis relating to the underworld (cf. Chapter 17 below). And, as already noted, the pain which is the tenor of that vehicle, 'the conceptual import' behind its 'pictorial envelope', was widely regarded as more acute than that associated with hell-fire in all of its insistent, irreducible materiality. The enduring strength of that metaphor, the power of its position within the scholastic economy of postmortem reward and punishment, can scarcely be exaggerated. And it encouraged and justified the generation of vast hordes of venomous infernal creatures – all those biting dragons, serpents, toads and frogs that lay in wait for the unredeemed sinner. In a

---

which enables visual delight) but rather something mixed with obscuring elements. *In IV Sent.*, dist. 50, art. 5, qu. 1 (IV, 707).

[13] As *The Prick of Conscience* succinctly puts it,
... sall þare be sere payns many ma,
Als þe boke says, and mare sorrow and wa   *woe*
Þan all þe men of erth, ald and yhong,
Moght think with hert or tell with tong .... (lines 7308-11).
Richard Morris's Prick of Conscience, prepared by Ralph Hanna and Sarah Wood, EETS os 342 (Oxford, 2013), p. 201.

[14] Cf. Chapter 9 above.

sermon he preached in 1406, Richard Alkerton refers both to the 'venemous wormes and naddris' which 'shul gnawe alle here membris' [i.e. the body-parts of the damned] withouten seessyng' and the 'worm of conscience, that is grutching in her conscience', which 'shal gnawe the soule'.[15] Thus he shifts with ease from sundry worms to the biggest worm of all, from corporeal pain to mental pain. Within sermon rhetoric, these creatures co-exist and collaborate in the infliction of suffering.

---

[15] G. R. Owst, *Literature and Pulpit in Medieval England* (Cambridge, 1933), p. 522. Cf. *The Prick of Conscience*, lines 6891-7004 and 7045-92, where the text shifts from one type of worm to the other. See further Mowbray, *Pain and Suffering*, p. 141. On Alkerton, a committed preacher who studied at Oxford in the 1370s and 1380s, see Siegfried Wenzel, *Latin Sermon Collections from Later Medieval England: Orthodox Preaching in the Age of Wyclif* (Cambridge, 2005), pp. 169-70.

CHAPTER 10

Negotiations of metaphor and materiality: from Latin to vernacular, and back again

No medieval text is more thoroughgoing in its meditations on the biggest worm of all than *The Prick of Conscience* (*c.* 1350), which enjoyed a circulation far in excess of that of any other Middle English poem[1] – an exceptional medieval success which, unfortunately, has compromised its modern reception, given that the intimidating number of mauscripts has deterred even the most hardy of potential editors. Although addressed to 'lewed men of Ingland, / Þat can noght bot Inglise undirstand' (lines 9544-5), the *Prick* is a highly sophisticated text in theological terms, if rather repetitive and gangly. While it does not wear its learning lightly, it is remarkably successful in expressing complicated doctrine in a cogent manner – and thus was well-suited to assist the priestly instruction of layfolk, which may have been a major reason for its popularity. Unsurprisingly, therefore, it is more reflective than *Sawles Warde*, and many of the popular visionary narratives, about the relationship of its hellish metaphors to materiality.

In the first instance, the poem offers a vivid description of how dragons and adders, toads and 'wode bestes grysely and grym', will with their teeth gnaw and bite on all the limbs that once took delight in sinful works, here on this earth, against the law of God and Holy Church (lines 6895-902). Many relevant biblical quotations are brought in, including Isaiah xiv.11 ('worms shall be thy covering'), Isaiah lxvi.24 ('Their worm shall not die'), and Judith xvi.21 ('[The Lord] will give fire, and worms into their flesh, that they may burn, and may feel for ever'), here nicely augmented with Deuteronomy xxxii.24 ('I will send the teeth of beasts upon them…'). Indeed, hell's vermin is much more grisly than what we

---

[1] All references to this text are to the revision of Richard Morris's edition which was prepared by Hanna and Wood; cf. p. 90, n. 13 above.

have in this present life, and therefore men ought to dread it all the more. By this means the divine law is exacted.

> It es right and skyll thurgh Godes lawe   *reasonable*
> Þat þe vermyn in hell ay þam gnawe.   *always*
> (lines 7003-4)

But, some people may ask, how can those creatures possibly be alive, following the final judgment?

> For men may in som boke wryten se
> Þat after þe gret dome þat last sall be,
> Na quyk creature sall lyf than,   *living*
> But anely aungell, devell, and man.
> How suld in hell þan or ourwhare ells,
> Any vermyn lyf, als men tells,
> Or any other best þat moght dere?   *hurt*
> (lines 6975-81)

For, as the poem goes on to say, when the heavens cease to move, all such life will die.

> ... moved noght, alle suld peryssch,   *perish*
> Both man and beste, foghel and fyssch   *bird and fish*
> And alle þat under þam may be
> Þat lyfes and growes, both gresse and tre.   *grass and tree*
> All suld be smored withouten dout,   *destroyed (lit. 'smothered'), doubt*
> Warne tha hevens ay moved obout ...   *unless*
> (lines 7594-599)

In one 'boke' which is a source of the *Prick*, its author could have found 'wryten' the statement that the worm of hell cannot be of a material kind: 'vermis ... nequaquam materialis est: quam nullum animal praeter hominem remanebit. Erit autem ibi vermis conscientiae, rodens animam, & non corpus'.² This is from a work which enjoyed a remarkably wide dissemination throughout the later Middle Ages and beyond, the *Compendium theologicae veritatis* which now is generally held to be the work of Hugh Ripelin of Strasbourg (d. *c.* 1270), a Dominican whose doctrine stays close to Aquinas's. However, the *Prick* poet prefers to amplify an explanation hinted at in his foundational source, the thirteenth-century Anglo-French prose treatise *Les Peines de purgatorie*: 'Mes quele menere [de vermine] la serra, ou deables en semblaunce de vermine ou autre manere, nous ne trovum pas escrist apertement'.³ All those biting little creatures are in fact devils in disguise.

> Þe vermyn þat sall be þan,   *vermin*
> Als I understand, noght ells es
> Bot devels in vermyn lyknes …   *appearance*
> Þus sall þe devels gnaw þam without
> In lyknes of vermyn all obout …
>
>   (lines 6984-90)

In this visceral way the devils exacerbate the sufferings of the damned, by acting on their bodies in whatever way is compatible with the degree of *impassibilitas* that God has permitted them (to expand a little what the poet is saying). If 'anely aungell, devell, and man' will remain in existence following the General Resurrection, as is generally believed, then devils (once fallen angels) are positioned to assume the appearances of venomous animals rendered extinct by the cessation of heavenly movement. Men do not need to imagine malevolent creatures attacking them, for the devils can render them directly present to their sight – though no doubt those devilish shapes will feature prominently in the

---

² *Compendium theologicae veritatis*, vii, 22. Cf. the editors' note to *Prick of Conscience*, lines 6973-94, on p. 349.

³ 'A critical edition of the Anglo-Norman and Latin versions of *Les Peines de purgatorie*', ed. Robert J. Relihan (unpub. Ph.D. diss., University of Iowa, 1978), p. 204. In the Latin version of the *Peines*, which apparently post-dates the Anglo-French text, the text reads: Quam tamen similitudinem, vel diabolicam vel aliam predictam, vermium multitude tenebit, in scriptis nulla tenus invenimus.

active imaginations of the incarnate damned, thereby increasing their suffering even more.

The *Prick* then moves away from the *Peines* to reflect the rationalization (as quoted above) offered by the *Compendium theologicae veritatis*, to the effect that the biggest worm in hell is the invasive *vermis conscientiae*.

> And þair conscience als vermyn   *like*
> Sall gnaw þam overall within ...
>
> (lines 6991-92)

Their conscience, like vermin (here the metaphorical understanding takes effect), shall gnaw the damned within, in their souls, while the devils shall gnaw their bodies 'without' (line 6989). 'Þe gnawing within / Of þair conscience' shall never cease,

> For within þam sall þe worme of conscience frete   *eat*
> Als withouten sall do vermyn grete,
> And swa sall þai evermare, withouten dout,
> Be gnawen and byten within and without.
>
> (lines 7047-50)

The *Prick* poet has resolved this stand-off between materiality and metaphor by having it both ways.[4]

But does this imply that devils have some material form, perhaps composed of dense and humid air, as Augustine once speculated? Aquinas spoke for many of the schoolmen by declaring that 'angels are not by

---

[4] He goes on to describe how the damned are published by 'glowand hamers huge and grete' (line 7008; cf. the 'striking hammers [prepared] for the bodies of fools'; Proverbs xix.29). The *Compendium theologicae veritatis* (vii, 22) had explained that these are to be understood not as material hammers but as the diversity of punishments with which the impious will be beaten. But that explanation is not offered here in the *Prick*.

nature conjoined with bodies'.[5] He asserts that certain 'early philosophers' went wrong in thinking that 'nothing existed except what could be sensed or imagined; and as nothing is imaginable except bodies, they thought that nothing but bodies existed'.[6] However, given the all-encompassing divine plan, the universe would be incomplete without some incorporeal creatures,[7] who do not need to acquire knowledge by sense experience.[8] Angels occupy that space – along with devils, since 'demons and angels are the same in nature'.[9] All of this having been said, the fact remains that, although angels are not by nature conjoined with bodies, they are quite capable of *assuming* bodies. This they do not for themselves (for angels have no need of anything corporeal) but for our sake – to render communication with humankind easier.

It is crucial to clarify what kinds of 'assumed' bodies Aquinas has in mind here. He is seeking to counter a tradition which is well expressed by a statement included in Isidore of Seville's account of the pagan gods: demons, Isidore says, 'flourish in accordance with the nature of aerial bodies' ('Hi corporum aeriorum natura vigent').[10] Indeed, 'before their fall they had celestial bodies'; by which he presumably means, bodies of fire, as appropriate to that elevated location. But, 'now that they have fallen, they have turned into an aerial quality (*in aeream qualitatem*), and they are not allowed to occupy the purer expanses of the air, but only the murky regions, which are like a prison to them, until the Day of Judgement'. So, then, demons have aerial bodies and they inhabit the worst possible expanse of the air. Peter Lombard credits Augustine as a source for a somewhat different tradition, that *all* angels once had aerial

---

[5] *Summa theologiae*, 1a, qu, 51, art. 1, resp. (IX, 32-3). Cf. the similar views of the highly influential Alexander of Hales, OFM (*c*.1186-1245), neatly summarized by Travis Dumsday, 'Alexander of Hales on angelic corporeality', *The Heythrop Journal*, 54/3 (2013), 360-70.
[6] *Summa theologiae*, 1a, qu. 50, art. 1, resp. (IX, 6-7).
[7] Ibid.
[8] *Summa theologiae*, 1a, qu, 51, art. 1, resp. (IX, 32-3).
[9] *Summa theologiae*, 1a, qu, 51, art. 1, 1 (IX, 30-31).
[10] *Etymologiae*, VIII.xi.16-17; Isidore of Seville, *Etymologiae*, ed. W. M. Lindsay, 2 vols (Oxford, 1911), unpag; trans. Stephen A. Barney *et al.*, *The Etymologies of Isidore of Seville* (Cambridge, 2006), p. 184.

bodies, 'formed from the purer and higher part of the air'.[11] Subsequently 'such bodies were preserved for the good angels, who remained steadfast'. Their bodies are of 'such fineness (*tenuitatis*) that they cannot be seen by mortals, unless they are clothed by some more dense form (*aliqua grossiori forma*)'. That is to say, good angels are seen when they occasionally and voluntarily take on such forms. In sharp contrast, 'the bodies of the evil angels in their fall were changed' into air of inferior quality – thicker, more opaque, dense. Just as they were cast down from a high place to a lower one, 'so their refined bodies were transformed into inferior and thicker ones (*deteriora corpora et spissiora*)'.[12] Having engaged in this Spiel, which reads like a conflation of bits of Augustine and bits of Isidore, Peter Lombard proceeds to cite an actual Augustine passage, the statement in *De Genesi ad litteram* that 'demons are called aerial animate beings because they are endowed with bodies of an aerial nature'.[13] Then the Lombard invites his readers to endorse the view that here Augustine did not express his own belief but reported an opinion – yet another instance of scholastic neutralization of the challenge presented by one of Augustine's problematic statements. 'Many Catholic writers have taught unanimously that the angels are incorporeal and do not have bodies united to them'. The crucial point is that they are not irrevocably attached to those bodies; angels take them on to perform certain services and set them aside when those services are completed.[14] Generations of *Sentences* commentators eagerly took up the invitation to reject the contrary view, Aquinas included.

---

[11] *II Sent.*, dist. 8, ch. 1 (43), 1 (II, 340; trans. Silano, II, 34).
[12] Ibid. Alexander of Hales's similar views on aerial bodies are discussed by Dumsday, 'Alexander of Hales on angelic corporeality', p. 366.
[13] *II Sent.*, dist. 8, ch. 1 (43), 2 (I, 340; trans. Silano, II, 34); cf. Augustine, *De Genesi ad litteram*, iii, 10, 14-15 (ed. Zycha, p. 74).
[14] *II Sent.*, dist. 8, ch. 1 (43), 3 (I, 341; trans. Silano, II, 34-5). Alexander of Hales went to far as to suggest that one of those services was 'literally engaging in physical combat with embodied demons, as part of their role as guardians': 'demons often assume bodies to kill us; and the angels, having assumed bodies, can stop them'. Dumsday, 'Alexander of Hales on angelic corporeality', p. 365.

But why did angels and demons *need* to take on bodies on those occasions? They do so only for 'our instruction (as regards the good angels) or for our deception (as regards the wicked angels)'. Therefore, in either case would an imaginative vision not be enough? The answer that Aquinas gives in his disputed question on miracles (dated 1265-6)[15] is that 'not only imaginary but also corporeal vision is useful for our instruction'.[16] Here Aquinas attempts to sort out the tangle between the assumed sensible bodies of angels, which are offered to the external or corporeal vision of humans, and the internal forms they produce in the imagination when 'they cause themselves to appear in imaginary visions'.[17] 'Rabbi Moses' (Maimonides) is credited with the belief that 'all the apparitions of angels related in the Scriptures are … imaginary visions, the seer being either awake or asleep'. But this, Aquinas claims, does not 'safeguard the truth of Scripture'. 'Since the Son of God took to himself a real body (*verum corpus*), in the sense of an external body, perceptible to the senses, and not an 'imaginary one (*phantasticum*) as the Manicheans falsely claimed, 'it was fitting that the angels also should appear to men by assuming real bodies'. How, then, was this done? An 'angel can assume a body from any element, as well as from several elements mixed together', Aquinas assures us.[18] However, air is the best one to use, since it 'condenses easily so as to take and retain shape and reflect various colours from other bodies, as may be seen in the clouds'.[19]

---

[15] *Quaestiones disputatae de potentia dei*, qu. VI, art. 7: *utrum angeli vel daemones possint corpus assumere*, ed. and trans. the English Dominican Fathers (Westminster, MD, 1932, rpt. 1952), html edition by Joseph Kenny at https://isidore.co/aquinas/QDdePotentia.htm.

[16] Qu. VI, art. 7, ad 2.

[17] Qu. VI, art. 7, resp.

[18] Qu. VI, art. 7, ad 7. It may be added (since Aquinas and his contemporaries generally assumed the point) that use of a single element distinguished aerial bodies from human bodies, which are composed of all four elements.

[19] Giles of Rome, whose *Sentences* commentary was composed at the beginning of the 1270s, discusses the three elements of fire, air and earth as possible candidates for the provision of material for assumed bodies, pronouncing air the winner. *In II Sent.*, dist. viii, qu. 1, art. 3, *dubiae* 1-3 and their *resolutiones*; *In secundum librum sententiarum quaestiones*, pars prima (Venice,

In his *Summa theologiae* also, Aquinas was eager to dismiss the suggestion that angels are simply the imaginations of certain prophets. What is seen in a person's imagination is solely present in the mind of that viewer; 'it is not a thing that anyone else can see at the same time'.[20] But sightings of angels have been attested by groups of people, Aquinas notes. Therefore we must assume the existence of some sort of body, which is independent of any individual's imagination. Such a body is made of air, he continues, which has been 'condensed by divine power in an appropriate manner'.[21] This representation is quite in line with the Scriptures' way of using the similitudes of sensible things to describe what is, rightly understood, only discernible by intelligence. (Here Aquinas is, of course, echoing Pseudo-Dionysius). To borrow (and reorganize) phrases from John Donne's 'Air and Angels', a poem published well over three hundred years later, 'an angel ... doth wear' a 'face, and wings / Of air, not pure as it, yet pure'.[22]

Applying all of this to the situation described in *The Prick of Conscience*, it would seem that devils can mutate their aerial bodies into the forms of venomous creatures, even as good angels can present themselves with handsome faces and beautiful wings. This is rendered possible by the pliable, flexible nature of air, which condenses easily so as to take on different shapes and reflect various colours. So then, materiality – of whatever kind or degree is held appropriate to the manifestations of devils – is at the very centre of this particular explanation; we are not dealing with imaginary forms conjured up in the souls of the tormented. And it is logical enough, given the widely-held belief that devils are capable of taking on the shapes of many kinds of

---

1581), pp. 358, 360-3. On the comparison with clouds see further pp. 118-20, 157-8 below.

[20] *Summa theologiae*, 1a, qu, 51, art. 2, resp. (IX, 36-7).
[21] *Summa theologiae*, 1a, qu, 51, art. 2, ad 3 (IX, 36-7).
[22] *The Songs and Sonets of John Donne*, ed. Theodore Redpath (London, 1967), p. 30. Donne applies the distinction to misogynistic effect, declaring that women's love, while pure as air, is not as pure as men's love, which may be compared to the incorporeality of angels.

creature.²³ Generally supported by scholasticism, this view survived its devaluation in the English Reformation and endured for centuries, attaining a particularly eloquent expression in John Milton's *Paradise Lost*.

> Spirits when they please
> Can either Sex assume, or both; so soft
> And uncompounded is their Essence pure;
> Not ti'd or manacl'd with joint or limb,
> Nor founded on the brittle strength of bones,
> Like cumbrous flesh; but in what shape they choose
> Dilated or condenst, bright or obscure,
> Can execute their aerie purposes,
> And works of love or enmity fulfill.
> (*Paradise Lost*, I, 423-31)²⁴

Subsequently we see Milton's Satan assuming the body of a snake, in order to deceive Eve. And, in one of the poem's most startling moments, God turns all the devils in hell into snakes (X, 538-47), to punish their role in bringing about the fall of mankind. It may be recalled that, in Old, Middle and Early Modern English, the word 'worm' could designate any animal that creeps or crawls; a reptile (including dragons); an insect.²⁵ In an 'evil hour' Eve listened to that 'false Worm', Satan (IX,

---

[23] On which see especially the recent contribution of Richard Firth Green, *Elf Queens and Holy Friars: Fairy Beliefs and the Medieval Church* (Philadelphia, 2016), pp. 55-6, 68-70, 82, 86-7 232n. According to the *Bonum universale de apibus* of Thomas of Cantimpré (d. *c.* 1270), a demon can manifest itself in the shape of 'a pig (especially black), or otherwise a dog, a cat, a cow, a calf's tail, monkey, or dragon', to follow Andrew Murray's summary. 'Demons as psychological abstractions', p. 180. If this can be done to torment humans in the present life, why not also in the afterlife?

[24] *The Poetical Works of John Milton*, ed. Helen Darbishire (London, 1963), p. 16.

[25] Cf. *OED*, s.v. worm, n. As Alan Bernstein emphasizes, the biblical worm was understood 'not just [as] the common earthworm, or even the maggot that attacks dead flesh, but an assortment of beasts that swim, fly, and crawl'. *Hell and its Rivals*, p. 74.

1068), so it is quite appropriate that the pride of his followers is humbled by being forced to assume the appearance of lowly creatures that creep upon the ground.[26] The same strategy of punitive humiliation – inflicted on fallen angels and damned souls – is at work in *The Prick of Conscience*.

---

[26] Here I echo Milton's expression at *Paradise Lost*, VII, 476.

CHAPTER 11

Likening spiritual to corporeal forms: vernacular theology's hellish imaginations

Staying with *Paradise Lost* for a moment longer: in the scene wherein Raphael, serving as God's emissary, attempts to recount something of 'the secrets of another World' (i.e. heaven) to Adam and Eve, he explains that he will delineate 'what surmounts the reach / Of human sense'

> 'By lik'ning spiritual to corporeal forms,
> As may express them best...' (V, 571-4)[1]

Then he adds the thought:

> '... though what if Earth
> Be but the shadow of Heav'n, and things therein
> Each to other like, more then on Earth is thought?' (V, 574-6)

Likening the operations of conscience to the bite of a worm affords a good example of how a spiritual form can effectively be likened to a corporeal one, through a metaphorical connection, while the postmortem torments of fire show just how alike earthly things the conditions in 'another World' (hell in this case) can be.

While schoolmen like Aquinas and Bonaventure were wary, indeed dismissive (however tactfully), of the Augustinian appeal to a *similitudo corporis* in the soul, any medieval writer of narrative poetry or prose who featured the soul in his story could hardly avoid likening spiritual to corporeal forms. The impulse towards 'somatomorphism' was 'irresistible' in that context, a point Carol Zaleski has made elegantly. 'For theologians both medieval and modern, the tendency to make the soul impersonate the body has been an embarrassment', but in 'both

---

[1] *Poetical Works of Milton*, ed. Darbishire, p. 114.

medieval and modern otherworld journey literature' it has been a necessity.[2] A necessity which, in fact, was recognized by many distinguished theologians. Hugh of St Victor said there should be nothing surprising in the fact that 'when souls have departed from bodies, certain signs (*signa*) similar to the corporeal are presented for the demonstration of the spiritual, which, unless they were seen in and through such a corporeal likeness would by no means be mentioned by those same souls when returned to bodies, living in bodies, and knowing only corporeal things'.[3] Two separate yet crucially related matters are being fused together here: the perceptive needs of visitors to the other world (the issue of manifestation), and those of the audiences to whom those travellers, having arrived back home, tell their stories (the issue of representation). Visionaries need to be shown corporeal likenesses (*signa*), and their spiritual experiences need to be recounted with the use of such signs. 'Although being stripped of bodies there' they are able to see wondrous things in bodily terms, and without the use of those means they could not share their adventures. Otherwise what 'might be told us' by those 'who depart and see' would 'always remain hidden' – an inestimable loss.[4] There are no signs of 'embarrassment' in this account.

---

[2] Carol Zaleski, *Otherworld Journeys: Accounts of Near-Death Experience in Medieval and Modern Times* (Oxford, 1988), p. 51. She adds, 'Regardless of how one conceives the distinction between spirit and matter, somatomorphism violates it; it is primitive, crude, even idolatrous'.

[3] *De sacramentis*, II.16.2; *PL*, LXXVI, col. 584A-B, trans. Deferrari, p. 437. Hoc quidem commemorare voluimus ne mirum videatur si animabus a corporibus egressis signa quaedam corporalibus similia ad demonstrationem spiritualium praesentantur, quae nisi in talibus et per talia ab animabus corpore exutis viderentur; nullo modo ab eisdem ad corpora reversis in corpore viventibus et corporalia tantum scientibus dicerentur.

[4] Quamvis enim illa aliter ibi a corporibus exutae videre possent, non tamen hic nobis aliter narrare possent, et manerent semper occulta illa; nec esset quod de illis nobis a redeuntibus diceretur, nisi exeuntibus, et videntibus secundum ista monstraretur. *PL*, CLXXVI, col. 584B. With this may be compared the general attitude evinced by St Gregory in the fourth book of his *Dialogues*, to the effect that the here narrated were both for the benefit of those experiencing them and of those hearing about them. See for example, *Dialogi*, IV, chs 32 and 36; *PL*, LXXVII, cols 372A-B and 385C-D.

The dilemma is amusingly addressed by William Langland (*c.* 1325-*c.* 1390) in *Piers Plowman*, when the narrator-figure encounters the soul itself, *Anima*. Which is described as 'a sotil thyng withalle – / Oon withouten tonge and teeth'.[5] The term 'sotil' is richly ambiguous; it can designate a person with a profound and penetrating intellect, but when related to a substance or thing it means 'light, thin, lacking in density', and so can be applied to 'air, fire, a spirit, soul, or resurrected body'.[6] Yet our Langland passage reveals that features of that same body are necessary in order to delineate for humans 'what surmounts the reach / Of human sense'. Raphael's predicament also makes itself felt in *Le Pèlerinage de vie humaine*, the first in the sequence of three allegorical poems composed and revised during the period 1130-58 by Guillaume de Deguileville – 'outside of St Bernard, ... probably history's most popular Cistercian poet'.[7] The pilgrim-figure, tired of being lectured by Reason, asks to be divested of his body, so that he may learn for himself what he has been

---

[5] *Piers Plowman* B, xv.12-13, in *William Langland: The Vision of Piers Plowman*, 2nd edn, ed. A. V. C. Schmidt (London, 1995), pp. 246-7. It has been argued (convincingly, to my mind) that Langland's view of the soul is heavily indebted to Augustinian tradition, the pseudo-Augustinian *De spiritu et anima* (on which, much more below) often being cited as a direct source. See especially Joseph S. Wittig, '*Piers Plowman* B, Passus IX- XII: elements in the design of the inward journey', *Traditio*, 28 (1972), 211-80 (pp. 212-4); A. V. C. Schmidt's two articles, 'A Note on Langland's conception of "anima" and "inwit"', *Notes and Queries*, n.s.15 (1968), 363-4 and 'Langland and scholastic philosophy', *Medium Ævum*, 38/2 (1969), 134-56; and James Simpson, *Piers Plowman: An Introduction to the B-Text* (London and New York, 1990), pp. 98-9.

[6] *MED*, s.v. *sotil* adj., especially 3c. (a). Thus *The Cloud of Unknowing* looks forward to the Day of Judgment, when we shall be made 'sotyl in body & in soule to-geders', and Thomas Norton's *Ordinal of Alchemy* contrasts 'the subtile soule, pure & immortalle', 'so light and clene', with the heavy and 'grose bodye'.

[7] Joseph M. Keenan, 'The Cistercian pilgrimage to Jerusalem in Guillaume de Deguileville's *Pèlerinage de vie humaine*', in *Studies in Medieval Cistercian History, II*, ed. John R. Sommerfeldt (Kalamazoo, MI, 1976), pp. 166-85 (p. 167).

told about the duality of body and soul.[8] However, in order to experience fully what is happening to him, the pilgrim needs the very bodily faculties of which he has just been stripped. As Marco Nievergelt nicely puts it, this episode reveals how Deguileville's pilgrim-persona's 'supposedly disembodied soul continues to rely on corporeally mediated sense perception', thereby raising 'profound, possibly insoluble, problems, given that sense perception is clearly impossible without reliance on the body's sense organs' – a conclusion which apparently validates Aristotle's views on that subject.[9] However, a major caveat should be entered: one should be careful not to allow Aristotelian epistemology inappropriate priority when evaluating the writings of a Cistercian monk imbued with the spirit of a spirituality which is foundationally Augustinian and in many ways resistant to Aristotelian intellectual hegemony[10] – a warning

---

[8] Here I refer to the earlier, and most popular, version of *Le Pèlerinage de vie humaine*, ed. J. J. Stürzinger, Roxburghe Club (London, 1893).

[9] Marco Nievergelt, 'Can thought experiments backfire? Avicenna's flying man, self-knowledge, and the experience of allegory in Deguileville's *Pèlerinage de vie humaine*', in *Medieval Thought Experiments*, ed. Knox, Morton and Reeve, pp. 41-69 (pp. 59, 64).

[10] I have in mind that spirituality which I shall describe below as characteristic of William of St Thierry, Isaac of Stella, and the anonymous *De spiritu et anima*. In that highly influential treatise we are assured that, when the soul passes from earthly life into death, it takes with it 'all its faculties: sense knowledge, imagination, reason, understanding and intelligence, the concupiscible and irascible powers'. Here is a distinctively Cistercian elaboration of the Augustinian *similitudo corporis* theory. Which rather complicates the perspective within which Deguileville's allegory may be interpreted. As I read Nievergelt's argument (reference in previous footnote) Deguileville's thought-experiment here has 'backfired' because the pilgrim's attempt to understand his soul in the absence of his body actually reveals his need for the very corporeal faculties of which he has been stripped. On the other hand, this episode could be interpreted as a success inasmuch as it proves a fact about the nature of the soul – following disembodiment, the soul bears with it a *similitudo corporis* that enables the experiencing of pleasure and pain. The fact that, to judge by Deguileville's pilgrim, 'human cognitive faculties are finally unable to dispose of corporeal *phantasmata*' (p. 63), is not necessarily problematic if viewed within an Augustinian (as opposed to an Aristotelian) perspective.

signal being issued when, during *Le Pèlerinage de vie humaine*, Lady Sapience robustly brings out the limitations of 'Aristote', who is subjected to rebarbative characterization at lines 2918-3300.[11] Moving away from that specific interpretative thicket: here the general question is prompted, in what form of words can one describe the spiritual experiences of a (briefly and temporarily) disembodied soul, and how does this relate to description of the experiences currently being undergone by those souls severed from their bodies by death?

That is the representational problem faced by the narrators of the tales of (for example) Tundale, Thurkill, The Monk of Eynsham, the 'Gast of Gy', and visitors to Saint Patrick's purgatory – and, of course, by Dante, the supreme poet of heaven, hell and purgatory. We are not dealing here with some division between the privileged Latin learning of professional theologians and the populist fare provided in the vernacular for the *simplices*. Dante's *Comedy* is hardly lacking in doctrinal complexity. Besides, many Latin versions of otherworld adventures enjoyed a quite wide dissemination, most obviously the *Visio Tnugdali* (dating from the mid twelfth century). According to Henry of Herford's chronicle entry for the year 1331, when Pope John XXII – an accomplished if often controversial theologian – had the tale of Tundale read to him, he experienced the vision afresh in a dream of his own, and declared that it was in accord with his own beliefs.[12] Whatever one makes of that claim,

---

[11] Deguileville's disrespectful attitude to Aristotle is well brought out by Stephanie A. Viereck Gibbs Kamath, 'Rewriting ancient *auctores* in the *Pèlerinage de la vie humaine*', in *Mittelalterliche Literatur als Retextualisierung: Das 'Pelerinage'-Corpus des Guillaume de Deguileville im europaischen Mittelalter*, ed. Andreas Kablitz and Ursula Peters (Heidelberg, 2014), pp. 321-41 (pp. 325-30), and by Marco Nievergelt, 'From *disputatio* to *predicatio* – and back again: dialectic, authority, and epistemology between the *Roman de la Rose* and the *Pèlerinage de vie humaine*', *New Medieval Literatures*, 16 (2015), 135-71 (pp. 154-9). See also Sarah Kay, *The Place of Thought: The Complexity of One in Late Medieval French Didactic Poetry* (Philadelphia, 2007), pp. 71-80.

[12] Nigel F. Palmer,'*Visio Tnugdali*': *The German and Dutch Translations and Circulation in the Later Middle Ages*, Münchener Texte und Untersuchungen zur mittleren deutschen Literatur des Mittelalters 76 (Munich, 1982), p. 22.

at least it shows that popular otherworld tales were not beneath the notice of the learned. Or, at least, the notice of Henry of Herford, a scholarly Dominican based in Minden, Westphalia, who in addition to his impressive *Liber de rebus memorabilioribus sive Chronicon* wrote a treatise on the conception of the Virgin Mary and a substantial compilation of philosophical and theological knowledge, the *Catena aurea entium*. An impressive resumé.

Therefore, it would be quite incorrect to postulate a hard and fast distinction between élite academic investigation and popular visionary narrative. In the first instance, one may note that many distinguished theologians included 'ghost stories' in their erudite writings. In his august *De sacramentis* Hugh of St Victor described an incident of which he himself had heard, concerning a certain man whom a venerable-looking but actually wicked apparition had deceived into committing suicide. Saint James prevented this unfortunate soul from being led to postmortem torments, whisked him off for a brief experience of heaven, and then returned him to life.[13] The large number of otherworld apparitions included in Gregory the Great's *Dialogues* did much to normalize the view that such events should be taken seriously, as a means of learning something about life after death. Besides, the inscription and dissemination of those visionary narratives was in the hands of churchmen, who could express initial scepticism about what they are recording, and the considerable amount of care they took to verify the credibility of their stories. Going beyond that, they can display an awareness of what the expert theologians have to say about such controversial matters. A telling example may be found in the prologue to the *Tractatus de purgatorio sancti Patricii* (c. 1179-81), where 'H. of

---

[13] *De sacramentis*, II.16.2 (*PL*, CLXXVI, cols 583A-84A; trans. Deferrari, pp. 436-7). The visionary saw many thousands of angels, but was unable to describe them because 'there was nothing like them (*simile illis*) in this world by which he could have expressed that quality which he had seen in them, unless fire and light, but that it itself was greatly different by far (*longe et valde dissimiliter*)'; *De sacramentis*, ii.16.2 (*PL*, CLXXVI, col. 584A; trans. Deferrari, p. 437). Hugh takes this as evidence of how in visionary experience 'certain signs similar to the corporeal are presented for the demonstration of the physical'.

Sawtry' – who gives us only his initial – explains that, in this account of the Irish knight Owein's experience of the afterlife, spiritual things are said to have been seen by a mortal man 'as it were in corporeal forms and images' ('quasi in forma et specie corporali').[14] At the beginning of this prologue, the Monk of Sawtry notes that Pope Gregory has recounted many things concerning out-of-body experiences, to a good end (frightening sinners and inflaming the just to devotion).[15] When they return to their bodies, visionaries speak in corporeal terms and about things which have similarities to bodies. So we hear about rivers, fires, bridges, ships, houses, woods, meadows, flowers, black and white men, and so forth, all to inspire love of heavenly reward and fear of hellish torment.[16] This is a verbatim (though not specifically acknowledged) citation of the passage which in Hugh of St Victor's *De sacramentis* introduces the story Hugh himself had heard concerning the suicide who, having been granted the blessing of a vision of heaven, was returned to life.[17]

[14] *Tractatus de purgatorio*, in *St. Patrick's Purgatory*, ed. Easting, p. 123. See further Robert Easting, 'Owein at St. Patrick's Purgatory', *Medium Ævum*, 55/2 (1986), 159-75, and Carol Zaleski, 'St. Patrick's Purgatory: pilgrimage motifs in a medieval otherworld vision', *Journal of the History of Ideas*, 46/4 (1985), 467-85.

[15] *Tractatus de purgatorio*, ed. Easting, p. 121. A more direct intervention by Gregory is postulated in the ninth-century *Visio Wettini*. During a brief initial vision Wetti, a monk in the monastery at Reichenau, talks with an angel. Following which he asks his brothers to read to him from Gregory's *Dialogues* (the last book, Book IV, is chosen – of course!). Whereupon he falls asleep, and experiences an extensive tour of the underworld. *Visions of Heaven and Hell before Dante*, ed. and trans. Edith Gardner (New York, 1989), pp. 66-68, 244.

[16] *Tractatus de purgatorio*, ed. Easting, pp. 121-2. As Zaleski remarks, 'Although they usually spare their audiences the epistemological niceties', medieval vision narratives often suggest that 'what the protagonist saw, though real, should not be accepted too literally' (p. 89). However, the Monk of Sawtry does wish to make his audience aware of at least some of those 'niceties'.

[17] *De sacramentis*, II.16.2 (*PL*, CLXXVI, cols. 582D- 83A; trans. Deferrari, p. 436). H. of Sawtry's use of Hugh was spotted by Easting, 'Purgatory and the Earthly Paradise', pp. 27-9.

The Monk proceeds to declare that the fires of hell are more than a metaphor. Saints Augustine and Gregory are named as saying that corporeal fire can inflict punishment on the incorporeal spirit – which seems to be confirmed by the following story of Owein ('ista uidentur etiam affirmari narratione').[18] This gets at least part of Gregory's position right. As far as Augustine is concerned, the Monk may have had in mind what the saint said about the materiality of punitive fire following the General Resurrection (which does not obviously resolve the issues relating to the separated soul),[19] or perhaps even his tentative speculation that both the images of the fire and the worm could denote material entities.[20] This adds up to a considerable amount of learning being pressed into the service of verifying a fresh miracle. The Monk of Sawtry is taking no less care, in presenting his other-worldly narrative, than Hugh of St Victor had done before him, and indeed he uses a piece of Hugh's justification to assist his own.

It seems quite clear that Le Goff's desire to separate academic theology from 'popular folklore' and 'the popular sensibility', which have a discernible imprint on tales such as Owein's, requires careful reconsideration, together with those aspects of Aron Gurevich's response to Le Goff's grand narrative which complicate the nature of that separation whilst in some manner reinforcing it.[21] Gurevich writes forcefully about 'a complex and contradictory confusion of popular beliefs and Christian doctrine, a peculiar product of the prolonged

---

[18] *Tractatus de purgatorio*, ed. Easting, p. 122.
[19] See above, Chapter 2.
[20] *De civitate Dei*, xxi, 9 (ed. Hoffman, II, 536; trans. Dyson, p. 1065).
[21] A persuasive move towards the establishment of a larger cultural perspective for the issues raised here has been provided by Brian Patrick McGuire, 'Purgatory, the communion of saints, and medieval change', *Viator*, 20 (1989), 61-84. McGuire argues that 'Purgatory was only part of an awareness that the spiritual and the material words were moving closer to each other and that the bonds between them were becoming more visible'. He predicts that 'a closer study of the development of ideas of the afterlife in the period 1250-1550 would probably show that popular belief in ghosts was much more in evidence than any conception of a distance place where souls were purified' (p. 83).

process of mutual activity and interaction between two forces, a product which can be designated as "popular Christianity" or "parish catholicism", professed by the great mass of the population of medieval Europe'.[22] I admire, and certainly would endorse, that statement, whilst preferring to use the term 'vernacular theology' – by which I wish to evoke notions of the non-standard and uncodified, the informal and indeed the unruly, the (at least partly) unofficial and non-institutional, which go beyond any distinction between hegemonic Latin and the diverse medieval vernaculars, since all of those features can be present in any of those languages, Latin not least of all.[23]

Attempts to date the 'invention' of purgatory constitute a major test-case for investigation of the boundaries and/or intersections of official and vernacular theology. Gurevich suspects that purgatory was 'pressed on the theologians': they were obliged to act in response to what had been for a long time 'an integral element of faith and popular culture, and only

---

[22] 'Popular and scholarly medieval cultural traditions: notes in the margin of Jacques Le Goff's book', *Journal of Medieval History*, 9/2 (1983), 71-90 (p. 80).

[23] See Alastair Minnis, *Translations of Authority in Medieval English Literature: Valuing the Vernacular* (Cambridge, 2009), esp. pp. 1-3, 10-12, 102-6, 208 notes 61 and 62. In its fullest and most comprehensive sense, I believe, 'vernacular' can rightly be used to denote 'acts of cultural transfer, negotiation, and appropriation' (p. 12). On the currency of the term 'vernacular theology' in recent scholarship see the masterly overview by Vincent Gillespie, 'Vernacular theology', in *Oxford Twenty-First Century Approaches to Literature: Middle English*, ed. Paul Strohm (Oxford, 2007), pp. 401-20. The work of Nicholas Watson has been of crucial importance; cf. his articles 'Censorship and cultural change in Late-Medieval England: Vernacular theology, the Oxford translation debate, and Arundel's Constitutions of 1409', *Speculum*, 70 (1995), 822-64; 'Visions of inclusion: universal salvation and vernacular theology in Pre-Reformation England', *Journal of Medieval and Early Modern Studies*, 27 (1997), 145-87; and 'The Gawain poet as a vernacular theologian', in *A Companion to the Gawain Poet*, ed. Derek Brewer and Jonathan Gibson (Cambridge, 1997), pp. 293-314. Among contributions following Gillespie's overview, of special substance and significance is Ian Johnson, *The Middle English Life of Christ: Academic Discourse, Translation and Vernacular Theology* (Turnhout, 2013).

much later became a problem' for them.²⁴ But, although the schoolmen did not 'invent' purgatory as such, they soon 'imposed their conceptual structure on the chaos of ideas hitherto dominant in the collective consciousness'. Gurevich then proceeds – and here he largely supports Le Goff – to pronounce a 'contrast between the new coherent structure of the other world worked out by theological thought, and the badly organized simplistic picture of this world as outlined in visionary literature'. This, he believes, is an expression of 'the profound difference between these two styles of medieval thought; between disciplined scholarly thought, and the mytho-poetical, folkloric popular tradition'. While I accept the usefulness of postulating two 'cultural traditions, scholarly and popular',²⁵ in developing certain arguments, any rigid demarcation between 'two styles of medieval thought'²⁶ is open to dispute, given the ideological concerns and hermeneutic procedures of the schoolmen, who were tasked with explicating a sacred book which often deployed discourse that may appropriately be called 'mythopoetical', and which recorded the preaching *ad populum* of the very founder of Christianity, who had a love of parable, metaphor, and imaginative language in general.

'Folk fantasy attributed all the signs of corporeality to the soul', says Gurevich.²⁷ Indeed, and the question of if and how this attribution could be done was a perennial concern of medieval theology. The popular visionary narratives, expressions of vernacular theology, raised the very same ontological problem with which the schoolmen wrestled in their efforts to understand and rationalize hellish imaginations. A fact of which Gregory the Great, Hugh of St Victor, and the Monk of Sawtry were acutely aware. Gregory in particular has (quite patronizingly) been criticised by certain modern scholars who have wondered how such a

---

[24] 'Popular and scholarly', p. 83. A fine summary of the different attitudes to purgatory held by Le Goff and Gurevich is provided by Wei, who extends their discussion by bringing in relevant views held by an array of Parisian masters. *Intellectual Culture in Medieval Paris*, pp. 185-220.
[25] Ibid., p. 88.
[26] Ibid., p. 83.
[27] Ibid., p. 79.

shrewd thinker and efficient papal administrator could possibly contribute 'to the propagation of these wild tales of demons and wizards and haunted houses, of souls made visible, of rivers obedient to written orders, of corpses that scream and walk'.[28] Even the angelic doctor, St Thomas Aquinas, has occasioned a modicum of disapproval for the supposedly 'inordinate amount of attention' he pays 'to stories of incubi, succubi, and ghosts' in his quodlibetal question on miracles.[29] Yet such 'signs of corporeality' feature in many revelations vouchsafed to living, practising visionaries of the later Middle Ages, including the holy women whose testimonies we shall consider later in this essay. Furthermore, it is salutary to remember that St Thomas himself, that most cerebral of schoolmen, had (according to his hagiographer Bernard Gui) experienced a vision of a deceased brother friar, Romanus by name. God allowed Romanus to appear before him in corporeal form on account of his, St Thomas's, merits. Having been assured that his works are pleasing to God, Aquinas then asks his visitor, 'What is the right solution of that problem we used often to discuss together, whether knowledge gained in this life remains in the soul after death?'[30] Unfortunately, and indeed

[28] F. Homes Dudden, *Gregory the Great: His Place in History and Thought*, 2 vols (London, 1905), I, 356. But it should be recalled that Augustine himself had treated seriously the vivid otherworld testimony of 'those who have been detached from the senses of the body, less totally indeed than if they had actually died, but still more profoundly than if they were just asleep'. *De Genesi ad litteram*, xii, 32,61 (ed. Zycha, p. 427; trans. Hill, p. 501). For a thorough, and positive, presentation of Gregory's handling of the miraculous see William McCready, *Signs of Sanctity: Miracles in the Thought of Gregory the Great*, Studies and Texts 91 (Toronto, 1984). More generally, see the crucial studies by M. Goodich, *Miracles and Wonders. The Development of the Concept of Miracle, 1150-1350* (Aldershot, 2007), and Robert Bartlett, *Why Can the Dead Do Such Great Things? Saints and Worshippers from the Martyrs to the Reformation* (Princeton, NJ, 2013), pp. 333-409.
[29] Bynum, *Resurrection*, p. 290.
[30] *The Life of Saint Thomas Aquinas: Biographical Documents*, ed. and trans. Kenelm Foster (London and Baltimore, 1959), p. 40. Gui's *vita* was published soon after Aquinas's canonization (1323-5).

somewhat ironically, Romanus leaves without giving a clear answer.[31] But stories like this indicate that belief in the ongoing recurrence of the miraculous (often affirmed in canonisation processes, one should recall)[32] was no impediment to 'disciplined scholarly thought', and frequently accompanied it, indeed could serve as a spur to it.

Many of the most prominent theologians were pastors also, who were confronted on a regular basis with the everyday fears and hopes of their flocks, the ubiquitous belief in ghosts, apparitions and visitors from purgatory, together with the constant threat posed by demons and the protective presence of angels. On many occasions they brought 'disciplined scholarly thought' to bear on those issues – revealing that they were certainly not unresponsive to the tales told by their charges, or insensitive to the issues raised by the popular visionary narratives. It was generally admitted that demons can fool and dupe the senses (the usual verb employed being *illudere*), and quite how they can do that was discussed assiduously. Such trickery had gone back a long way, into pagan antiquity, as was exemplified by old tales like Circe's transformation of Ulysses' companions into beasts and the fate of certain Arcadians who, having swum across a mysterious lake, were changed into wolves. Furthermore, after the destruction of Troy Diomede was prevented from returning to his own people, with his companions being turned into

---

[31] Gui also tells the story of how, on another occasion, Aquinas's deceased sister appeared in a vision to him, to request masses and prayers so that she might progress through purgatory; the requisite arrangements having been made, she appears once again to reassure him that she is 'now in glory, as a result of this help'. *Life of Saint Thomas Aquinas*, ed. Foster, p. 41. Thomas was also credited with experiencing a vision of a 'venerable figure' whom some identified as the very founder of his order, St Dominic (p. 118).

[32] Cf. Goodich, 'Theory and public policy: canonization records' in idem, *Miracles and Wonders*, pp. 69-87; Bartlett, *The Natural and the Supernatural*, pp. 9-12, 23; and Aviad Kleinberg, 'Proving sanctity: Selection and authentication of saints in the Later Middle Ages', *Viator*, 20 (1989), 183-205 (pp. 200-5). Stefan Dragulinescu has illustrated the longevity of Augustine's view of miracles in opposition to Aristotelian rationalism in his fine essay, 'Thomas of Hereford's miracles – between Aquinas and Augustine', *Journal of Medieval History*, 44/5 (2018), 543-68.

birds, an incident narrated by both Virgil and Ovid.[33] Augustine had confronted these strange apparitions in his *De civitate Dei*, uttering the confident assertion, 'I do not ... in the least believe that either the body or the soul can be transformed into the members and lineaments of beasts by the art or power of demons'.[34] So, then, illusion was being practiced, but how was it effected? Following Augustine's lead, Aquinas declared that 'imaginary apparitions' rather than actual material things were involved here.[35] By interfering with our animal spirits and humours, natural vapours and fluids, demons can cause 'the power of the imagination or the external senses' to perceive things that are not actually there.[36]

But that power is limited, inasmuch as demons cannot cause the production of brand-new images. For instance, they are unable to 'make a man born blind imagine colours or a person born deaf imagine sounds'. Rather they can create 'new' images in the sense of composite images, by means of the compositive power of the human imagination. 'A person [may] imagine gold mountains never before seen'; 'because the person has seen gold and mountains, he can by a natural movement imagine the image of a gold mountain'.[37] Here Aquinas deploys, once again, an illustration which became commonplace. In his version of the same fundamental *quaestio*, Richard of Middleton offers the example of how a person can imagine a green sun; since in part of his imagination he holds the likeness of the sun and in another part that of greenness, a composite image can be formed from the two.[38] This is exactly how demons operate: by presenting 'new things to the imagination of human beings' through

---

[33] All these stories are recounted by Augustine, *De civitate Dei*, xviii, 16-17 (II, 287-9; trans. Dyson, pp. 842-3). Cf. Virgil, *Aeneid*, xi. 252ff.; Ovid, *Metamorphoses*, xiv. 455ff.
[34] Augustine, *De civitate Dei*, xviii, 18 (II, 290; trans. Dyson, p. 843).
[35] Aquinas, *De malo*, qu. xvi, art. 9, ad 2 (ed. Regan and Davies, pp. 928-31).
[36] Aquinas, *De malo*, qu. xvi, art. 11, resp. (ed. Regan and Davies, pp. 946-7).
[37] Aquinas, *De malo*, qu. xvi, art. 11, ad 9 (ed. Regan and Davies, pp. 948-9).
[38] *Questiones disputatae*, 31: *utrum mali angeli possint ludificare sensus nostros*, in *Richard de Mediavilla: Questions disputées, tome IV, 23-32: Les démons*, ed. with French trans. by Alain Boureau (Paris, 2011), pp. 350-51.

'different compositions of movement and forms, certain seeds (*seminum*) as it were, hidden in sense organs, whose potential devils know'.[39]

But, do demons and angels impress 'already-formed visions' on the human spirit, thus enabling it to perceive images they have fashioned, or do they form 'in the imagination of human beings images of the things they reveal'? The latter hypothesis seems the 'more probable', Aquinas says, because angels and demons themselves lack the *virtus imaginativa* – 'there is no power of imagination without a bodily organ', which immaterial creatures do not have[40] – and so they have to exploit the compositive abilities of the human imagination.[41] This explanation takes care of many of the supposed occurrences quoted above. But not, Aquinas admits, the case of Diomedes' companions being turned into birds – this 'involved more than an imaginary apparition'. If fact, those companions had actually drowned, and 'demons procured birds to substitute' for them, a far cry from turning men into birds.[42]

---

[39] Aquinas, *De malo*, qu. xvi, art. 11, ad 9 (ed. Regan and Davies, pp. 948-9). In the following article, Aquinas argues that 'good or bad angels can somehow internally dispose and arrange forms of the imagination insofar as such dispositions and arrangements are appropriate for apprehending intelligible things. And good angels indeed arrange forms of the imagination for human beings' good. And devils do likewise for their evil. Devils arrange forms of the imagination whether to desire sin, namely, as the things human beings apprehend induce them to pride or some other sin, or to present true understanding itself, as things apprehended lead human beings into doubts they do not know how to resolve, and then into error'. *De malo*, qu. xvi, art. 12, resp. (ed. Regan and Davies, pp. 954-5).

[40] *De malo*, qu. xvi, art. 1, 16 (ed. Regan and Davies, pp. 806-9). Cf. *Summa theologiae*, 1a, qu. 111, ad 2: 'Angels induce change in the imagination not by impressing a kind of imaginary form that has never been previously received through the senses (for they cannot make a blind man imagine colours) but rather by local movement of the spirits and humours ...' (XV, 29).

[41] Hence angels and demons 'make clear to the human imagination *what* they know, but not in the way *in which* (*eo modo*) they know'. *Summa theologiae*, 1a, qu. 111, art.3, ad.1 (XV, 29).

[42] Aquinas, *De malo*, qu. xvi, art. 9, ad 3 (ed. Regan and Davies, pp. 930-31). Cf. Augustine, *De civitate Dei*, xviii, 18 (ed. Hoffman, II, 292; trans. Dyson, p. 845).

In such discussions the schoolmen applied the best scientific knowledge then available to phenomena that troubled people who had grown up with 'stories of incubi, succubi, and ghosts'. Given the ubiquity of such fears, the amount of time the theologians devoted to them seems appropriate rather than 'inordinate' – though admittedly the solutions they came up with would have gone over the heads of many of the *simplices*.

CHAPTER 12

Images of air: *Purgatorio* XXV and the Cistercian *similitudo corporis*

There certainly is no lack of 'disciplined scholarly thought' in Dante's vernacular theology of purgatory, a fictional but truth-telling narrative where the issue of the creation of the human soul within the body, and its survival after death, is addressed with remarkable vigour. In particular, the Dante-persona is puzzled by the fact that the souls on the terrace of gluttony look emaciated: how can this be, when they are disembodied, not in need of food and unaffected by the lack thereof? The shade of Statius, having been called upon to speak by Dante's spirit-guide, Virgil, offers an account of how human embryos are formed, moving on to how the First Mover joyously breathes a *spirito novo* into the soul, a new spirit that will unite its different parts (vegetative, sensitive, and intellective) in a single rational substance – and finally, he explains how, in the afterworld, souls can take on the virtual shapes which enable Dante to see them, aerial semblances of human bodies having been created.[1]

> 'E come l'aere, quand' è ben pïorno,
> per l'altrui raggio che 'n sé si reflette,
> di diversi color diventa addorno;
> cosí l'aere vicin quivi si mette
> e in quella forma ch'è in lui suggella
> virtüalmente l'alma che ristette ...' (*Purgatorio* XXV, 91-6)[2]

---

[1] Christian Moevs summarises this transition nicely: 'upon death, human souls, carrying with them both "the human and the divine" (both the nutritive-sensitive and the intellective powers), unfold their powers of life and sensation as temporary aerial bodies, through which they act and feel'. *The Metaphysics of Dante's 'Comedy'* (Oxford, 2005), p. 131.

[2] All *Comedy* references are to Dante Alighieri, *La Commedia secondo l'antica vulgata*, ed. Giorgio Petrocchi, 4 vols, rev. repr. edn (Florence, 1994); I have drawn on the translation included in *The Divine Comedy*, ed. and trans. Charles S. Singleton, 3 vols, rev. repr. edn (Princeton, NJ, 1977), but with

['And as the air, when it is full of moisture becomes adorned with various colors by another's [i.e. the sun's] rays which are reflected in it, so there, where the soul stopped, the nearby air takes on the form that the soul virtually impressed upon it...']³

Aquinas had asked, how can angels possibly assume bodies formed of air, given that air lacks shape and colour? His answer is that compressed and concentrated air 'can have shape and colour, as in the clouds'; by the same token, angels can indeed take on aerial bodies, with the air having been duly 'condensed by divine power in an appropriate manner'(cf. p. 99

---

occasional alterations. In what follows I have benefited particularly from the following discussions (here listed in date order): Bruno Nardi, *Studi di filosofia medievale* (Rome, 1960), p. 58, along with his 'Il Canto XXV del Purgatorio', in *Lecturae et altri studi danteschi*, ed. Rudy Abardo (Florence, 1990), pp. 139-50; Étienne Gilson, 'Dante's notion of a shade: *Purgatorio* xxv', *Mediaeval Studies*, 29 (1967), 124-42; Vittorio Russo, 'A proposito del canto xxv del *Purgatorio*', in idem, *Esperienze e/di letture dantesche* (Naples, 1971), pp. 101-58; Anna Cerbo, '"Sangue perfetto" e "virtute informative". Il canto XXV del *Purgatorio*', in idem, *Poesia e scienza del corpo nella 'Divina Commedia': 'dicer del sangue e de le piaghe...'* (Naples, 2001), pp. 25-42; Adriano Lanza, 'La dottrina dantesca della generazione umana e dei corpi aerei (Canto XXV del *Purgatorio*)', in idem, *Dante eterodosso: una lettura diversa della Commedia* (Bergamo, 2004), pp. 170-79; and Manuele Gragnolati, *Experiencing the Afterlife: Soul and Body in Dante and Medieval Culture* (Notre Dame, IN, 2005), esp. Ch. 2: 'Embryology and aerial bodies in Dante's *Comedy*', on pp. 67-77. However, none of these accounts address the influence of Cistercian spirituality, which I will prioritize below. Other illuminating treatments of aspects of this science-heavy canto, and its larger consequences for the poem, include Giuseppe Mazzotta, *Dante, Poet of the Desert: History and Allegory in the 'Divine Comedy'* (Princeton, NJ, 1979), pp. 211-26; Patrick Boyde, *Dante, Philomythes and Philosopher: Man in the Cosmos* (Cambridge, 1983), pp. 271-81; Piero Boitani, '"Trattando l'ombre come cosa salda": fisiologia, metafisica e poetica dell'ombra', in *Elogio dell'ombra*, ed. Stefano Colmagro (Venice, 1995), pp. 33-47; and Rachel Jacoff, 'Our bodies, our selves: the body in the *Commedia*', in *Sparks and Seeds: Medieval Literature and its Afterlife. Essays in Honor of John Freccero*, ed. Dana E. Stewart and Alison Cornish (Turnhout, 2000), pp. 119-38.

³ The translation of lines 94-6 is my own.

above).⁴ Bonaventure offers a similar explanation.⁵ Just as water solidifies into crystal or ice on account of the cold, so it happens that air can be condensed (more and less) according to an angel's will; in the process this body of air takes on a shape and outward appearance (*figuram et effigiem*) which makes it look like an organic body. However, this does not account for the presence of colour in angelic appearances, so Bonaventure goes further. While the assumed body is understood as having been formed principally by the air, some 'earthly or watery vapour' (*vaporis terrei vel aquosi*) also features in its production, involving variety in the condensation process and enabling a range of colours. This does not require any extra activity on behalf of the angel, he adds, because the air has already been commingled with vapours.

Probably influenced by such discussion, Dante has enlisted the analogy with clouds to clarify how air can assume the shape impressed on it by the divinely-enabled power of the separated soul. This may seem some distance away from the behaviour of angels, but in scholastic thought those two entities are often directly compared in respect of their modes of cognition – so, why not also compare them in respect of their modes of self-manifestation? And it is reassuring to note that the connection has long been recognized in Dante scholarship, going back to the commentaries of Giovanni da Serravalle (1416-17)⁶ and P. Pompeo Venturi (1732).⁷

4   Cf. the insightful remarks by Zygmunt Barański, 'Canto XXV', in *Lectura Dantis Turicensis*, ed. Georges Güntert and Michelangelo Picone, vol. 2: *Purgatorio* (Florence, 2001), pp. 389-406 (especially p. 405).
5   *In II Sent.*, dist. 8, pars 1, art. 2, qu. 2, con. (*Bonaventurae opera*, II, 217-18).
6   ... virtus formativa facit de aiere circumstante illas animas, sicut dicitur quod angeli faciunt quando volunt apparere alicui persone; formare de aiere eos circumstante aliqua corpora aerea, et ita loquuntur, etc. *Fratris Johannis de Serravalle Ord. Min. Episcopi et Principis Firmani Translatio et Comentum totius libri Dantis Aldigherii*, ed. Marcellino da Civezza and Teofilo Domenichelli (Prati, 1891), consulted via The Dartmouth Dante Project, https://dante.dartmouth.edu/.
7   Dante dunque finge, che dall'anime separate si assumano corpi aerei: e passi per finzione poetica, non essendo vero il fatto, benchè non sia di sua natura impossibile, poichè, se ciò possono gli Angeli, perchè non l'Anime separate?

Having attained its visibility and appearance from air, this new semblance is called a shade (*ombra*). And out of air it forms virtual organs for all the senses.

> '... e quindi organa poi
> ciascun sentire infino a la veduta'. (*Purgatorio* XXV, 101-2)
> ['... therefrom it forms the organs of every sense, even to the sight'.]

Their specific shapes are determined by the 'desires and the other affections [which] prick us', Statius continues, and this explains the emaciated appearance of those spectres on the terrace of gluttony.[8] The purgatorial punishments they endure are marked upon their aerial bodies, their sins rendered visible to the viewer without any possibility of concealment.[9] Metaphor is not in play here; we are dealing with materiality, though of a kind which bespeaks a virtual reality as delicate and fragile as the rainbow created when the sun's rays fall on moisture-laden clouds.

An astonishing aspect of that (partial, tentative) materiality is the aerial bodies' ability to speak and laugh – and indeed, to produce the

---

La 'Divina Commedia' di Dante Alighieri...col comento del P. Pompeo Venturi (Florence, 1821), consulted via The Dartmouth Dante Project, https://dante.dartmouth.edu/. Cf. Gardner, p. 198 note 100.

[8] The commentator known as the Anonymus Lombardus (1325?) explains the matter neatly: ... secundum quod affligimur a desideriis seu aliis affectibus, figuratur umbra nostra, sicut figuraretur verum corpus. *Chiose di Dante le quali fece el figliuolo co le sue mani*, ed. F. P. Luiso, vol. II (Florence, 1904), consulted via The Dartmouth Dante Project, https://dante.dartmouth.edu/.

[9] Aquinas explains that, thanks to the ordering of divine justice, the fire of hell (which, of its own power, cannot torture some individuals more and others less) is able to follow the mode of guilt in the person punished – just as the fire of a furnace is regulated by the craftsmanship of the smith, in accord with what his art requires at a given moment. *In IV Sent.*, dist. 44, qu. 3, art. 2, qc. 1, ad 3. Here Dante shows such modulations of punishment in a highly original way – by imaging them through misshapen aerial bodies. Two different iterations of craftsmanship, in the shared attempt to express the mysteries of divine justice.

teardrops and the sighs which the Dante-persona, a presence of 'opaque flesh in a world of diaphanous spirit',[10] may have heard previously.

> 'Quindi parliamo e quindi ridiam noi;
> quindi facciam le lagrime e ' sospiri
> che per lo monte aver sentiri puoi'. (*Purgatorio* XXV, 103-5)
> ['By this we speak and by this we laugh, by this we make the tears and sighs which you may have heard all around the mountain'.]

At least a partial parallel (and/or indeed the inspiration?) for this may be found in scholastic accounts of how the resurrected body, having been rejoined by its once-separated soul, may physically express emotion. In his *Summa contra gentiles* (as quoted above) Aquinas explained that, while the impassible body cannot lose moisture in the form of tears, nevertheless the 'perturbation of the eyes and head which usually accompany weeping' will indeed occur, this being indicative of 'the sorrow of the heart'. Similarly, in his *Sentences* commentary Aquinas suggests that, just as 'in corporeal weeping' there occurs 'a certain commotion and disturbance of the head and eyes', so in that respect 'weeping will be possible in the damned after the Resurrection': that is to say, certain physical movements will be discernible, expressive of the internal torment which racks the bodies of the damned.[11] It would seem that Dante has appropriated, and elaborated upon, such thought in his description of the pre-resurrection bodies of the residents of purgatory.

Dante's creation of *ombre* from ideas derived from angelology and Resurrection theology is driven by a confidence in – and indeed a celebration of – the mental powers and activities of separated souls. When 'the soul is loosed from the flesh' certain faculties' will become 'mute'(*mute*), but

---

[10] To borrow an elegant phrase from Philip R. Berk, 'Shadows on the Mount of Purgatory', *Dante Studies*, 97 (1979), 47-63 (p. 52).
[11] *In IV Sent.*, dist. 50, qu. 2, art. 3, qc. 3 co.

> '... memoria, intelligenza e volontade
> in atto molto piú che prima agute'. (*Purgatorio* XXV, 83-4)
> ['memory, intellect and will [shall be] far more acute in action than before'.]

That is to say, while the sensory and appetitive powers will be muted (until their reactivation at the General Resurrection), since they no longer have any bodily organs with, and through, which to function, the rational powers of memory, intelligence and will shall survive – and, indeed, be even more vigorous than before.[12] Here Dante invokes the three faculties of Augustinian psychology, which the saint regarded as a series of analogies or images of the three persons in one God.[13]

Aquinas's view of the mental activities of the separated soul has been vividly summed up by Denys Turner: 'For Thomas, the human soul separated from the body is a functioning store of memories that it can continue to tell but can no longer edit, add to, or revise; it is a life frozen

---

[12] Giovanni da Serravalle, staying close to Dante's text, explains the lines thus: Alie potentie omnes mute, idest sunt, sicut sentire, vegetare, audire, videre, digerire, etc.; sed memoria, intelligentia et voluntas in actu multo plus acute, scilicet sunt ad operandum. Nota quod aliquas operationes habet anima in sua potestate, quas non potest exercere nisi cum organis corporalibus, et in hiis anima separata, ratio idest, quiescit. Aliqua sunt opera anime nostre, que potest exercere etiam sine organis corporalibus; et in hiis anima, separata a corpore, multo melius exercetur, sicut intelligendo, volendo et memorando, quia ad hoc exercendum anima separata est liberior. The notion that, after death, certain activities of the soul – including its memorative power – shall actually be enhanced, is well expressed here. *Johannis de Serravalle ... Translatio et Comentum totius libri Dantis Aldigherii*, ed. da Civezza and Domenichelli, consulted via The Dartmouth Dante Project.

[13] Pointed out by Nardi, *Studi di filosofia medievale*, p. 58. Cf. *De trinitate*, x, 11; also xii, 15 and xiv, 7-8. As Ronald Teske notes, in *De trinitate* 'Augustine finds in the memory, understanding, and will of the human soul a series of psychological analogies or images of the three persons in one God'. 'Augustine's Philosophy of Memory', in *The Cambridge Companion to Augustine*, 1st edn, ed. Eleonore Stump and Norman Kretzmann (Cambridge, 2001), pp. 148-58 (p. 148).

into the shape it possessed at the moment of death'.[14] Dante seems to be attributing active powers to separated souls that are far in excess of that estimate. Even more daringly, he is suggesting that those souls can shape virtual bodies that experience and express sensations (in their actions of speaking, laughing, weeping and sighing, etc.). Both these moves, especially the latter, seem quite contrary to the schoolmen's efforts to use Aristotelian philosophies *de anima* to solve the problem. The soul's operations which are not exercised through bodily organs certainly remain in the soul when it leaves the body, declares Aquinas in his *Summa contra Gentiles*; he has in mind the operations of willing and understanding. Indeed, 'the more the soul is freed from preoccupation with its body, the more fit does it become for understanding higher things'.[15] On the face of it, this statement resembles Dante's claim that after death 'memory, intellect and will [shall be] far more acute in action than before'. But Aquinas is concerned to emphasize disjunction rather than continuity: 'it must be borne in mind that the soul understands in a different manner when separated from the body and when united to it'. 'The mode of understanding vouchsafed to us in the present life' will cease 'upon the death of the body', to be replaced by 'another and higher mode of understanding' – by which Aquinas means the reception of knowledge from above, divine infusion (as occurs in the case of angels). While, in this life, the soul cannot think without an image (cf. the triumphal Aristotelian moment cited on p. 34 above), images are not necessary, and indeed cannot be generated, in the next life as currently they are constituted. In his *Sentences* commentary Aquinas does allow that, following the return of the body to the soul at the General Resurrection, the imagination will once again form and use phantasms. 'But then the body will be entirely under the rule of the soul'.[16] As Anton C. Pegis says, 'St. Thomas clearly wishes to cut the intellect from its dependence on phantasms', because of an obvious fear: if we imply that,

---

[14] Turner, *Thomas Aquinas: A Portrait* (New Haven and London, 2013), pp. 79-80.
[15] *Summa contra gentiles*, II, 80-1, 12; trans. James F. Anderson, https://dhspriory.org/thomas/english/ContraGentiles2.htm.
[16] Pegis, 'Separated soul and its nature in St. Thomas', p. 139.

for the soul, 'embodiment means ... that it cannot in any way understand when it is separated from the body', then we 'render the separated soul operationless' and indeed 'threaten it with nonexistence'.[17] A high risk indeed.

Dante, however, does not see things that way, being quite taken with the idea that the memory, intellect and will shall function perfectly well in the afterlife, indeed in a manner superior to the way in which they do at present (when they need the constant input of sense-data), and that their eager operations can work in association with, and be manifest by, the *ombre* which their respective souls shape out of air, virtual bodies which perform certain actions normally associated with our earthly bodies. And if his apparent deviation from the heavily Aristotelian teaching of Aquinas and Bonaventure is troubling, it may be noted that this was not, so to speak, the only show in town. As we have seen, there was another tradition, which was quite willing to conceive of the possibility that after death the soul retains the capacity to engage in various mental activities, including imagination. The continuing popularity of the treatise *De spiritu et anima*, a twelfth-century pseudo-Augustinian text (probably of Cistercian origin) which during the thirteenth century served as a counterbalance to aspects of Aristotelianism, is salutary.[18] Here we are assured that the soul withdraws from the body

---

[17] Ibid., p. 140.

[18] Text printed in *PL*, XL, cols 779-832. See further Joan Martínez Porcell's partial edition and modern Spanish translation; 'Introducción y traducción del *De Spiritu et Anima*, un opúsculo inédito atribuido a Alcher de Clairvaux', *Espíritu*, 67, issue 155 (2018), 265-90; Teresa Regan (Sister Frances Carmel), 'A Study of The *Liber de spiritu et anima*: Its Doctrine, Sources and Historical Significance' (unpub. Ph.D. diss., University of Toronto, 1948); and L. Norpoth, 'Der pseudo-augustinische Traktat "De spiritu et anima"'(unpub. Ph.D. diss., Cologne, Institut für Geschichte der Medizin, 1971). The attribution to Alcher of Clairvaux is now widely discounted, though Cistercian origin remains a strong possibility, and is affirmed by Bernard McGinn in his edition and translation of texts, *Three Treatises on Man: A Cistercian Anthropology* (Kalamazoo, MI, 1977), pp. 63-74. In the context of a discussion of whether the acts of the sensitive powers remain in the separated soul, Aquinas declares that the treatise 'is ascribed to

... secum trahens omnia; sensum scilicet, imaginationem, rationem, intellectum, intelligentiam, concupiscibilitatem, et irascibilitatem: et ex his secundum merita afficitur ad delectationem, sive ad dolorem. [... taking with it all its faculties: sense knowledge, imagination, reason, understanding and intelligence, the concupiscible and irascible powers. And from these, according to its merits, the soul passes over to either joy or pain.][19]

In a subsequent chapter the anonymous author goes on to offer an extraordinary elaboration of Augustine's account of the *similitudo corporis* – which may be deemed a coarsening of the saint's cautious and understated account, though (from a different viewpoint) it does spell out the implications of what he had said in a way which brings the discussion closer to the language of the Gregorian visionary tradition and

---

a Cistercian who compiled it from Augustine's works and added things of his own'. *In IV Sent.*, dist. 44, qu. 3, art. 3, qc. 2, ad 1. On the issue of authorship see further Regan, 'Study of The *Liber de spiritu et anima*', pp. 271-82; G. Théry, 'L'Authenticité du *De spiritu et anima* dans Saint Thomas et Albert le Grand', *Revue des sciences philosophiques et théologiques*, 10/3 (1921), 373-77; and especially Constant Mews, 'Debating the authority of Pseudo-Augustine's *De spiritu et anima*', *Przegląd Tomistyczny*, 24 (2018), 321-48, who robustly states that 'the hypothesis of Alcher's authorship should not be dismissed out of hand' (p. 349). Albert initially went along with the attribution to Augustine, but came to reject it. Alexander of Hales and Bonaventure accepted it (the text's Neoplatonism made it attractive to Franciscans), and drew on the treatise substantially. Despite a rather negative attitude to *De Spiritu et anima* as a mere 'compendium of old and new' which lacks originality (in contrast with other, more innovative, Cistercian treatises which failed to achieve its high level of dissemination), McGinn affirms that it was of crucial importance 'in assuring Cistercian anthropology a real influence in the history of medieval theology' (*Three Treatises on Man*, p. 93). Mews offers a measured judgment, stating that the treatise should not be denigrated as a 'derivative compilation', for 'the author does try to create a synthesis from a wealth of texts from which he quotes' ('Debating the authority', pp. 343, 349).

[19] *De spiritu et anima*, cap. 15, in *PL*, XL, col. 791. Cf. the translation by McGinn, *Three Treatises on Man*, p. 206, which I have not followed at this point.

the needs of those tasked with validating recent adventures in the underworld.

> Porro anima non est corpus, quia non omnis similitudo corporis corpus est. Dormienti enim tibi in somnis velut corpus apparebit, neque id corpus tuum, sed anima tua; nec verum corpus, sed similitudo corporis tui. Jacebit enim corpus tuum, ambulabit illa. Tacebit lingua corporis tui, loquetur illa. Clausi erunt oculi tui, videbit illa. Et ita in ea tota et integra cernetur similitudo carnis tuae. In hac similitudine quasi per loca cognita vel incognita discurrit, et sentit laeta vel tristia. Anima etiam mortui, sicut dormientis, in ipsa similitudine corporis sui sentit, seu bona seu mala: non sunt tamen corporalia, sed corporalibus similia, quibus animae corporibus exutae afficiuntur, seu bene seu male, cum et ipsae suis corporibus similes sibimet appareant ...
>
> [Now the soul is not a body, since not every likeness of a body is a body. When you sleep, something like a body may appear which is not your body, but your [body as envisaged by your] soul. Nor is it a true body, rather the likeness of your body. While your body is reclining [i.e. in sleep] that likeness can be walking about [i.e. in your dream]. Your bodily tongue may be silent, the likeness will speak. Even if your eyes are shut, the likeness has vision. And so in that likeness you can recognize a detailed replica of your flesh. In that likeness your soul can wander over familiar or unknown places, capable of feeling joy or sadness. In the likeness of its body the soul of a dead man, like that of a sleeping man, can experience good and bad things. The things to which souls deprived of bodies become attached, for better or for worse, are not corporeal, but similar to corporeal things ...][20]

Aspects and adumbrations of the ideas in *De spiritu et anima* are to be found not only in the authentic Augustine but also in Gregory the Great, Hugh of St Victor, and William of Auvergne, and not forgetting the

---

[20] *De spiritu et anima*, cap. 23, in *PL*, XL, col. 796-7; trans. McGinn, *Three Treatises on Man*, p. 215.

subversive Avicenna.²¹ Indeed, Hugh of St Victor and Avicenna are generally regarded as sources of the treatise, and Vincent of Beauvais attributed it to Hugh of St Victor; a shorter version was regularly copied under Hugh's name.²² There are definite academic precedents, then, for at least some of Dante's creative decisions.

The claims of this intellectual tradition were recognized by Dante's son Pietro Alighieri in the final version of his gloss on *Purgatorio* XXV (written 1359-64), where he quotes the passage from *De spiritu et anima* about how the soul, on withdrawing from the body, takes with it all its faculties, and immediately follows it up with Augustine's advocacy of the *similitudo corporis*.²³ However, Pietro also partially quotes and partially summarizes a passage from Aquinas's *Summa theologiae* which affirms an opposing position, contending that when the body-soul composite is destroyed the sensory powers do not remain in the soul actually (*actu*) but only virtually (*virtute tantum*), 'as in their principle or root (*in principio vel radice*)'. In the same *quaestio* Aquinas, having quoted that very same passage ('secum trahens omnia ...') from *De spiritu et anima*, which he will proceed to refute, attacks the entire treatise as lacking in authority and denies its attribution to Augustine.²⁴ Pietro does not quote

---

²¹ The influence of Avicenna (perhaps via the twelfth-century Toledan scholar Dominicus Gundissalinus) on the theory of divine illumination followed in this text is argued by Regan.
²² *Three Treatises on Man*, trans. McGinn, pp. 71-2; Mews, 'Debating the authority', pp. 334-5.
²³ Pietro Alighieri, *Comentum super poema Comedie Dantis: A Critical Edition of the Third and Final Draft of Pietro Alighieri's Commentary on Dante's 'Divine Comedy'*, ed. Massimiliano Chiamenti (Tempe, AZ, 2002). Accessed through The Dartmouth Dante Project, at https://dante.dartmouth.edu/. Cf. the *Codice cassinese* (1350-75[?]) on *Purgatorio* XXV.84, where the *De spiritu et anima* passage is also quoted. *Il codice cassinese della Divina commedia...per cura dei monaci benedettini della badia di Monte Cassino* (Monte Cassino, 1865), again consulted via The Dartmouth Dante Project.
²⁴ Aquinas, *Summa theologiae*, 1a, qu. 77, art. 8, 1 and ad. 1 (XI, 116-17). Aquinas quotes and critiques the same passage at *In IV Sent.*, dist. 44, qu. 3, art. 3, qc. 1, arg. 1, *In IV Sent.*, dist. 44, qu. 3, art. 3, qc. 2 ad 1, and *Quaestiones disputatae de anima*, art. 19, ad 3. Apparently it attained a certain popularity, indeed notoriety, as a succinct statement of a highly controversial

that indictment though presumably he had read it. So, then, he would have been perfectly aware of the controversy into which his father had ventured, but does not suggest any resolution, preferring to let *De spiritu et anima* have its say and to back it up with a supportive statement by the genuine Augustine.

Aquinas's phrase *virtute tantum* merits careful examination because it seems to match line 80's *in virtute*,[25] which no doubt is one of the reasons why Pietro cited it: when the soul leaves the body, says Statius, it carries

> position. It is at the head of a double *quaestio* on whether sensitive powers remain in the separated soul, which is included in the *Sentences* commentary of Peter of Tarantasia, a contemporary of Aquinas's who commented on the *Sentences* during 1257-9 (and became Pope Innocent V in 1276, shortly before his death). Peter offers several versions of a negative response. Some say the sensitive powers are accidents of the soul, which communicate with the body when joined to it but remain when it is separated: however, in their case neither act nor power (here the same thing) cannot exist without that conjunction with the body. Others say (and here he echoes Aquinas) that the sensitive power is not in the soul *ut subjecto* but *ut coniuncto*: but it flows from the soul, as its origin (*principio*), just as natural properties of a thing flow from its form, and therefore when the soul is separated from the body, they do not remain in the soul *in subiecto*, but solely *in radice et in principio*. Others postulate twofold sensitive powers, some which have their origin in the soul, and which remain, and others which have their origin in the body, which do not. *In IV Sent.*, dist. 44, qu. 2, art. 5, in, *Innocenti quinti .... in IV libros sententiarum*, 3 vols (Toulouse, 1649-52), III, 426-7. Peter's views on the body-soul relationship are discussed comprehensively by Emanuel C. Buttigieg, 'The Definition of the Human Soul in the *Commentary on the Sentences of Peter Lombard* by Peter of Tarantasia, O. P.' (unpub. Ph.D. diss., Marquette University, 1984). Richard of Middleton addresses the statement in *De spiritu et anima*, cap. 13, that the soul (always in motion) is called 'soul' (*anima*) when it enlivens and 'spirit' (*spiritus*) when it contemplates, which indicates that the sensitive powers continue to be present in the soul when it leaves the body; since these powers are active (*non ociose*), knowledge based on sense perception is gained by the soul. Richard goes on to conclude that the sensitive powers cannot actually operate in the separated soul, given its lack of bodily organs, but will resume their functions following the Resurrection. *In IV Sent.*, dist. 50, art. 1, qu. 1 (IV, 692-3); cf. *PL*, XL, cols.788-9.

[25] As pointed out by Nardi, *Studi di filosofia medievale*, p. 58, and reiterated in subsequent Dante scholarship.

with it, 'in potency (*virtute*), both the human and the divine', with memory, intellect and will being more 'acute in action than before', though other faculties ('l'altre potenze') are muted ('mute'; lines 80-4). In this case Aquinas was following Albert the Great, who in his *Sentences* commentary had argued that in the separated soul the root (*radix*) of the senses and affections is present, although acts of hearing, seeing and imagination are not possible, and neither do they exist in terms of being (*in esse*), since the soul is severed from the corporeal organs with which it once functioned.[26] The *Summa theologiae* passage is a more positive iteration of the opinion which Aquinas cites, and gives rather lukewarm approval to, in his *Sentences* commentary: 'others say that the sensitive and other similar powers do not remain in the separated soul except in a limited sense, namely as a root (*in radice*), in the same way as a result lies in its [originating] principle: because there remains in the separated soul the ability to pour out (*efficacia influendi*) these powers should it be reunited with the body... . And this opinion appears to be the more reasonable'.[27]

Here we see these masters (and Dante after them) being caught between the Scylla of Aristotelian psychology and the Charybdis of mandatory belief in the future reinstatement of the body-soul composite. The matter was a straightforward one for Aristotle, who did not believe in a future General Resurrection; in his opinion, at death the body together with its sensory faculties perished completely, never to return. But his scholastic successors were tasked with explaining what the separated soul could do before it rejoined its body, and how those operations related to what it would do following that reunion, when the senses would be reactivated, 'unmuted' (to echo Dante's term). The notion that the resurrected body's powers had to start up from scratch, perhaps even *ex nihilo*, was difficult if not impossible to rationalize in philosophical terms – and indeed in terms of Christian faith, for the idea of a second creation of humankind (in parallel with the creation of Adam and Eve) presented enormous difficulties. Therefore, some measure of

---

[26] *In IV Sent.*, dist. 44, G, art. 43, resp. (XXX, 600-1).
[27] *In IV Sent.*, dist. 44, qu. 3, art. 3, qc. 1 co.

continuity had to be accepted. And so, the schoolmen hit on the discourse of *in principio vel radice*. As Mowbray says, 'recognizing that the soul was the root of sensitive powers was one way in which the soul could be said to possess some powers of the senses', and by this means 'the Platonic idea that the soul possessed some sensitive powers independent of the body' was defused.[28] Of course, for Plato and his followers that idea fitted within a belief-system that envisaged the pre-existence of souls and their transmigration following each death of their host-bodies. That was a doctrine which no orthodox Christian theologian could accept.

Relating this to Dante: one might say that in his aerial bodies we see the separated soul eagerly unmuting and pouring out its powers on maleable air, thanks to the *efficacia influendi* which it has retained, and maintains, after death, an efficacy which shall enjoy its complete fulfillment when it gets to work on actual bodies following the General Resurrection. But was there enough, in this rather minimalist proposition of deep-down *radix* and hidden *principium*, to have motivated Dante's vision of the vigorously functioning powers of the separated soul through its aerial body? I think not. And neither, I believe, did the erudite Pietro Alighieri. He looked farther afield, to *De spiritu et anima*, a passage from which (as I have noted above) he provocatively juxtaposed with a contrary statement from Aquinas's *Summa theologiae*. The relevance of this probably Cistercian text – together with related treatises of clearly Cistercian origin – for a reading of *Purgatorio* XXV, and its potential attractiveness to any Dante commentator, is manifested by a passage which Pietro does not actually quote, but which he must have read since it follows on immediately from what he *does* quote. After its death, the body, having 'previously been integrated like a well-tempered instrument (*organum*), ever ready to produce music at the least touch', now 'lies broken and useless'. Its bodily organs being gone, 'the soul no longer has an instrument upon which to exercise its faculties'. (Here the author is punning on the Medieval Latin meanings of *organum* as either a musical instrument or a body part). But that does not mean that its beautiful

---

[28] *Pain and Suffering*, p. 109.

music has ceased – far from it. 'Even though the instrument had been destroyed, yet the melody (*melos*) has not ended, nor has the player perished'.[29]

This entire discussion in *De spiritu et anima* – the affirmation of the survival of the faculties of sense knowledge, imagination etc. after death ('secum trahens omnia ...') followed by the metaphor of the body as the soul's musical instrument – is clearly dependent on the *Epistola de anima* which the Cistercian Isaac of Stella composed around 1162, or perhaps a little earlier (whereas *De spiritu et anima* has plausibly been dated to some time after 1170).[30] A version of that same metaphor may also be found in the treatise *De natura corporis et animae* (*c.* 1140) which was produced by another author who exercised a major influence on Cistercian thought, William of St Thierry.[31] So, then, the Cistercian pedigree of these ideas is palpable, and their claim on our attention as interpreters of a poet who afforded a major leader of that order, St Bernard of Clairvaux, pride of place as guide to the Empyrean Heaven, is unquestionable.[32]

---

[29] ... quoniam etsi organum periit, sed non melos, nec quod organum movebat. *De spiritu et anima*, cap. 15, in *PL*, XL, col. 791; trans. McGinn, *Three Treatises on Man*, p. 206.

[30] *Epistola de anima*, cap. 13; in *PL*, CXCIV, cols 1882C-83B; trans. McGinn, *Three Treatises on Man*, p. 166. The debt of *De spiritu et anima* to Isaac is well brought out by Mews, 'Debating the authority'.

[31] *De natura corporis et animae*, Book II, cap. 3, in *PL*, CLXXX, col. 721B-D; trans. McGinn, *Three Treatises on Man*, p. 130.

[32] On which see especially Steven Botterill, *Dante and the Mystical Tradition: Bernard of Clairvaux in the 'Commedia'* (Cambridge, 1994), though he prefers the term 'sponsor' to 'guide' – a position critiqued by Peter S. Hawkins in his review, in *Speculum* 71/ 1 (1996), 127-9. Neither Botterill's book, nor its predecessor, Alexandre Masseron's *Dante et Saint Bernard* (Paris, 1953), considers the possibility of the influence of Cistercian spirituality on *Purgatorio* XXV. However, Botterill offers the insightful statement that, 'As a rule, Cistercian authors of the twelfth and thirteenth centuries remained isolated from the mainstream of scholastic activity, in keeping with the generally anti-intellectual tenets of the Order's originators (Bernard himself prominent among them); and they also tended to keep their distance from the emergent universities' (p. 27). 'Bernard's position as an *auctor* in scholastic thought was always equivocal', Botterill continues; 'His own approach to theology, coupled with his low opinion of the value of

Dante may be characterized as also having believed (in due Cistercian fashion) that the soul's sublime melody does not need an earthly body in order to play: and proceeding to show it exercising its faculties upon, and through, an aerial body.

It may be added that Augustine's account of the faculties of 'memory, intellect and will', as explicitly referenced in *Purgatorio* XXV, 83-4, is enthusiastically elaborated in Cistercian spirituality. William of St Thierry found it particularly attractive; indeed, the Trinitarian structure of his theory of mystical ascent has been judged his most original contribution.[33] *De spiritu et anima* follows Augustine's identification of those powers as evidence that the soul 'bears a certain image of the Holy Trinity'. One in three, and three in one ... 'Having but one nature, the soul nevertheless has three faculties. These are the intellect, the will, and the memory'.[34]

> unaided human reason, was not guaranteed to earn him sympathy among the scholastics, founded as it was on a tradition more mystical than rational, a staunch doctrinal conservatism suspicious of novelty, and a sound measure of scorn for anything smacking of "pagan" learning'. On this argument, it is hardly surprising that certain scholastics – pre-eminently Thomas Aquinas – seem to display 'a certain scepticism about the value of Bernard's intellectual achievements' (p. 28). Dante's decision to value Cistercian soul-theory (doctrine of a conservative, Augustinian bent) when rationalizing his representation of separated souls is of a piece, I would argue, with the conclusive honour he bestowed upon a figure whose mysticism transcended contemporary appropriations of the best of pagan philosophers, Aristotle – even as he sought to transcend Virgil, the highest of pagan poets. And, in terms of the hierarchy of ultimate values, the elevated position afforded St Bernard proclaims the superiority of love over all human reason and 'intellectual achievements'.

[33] By O. Brooke, 'The trinitarian aspect of the ascent of the soul to God in the theology of William of St. Thierry', *Recherches de théologie ancienne et médiévale*, 26 (1959), 85-127. Cf. McGinn, *Three Treatises on Man*, pp. 44, 96. Isaac of Stella developed his own distinctive version; see his *Epistola de anima*, cap. 7-13, in *PL*, CXCIV, 1879B-83B; trans. McGinn, pp. 161-7.

[34] *De spiritu et anima*, cap. 35, in *PL*, XL, col. 805; trans. McGinn, *Three Treatises on Man*, p. 237. Moving beyond the *Comedy*, it may be noted that a good case for the influence of the love-doctrine in *De spiritu et anima*, along with Richard of St Victor's 'Four grades of violent love', on Dante's *Canzone*

That said, there is nothing in either *De spiritu et anima* or in any other treatise on the soul known to me (Cistercian or otherwise) to support Dante's contention that the powers supposedly active in the separated soul, however they may be detailed and described, can function though organs formed of air. It is hardly surprising that even the learned Pietro Alighieri is unable to come up with anything relevant. Generally speaking, at this point the early Dante commentators tend to content themselves with literalistic restatement of what their text is saying – though Giovanni da Serravalle's comparison of Dante's *ombre* with the way in which angels use air to manifest themselves to humans should be given its due (cf. p. 119 above). So, then, it might be concluded that Dante has moved beyond even the robustly resistant Augustinianism represented by *De spiritu et anima,* and even farther away from the Aristotelianism of Aquinas and Bonaventure, while noting that this was a quite reasonable (and certainly well-informed) move to make, given the precedents afforded by angelology and resurrection theology.

> From dream to dream and rhyme to rhyme I have ranged
> In rambling talk with an image of air ...[35]

W. B. Yeats's words have resonance in any attempt to interpret Dante's aerial bodies, and prompt the question of the relationship between philosophy and poetry in *Purgatorio* XXV.

Montanina ('Amor, da che convien pur ch'io mi doglia') has been made by Carlos López Cortezo, *'Amor, da che convien pur ch'io mi doglia.* Alcune precisazioni', in *Le Rime di Dante,* ed. Claudia Berra and Paolo Borsa (Milan, 2010), pp. 213-9.

[35] From W. B. Yeats, 'Broken Dreams', in *The Collected Poems of W. B. Yeats,* ed. Richard J. Finneran, rev. 2nd edn (New York, 1996), pp. 153-4.

CHAPTER 13

Dante, poet of material perfection

The issue of manifestation, how the spiritual can render itself perceptible, in this fascinatingly learned canto raises major interpretive problems, to which we may now turn. For whose edification, to what end, is this grotesque mimicry of speaking and laughing, this performance of corporeal emaciation, this perceptible externalization of the desires and affections which trouble the suffering souls? Are they materialising for the persona's benefit, so he can communicate with them (as a temporarily separated soul whose experience resembles that of a dream), or for their own, as a regular feature of their existence in purgatory?

Perhaps Saint Gregory can help us out here, even as he assisted the Monk of Sawtry when he sought support for his endorsement of Owein Miles' vision. For Gregory usefully explains how one Repartus was granted a vision wherein he encountered things with which he, and by extension we, could feel a certain familiarity; crucially, 'he saw not all these things for himself (*non sibi viderit*), but for us that yet live, and have time granted to amend our wicked lives (*a malis operibus emendare*)'.[1] That is to say, Repartus experienced something in terms that he could understand, and thus was enabled to pass on that experience in terms that we can understand. No claim is being made here that the underworld is really like that (though fire will always be fire, both here and there). As Patrick Gardner puts it, 'this and all other supposed visions of the otherworld have no implication for the corporeality of that state, but are merely images introduced directly into the sensitive powers of the one having the vision, as in a dream'.[2] Likewise, everything that Dante is describing is supposed (according to the poem's narrative) to have happened in his own head and not beyond; we have been invited to share his personal psychomachia. Quite a show to have been put on for one

---

[1] *Dialogi*, IV, 32 (*PL*, LXXVII, col. 372A-B).
[2] Patrick Meredith Gardner, 'Dante and the suffering soul' (unpub. Ph.D. diss., University of Notre Dame, 2009), p. 66.

man, one might say: but it seems more appropriate to say that Dante is the man whose mind is putting on the show. His single and singular consciousness is the theatre in which the shades, *his* shades, go through their motions, enact their mimesis.³

Support for such a reading may be found in a much later passage of the *Comedy*, where Beatrice explains to Dante that the seraphim and saints that he has seen, and will see, are not actually there in material form.

> 'Così parlar conviensi al vostro ingegno,
> però che solo da sensato apprende
> ciò che fa poscia d'intelletto degno'. (*Paradiso* IV, 40-2)
> ['It is needful to speak thus to your faculty, since only through sense perception does it apprehend that which it afterward makes fit for the intellect'.]

'For this reason Scripture condescends to your capacity', Beatrice continues, as when it attributes 'hands and feet to God', and 'Holy Church represents to you with human aspect' angels like Gabriel, Michael, and Raphael⁴ (presumably a reference to church paintings). This echoes, tacitly and perhaps deliberately, the defences of scriptural metaphor offered by Aquinas (with a little help from Pseudo-Dionysius) at the beginning of his *Summa theologiae* (and quoted on pp. 28-9 above).

---

3   Simon Gilson speaks of how Dante 'foregrounds the pilgrim's bodily processes and reactions', filtering 'the narrative through the physical sense of the pilgrim, especially his sight and hearing'; 'The anatomy and physiology of the human body in the *Commedia*', in *Dante and the Human Body: Eight Essays*, ed. John C. Barnes and Jennifer Petrie (Dublin, 2007), pp. 11-42 (pp. 11-12). This rather implies that there is some material reality external to the Dante-persona's mind, which he perceives and to which he reacts. The argument being outlined above (which I shall question) is quite different: there is no external reality beyond the persona's mind; the narrative is supposed to be recording (and making public) internal adventures which are the product of his individual psyche.
4   Raphael being the 'one' who restored the sight of old Tobit; cf. Tobit xi.1-15.

Similarly, the shade-bodies of *Purgatorio* XXV condescend to the capacity of the Dante-persona – his *ingegno*, his perceptive and representational needs – albeit as a representative of humankind in general.

Against this 'subjective' reading may be adduced the controversial passage concerning the spirit's formation of the *ombra*, which seems to be making an objective statement about the shadowy corporeality of its infernal existence.

> '... e quindi organa poi
> ciascun sentire infino a la veduta'. (*Purgatorio* XXV, 102-3)
> [' ... therefrom it forms the organs of every sense, even to the sight'.]

It is hard not to read this as meaning: out of air organs for every sense are made, even up to and including sight. Sight was often described as the noblest, strongest and most subtle of the senses, and identified as the one which will enjoy the most intense of all sensory experiences in the resurrected body.[5] Therefore, if the means of seeing is included in this re-shaping of what the body had before, the production of a functioning facsimile of its living members (that being a plausible way of reading line 90, 'così e quanto ne le membra vive'), it would seem that the soul's *virtù formativa* (line 89) really wants to create a complete and comprehensive semblance of the body. (Augustine's *similitudo corporis* comes to mind. It certainly came to the mind of Dante's son Pietro, as already noted.)[6] We are dealing not with the metaphorical depiction of spiritual beings in writing or in painting but with the making of virtual bodies that exist irrespective of the perceptive and representational needs of any human mind, and constitute an elaborate social network that functions irrespective of who may be witnessing it.[7] The inhabitants of Dante's

---

[5] Minnis, *From Eden to Eternity*, pp. 198-9, 313-4 n 260.
[6] Pietro Alighieri, *Comentum super poema Comedie Dantis*, ed. Chiamenti, consulted via The Dartmouth Dante Project.
[7] Heather Webb sees the social arrangement of purgatory as comprising a community of aerial bodies communicating with each other through speech and gesture; by means of 'words, smiles, tears, and sighs, they relate to others'. 'Aerial bodies are not intended principally to effect suffering', Webb

purgatory seem to take pleasure in taking on bodies of air themselves and in witnessing each other's materialisations.

This 'objective' type of reading has been contested in Patrick Gardner's exigent interpretation of *Purgatorio* XXV. In his view, when Dante came to consider the 'possible union of separated souls to aerial bodies', he advocated 'not a formal union allowing for sensation, but a virtual one allowing for manifestation which is precisely parallel to angelic appearances'.[8] The suffering souls encountered by the Dante-

claims; 'rather, their principal purpose is to share suffering as joy, as the process of purgation reveals that suffering in a penitential mode does not isolate sufferers, but rather brings them into concert with their neighbours'. *Dante's Persons: An Ethics of the Transhuman* (Oxford, 2016), p. 43. In sharp contrast, in hell 'gesturality does not recognize its dependence upon neighbours; whether striking out or withholding itself, it does not elicit or expect reciprocity of communication' (p. 38). It was commonly supposed that hell is a place where hatred, wrath and envy rule, friendship and sociability being impossible. The damned despise each other and would fight and strangle each other if they could, to quote the graphic (and quite representative) account in *The Prick of Conscience*, lines 8400-43, 8466-81. The contrast between the two places of torment is well brought out by Eamon Duffy, who emphasizes the fellowship and sociability shared by souls in purgatory who are confident of their ultimate salvation and know their punishment is not eternal. *Stripping of the Altars*, pp. 348-50. Scholastic advocacy of the presence of hope in purgatory has been noted above. However, a much harsher estimation of purgatorial experience was carried by popular visionary narratives (certainly known to Dante), which the schoolmen often reacted against. This crucial point is made very well by Easting, 'Purgatory and the Earthly Paradise', who corrects Le Goff's reading of the *Tractatus de purgatorio sancti Patricii* and the *Visio Tnugdali*. It would seem that, in presenting the socially cohesive aspects of existence in purgatory, Dante sided with the schoolmen rather than with the popular narratives. But the extent to which 'sociality and relationality' (Webb's terms) are features of purgatory in Dante's account, and elsewhere, should not be exaggerated. The intense pain and suffering experienced in purgatory is unmitigated, and the theologians were quite clear that only blessed souls truly benefit from the God-given gifts of *amicitia* (friendship), *concordia* (concord), and *gaudium* (joy); cf. Minnis, *From Eden to Eternity*, p. 300 note 91.

[8] Gardner, 'Dante and the suffering soul', dissertation abstract.

persona are not to be 'understood as capable of sensing their apparent torments', but rather as 'capable of manifesting their intellectual torment physically'. It's all a matter of appearances, laid on for the benefit of the human viewer and witness, 'the only one who can see them, the only subject of sensation',[9] in a manner comparable to the way in which angels currently make themselves known to sense-dependent humans. 'Angels must form eyes, ears, and so forth, in order to present a human appearance, for the sake of being seen',[10] though they themselves have no use for such organs; by the same token, the shade-bodies are not produced to experience sensation but for the purpose of manifestation.

But what about lines 102-3, where it is said of the *ombra*, 'e quindi organa poi / ciascun sentire infino a la veduta'? This, argues Gardner, could designate not 'actual powers of sensation' as granted to an aerial condensation 'but merely the appearance of those organs to one who does have the faculty of sight in body and in truth', the Dante-persona himself.[11] If 'the shades form organs "even to the sight" the question is, to whose sight?'[12] Are we dealing with the shade's power to see (a 'philosophical absurdity', on Gardner's reading)[13] or its capacity to make itself visible, to be seen?[14] Gardner admits that the former is a 'natural reading', but holds out the possibility of an 'unappreciated ambiguity' in the text's formulation.[15] Dante, he claims, would have expected the 'most common' reading of the statement in lines 102-3 to be that the shade forms aerial organs for each and every sense, thereby enabling the full

---

[9] Gardner, 'Dante and the suffering soul', p. 205. On the ways in which the dead made themselves visible to the living see especially Peter Dinzelbacher, 'Il corpo nelle visioni dell' aldilà', in *Micrologus. Natura, scienze e società medievali (Nature, Sciences and Medieval Societies)*, Rivista della Società Internazionale per lo Studio del Medio Evo Latino, 1 (Turnhout, 1993), pp. 301-26.
[10] Gardner, 'Dante and the suffering soul', p. 203.
[11] Ibid., p. 204.
[12] Ibid., p. 200.
[13] Ibid., p. 202.
[14] Ibid., p. 293.
[15] Ibid., p. 200.

range of sensation, *but* 'he also phrased it in such a way' as to allow the other interpretation.[16]

Some support may be found for that other interpretation in scholastic angelology – assuming, of course, the doctrine in question may be applied directly to Dante's *ombre*. Here we must return to issues concerning the materialisation of spiritual forms previously considered in respect of *The Prick of Conscience*'s venture into demonic shape-shifting, since Dante's intervention in this sphere is at once more complicated and daring. According to a tradition associated with Augustine and Isidore of Seville, once upon a time (or, rather, before time as we know it) both angels and demons had aerial bodies. Nowadays they take such bodies upon themselves – the good angels having the better deal in terms of aerial purity, of course – when they have to perform some divine service (in the case of the good angels) or some wicked intervention (in the case of demons). As already noted, Isidore declared that demons 'flourish in accordance with the nature of aerial bodies' ('Hi corporum aeriorum natura vigent'). The popularity of Isidore's *Etymologiae* endured,[17] and the doctrine in question was transmitted in the major late-medieval encyclopedias.[18] Bartholomew the Englishman's *De proprietatibus rerum* directly channels Isidore of Seville:

> Hi corporum aereorum natura vigent. Ante transgressionem celestia corpora gerebant: lapsi vero in aeream qualitatem conuersi sunt. Et ista aeris caliginosi spacia tenere permissi sunt, qui eis carcer est vsque ad iudicium.

---

[16] Ibid., p. 202.

[17] In his commentary on the *Inferno* (1327-8?) Guido da Pisa quotes Isidore when seeking to explain Canto XXXIV, 16-21, where the Dante-persona sees the *ombre* who inhabit the innermost circle of hell 'wholly covered', as in a thick fog, 'showing through like straw in glass', and experiences the presence of Satan himself as a giant, occluded shape. *Expositiones et glose super Comediam Dantis, or Commentary on Dante's 'Inferno'*, ed. Vincenzo Cioffari (Albany, NY, 1974); consulted via The Dartmouth Dante Project.

[18] See for example Vincent of Beauvais, *Speculum naturale*, i, 79; *Speculum doctrinale*, ix, 117 (*Speculum maius*, I, 72-3; II, 849-50).

[Þese fendis liueþ in kynde of bodies of aier; for tofore þe trespas þey bere heuenliche bodies, and siþ þey buþ islyde and ifalle þey buþ iturned into qualite of aere, and þey buþ isuffred to holde þis spaces of derk aer þat is to hem a prisoun anon to þe dome.][19]

But – and this is the crucial point for our purposes – Bartholomew affirms the view that appearances of angels and demons to humankind involve merely temporary conjunctions of a spiritual entity and an aerial body. To continue with our quotation from the fourteenth-century English translation by John Trevisa (1397), 'an angel whan he wole takeþ a body conuenabil to his worchinge, þat he may be iseye; and whanne he hath ido his office, he leueþ þat body that was itake'. Once the job is done, the aerial body is discarded; neither angels nor demons desire it, take pleasure in it, need it for any purpose of their own. Wholly and simply, we are dealing with a manifestation, a necessity for interaction with human beings and nothing else. That view had been offered up for approval in Peter Lombard's *Sentences*; generations of commentators, and compilers like Bartholomew, happily gave it.[20]

---

[19] *De proprietatibus rerum*, ii, 19, unfol. (my punctuation inserted); *On the Properties of Things: John Trevisa's Translation of Bartholomaeus Anglicus De proprietatibus rerum*, ed. M. C. Seymour *et al.*, 3 vols (Oxford, 1975-88), I, 86.

[20] As when Bonaventure asserts that angels do not naturally have aerial bodies united to them, though they may voluntarily take them on, not for any purpose of their own but in order to minister to others. *In II Sent.*, dist. viii, pars 1, art. 1, qu. 1 (*Bonaventurae opera*, II, 209-12). Do angels ever assume bodies for themselves, on their own account? No, answers Bonaventure. There is a twofold force in angels, namely the contemplative and the administrative or operative. 'According to the contemplative they are turned completely toward God, and thus they do not need the solace of an assumed body'. However, 'according to the administrative [force] they descend to us, and condescend to us', taking on human bodies as instruments, signs, and dwellings, thereby manifesting themselves to us in order to gladden or comfort us. In that way and for that purpose, they *do* need 'the solace of an assumed body': only in the context of serving human beings. *In II Sent.*, dist. viii, pars 1, art. 1, qu. 2 (*Bonaventurae opera*, II, 212-13).

So, then, this temporary aerial body is a thing without life; 'þey an angel take a body for eny nedeful doinge, he makeþ it noȝt liue, neþer ȝeueþ þerto lif, but onliche he meueþ it'.[21] The angel merely moves its aerial construction rather than animating it as the soul animates the human body (to expand Bartholomew's statement a little).[22] Bonaventure argues that angels do not exercise the activities associated with the senses (*actus sentiendi*) through an assumed body, even though that body may possess all the human organs (because any lack in this regard would not fittingly manifest the perfection and completeness associated with an angelic spirit).[23] Although those organs may be complete they are there not to sense (*ad organorum sensificationem*) but rather for the purpose of the angel's self-manifestation (*ad sui ipsius ostensionem*). Hence the 'eye' in such a body may be so-called only in an 'equivocal' sense, because it is not used for the purpose of seeing. Similarly, Aquinas roundly rejects the proposition that 'angels have sensations through the organs of the bodies they assume'.[24] However, those organs are not simply superfluous,

---

[21] *De proprietatibus rerum*, ii, 18, unfol.; trans. Trevisa, ed. Seymour, I, 84.

[22] This contrast between angels and demons merely moving, as opposed to animating, an aerial body had become an academic commonplace. On Alexander of Hales' (quite typical) views see Dumsday, 'Alexander of Hales on angelic corporeality', p. 365. Addressing the issue of whether in their assumed bodies angels employ bodily sense-faculties like sight and hearing, Alexander vacillates a little, saying that this is unlikely, 'but if they do it is not because they need them to access information that would otherwise be unavailable to them' (p. 366). Angels are never dependent on sense faculties for gaining knowledge, because their noble cognitive activities, which are far beyond the capacities of mere mortals, do not need that constant processing of sense-data which is necessary (on the Aristotelian model) for standard human cognition.

[23] *In II Sent.*, dist. viii, pars 1, art. 3, qu. 2: *utrum angeli in corporibus assumtis exerceant operationes convenientes potentiae sensitivae* (*Bonaventurae opera*, II, 221-3).

[24] *Summa theologiae*, 1a, qu. 51, art. 3 (IX, 38-43). Affirming the same doctrine, Aquinas answers in the negative his question on 'whether an angel or demon by means of an assumed body can exercise the functions of a living body.' Angels do not experience sensations when they assume aerial bodies, and when speech is ascribed to them this is 'not really natural speech but an imitation thereof by producing a like effect: and the same applies to eating'

because they perform the function of signifying the angels' spiritual faculties; the eyes image angelic knowledge, for instance, and the other organs other spiritual powers. (Here Aquinas makes an appeal to Pseudo-Dionysian metaphorical interpretation – on which, more later). But are there not many examples in Scripture of angels speaking through their assumed bodies? Angels do not really speak in this way, Aquinas explains; they merely 'imitate speech (*aliquid simile locutioni*), forming sounds in the air corresponding to human words'.[25] All of this is just for the benefit of their human witnesses. However much they may have disagreed on the details, the schoolmen agreed that, as pure intelligences, angels share a mental 'language' which consists in purely intellectual activity, and

> (*Quaestiones disputatae de potentia dei*, qu. VI, art. 8, resp.) Similar views are put forward in the question *de demonibus* which forms the final part of Aquinas's *De malo*. The article, 'can demons cause the local movement of material substances (*possent corpora mouere localiter*)?', is answered in the affirmative (art. 10, resp.). But this movement – required for manifestation to human beings – can be done without demons actually animating aerial bodies (art. 1, resp.). No aerial material substance can be animated, become a living thing (*nullum corpus aereum possit esse animatum*; art. 1, resp.); it cannot experience sense perception through a demon's power. Demons (and angels) themselves do not have senses, since they lack the necessary corporeal organs (art. 7,12). Therefore, when they occasionally and temporarily assume aerial bodies this does not mean that they are joined to them naturally. Demons cannot 'live' through them in a relationship comparable to the one whereby a human soul animates its body. *De malo*, ed. Regan and Davies, pp. 812-15, 900-1, 937.

[25] Unfortunately, Aquinas does not go into detail here. There was a long-standing grammatical tradition that, as Donatus put it, 'speech sound (*vox*) is struck air (*aer ictus*) perceptible to hearing'; Priscian cites the definition of 'the philosophers' of 'spoken utterance (*vox*) as very thin struck air (*aerem tenuissimum ictum*) or its property perceptible to hearing, that is, what properly strikes the ears'. A vernacular echo of this teaching is found in Geoffrey Chaucer's *House of Fame*, line 765, 'Soun ys noght but eyr ybroken'. Donatus, *Ars grammatica*, and Priscian, *Institutiones grammaticae*, in *Grammatici latini*, ed. Henry Keil, 8 vols (Hildesheim, 1961), IV, 367 and II, 5; cf. Martin Irvine, 'Medieval grammatical theory and Chaucer's *House of Fame*', *Speculum*, 60/4 (1985), 850-76. So, perhaps it may be inferred that an angel, having taken on a body of air, is able to create that percussion or breaking of air which is necessary for human hearing.

reveal their thoughts to each other (as they certainly wish to, given heavenly sociability) without sound, since they lack bodily organs.[26]

So then, might not all of this be applied to the aereal bodies of separated souls, as presented by Dante? Partially, certainly: but there is a

---

[26] The matter of how angels can communicate with each other, as opposed to communicating with the humans in their care, is beyond the scope of this essay. Excellent discussions include: Tiziana Suarez-Nani, *Connaissance et langage des anges selon Thomas d'Aquin et Gilles de Rome* (Paris, 2002); Harm Goris, 'The Angelic Doctor and angelic speech: the development of Thomas Aquinas's thought on how angels communicate', *Medieval Philosophy and Theology*, 11 (2003), 87-105; Theo Kobusch, 'The language of angels: on the subjectivity and intersubjectivity of pure spirits', in *Angels in Medieval Philosophical Inquiry*, ed. Iribarren and Lenz, pp. 131-42; and Bernd Roling, 'Angelic language and communication', in *A Companion to Angels in Medieval Philosophy*, ed. Hoffmann, pp. 223-60. This leads into the issue of mental language (*lingua mentalis, oratio mentalis*, etc.), on which see *Le langage mental du moyen âge à l'âge classique*, ed. Joël Biard (Leuven, 2009); *Knowledge, Mental Language, and Free Will*, ed. Gyula Kilma and Alexander W. Hall (Newcastle upon Tyne, 2011); and *Mental Language: from Plato to William of Ockham*, ed. Claude Panaccio, trans. Joshua P. Hochschild and Meredith K. Ziebart (New York, 2017). One particularly interesting aspect is, how do angels praise God if they cannot produce sounds? Bonaventure discusses but does not pronounce decisively on the matter, saying that certitude is not to be had here, different points of view being probable and held by different authorities. Because they are spiritual substances, lacking corporal organs, angels cannot form a spoken word (*vox*). Further, a spoken word is formed out of the percussion and breaking of the air (see the previous note), but there is no air in the empyrean. So, it would seem that there cannot be a spoken word or a sound there. But might there be some substitute for air? Maybe not, and perhaps corporeal praise (*laus vocalis*) will have no place in the empyrean, since the praise of the mind (*laus mentalis*) shall be so great. 'Because [angels] are incorporeal through their own nature, naught suits them but the praise of the mind'. However, when 'they minister to us' angels 'assume bodies for our solace and in them sometimes speak and form spoken words for our instruction' – 'so also in them they praise God vocally for our consolation'. In brief, angels may sing to us, in the sense of making sounds perceptible (and superlatively pleasing) to our hearing, but not to each other. *In II Sent.*, dist. 2, pars 2, dubia circa litteram Magistri (*Bonaventurae opera*, II, 84-6). For Henry of Ghent's discussion of empyrean acoustics see Minnis, *From Eden to Eternity*, pp. 203-4.

major contrast, which makes all the difference. Angels already enjoy their state of perfection, and at the General Resurrection they are to stay the same as they are now. Never having had material bodies, they do not long for their return – indeed, to be clothed in flesh would mean a diminution of ontological status – whereas the *ombre* do precisely that. In *Purgatorio* XXV the materialising impulse and desire of the soul's formative power is presented as being so strong that it wishes to anticipate the point at which the soul will rejoin and re-animate its body – a moment of great joy, which is celebrated in Canto XIV of the *Paradiso*. Speaking here for all the virtuous souls in the sphere of the sun, Solomon eagerly looks forward to the paradise beyond death,

> 'Come la carne glorïosa e santa
> fia rivestita, la nostra persona
> piú grata fia per esser tutta quanta ...' (43-5)
> [' ... when our flesh, sanctified and glorious, shall clothe our souls once more, our person then will be more pleasing since it is complete...'][27]

In the meantime, do such souls indeed 'have sensations through the organs of the [aerial] bodies they assume'? That would be to go along with what Gardner calls a 'natural reading' of lines 102-3, the 'most common' possible, viz. that the formation of virtual 'organs of sense' implies that those same organs are capable of sensing.

That is certainly an obvious literal interpretation of the passage in question. But it is also a deeply, though richly, troubling one. We have seen how medieval theologians regularly emphasize that angels are not naturally connected to the aerial bodies which they temporarily deploy.

---

[27] Here I follow the translation by Mark Musa, *The Divine Comedy, vol. 3: Paradise* (Harmondsworth, 1986), p. 169, since I prefer his rendering of *più grata* as 'more pleasing' (intimating the sheer joy of the re-embodied souls' greater spiritual happiness and fulfillment) as opposed to Singleton's rather anaemic 'more acceptable'. Of course, the long-suffering souls in hell can hardly share that enthusiasm, given the prospect of new, or at least enhanced, forms of torment.

When they do take on such forms, they merely move around matter which is somewhat cumbersome to them, mimicking human actions such as seeing, hearing and speaking for as long as their divine mission requires. Angels do not 'have sensations through the organs of the bodies they assume';[28] they cannot 'live' through them in a relationship comparable to the one whereby a human soul animates its body. *Assuming* a body is a very different thing from *animating* it. Dante, however, seems to be going some distance towards suggesting that his *ombre* are able to animate the materials they have shaped to suit their needs.

Does he actually reach that point, go quite that far? That, in my view, is unclear. If that indeed is what he is up to, he is flying in the face of the common scholastic belief (well supported by the science of the day) that an aerial body is incapable of animation. No aerial material substance can be animated, declares Aquinas; it cannot become a living thing (*nullum corpus aereum possit esse animatum*).[29] Here Aquinas is talking about the inability of a demon to animate an aerial body. But *mutatis mutandis* this principle could also be applied to what a separated soul can and cannot do with a body of air. On this reckoning, then, while 'the organs of every sense' may well be formed from air, they would be incapable of functioning as actual sense-organs.

That fails to satisfy, as a reading of the relevant lines in *Purgatorio* XXV. Besides, given the enthusiasm with which Statius proclaims the formation of aerial bodies, it seems difficult to accept that he has just in mind that mimicry of human actions which is all that angels can manage (however much it may be conceded that they can put on a good show). Separated souls are not angels; they have psychosomatic needs all of their own, an extraordinarily powerful desire for embodiment which will be satisfied fully only at the General Resurrection. In the meantime, the creative virtue (*virtù formativa*) which they channel will exert its power to shape the nearby air into appealing forms (cf. lines 88-90). Aquinas states that 'bodies can only be organic if they in themselves can have limit

---

[28] Aquinas, *Summa theologiae*, 1a, qu. 51, art. 3 (IX, 38-43).
[29] *De malo*, qu. xvi, art. 1, resp. (ed. Davies, pp. 814-5).

and shape', a property which air lacks; itself incapable of being limited, a segment of air cannot be isolated and 'distinguished from the surrounding air'.[30] A possible counter-argument would be that the *virtù formativa* at work in *Paradiso* XXV is perfectly capable of distinguishing some part of the air from its surroundings, imposing the limits necessary for some measure of organicism.

But Dante's intention on that front remains opaque. What *is* evident is that he is offering a high estimation, indeed engaging in a robust celebration, of the activities which separated souls can perform. That is clearly true, I believe, irrespective of the extent to which he supposes those activities can be conducted through aerial bodies – indeed, that issue might be deemed incidental, in comparison with what he is implying about what powers the soul carries with it from this life into the next. Dante has taken the *umbrae* of Virgil's underworld[31] and not only

---

[30] Ibid.

[31] That most important of all poetic intertexts for the *Comedy*, Virgil's *Aeneid*, includes reference to the shades of the dead, described as mere shadows, as diaphanous as 'the light breath of a breeze or vanishing dream' (*Aeneid*, VI, 290-4; VI, 700-2). As Étienne Gilson notes, 'the similarity between the *umbrae* of Virgil and the *ombre* of Dante is striking'. 'Dante's notion of a shade', pp. 140-1; see further Andrew Hui, 'Dante's book of shadows: *ombra* in the *Divine Comedy*', *Dante Studies*, 134 (2016), 195-224. It is quite telling that, in his 1359-64 gloss on *Purgatorio* XXV, 61-108, Dante's son Pietro ends his compilation of authorities concerning the separated soul with the *Aeneid*, VI, 730ff., where Virgil describes his underworld dwellers as having originated in heaven yet being hampered by the body's evil: 'all evil and all the ills of the body still do not entirely pass from the sad soul', for 'many engrafted faults have long been mysteriously hardening within' and accordingly souls 'pay in punishment for their old offences' (trans. W. F. Jackson Knight [Harmondsworth, 1968], p. 169). Pietro Alighieri, *Comentum super poema Comedie Dantis*, ed. Chiamenti, consulted via The Dartmouth Dante Project. The Virgil passage is also cited in the first version of Pietro's commentary (1340-2), glossing *Purgatorio* XXV, 103-6. *Petri Allegherii super Dantis ipsius genitoris Comoediam commentarium*, ed. Vincenzo Nannucci (Florence, 1845), again consulted via The Dartmouth Dante Project.

Christianized them via Statius[32] but also enriched their conceptualization with ideas from the latest theological teaching. 'The Most High Poet has adapted to the needs of his own universe the data provided by the theology of his time', as Étienne Gilson says, thereby boldly providing a compelling 'explanation of those creatures of his imagination'.[33] Creatures which seem to have retained their power of associational, compositive imagination (to apply the scholastic theory), as now exercised through their assumed bodies. Just as (to push the argument further) they chose to converse through the speech-organs of those bodies as a matter of course, rather than being content – and what a high degree of contentment that would be! – with the sublime 'language' of angels. Those bodily features, that conversation, do not constitute a performance just to meet the human cognitive needs of the Dante-persona. Their significance goes far and beyond that – in affirming the truth of the Resurrection. Shadows the *ombre* may be, but they foreshadow a future time when separated souls will be reunited with their complete, fully-functioning, bodily organs.

In seeking to understand *Purgatorio* XXV, 79-108, we need not be troubled by the thought that Dante has engaged in 'theologically-facetious *legerdemain*' which cannot be justified philosophically, and

---

[32] The fact that it is Statius who mediates this Christianizing transition is surely significant. Statius's reading of the *Aeneid*, he declares at *Purgatorio* XXII, 73, made him not just a poet but a Christian; hence he benefited from an 'illumination' (line 66) that his author Virgil could not enjoy. (I am indebted to Kenneth Clarke for this thought.)

[33] Gilson, 'Dante's notion of a shade', pp. 134, 142. Cf. Marc Cogan, *The Design in the Wax: The Structure of the 'Divine Comedy' and its Meaning* (Notre Dame, IN, 1999), p. 129: 'In formulating his solution Dante relies on familiar philosophical and theological authorities, but interprets them in a unique way, consistent with the letter of what they have said but manifesting a whole new spirit than would have conventionally been discovered in these texts'. I myself would argue that Dante follows the spirit of at least some of the theological texts he was aware of, whilst moving beyond 'the letter' of what they said. Besides, given the complexities of certain 'familiar philosophical and theological authorities' on the issues in question, what their readers found therein often went far beyond the 'conventional', if by that is meant passive and perfunctory response.

therefore we must fall back, almost as a last resort, on an appeal to 'poetic license'.[34] Such binary thinking is, in my view, unhelpful in approaching a writer who was interested not only in resurrection bodies and their aerial antecedents (or prefigurations, one might say) but also in the resurrection of 'dead poetry' (cf. *Purgatorio* I.7, 'Ma qui la morta poesì resurga …'). Neither should Dantean *ombra*-production be designated 'in orthodox terms probably a heretical idea'.[35] Any poetic license exercised here has clearly identifiable, and non-heterodox, theological precedents, or at least analogues, and hence rests on a plausible ideological basis. Quite specifically and (I think) self-consciously, Dante has taken ideas relating to angelic cognition and manifestation on the one hand and to the physical expressions of emotion expected of the resurrected body on the other, and applied them to his separated souls. Those ideas have an obvious intellectual valence, and are skilfully used to help make sense of how the 'creatures' of his 'imagination' can materialise to an extent, and in a way, that enables them to express (maybe even to experience?) sensation.

Any suspicion of intellectual sleight-of-hand is further alleviated if we look beyond the relevant views of Aquinas and Bonaventure (the former in particular) and engage with the revalorisation of Augustine's views on the separated soul which is a feature of Cistercian spirituality. Of particular significance is the role afforded to the imagination, that faculty

---

[34] Here I borrow some phrasing from Gardner, 'Dante and the suffering soul', dissertation abstract.

[35] As suggested by Robert M. Durling in his note on *Purgatorio* XXV, 88; *The 'Divine Comedy' of Dante Alighieri, vol.2: Purgatorio*, ed. and tr. Robert M. Durling, with Ronald L. Martinez (Oxford, 2003), p. 434. Durling claims that the 'falling' action of the soul 'to the embarkation points sets the production of the airy body …within Dante's fiction or myth, insulating it from awkward questions'. In my view, this is an unnecessary *apologia* for what Dante has done, no insulation being necessary. The matter merits questioning and answering in well-established theological terms, there being nothing inherently 'awkward' about it. Durling proceeds to acknowledge that the idea is 'so central to his poetics and his view of the relation of soul and body, and is given such prominence here, that it demands to be taken seriously'. Indeed. And this involves taking it 'seriously' in theological terms.

which Augustine saw as being hyper-active in the sensorium characteristic of dreams and out-of-body experiences, and which, being independent of material bodies, will survive death. Bernard McGinn has emphasized that Isaac of Stella was particularly 'interested in the role of imagination, particularly in the crucial role that it plays on the border line between the material and the spiritual levels of reality'.[36] Isaac, and the *De spiritu et anima* author, envisaged this power as a crucial part of what remains in the soul when it is severed from the body. The latter text describes a process whereby imaginative activity is 'purified and made keen to such an extent that it is joined to the spirit with no other substance intervening, while all along it truly retains the nature and properties of a body. ... Seen thus, the imagination is a likeness of the body'.[37] *Est itaque imaginatio similitudo corporis.* Here the imagination is elevated in language reminiscent of the discourse Augustine had used to describe the entire likeness (including but certainly not identifiable with the imagination) of the body which the soul bears with it into the next world and which is necessary for its feelings of pleasure or pain there. The anonymous author proceeds to qualify and contextualize its position by describing it as 'so lofty (*sublime*) a thing ... that the next above it is reason itself'.[38] Sublime indeed, though (of course) subordinate to a superior noetic faculty.

The controversial nature of such views in late-medieval thought should be appreciated. Albert the Great writes contemptuously of those who wish to introduce a 'new philosophy' which holds that the separated soul 'sees and hears and imagines, and bears with it the corporeal imaginations which it received whilst in the body'; he can't be bothered to talk about how they prove this, for it is a derisory proposition rather than a true judgment.[39] In similar vein, Aquinas denigrates *De spiritu et*

---

[36] *Three Treatises on Man*, trans. McGinn, p. 56.
[37] *De spiritu et anima*, cap. 33, in *PL*, XL, col. 802; trans. McGinn, *Three Treatises on Man*, p. 231.
[38] *PL*, XL, col. 802; trans. McGinn, *Three Treatises on Man*, p. 232.
[39] Nota tamen, quod quidam volunt novam philosophiam inducere, quod anima exuta videt et audit et imaginatur, et secum defert imaginationes corporis quas recipit in corpore: quod qualiter probant, non oportet dicere,

anima by name, saying 'what is written in it can be disregarded as lightly as it was expressed to begin with'.[40] These reactions are anything but 'light' — and hardly surprising, given that the writings in question resolutely stood in direct opposition to the Aristotelian noetics of which Albert and Aquinas were stout defenders.[41] The virulence of their remarks in fact testifies to the continuing strength of a spiritual tradition which was, at least in some ways, contrary to theirs, a neo-Augustinianism possessed of a resilient Neoplatonism and newly vitalized in many strands of Arabic philosophy.[42] Besides, Dante was not one to shirk controversy, intellectual or otherwise, being a man who (in the exquisite formulation of his biographer Giovanni Boccaccio) 'did not think himself to be worth less than he actually was'.[43] His choice of St Bernard as possessing the

quia potius derisio est, quam sententia veritatis. *In IV Sent.*, dist. 44, G, art. 43, nota (*Alberti opera*, XXX, 601).

[40] *Summa theologiae*, 1a, qu. 77, art. 8, ad 1 (XI, 116-17).

[41] Hence we must disagree with A. V. C. Schmidt's statement that *De spiritu et anima*, along with other 'pre-scholastic' treatises on the soul which have 'a strong Augustinian bias', were popular and influential because their doctrine tended to be 'synthetic and non-controversial'. 'Langland and scholastic philosophy', p. 144. On the contrary, they were at the very centre of controversy concerning the nature of the soul, presenting a challenge (and occasional irritant) to Aristotelian theorizing.

[42] Thus Constant Mews has judiciously characterized *De spiritu et anima* as 'offering a vision of the human person influenced by Platonist tradition, before the writings of Aristotle on the soul and its powers had become widely known'. Even after Aristotle's writings had become widely known, it held its ground. Noting its popularity among Franciscans, Mews sees the treatise as having 'formulated' an attractive vision of 'the divine as present in all creation'. 'Debating the authority', p. 343.

[43] *Trattatello in laude di Dante*, 165, trans. David Wallace in Minnis and Scott, *Medieval Literary Theory and Criticism*, p. 501. The issue of how Dante, as a layman, might have gained his knowledge of abstruse philosophical and theological matters is a fascinating one. Particularly important discussions have been offered by Ruedi Imbach, *Dante, la filosofie et les laïcs* (Fribourg and Paris, 1996); Zygmunt G. Barański, 'On Dante's trail', *Italian Studies*, 72/1 (2017), 1-15; and Lorenzo Dell'Oso, 'Per la formazione intellettuale di Dante: i cataloghi librari, le tracce testuali, *il Trattatello* di Boccaccio', *Le Tre Corone: Rivista internazionale di studi su Dante, Petrarca, Boccaccio*, 4 (2017), 129-61. In his *Convivio* (ii, 13) Dante tantalizingly alludes to how, following

soul who gets closest to God (elevated above Albert, Bonaventure and Aquinas) may be read as indicative of certain overriding spiritual preferences. At the very least, the Cistercian espousal of the lofty imagination is reminiscent of Dante's valorisation of *alta fantasia*, high imagination,[44] which in the *Paradiso* occupies a liminal position in noetic terms comparable to that occupied by St Bernard in narrative terms.

Viewed thus, the gap between poetry and philosophy in *Purgatorio* XXV seems to narrow. It is true that, especially in respect of his presentation of aerial bodies with 'the organs of every sense' (line 103), Dante is going beyond some of the specific propositions of theological thought considered in this essay. Yet he seems inspired by them, composing in a way which is true to their spirit if not always to their letter. And the way in which he bestows an appearance of consistency on the rival authorities is impressive; his Statius does not miss a beat. In the final analysis, neither disjunction nor distance but rather continuity and enhancement is envisioned between this life and the next, of a kind vividly and appealingly anticipatory of the startling improvements to the re-ensouled body in particular, and to the body-soul relationship in general, which shall occur at the General Resurrection.[45] Here we approach a general truth concerning Dante's somatomorphism,[46] the sophisticated way in which he manifests the spiritual through the physical. Something of the power, the awe, of that moment when 'our

> Beatrice's death in 1290, he sought out where philosophy was revealed by attending the 'schools of the religious orders' and 'the disputations of the philosophers'. This may include reference to the quodlibetal disputations held at that time in the Florentine Mendicant convents, which were open to the public. The quodlibetal questions of Peter of Trabibus, who was lector in Santa Croce in Florence between 1295 and 1297, are enjoying attention currently; see especially Sylvain Piron, '*Ut philosophia poesis*', in *Questions philosophiques dans l'oeuvre de Dante, Pétrarque et Boccacce*, ed. Joël Biard and Fosca Mariani Zini (Paris, 2008), pp. 73–112. A recent conference at the University of Notre Dame (April 26-27, 2019) was devoted to 'Quodlibetal Culture in Dante's Time'; see https://italianstudies.nd.edu/research/devers-program/quodlibetal-culture-in-dantes-time/.

[44] At *Paradiso* XXXIII, 142.
[45] Cf. Minnis, *From Eden to Eternity*, p. 166.
[46] Cf. my discussion of this concept on pp. 102-3 above.

flesh, sanctified and glorious, shall clothe our souls once more',[47] a moment presaged by the souls' irresistible urge to clothe themselves with aerial bodies, impels the poetics of the *Comedy*. Dante has had many epithets bestowed upon him. To the long list may be added: the poet of material perfection.

I myself cannot find any 'philosophical deficiency' in *Purgatorio* XXV,[48] though Dante is certainly not being circumscribed by the then-prevailing philosophies. But might it be said that here was a *determinatio* waiting to happen? There is some traction in that proposition. In the first instance, it was commonly believed that souls of the dead could manifest themselves to the living, leaving their current locations to do so. At least *some* souls. Bonaventure notes that the lives of the saints provide many instances of the true apparition (*vera apparatio*).[49] As far as demons are concerned, they go forth among us and harass us, despite the fact that they deserve more punishment than damned souls and therefore should more appropriately be confined to their places of punishment – so, why cannot damned souls appear to us? Bonaventure rejects that comparison between demons and the damned, because the former have the job of harassing us while the latter do not. Punishment is dependent on place, but glory is not. Whereas the damned are confined to their places of punishment, totally restricted in their operations, the souls of the blessed come and go as they please, recalling, teaching, strengthening and liberating us. Aquinas totally agrees with Bonaventure's point about the souls of the saints; by virtue of their glory, they can appear whenever they wish to the living.[50] But he differs in respect of the separated souls of the damned. They can indeed manifest themselves – though not as they please, but only through special divine permission. Perhaps they have little desire to appear to others because they are so oppressed by their

---

[47] Cf. p. 144 above, the reference being to *Paradiso* XIV, 43-4.
[48] To use one of Gardner's terms; 'Dante and the Suffering Soul', dissertation abstract.
[49] *In IV Sent.*, dist. 50, pars 1, art. 2, qu. 2 (*Bonaventurae opera*, IV, 1041).
[50] *In IV Sent.*, dist. 45, qu. 1, art. 1, qc. 3 co. Aquinas describes this as a further expression of the gifts of healing and effecting wondrous works which the saints exercised while living in the flesh.

punishments: but appear they can, and they do. 'For man's instruction and intimidation they [may] be permitted to appear to the living; or again in order to seek our suffrages, as to those who are detained in purgatory, as evidenced by many instances related in the fourth book of the *Dialogues*'. The greater prominence, in the later Middle Ages, of the idea of purgatory, made it much easier to account for visits to the living paid by the dead; leaving purgatory was a lot easier than leaving hell. And here Aquinas specifically identifies the relevant escapades in Gregory's *Dialogues* as involving apparitions of souls who are suffering in purgatory – which Gregory himself had not (unsurprisingly, given that in the seventh century the full paraphernalia of purgatory had not yet developed).[51]

---

[51] In his *conclusio* Aquinas quotes from Augustine's *De cura pro mortuis* the story of how the martyr Felix appeared visibly to the people of Nola when they were besieged by the barbarians. *In IV Sent.*, dist. 45, qu. 1, art. 1, qc. 3, co.; cf. *De cura pro mortuis*, cap. 16 (19), *PL*, XL, col. 606. For Aquinas this is yet another example of a soul leaving its place of abode to visit the living. However, while admitting the possibility that certain imaginary visions may be the result of angelic operations through the dispensation of divine providence, Augustine was highly sceptical concerning the possibility of genuine visitations by the dead in dreams. If this could happen, then his loving mother (Monica), who in life had followed him by land and sea in order to live with him, would not for a single night fail to appear. Aquinas quotes this as a contrary opinion; *In IV Sent.*, dist. 45, qu. 1, art. 1, qc. 3, arg. 1; cf. *De cura pro mortuis*, cap. 13 (16); col. 604. In fact, this treatise is a balanced, and quite cautious, exploration of the problem, which (*inter alia*) offers the argument that separated souls are not interested in the affairs of the living 'by their proper nature', of their own volition, but only as and when God wills that they should take an interest (cap. 16 [19]; cols 606-7). Elsewhere, in Letter 159 to Evodius (*PL*, XXXIII, cols 698-701) Augustine reports how Gennadius, a reputable physician who had doubts as to whether there was any life after death, experienced a vision in which a young man appeared to him, and said, 'as while you are asleep and lying on your bed these eyes of your body are now unemployed and doing nothing, and yet you have eyes with which you behold me, and enjoy this vision, so, after your death, while your bodily eyes shall be wholly inactive, there shall be in you a life by which you shall still live, and a faculty of perception by which you shall still perceive' (cap. 4). Augustine refuses to make a definite pronouncement on this matter, but invites any man to think of his own

Relating all this to the *Comedy*, one might imagine a schoolman pursuing the matter thus. If separated souls can manifest themselves to the living, in order to instruct us, strengthen our faith, intimidate us, etc., there seems no reason to doubt that they can manifest themselves to the Dante-persona, as a living being (though he is visiting them rather than them visiting him). On the same argument, separated souls can manifest themselves to each other. Here an excursus would be necessary on *why* they would wish to do this, given that aerial bodies are not necessary for the interaction and communication in which souls engage with each other. Our hypothetical schoolman could easily invoke the overwhelming desire of the separated soul to be embodied. This argument works well, whether it is said that sensory faculties exist in the separated soul only *in principio vel radice* or whether 'sense knowledge, imagination, reason, understanding and intelligence', together with 'the concupiscible and irascible powers', are supposed to remain and function in the soul following the body's death, as *De spiritu et anima* would have it. I would have him argue that the latter, more flamboyant (and Aristotelian-baiting), position accords better with Dante's *ombre*.

So far, so good. But there is yet another problem, insofar as Bonaventure and Aquinas – somewhat surprisingly, and rather annoyingly – do not investigate the matter of *how* separated souls manifest themselves to the living (apart from their appearances in dreams, of course, which can be attributed, with relative ease, to spiritual influence on the imagination). And how, then, do they manifest themselves to the Dante-persona and to each other; what type of materialisation is involved? One and the same answer solves both versions of the problem: they shape aerial bodies. At this point our schoolman

> dreaming experience of 'things which, while not material bodies, do nevertheless resemble the forms, properties, and motions of material bodies' – and come up with an answer if he can. He himself is confident that such semblances of material bodies are not produced by the body, though they are perceived as if they were seen by the bodily senses. His addressee, Evodius, is referred to Book XII of *De Genesi ad litteram* for an extensive discussion. No doubt Augustine had particularly in mind the account there provided of the *similitudo corporis*.

would cite the precedents of angelic manifestation (if angels can use air, why cannot separated souls?) and the material expressions of internal agitations envisaged for the resurrected bodies of the damned.

This hypothetical *quaestio* has, I believe, much to commend it. But some may feel that in *Purgatorio* XXV we are dealing not with a viable contribution to scholastic debate (or at least, something which the professional debaters would have found intellectually provocative and/or entertaining) but rather with an enterprise akin to science fiction of a kind which goes some distance beyond the current boundaries of belief and possibility. To which the rejoinder would be: if that is the case, the extent to which this canto is informed by what was then recognized as legitimate scholastic analysis is impressive, the aura of authenticity compelling. *Quot homines tot sententiæ*: but whatever position one takes, it is evident that Dante has raised somatomorphism to a fine art.[52]

---

[52] On the 'somatomorphic' soul in the *Comedy* see Bynum, *Resurrection*, pp. 299-302, and Gragnolati, *Experiencing the Afterlife*, pp. 53-87 (esp. pp. 74-77).

CHAPTER 14

Metaphor and the limits of language

Dante's standing as the poet of material perfection becomes even clearer when his constructions are compared with the apotheosis of metaphor in the Pseudo-Dionysian tradition – a tradition from which he crucially diverges. The modus operandi in his greatest literary achievement is marked by a strong impulse towards materialisation, a drive which is at once inescapable, exciting, and consuming.[1] And which, by its very nature, involves a resistance towards singularly metaphorical solutions (which is not to be confused with a resistance towards metaphor itself).

Aristotle held that a good metaphor involves an acute perception 'of the similarity in dissimilars', as already noted.[2] But, paradoxically enough, according to Pseudo-Dionysian theology the best similes are the ones that highlight the greatest dissimilarity, because if heavenly things are imaged by lowly figures it is much harder to fall into the trap of supposing that they are really like that. As Robert Grosseteste (Bishop of Lincoln, 1235-53) puts it in his commentary on *The Celestial Hierarchy*, even those who can easily believe that 'the heavenly beings have the glitter of gold, or shine with the splendour of the fire and sun', will baulk at the notion that 'other celestial beings are like horses or cattle or lions or some

---

[1] Nancy Lindhelm has expressed the thought that 'the primary significance of Statius' speech' in *Purgatorio* XXV 'lies in its justifying' a kind of poetry that 'does not have to apologize for or repent its connections with the body', while Caroline Walker Bynum goes even further, in saying that Dante's reader comes to see that 'poetry making itself is a process of giving body'. Lindheim, 'Body, Soul, and Immortality: Some Readings in Dante's *Commedia*', *Modern Language Notes*, 10/1, Italian Issue (1990), 1-32 (p. 15); Bynum, *Resurrection*, p. 306. I myself believe that, more than any other medieval poet, Dante substantiates Howard Nemerov's claim that 'poetry exists by a continuing revelation in a world always incarnate of word and flesh indissolubly, a world simultaneously solid and transpicuous'. *A Howard Nemerov Reader* (Columbia, MI 1991), p. 171.

[2] *Poetics*, 22 (1459a), trans. Bywater in *The Complete Works of Aristotle*, ed. Barnes, II, 2334-5. Cf. p. 7 above.

other such creatures'. 'By the evidence of their materiality and corruptibility [they] manifestly cry out that they are not the divine beings, but very far removed from them and very unlike them'.[3] It has well been said that 'Metaphors stretch language beyond its elastic limit';[4] that process reaches its extreme limit in the apophaticism here in play.

Seeing how Pseudo-Dionysius treats imagery close to Dante's is intriguing.[5] In chapter 25 of his *Celestial Hierarchy* he goes to great lengths to rationalize the many ways in which holy Scripture assigns human forms, emotions and senses to angels, why they are sometimes described as being unshod or clothed, and why they are described in terms of fire, winds, and clouds, etc.[6] Take clouds, for example, that natural phenomenon of such importance in Dante's attempt to explain the *ombre*. Cloud is 'the mother of rain', explains Grosseteste, 'and, by sending showers to the bosom of the earth makes the earth conceive, bring forth, bud, and give life, growth, and maturity to its products…'.

[3] J. S. McQuade, 'Robert Grosseteste's Commentary on the "Celestial Hierarchy" of Pseudo-Dionysius the Areopagite: an edition, translation, and introduction to his text and commentary' (unpub. Ph.D. diss., The Queen's University of Belfast, 1961), pp. 65, 70-1. Cf. *Medieval Literary Theory and Criticism*, ed. Minnis and Scott, p. 171, and see further, *Angelic Spirituality*, trans. Chase, pp. 44-6, 222-3.

[4] Ortony, 'Role of Similarity', p. 200.

[5] Dante's angelology, with reference to the Pseudo-Dionysian tradition, is discussed extensively by Susanna Barsella, *In the Light of the Angels: Angelology and Cosmology in Dante's 'Divina commedia'* (Florence, 2010). However, her stated parameters do not include the issues which are the focus of the present essay.

[6] For the version of this disquisition in the *Extractio* or summary of *The Celestial Hierarchy* by Thomas Gallus, see Minnis and Scott, *Medieval Literary Theory and Criticism*, pp. 169, 182-92. The last in the line of great Victorine scholars, and heavily influenced by Hugh of St Victor's Pseudo-Dionysian scholarship, Gallus sought to provide a clarifying summary of this sublimely obscure work, working from the Latin translations from the Greek by John Scotus Eriugena (*c.* 810 - *c.* 877) and John the Saracen (*fl.* 1167). His more extensive treatment of *The Celestial Hierarchy*, the *Explanatio* or commentary thereon, has been edited by Declan Lawell as one of the texts in Thomas Gallus, *Explanatio in libros Dionysii*, CCCM 223 (Turnhout, 2011).

Having been 'immaterially filled to overflowing' with the divine light, the angels, as superior beings, 'bring it down plentifully to those below, giving them the maximum amount they can take'. That is to say, the downward dissemination by angels of divine truth and wisdom may, 'physically understood', be likened to the way in which clouds 'conceive the rain physically and send the derivative showers' down to the earth.[7] Further, 'It is possible to create images appropriate to designate the heavenly powers seen in terms of the individual parts of the body', affirms Thomas Gallus (Abbot of St Andrews, Vercelli, 1219-46)[8] in his *Extractio* on the same chapter of *The Celestial Hierarchy*.[9] Human eyes designate the 'very clear gaze' of 'celestial minds ... upon the divine light'. Likewise, their receptivity to all they see signifies 'the pure and open acceptance of illuminations sent by God, without any rejection'. The dividing and separating power of human teeth (as when food is masticated) signifies 'the divisible power of perfect light, which is thrown upon each superior mind and nourishes it, to be passed down to a lower intelligence'. In other words, celestial intellects receive 'the light of the intellect which has been poured down upon it from above, just like a piece of dough', and

---

[7] Trans. Minnis and Scott, *Medieval Literary Theory and Criticism*, pp. 193-4.

[8] Gallus has been credited with promoting an 'affective' interpretation of Pseudo-Dionysius's work, which exercised a profound influence on later mystical writings in both Latin (e.g. by Bonaventure and Hugh of Balma) and several vernaculars (e. g. the Middle English *Cloud of Unknowing*). See Alastair Minnis, 'Affection and imagination in *The Cloud of Unknowing* and Walter Hilton's *Scale of Perfection*', *Traditio*, 39 (1983), 323-66; Bernard McGinn, 'Thomas Gallus and Dionysian Mysticism', *Studies in Spirituality*, 8, (1998), 81-96; Boyd Taylor Coolman, 'The medieval affective Dionysian tradition', in *Modern Theology*, 24/4 (2008), 615-32; and Declan Lawell, 'Affective excess: ontology and knowledge in the thought of Thomas Gallus', *Dionysius*, 26 (2008), 139-73.

[9] *Extractio*, 25, trans. Minnis and Scott, *Medieval Literary Theory and Criticism*, pp. 182-92. For the Latin text see *Dionysiaca: recueil donnant l'ensemble des traductions latines des ouvrages attribués au Denys de l'aréopage*, ed. P. Chavellier, 2 vols (Paris, 1937), II, 1062-6.

divvy it up 'for the elevation of the lower intelligences proportionally according to the power of each'.[10]

Similar treatment was afforded to the human intellect, the internal mental processes through which the body acts in conjunction with the soul, and the emotions and cognitions thereby generated, all of which are central to Dante's discourse in *Purgatorio* XXV. In *De divinis nominibus* Pseudo-Dionysius states that the evil in demons is 'an irrational rage, a demented desire, and a shameless imagination (*fantasia*)'.[11] But these belong to the sensory part of the soul, 'which possesses the power of imagination and the irascible and concipiscible powers'. Aquinas, whose quotation of Pseudo-Dionysius I am quoting here, goes on to ask, 'since the sensory part of the soul does not exist apart from a body', does it not follow that 'demons have bodies joined to them by nature (*naturaliter*)'?[12] This conclusion seems to be supported by Augustine's statement that 'through their knowledge of future events' they pre-form 'in their own spirit' the 'likenesses of bodily things',[13] an indication that demons and angels possess the *virtus imaginativa*. Aquinas uses Pseudo-Dionysian deconstructive technique to make short work of those hypotheses. The author was speaking metaphorically (*metaphorice*), he declares; 'we ascribe anger and desire to the holy angels in a metaphorical sense'. Likewise (here turning to Augustine's remark), we metaphorically 'ascribe to devils the power of imagination, which gets its name from vision, as the *De anima* says, just as we ascribe vision to the intellect'.[14] Angels and demons, then, have (properly speaking) no imagination (cf. p. 115 above).

---

[10] Trans. Minnis and Scott, *Medieval Literary Theory and Criticism*, p. 185. A hierarchy relating to the dissemination of divine truth is being described here, with the higher angels implanting wisdom in the intellects of lower angels and in human minds.
[11] *De divinis nominibus*, iv, 22 (*PG*, III, col. 725B-C). Cf. *Pseudo-Dionysius: The Complete Works*, trans. Luibheid, p. 91.
[12] *De malo*, qu. xvi, art. 1, 3 and ad 3 (ed. Regan and Davies, pp. 802-3, 814-17).
[13] *De Genesi ad litteram*, xii, 22,48 (ed. Zycha, p. 414; trans. Hill, p. 490).
[14] *De anima*, iii.3 (429a3-4).

At this point, one may note, we have moved into the sphere of 'similar similes', and (as the Pseudo-Dionysian narrative has it) run the risk of confusing metaphorical vehicle with tenor, falsely supposing that the images in question accurately signify heavenly realities; speaking of 'vision' is potentially very confusing, since it may blur the distinction between the corporeal and the spiritual. According to Pseudo-Dionysian hermeneutics, it's better, safer, to work with images 'like horses or cattle or lions or some other such creatures'. This imagery may surprise by its ugliness but it will not deceive.[15] Here, one might say, is the apotheosis of metaphor, and a quite paradoxical one at that – metaphor is valued most highly when its failure to connect the visible with the invisible is most marked. Indeed, that failure is the very basis of its value, since it calls attention to, and affirms, the unbridgeable distance between those two realms of being.[16]

Pseudo-Dionysian 'anagogical' or 'mystical interpretations of sensible forms'[17] systematically read material entities as metaphors for immaterial things, with the far-fetched nature of the comparisons being intimated – though, admittedly, in the event some dissimilarities cry out more loudly than others that we are not dealing with divine beings. What is fundamentally at issue here, in these intense stretchings of language, is the question of *why* (in anagogic terms) angels manifest themselves in these forms rather than in *how* they do so, what kind of material they appropriate in order to make themselves seen. Discussion of that issue took place elsewhere, in *quaestiones* like those of Bonaventure and Aquinas (as quoted above), excursūs of a kind which (in my view) influenced Dante in composing *Purgatorio* XXV. In such analyses the processes of logical deduction are undergone rigorously, and the best science then available is deployed. The emphasis is on literalism, which often involves a strong interest in materiality. A common scholastic dictum is that a formal argument can be drawn only from the literal sense, and not from the other senses of Scripture – certainly not from the

---

[15] Cf. Minnis and Scott, *Medieval Literary Theory and Criticism*, p. 171.
[16] Or, as secular linguistic theory relating to 'conceptual metaphor' would have it, 'between these two conceptual domains'. Cf. p. 217 below.
[17] Cf. Minnis and Scott, *Medieval Literary Theory and Criticism*, p. 183.

anagogic sense, given its deconstruction of apparent description of material things as metaphoric discourse. 'Truths which are taught under the guise of metaphor in one part of Scripture are explained more explicitly in other parts', declares Aquinas.[18] And those 'other parts' are to be sought out by the dialectician – an undertaking which, in large measure, is a quest for, a prioritization of, the material. Does not Saint Dionysius say at one point that 'the devil's evil consists of irrational rage'?[19] Aquinas briskly brushes that affront to rationality aside. Here Dionysius is speaking metaphorically (*metaphorice*) about the devil's rage – 'and we do not ascribe sound arguments to such figures of speech.' *Ex talibus locutionibus non trahitur conueniens argumentatio.*[20]

Those words would seem to identify Aquinas as an exponent of what Mark Johnson has identified as the 'comparison theory' of metaphor, which holds that 'the similarities revealed through the metaphorical transfer exist objectively in the world and are expressible in literal propositions'. On this view, there is 'no such thing as an irreducible metaphorical concept or proposition. There are only metaphorical utterances and thought processes whose meaning reduces to sets of *literal* propositions'.[21] At this point it must be conceded that Aquinas was relatively uninterested in matters symbolic and poetic, as one of the most perceptive of his recent interpreters, Marie-Dominique Chenu, frankly

---

[18] *Summa theologiae*, 1a, qu. 1, art. 9, resp., 2; trans. in Minnis and Scott, p. 240.
[19] *De malo*, qu. xvi, art. 6, 15 (ed. Regan and Davies, pp. 884-5).
[20] *De malo*, qu. xvi, art. 6, ad 15 (ed. Regan and Davies, pp. 894-5).
[21] *The Body in the Mind: The Bodily Basis of Meaning, Imagination, and Reason* (Chicago, 1987), pp. 66, 68. St Thomas's apparent approval of a reductive literalism (which, it should be emphasized, is here the abstract definition of a principle rather than an attempt to set limits on exegetical practice) was developed further by the fearsome Girolamo Savonarola (d. 1498); see Alastair Minnis, 'Fifteenth Century versions of literalism: Girolamo Savonarola and Alfonso de Madrigal', in *Neue Richtungen in der hoch- und spätmittelalterlichen Bibelexegese*, Schriften des Historischen Kollegs Kolloquien 32, ed. Robert Lerner (Munich, 1996), pp. 163-80. But, generally speaking, medieval attitudes to the matter were more complicated than Johnson would allow, a point I shall go on to make.

admits.[22] In this he differed from the likes of Bonaventure, Henry of Ghent, Thomas Gallus and Robert Grosseteste, though he did manage a (somewhat perfunctory) commentary on Pseudo-Dionysius's *De divinis nominibus*, and (as we have seen) drew on Dionysian theology when it suited him. Indeed, here he also differed from his master and mentor, Albert the Great. Take Albert's discussion of which images are most memorable, if what is 'proper', literal, affects a person more easily than what is non-literal.[23] His answer is that 'although literal words' (*propria*) make for more accuracy in respect of some particular thing or other, nevertheless 'metaphors (*metaphorica*) move the soul more and thus convey more to the memory'. 'What is marvellous (*mirabile*) is more moving than what is ordinary', Albert continues, 'and so when images of this metaphorical sort are made up out of marvels (*ex miris*) they affect memory more than commonplace literal matters'. Which is why the 'early philosophers translated their ideas in poetry', as 'the Philosopher' says.[24] The reference is to Aristotle's statement that knowledge began with wonder, the 'lover of myth' or fable (*philomites*) being 'a lover of wisdom'. What is wonderful 'causes questioning, and thence gives rise to investigation and recollection'. This seems to be quite at variance with Aquinas's somewhat dour claim that images of things which have no basis in reality, and which therefore can be dismissed as fictions, are less affecting than those which have direct referents in the present world (cf. p. 68 and note 20 above).

In line with this capacious concept of wisdom, and in enthusiastic pursuit of it, a major trend in thirteenth-century biblical exegesis affirmed that, in contrast with the methodologies of merely human means of seeking knowledge, 'the way in which theology proceeds is poetic or historical or parabolical' and that, ultimately, 'wisdom resides

---

[22] Chenu, *Toward Understanding Saint Thomas*, trans. A. M. Landry and D. Hughes (Chicago, 1964), pp. 169-70, 228.

[23] Albert, *Summa de bono*, tract. IV, qu. 2, art. 2, 16 & 17 and ad 16 & 17. Trans. by Carruthers, *Art of Memory*, pp. 272-3, 279-80; cf. Frances A. Yates, *The Art of Memory* (1966, rpt. Harmondsworth, 1969), pp. 76-8. Albert wrote this *Summa* in Paris *c.* 1243.

[24] *Metaphysics*, i.2 (982b15-20).

in the mysterious', far beyond any earthly referent and not simply reductive to the material.²⁵ The gnawing actions of worms and other venomous creatures as a form of postmortem punishment, the pain inflicted by fire on a separated soul, Dives's plea for a drop of cooling water ... Those, and many other, interpretive cruxes in biblical exegesis posed a question both tenacious and compelling: is that a metaphor or not, and, if so, what is its profound significance?

Besides, Aquinas has his moments. In a movingly eloquent one, he describes the human soul as being 'situated on the boundary line between corporeal and incorporeal substances, as though it existed on the horizon of eternity and time'.²⁶ Thanks to metaphor's ability to cross boundary lines by positing unexpected and arresting similarities, not revealing 'a sameness that was there all along so much as [creating] the sameness in our imaginations',²⁷ investigation of the relationship between corporeal and incorporeal substances was greatly facilitated and the nature of the human soul itself rendered more comprehensible (on some level or other) and/or more fit for devotional purpose. In the ascent towards God the power of even the highest form of imagination will ultimately fail, as Dante breathtakingly reveals at the very end of his *Comedy*.²⁸ But in the meantime, while we remain in the body, metaphor maintains its power to connect vehicle and tenor.

That power can make philosophy deeply suspicious, and feel under attack. Hence Paul de Man, who argued that all language contains the

---

²⁵ *Summa Halensis*, tract. introd., qu. 1, ch. 4, art. 1; trans. Minnis and Scott, *Medieval Literary Theory and Criticism*, pp. 213-14. On these large issues, particularly the valorisation of poetic, figurative and metaphorical speech in biblical exegesis, see Alastair Minnis, 'The trouble with theology: ethical poetics and the ends of Scripture', in *Author, Reader, Book: Medieval Authorship in Theory and Practice*, ed. Stephen Partridge and Erik Kwakkel (Toronto, 2011), pp. 21-37.
²⁶ ... in confinio corporum et incorporearum substantiarum, quasi in horizonte existens aeternitatis et temporis, recedens ab infimo, appropinquat ad summum. *Summa contra gentiles*, II, 80, n.13; tr. Anderson.
²⁷ Adam B. Seligman and Robert P. Weller, *How Things Count as the Same: Memory, Mimesis, and Metaphor* (New York and Oxford, 2019), p. 80.
²⁸ *Paradiso* XXXIII, 142.

instability of metaphor, declared that 'philosophy either has to give up its own constitutive claim to rigor in order to come to terms with the figurality of its language or ... it has to free itself from figuration altogether'.[29] Wittgenstein, like John Locke before him, longed for such freedom, searching for 'a logically rigorous and coherent language that could avoid the ambiguities and logical jumps that are inherent in a process like metaphor'.[30] But theology has as its primary task the interpretation of scriptural discourse, which includes a rich abundance of figurative language that includes many ambiguities and logical jumps, and so cannot be confined by the objectives and purposes of philosophy, which (as the schoolmen often stated) needs literal expression, whatever is 'properly' spoken (*proprie dicta*), to work with.[31] Scholastic exegesis does not narrowly exemplify what Mark Johnson defines as the 'literal-truth paradigm', which holds that 'metaphor is a deviant form of words in other than their proper senses, which accounts for its tendency to confuse and to deceive'.[32] While aware of ancient and medieval defences

[29] Paul de Man, 'The epistemology of metaphor', in *On Metaphor*, ed. Sacks, pp. 11-28 (p. 11).
[30] Seligman and Weller, *How Things Count as the Same*, p. 78.
[31] Cf. *Medieval Literary Theory and Criticism*, ed. Minnis and Scott, pp. 204, 242.
[32] 'Introduction' to *Philosophical Perspectives on Metaphor*, ed. Mark Johnson (Minneapolis, MN, 1981), pp. 3-47 (pp. 11-12). It may be noted that even the astute Johnson shares the tendency of many cognitive linguists to simplify centuries of debate on metaphor theory in their zeal to affirm the importance of their own research, as when he remarks that the 'literal-truth paradigm' has 'been challenged only in the last few years, and only in certain philosophical movements' ('Introduction', p. 11). At least partial challenges may be found in the medieval treatments of biblical figurative language explored by M.-D. Chenu, *La Théologie comme science au XIIIe siècle*, 3rd edn, Bibliothèque Thomiste 33 (Paris, 1969), and Ulrich Köpf, *Die Anfänge der theologischen Wissenschaftstheorie im 13. Jahrhundert*, Beiträge zur historischen Theologie 49 (Tubingen, 1974). The debates on the hierarchy of knowledge discussed in these books reveal an acute interest in the differences between biblical discourse (with its many 'literary' modes of procedure) and the language which is characteristic of sciences which, lacking revelation, involve 'definition, division and collection' (i.e. identifying a subject, dividing it up for analysis, and gathering together propositions,

of metaphors in Scripture, Johnson unfortunately believes that, even here, the prevailing view is that 'metaphor is a *deviant* use of a *word* to point up similarities'. This he elides with Thomas Hobbes' disputacious view that 'we deceive others' when 'we use words metaphorically, that is, in other sense than that they are ordained for': reasoning based on 'metaphors, and senseless and ambiguous words' is 'wandering amongst innumerable absurdities; and their end, contention and sedition, or contempt'.[33] Nothing could be farther from the capacious interpretive principles followed by late-medieval exegetes, who, in their discussions of the hierarchy of the sciences (here understood as bodies of reliable knowledge), placed theology above all thought based on philosophical reasoning and (profoundly influenced by the Pseudo-Dionysian tradition) affirmed the value of metaphors whilst entering the caveat that ultimately they had to be transcended.

'Without metaphors it is impossible to express a single thought. All effort to rise above images is doomed to fail. To speak of our most ardent aspirations only in negative terms does not satisfy the cravings of the human heart, and where philosophy no longer finds expression, poetry comes in again'.[34] Thus Johan Huizinga, who is (probably by chance) echoing the Aristotelian/Thomistic pronouncement that the soul never thinks without an image. That certainly is true of the embodied soul, and who can tell what goes on in the separated soul, during its time of

engaging in ratiocination)'. For discussion see Alastair Minnis, *Medieval Theory of Authorship: Scholastic Literary Attitudes in the Later Middle* Ages, reissued second edn with a new preface (Philadelphia, 2009), pp. 122-3, 144-7.

[33] *Leviathan* (1651), Part 1: Of Man, chs 4 and 5; ed. Mark C. Rooks (Charlottesville, 2000), pp. 20, 38. Here Hobbes is insisting that, in demonstration, words must be purged of ambiguity. Cf. Ch. 8: '[As] for metaphors, they are in this case [in demonstration] utterly excluded. For seeing they openly profess deceit; to admit them into counsel, or reasoning, were manifest folly' (p. 58).

[34] *The Waning of the Middle Ages*, trans. F. Hopman (Harmondsworth, rpt. 1965), p. 214. Here Huizinga is addressing what he regards as the limitations of apophatic theology. 'Mysticism has always rediscovered the road from the giddy heights of sublime contemplation to the flowery meadows of symbolism'.

disconnection from the body? Perhaps, as joined to an aerial body, it can speak, laugh, cry and sigh – if we are to accept Dante's daring hypothesis. But that is to engage in imagination, of an (authentically medieval) associational and compositive kind. 'Abstractions are too thin and bloodless to breathe in the lush atmosphere of the imagination'.[35] They must be joined to some iteration of the material. As Aquinas once remarked, 'nothing is imaginable except bodies' (cf. p. 96 above). To be more precise, nothing is imaginable, and therefore thinkable (in this life at least), without the aid of the corporeal – a line of inquiry which has fascinatingly been pursued in recent 'second generation cognitive science' studies, as when George Lakoff and Mark Johnson argue that the very structure of our thinking comes from the nature of the body.[36]

[35] Zaleski, *Otherworld Journeys*, p. 52.
[36] George Lakoff and Mark Johnson, *Philosophy in the Flesh: The Embodied Mind and its Challenge to Western Thought* (New York, 1999). They argue that, given the embodiment of mind, nearly all of the unconscious metaphors we use on a daily basis are based on common bodily experiences, and even abstract concepts are mostly metaphorical. See further Johnson, *The Body in the Mind*, where the lack of interest demonstrated by dominant theories of meaning and rationality in the imagination – 'without which nothing in the world could be meaningful' – is decried (pp. ix-x), and metaphor is identified as 'a pervasive principle of human understanding that underlies our vast network of interrelated literal meanings' (p. 65). A book co-authored by Lakoff and Johnson, *Metaphors we live by* (Chicago, 1980), did much to establish the study of conceptual metaphor (or cognitive metaphor) as a major research area within cognitive linguistics, the primary focus being on how one conceptual domain is used to describe another. For example, certain sporting events frequently are described with metaphorical reference to the most violent of activities, including warfare. Hence a losing team in (American) football, soccer, or rugby can be described as having been beaten, mauled, thrashed, hammered, wiped out, annihilated, and so forth; a manager can be said to have fired every gun in his arsenal when he selected a winning team. Such deployment of metaphors (which sometimes are not even recognized as such) can powerfully influence the way in which we think about the original activity, even to the point of being socially disruptive and dangerous. Given that different languages often employ the same metaphors, some have hypothesized that there is a correspondence between the metaphorical connection of domains and neural mappings in the human brain. Recent debates and controversies in cognitive linguistics research are

That is obviously, vividly, true of the structure of the thought which drives medieval other-worldly visions, whether populist, academically authorized, or fictional, whether their doctrine was institutionally sanctioned or vernacular. In an array of texts which included items as diverse as St Gregory's *Dialogues*, the *Tractatus de purgatorio Sancti Patricii*, and Mechthild of Hackeborn's *Liber specialis gratiae* (one of the major texts discussed in the next section), the separated souls who journey through esoteric visionary landscapes need some form of embodiment to enable their narrative functions. For the same reason, Dante's persona needs to encounter distinctive shades in his other worlds, to talk with images of air. And – to look more broadly at the intersecting, overlapping traditions of representing the unrepresentable – those ubiquitous worms, serpents and toads serve as potent vehicles for the persistent torments that are constitutive of hell. Metaphor is necessary, insistent, and unavoidable. Here we encounter the limits, perhaps the very nature, of language itself.

well illustrated by the contributions to *The Cognitive Linguistics Reader*, ed. Vyvyan Evans, Benjamin K. Bergen and Jörg Zinken (London and Oakville, CT, 2007).

CHAPTER 15

Hellish imaginations from the midwives of purgatory

That conclusion is endorsed and enhanced by writings by, and about, many of the holy women of the later Middle Ages – those 'midwives of purgatory', to return to Barbara Newman's felicitous formulation, who created some of the richest metaphorical language to stem from the period. Their testimony complicates the distinctions made above between professional theology and popular piety, the *provectos* and the *simplices*, for we are dealing with people who had some access (however mediated) to the formal theological discourses discussed above, yet were graced with their own inspired, privileged sources of knowledge.

Sarah Beckwith has spoken shrewdly of 'a very material mysticism', this being a reflex of the way women's 'access to the visionary' derived 'from the very specific representative function given to them in medieval culture, the specific representation of themselves as associated with the debased matter of the flesh' – which they saw 'valorized and redeemed in Christ's torture on the cross, a redemption through physicality'.[1] A redemption which, as a sacred cause and calling, many *mulieres sanctae* served through their own physical suffering. Learning and teaching by experience rather than by textbook, they turned their bodies into sensoria in which the most salvific forms of torment could be discovered and self-inflicted. That pain was supposed to continue from this world into the next, in an almost seamless transition. Catherine of Genoa lucidly expresses the notion of purgatory *in via*, experienced in this life: 'I see my soul in the midst of my body as in a purgatory, conformed and like to the true purgatory, in measure, however, that the body may be able to endure it and not die; yet the pain goes on increasing gradually until

---

[1] 'A very material mysticism: The medieval mysticism of Margery Kempe', in *Gender and Text in the Later Middle Ages*, ed. Jane Chance (Gainesville, FL, 1996), pp. 195-215 (p. 206).

death'.² However, enduring as much purgatorial cleansing as possible on earth rather than in purgatory was highly advisable, since infernal pain was widely supposed to be infinitely worse than anything that could be encountered in this life.³

The materiality of this continuum of pain perhaps left little psychic space for consideration of the differences between the suffering of the embodied soul and that of the separated soul, and in any case even the best-educated of holy women lacked full access to the analytical techniques and jargon of academe. Their spiritual discourses are far removed from the scholastic creation of a soul encased in incessant fire, not actually being burned yet enduring agony on account of it – a product of febrile abstraction and academic circle-squaring which might

---

² *Trattato del purgatorio*, 17, ed. Trovato, p. 141. As Caroline Walker Bynum has said so well, 'Purgatory was not primarily, to these women, a physical place somewhere '; 'it simply *was* suffering – redemptive suffering'. 'Purgatory was ... the fact of suffering', rather than 'a place in the cosmos or a counting house where deeds are measured and exchanged'. *Holy Feast and Holy Fast: The Religious Significance of Food to Medieval Women* (Berkeley, CA, 1987), pp. 120, 235.

³ A commonplace belief, often stated. Its ubiquity may be attributed, in some measure at least, to the statement in the highly popular pseudo-Augustinian text, *De vera et falsa poenitentia*, that purgatorial pain, although not eternal, is painful in a miraculous manner, and exceeds all the pains that can possibly be suffered in this life. *De vera et falsa poenitentia*, xviii, 34; *PL*, XL, col. 1128. For discussion see, for example, Cohen, *Modulated Scream*, pp. 36, 49, 189; Wei, *Intellectual Culture in Medieval Paris*, pp. 219-20; Matsuda, *Death and Purgatory in Middle English Didactic Poetry*, pp. 17, 39-40, 50, 56, 85, 92-3; Richard Kaeuper, *Holy Warriors: The Religious Ideology of Chivalry* (Philadelphia, 2009), p. 59; Linda S. Olson, 'Visions of the other world (heaven, hell, purgatory) in Medieval French saint's lives and other didactic literature' (unpub. Ph.D. diss., University of Wisconsin-Madison, 1996), II, 464; Scott E. Pincikowski, *Bodies of Pain: Suffering in the Works of Hartmann von Aue* (New York, 2002), pp. 16-17. To offer one example among many, *The Prick of Conscience* says that in hell the pain caused by 'fyre and vermyn'
... es mare to fele and se
Þan all þe paynes þat may be
In þis werld here ... (6965-71).

have satisfied the theoreticians yet which stands in firm contrast to the actual experiences of female 'living saints'.[4]

Denied entry to the supposedly 'public' space of the university classroom, and canonically barred from formal preaching, holy women carved out a niche of their own by fast-tracking the souls of their clients through purgatory (thanks to the efficacy of their substitute suffering and the power of their devout prayers),[5] and by reporting back about the conditions appertaining in the other world – in which respect they claimed a position traditionally occupied by the protagonists of the popular visionary narratives. In the *vita* of Christina of Sint-Truiden (Christina Mirabilis) which he wrote shortly after 1232, Thomas of Cantimpré records how, when this rather vexing figure seemed to die and experience a vision of purgatory, God offered her a choice. Either she could remain with Him in heaven, or return to her body to endure sufferings which would enable souls to be delivered from purgatory; further, by her way of life and example she could 'convert living men to

---

[4] As they have recently been called. See especially the introduction to *Living Saints of the Thirteenth Century: The Lives of Yvette, anchoress of Huy; Juliana of Cornillon, author of the Corpus Christi feast; and Margaret the Lame, anchoress of Magdeburg*, ed. Anneke B. Mulder-Bakker and trans. Jo Ann McNamara (Turnhout, 2011).

[5] On purgatory as an empowering doctrine for female ministry (what she calls 'service') see Bynum, *Holy Feast and Holy Fast*, pp. 120-1, 127, 129, 133, 171, 234, 242, 281, 235. By their special non-priestly activities, some medieval women 'bypassed certain forms of clerical control that stood between them and God', and forged for themselves 'roles as healers, teachers and savers of their fellow Christians that were in explicit contrast to the characteristic forms of male leadership' (p. 227). Barbara Newman has written in similar terms, remarking that their interventions 'constituted a safe, invisible, contemplative mission that could put women's devotion and compassion to work without violating any gender taboos'. Newman, 'On the threshold of the dead', p. 111. Cf. Alastair Minnis, 'Religious roles: public and private', in *Medieval Holy Women in the Christian Tradition, c. 1100 - c. 1500*, ed. Alastair Minnis and Rosalynn Voaden (Turnhout, 2010), pp. 47-81 (pp. 73-4). All of this should be seen within the full context of late-medieval care for the dead. One of the clergy's chief liturgical activities had become masses for the dead, work which in England largely came to an end in 1547, when the chantries were abolished by Parliament.

me and make them turn away from their sins'.⁶ Of course, Christina opts to return to her body. Her terms of reference are in part reminiscent of the preface to the *Tractatus de purgatorio sancti Patricii*, where the Monk of Sawtry enlists St Gregory's support in claiming that tales like this frighten sinners and inflame the just to devotion. Yet Christina offers much more than that – she is an eager proxy sufferer whose worthiness in the eyes of God gives her the power to petition, and successfully negotiate with, the almighty.⁷

Another highly efficient proxy sufferer was Mechthild of Hackeborn (1241-98), a nun at the illustrious convent of Helfta in Saxony, where Gertrude the Great (1256-c. 1301/2) was abbess and Mechthild of Magdeburg (d. c. 1282/94) spent her last days. Recounting a vision of souls she was in the process of rescuing from purgatory through her prayers, Mechthild builds on the biblical reference to the worm that never dies (Isaiah lxvi.24 yet again), duly identifying it as a metaphor for the human conscience. Yet she was not content to stay with that straightforward vehicle. The hearts of all her prayer-clients having been exposed to her gaze, Mechthild sees in each of them a creature resembling a worm, with the head of a dog, and four feet; this composite creature gnaws their hearts without ceasing and torments them with the scraping

---

6   *Thomas of Cantimpré: The Collected Saints' Lives: Christina the Astonishing, Lutgard of Aywières, Margaret of Ypres and Abbot John of Cantimpre ́*, ed. Barbara Newman and trans. Margot H. King and Barbara Newman (Turnhout, 2008), p. 131. In the fifteenth-century Middle English translation, God says to Christina, 'now I putte to the choys of two thinges: that is to seye, whether thou hast leuer dwelle stille with me now or turne ageyn to thy body, there to suffer peynes of an vndeedly soule by a deedly body withouten harme of hitselfe and to delyuere with thy peynes all ethos soulless of the whiche thou haddest pite in the place of Purgatorie. ¶ And also with ensaumple of thy peyne and lyfe, to stire men to repentauns and panauns, and to forsake her synnes and be trewly turnyd to me. And after alle this is doon, then thou schalte come ageyne to me with many medys'. *Three Women of Liège: A Critical Edition of and Commentary on the Middle English Lives of Elizabeth of Spalbeek, Christina Mirabilis and Marie d'Oignies*, ed. Jennifer N. Brown (Turnhout, 2008), p. 56.
7   On 'substitute' suffering see especially Bynum, *Holy Feast and Holy Fast*, pp. 127, 129, 171, 234.

of its claws. Here the metaphorical discourse has moved away from the negative, physically repellent features of a worm to enlist the much more positive connotations of a faithful dog, which never stops trying to show its master the best course of action. The gnawing, biting action of the conscience has never seemed so positive – quite a feat, given the grotesquerie of the image.

Here is the relevant passage in the *Liber specialis gratiae*, together with its rendering in the fifteenth-century Middle English translation, *The Booke of Gostlye Grace*:

> Hic vermis propria erat conscientia cujuslibet, qui ideo faciem canis prætendebat, quia fidele animal est canis, et conscientia semper corrodit et arguit animam, pro eo quod dulcissimo et benignissimo Deo suo extitit infidelis, nec ad eum absque impedimento post mortem meruit evolare.
> [This worme was the conscience of eche sawlle whiche schewede a face of a hounde, for a hounde es a [trewe] beste. Ryght so the conscience eueremore freteth ande vnderenymeth þe sowlle, foralsmoche as he was vntrewe to his goode benygne God ande for he deservede now3t / to goo evene streyght to his God aftere his deyde withoutene lettynge.][8]

By the four feet are figured all the wicked desires and evil ways that drove away the soul from his God. But Mechthild is more interested in what the tail of this horrid hybrid signifies. Some worms have smooth and plain tails, while others are sharp and rough; she reads the former as the good reputation which some souls leave behind after their death, and for which they are given due credit, while the latter signifies the bad reputation which never dies and torments the soul (for its own good, of course) until it enters heaven.

---

[8] *Liber specialis gratiae*, v, 17, in *Revelationes Gertrudianae ac Mechtildianae*, ed. Louis Paquelin and the monks of Solesmes, 2 vols (Poitiers and Paris, 1875-7), II, 346; *The Booke of Gostlye Grace of Mechtild of Hackeborn*, ed. Theresa A. Halligan (Toronto, 1979), p. 573.

Hic vermis etiam habebat caudam longam: quorumdam erat lenis et plana, quorumdam vero hispida et hirsuta. Per hanc caudam notabatur fama quam reliquerant in terris. Quæ vero bonam famam reliquerant, eorum cauda erat lenis, et ex hoc quoddam habebant remedium. Quæ autem malam post mortem reliquerant, earum vermium cauda hispida erat et retorta, crucians animam vehementer. Hic vermis nunquam moritur [Isaiah lxvi.24], nec anima inde liberatur, donec intret in gaudium Domini sui, foedere indissolubili Deo juncta.

[This worme hadde also a longe tayle, botte the taylle of some wormes was smoyth ande playne, ande of some wormes þe tayle was scharpe ande rowȝh. Be the smoyth ande softe tayle was betokenede þe goode faame whiche some sawlles lefte behynde þame aftere þare deyde, ande by þat goode fame for þare goode ensample þaye hadde some remedye. Ande the taylle of þame þat lefte an evylle fame was scharpe and rowhȝ whiche greuouslye tormentede the sowlle. This worme dyeth neuere ande the sowelle es neuer delyuerede fro þat worme into the tyme þat the sawlle entere into the blysse of his lorde.][9]

Mechthild prays with all her might that our Lord should deliver all the souls from pain and give them full remission and forgiveness. Immediately all the worms die ('anone the wormes of eche sawlle felle downe and deyde'), and the souls joyfully pass into heavenly bliss. After this, the Lord affords Mechthild a vision of purgatory in which souls emerge from the fires, burned and ugly to see, but on being delivered from their pain they take on the shape and habit that they had whilst on earth.[10] Perhaps this re-materialisation is intended as an anticipation of the glorious event at the General Resurrection when souls shall take on flesh again, rejoining their earthly bodies (though in perfected versions thereof). At any rate, it is a striking *coup de theatre*.

---

[9] *Liber specialis gratiae*, v, 17, ed. Paquelin, II, 346; *Booke of Gostlye Grace*, pp. 573-4.
[10] ... quaelibet formam et habitum suum qualis fuerat in terris recipiebat ... (Paquelin, II, 347); ... toke here schape ande habyte whiche þaye hadde in erthe ... (*Booke of Gostlye Grace*, p. 574).

The doggy worm created in Mechthild's vision allegedly influenced the expression of a vision of purgatory recorded by an unnamed fifteenth-century Englishwoman from Winchester, who dreamed of the purgatorial punishments endured by the soul of a woman she used to know, a nun named Margaret.[11] Here the worm of conscience is accompanied by two other creatures, a ferocious little dog and cat, all of whom are allies in the infliction of pain.

> ... þe lyttill hounde and þe catt sulde euer be with hir in fyre to encrese hir paynes, and ... þe worme of conscience sulde euer gnawe hir with-ine.[12]

The hapless Margaret then identifies the worm of conscience as the source of greatest pain.[13] Subsequently we hear of how a devil takes 'worms and pitch and tar' and makes Margaret ringlets of them. Whereupon the little dog and cat viciously join in the torment, 'ripping apart her legs and her arms'. The Devil of Pride declares that they 'shall continuously tear' at her whilst she is there because of the 'unreasonable love' she bestowed upon 'stinking pride and boastfulness' whilst on earth.[14] An explanation of the presence of those two creatures, quite atypical in visions of purgatory, is eventually offered:

> [As] touchynge the lyttil hounde and þe cate, þay were hir mawemetts [idols] þe whils scho was one lyfe and scho sett hir herte to mekill [too much] one swylke foulle wormes. 'And þar-{for} þat folowe me to encrese my paynes ay till þe bandes of syne be worne in-sondir'.[15]

When she is cleansed from all vestiges of sin, Margaret continues, 'this dog or this cat shall never follow me more'. It would seem, then, that this

---

[11] *A Revelation of Purgatory*, ed. and trans. Liz Herbert McAvoy (Cambridge, 2017).
[12] Ibid., pp. 95-6.
[13] Ibid., pp. 96-7.
[14] Ibid., pp. 100-5.
[15] Ibid., pp. 132-3.

nun expended too much love and attention on a pet dog and cat, in effect idolizing them. And now she is being held to account.

A partial analogue may be found in the *Livre pour l'enseignement de ses filles du Chevalier de La Tour Landry* (1371-2), where Geoffroy IV de la Tour Landry tells the tale of a lady who took pleasure in feeding her two little dogs with dishes of milk-sop and meat. Although warned by a friar that it was wicked to make her pets fat while poor people were lean and hungry, she persisted in her bad behaviour. When she was dying, there was an amazing spectacle:

> Sy advint que la dame acoucha au lit malade de la mort, et y avint telles merveilles que l'en vit tout appertement sur son lit deux petiz chiens noirs, et, quant elle transit, ilz estoient entour sa bouche et lui lechoient le bec, et, quand elle fut transie, l'on lui vit la bouche toute noire, que ilz avoient lechée, comme charbons ...
> [And after she happed she deied, and there fell a wonder meruailous sight, for there was seyn euer on her bedde .ij. litell blake dogges, and in her deyeng thei were about her mouthe and liked [licked] it, and whanne she was dede, there the dogges had lyked it was al blacke as cole ...][16]

Whether those black dogs are her actual pets or their fiendish equivalents is unclear; the belief that the devil could appear in the shape of a dog goes back a long way.[17] That very ambiguity contributes to the horror of the

---

[16] *Le Livre du Chevalier de la Tour Landry pour l'enseignement de ses filles*, ed. M. A. de Montaiglon (Paris, 1854), pp. 44-5; *The Book of the Knight of La Tour-Landry*, ed. Thomas Wright, EETS os 33, rev. edn (London, 1906), pp. 28-9. This English translation was printed by William Caxton in 1484. For a diatribe against how the wealthy provide for their dogs more readily than for the poor see John Bromyard, *Summa praedicantium*, s.v. *servire*, quoted by Owst, *Literature and Pulpit*, pp. 327-8.

[17] See B. Allen Woods, 'The devil in dog form', *Western Folklore*, 13/4 (1954), 229-35. On the appearance of the devil in cat form, see Lyndal Roper, *The Witch in the Western Imagination* (Charlottesville, 2012), p. 171, and also pp. 138, 143-5. For the association of the cat with heresy, and hence with the devil, see Sara Lipton, 'Jews, heretics and the sign of the cat in the *Bible*

scene. But it is evident that their actions anticipate purgatorial punishments for the wealthy woman's failure to distribute alms. Creatures which, in life, might have licked their owner's face, to her great pleasure, now reveal the darkness of death, bodily corruption, and the appropriate punishment of the soul.

One may also compare Geoffrey Chaucer's portrait of his somewhat affected Prioress, who feeds her small hounds with rich fare – roasted meat, milk and fine white bread – and weeps sorely if one of them is beaten or dies.[18] That statement may be read as an aspect of Madame Eglentyne's 'counterfeiting' of 'cheere / Of court' (*Canterbury Tales*, I(A), 139-40), i.e. imitation of aristocratic manners and fashions. The keeping of pets, animals with no functional purpose that were valued for affection and companionship, was an identity-marker of upper-class women, a symbol of wealth and conspicuous consumption. Small dogs were the most popular companion, but cats could also be kept in pampered and privileged conditions – as were singing and talking birds, plus the occasional monkey.[19] Margaret may have lavished too much sentimental emotion on her pets, in detriment to her duties as a nun, and now their

---

moralisée', *Word & Image*, 8/4 (1992), 362-77. Alan of Lille records the accusation that 'Cathars are called after the cat, because they kiss the posterior of a cat in whose shape, it is said, Lucifer appears to them ... '. *Contra hereticos*, *PL*, CCX, col. 366A; cited by Lipton, pp. 368-9. A useful overview of feline imagery has been provided by Douglas Gray, 'Notes of some medieval mystical, magical and moral cats', in *Langland, the Mystics and the Medieval English Religious Tradition: Essays in Honour of S. S. Hussey*, ed. Helen Philipps (Cambridge, 1990), pp. 185-202.

[18] General Prologue to *The Canterbury Tales*, I(A) 146-9; *The Riverside Chaucer*, ed. Larry D. Benson (Boston, MA, 1987). It may be added that the worm of conscience puts in an appearance at the end of Chaucer's *Physician's Tale* (VI(C) 280-2). For a persuasive explanation of this difficult passage see the crucial article by Marta Powell Harley, 'Last things first in Chaucer's *Physician's Tale*: final judgment and the worm of conscience', *Journal of English and Germanic Philology*, 91/1 (1992), 1-16.

[19] Here I am indebted to the work of Kathleen Walker-Meikle: 'Late medieval pet keeping: gender, status and emotions' (unpub. Ph.D. diss., University College London, 2008); idem, *Medieval Pets* (Woodbridge, 2012).

avatars are participating in her punishment. Recognizing her fault, she dismisses her former friends as 'foulle wormes', things of no value.

This is some distance away from Mechthild's image of a worm-like creature with a dog's head. Therefore I would question Liz Herbert McAvoy's suggestion that, as a mark of Mechthild's influence, in the woman of Winchester's vision the worm, cat and dog have 'become conflated into one monstrous and hybrid body', such is the degree of their 'close collaboration'.[20] Their status is quite different, it seems to me. Moreover, they function separately as well as together – as when, in the judgment scene which ends the treatise, the Virgin Mary asks the devil to testify what he can say against Margaret, whereupon he produces a 'grete worme', identifying it as 'þe worme of conscyence'.[21] Then (rather underwhelmingly) the devil specifies that it shall torment her for a single past sin of omission, namely that 'she made a vow of pilgrimage and failed to fulfil it'. The Blessed Virgin, 'Queen of Heaven and of Earth, Empress of Hell and of Purgatory', quickly dismisses this charge, saying that the debt has been paid (masses and prayers having been said), whereupon the devil and the worm make 'a great cry' and disappear from sight, leaving Margaret's soul to enter the bliss of heaven.[22] The worm is a permanent fixture of purgatory and hell, telling truths about the sins of its suffering souls, whereas the dog and cat are unique vestiges of Margaret's prideful and vain life, which have come back to haunt her.[23] Here is a colourful

[20] *Revelation of Purgatory*, ed. McAvoy; Introduction, p. 61.
[21] *Revelation of Purgatory*, ed. McAvoy, pp. 150-1.
[22] By way of the Earthly Paradise, as a stop *en route*. On the continued appearance of this place of the dead in visionary literature (despite the appeal of the three-place model, of hell, purgatory and heaven) see Easting, 'Purgatory and the Earthly Paradise', esp. pp. 43-8.
[23] Might this transformation of Margaret's erstwhile pets into devilish surrogates have been influenced in some way by superstitions concerning the familiars of witches? In 1324 a Kilkenny woman, Alice Kyteler, was accused of having conversed with the devil in the forms of a hairy black dog and a cat; her incubus, Robert or Robin son of Art, might assume these appearances when visiting her for sex. *A Contemporary Narrative of the Proceedings against Dame Alice Kyteler, Prosecuted for Sorcery in 1324 by Richard de Ledrede*, ed. Thomas Wright, Camden Society (London, 1843), pp. 2-3. See further Maeve Brigid Callan, *The Templars, the Witch, and the*

application of the principle expressed at Wisdom xi.17, 'by what things a man sinneth, by the same also he is tormented'.

However one may interpret this intriguing text, the Dominican tertiary Catherine of Siena (1347-80) goes one farther in respect of canine imagery, in presenting a fully-developed metaphor of the dog of conscience – conceived as a fundamentally loyal and useful creature, in contrast with the nun Margaret's faithless pet.[24] Here the *in bono* interpretation of the creature's characteristics clearly outweighs the *in malo* one, the image being disambiguated.[25] Because shepherds who fail

Wild Irish: Vengeance and Heresy in Medieval Ireland (Ithaca, NY, 2014). Richard Firth Green, to whom I owe the Kyteler reference, tells me that 'there seems to be a general consensus that familiars are commoner in the British isles than on the Continent and that though they probably have roots in folk beliefs reaching way back in time they aren't recorded much before the fourteenth century'. 'It's interesting to see how many (particularly Continental) records *don't* mention familiars: they're not in the Templar trials, for instance, nor are they in the *Malleus maleficarum*. English trial procedure put far more emphasis on physical evidence than inquisitional procedure, which may be why familiars, witches' marks, etc. feature more prominently in England' (personal communication). The possibility of influence is certainly worth considering.

[24] There is some precedent. The French Benedictine abbot William of St Thierry (d. *c.* 1148) also uses the dog metaphor to illustrate an essential aspect of conscience. Initially he refers to Christ's abrupt rejection of the Canaanite woman at Matthew xv.21-8. 'It is not good to take the bread of the children, and to cast it to the dogs', Christ declares harshly, whereupon she replies, 'the whelps also eat of the crumbs that fall from the table of their masters' (26-7). Like that woman, William has initially been rebuffed, but he will return, even as a whelp that has been chased with blows will return immediately and, hanging watchfully about the place, receive its daily bread. Likewise, conscience, by its very nature, 'hangs around' God. William then draws attention to a second aspect of conscience illustrated by this metaphor. A dog is a faithful companion that cannot live without human companionship; likewise William's soul cannot live without God. Thomas X. Davis, 'The Trinity's Glorifying Embrace: *Concientia* in William of Saint-Thierry', in *A Companion to William of Saint-Thierry*, ed. F. Tyler Sergent (Leiden, 2019), pp. 131-59 (p. 140).

[25] Discourse concerning the roles and duties of preachers was rife with comparisons of them to hounds who, with their relentless bark, protect 'the

to guide their flocks are evil they fail to 'have a dog that will bark when it sees the wolf coming. No, their dog is no better than themselves'.[26] Here the text is extrapolating from Isaiah lvi.10, where ignorant watchmen are denounced as 'dumb dogs not able to bark'. The conscience of these 'careless ministers' does 'not bark to reproach them for their own sins', complains God to Catherine, 'and they do not reprove the sheep either when they see them going astray', easy prey for 'the infernal wolf'. 'So weakened for want of feeding' is the dog of such a man's conscience that it cannot bark'. The food with which it must be fed is 'the blood of the Lamb, my Son'. Thus nourished, the invigorated conscience stands guard, barking 'like a dog, excitedly, until it rouses reason'. The Middle English translation of Catherine's *Dialogo, The Orcherd of Syon*, apparently prepared around 1420 for the first generation

sacred sheepfolds from wolves'. Alternatively, prelates could be criticized for *not* engaging in exemplary hound-behaviour, as when 'they leave the flocks, and elect to spend their days in the courts of the mighty, to eat the flesh of fat beasts'. Thus they become 'not faithful sheep-dogs but lap-dogs, eating up the luscious tit-bits that lords and ladies throw to them'. In late-medieval England, bishops could be termed 'dumb dogs' (cf. Isaiah lxvi.10) for their lack of preaching, and parish priests accused of hindering the activities of preaching friars: 'they neither cherish nor support such dogs, that is, the preachers, but rather hinder and harass them'. All these statements are from the voluminous *Summa praedicantium* of John Bromyard, OP (d. *c.* 1352), as quoted by G. R. Owst, *Preaching in Medieval England: An Introduction to Sermon Manuscripts of the Period c. 1350-1450* (Cambridge, 1926), pp. 7, 41 note 2, 67, 75. In his *Liber de eruditione praedicatorum*, Humbert of Romans, Master General of the Dominicans during the period 1254-63, cites the reference at Isaiah lvi.10 to 'dumb dogs which cannot bark' and interprets that barking as preaching, the implication being that preachers should certainly not be 'dumb' in this sense. Humbert goes on to say that 'the preacher is called a dog, and therefore he ought to wander round hither and thither like a hungry dog, eager to swallow up souls into the body of the church'; 'they will feel hunger like dogs and go about the city' (Psalm 58.7). Trans. Simon Tugwell in *Early Dominicans: Selected Writings* (New York and Mahwah, NJ, 1982), p. 226.

[26] *Dialogo*, 129, ed. Matilde Fiorilli, *Libro della divina dottrina: volgarmente detto Dialogo della divina Provvidenza* (Bari, 1912), p. 278; trans. Suzanne Noffke, *Catherine of Siena: The Dialogue* (New York and Mahwah, NJ, 2017), p. 257.

of Bridgettine nuns at Syon Abbey, offers a lively rendering: 'as soone as ony enemy of þe soule, which is synne, wil entre yn, anoon þe conscience as an hound berkeþ aȝeins it & exciteþ resoun to helpe hym for to do riȝtwiisnesse aȝens hym. For he þat haþ conscience hath riȝtwiisnesse ...'.[27]

However, the worm of conscience was too persistent a metaphor to be replaced with the vehicle of a different creature; the attributes associated with other animals simply could not compete, given its biblical valorisation and centuries of reiteration in Christian teaching. It does put in occasional, and quite striking, appearances in Catherine's *Dialogo*. Having been asleep, the worm is shocked into action by the reality of damnation. Then it will gnaw away, with devils screaming at the soul, seeking to bring it into despair; 'your conscience reproaches you in the horrible appearance of the demons'.[28] False Christians fare much worse than pagans, for 'the fire of divine justice torments them the more; burning without consuming; and in their torment they feel themselves being eaten by the worm of conscience, which eats away without eating up – for the damned for all their torment cannot cease to exist'.[29] In this deft rhetorical move, the actions of gnawing and the burning are united in their ability to cause pain which never reaches a natural end, which

---

[27] *The Orcherd of Syon*, ed. Phyllis Hodgson and Gabriel M. Liegey, EETS os 258 (London, 1966), p. 299.

[28] *Dialogo*, 132, ed. Fiorilli, pp. 291-2; trans. Noffke, pp. 268-9. Elsewhere, Catherine likens worldly people to 'animals running loose, running on 'from bad to worse, from sin to sin, from wickedness to wickedness, from darkness to darkness, from death to death. They finally end up in death's ditch with the worm of conscience constantly gnawing away at them'. *Dialogo*, 156, ed. Fiorilli, pp. 369-70; tr. Noffke, p. 333.

[29] ... e più el consuma el fuoco senza consumare, per divina giustizia, cioè affligge, e afliiggendo si sentono consumare col vermine della coscienzia e nondimeno non consuma, perché i dampnati non perdono l'essere per veruno tormento che ricevano. *Dialogo*, 15; ed. Fiorilli, p. 37; trans. Noffke, p. 54. Cf. *The Orcherd of Syon*: þe peynful flawme of fier brenneþ hem wiþouten waastynge; and so þei feele afflixioun and turment þoru ful cruel fretynges & bitinges of her owne consciences; and ȝit þe fier waasteþ hem not, for þei þat ben dampnyd lesen not her beyng for ony turment þat þei haue (p. 55).

lacks an inbuilt point of cessation. Similarly, when Catherine comes to list the torments of hell, its fire is described as burning 'without consuming, for the soul cannot be consumed, since it is not material (such as fire could consume) but spiritual'. 'In my divine justice', God explains to Catherine, 'I allow the fire to burn these souls mightily, tormenting them without consuming them'.[30] Here is the crucial passage, together with its Middle English translation in *The Orcherd of Syon*:

> Questo fuoco arde e non consuma, però che l'anima non si può consumare l'essere suo; e non è cosa materiale, la quale materia el fuoco la consumasse, però che ella è incorporea. Ma Io per divina giustizia ho permesso che 'l fuoco gli arda affliggitivamente,' che gli affligge e non gli consuma. E affliggeli e ardeli con grandissime pene, in diversi modi, secondo la diversità de' peccati; chi più e chi meno, secondo la gravezza della colpa.
> [Þis fier ceessiþ neuere of brennynge, and ȝit he wasteþ not, for þe beynge of þe soule may nott be wasstid, and may not waste þe materie of þe fier, for it [i.e. the soul] is not bodily. Naþelees I suffer hem be brend of þat fier by myn dyuyne riȝtwiisnes, as by wey of turment. Which fier turmenteþ hem and not waasteþ; and turmenteþ and brenneþ hem wiþ grete peynes by manye dyuerse weyes, aftir þe dyuersite and multitude of synnes.][31]

At this point Catherine's God is echoing what generations of theologians (going back to Augustine at least) had said concerning the impossibility of the spiritual soul being consumed by material fire; she also shows herself aware of the doctrine that the operation of divine justice (the *ordo divinae iustitiae*) is not constrained by the natural order.[32] Here she

---

[30] *Dialogo*, 38; ed. Fiorilli, p. 70; trans. Noffke, p. 81. The torments of hell are listed as: the deprival of the sight of God, the worm of conscience, the sight of the devil, and the fire.
[31] *Dialogo*, 38, ed. Fiorilli, p. 70; *The Orcherd of Syon*, ed. Hodgson and Liegey, p. 89.
[32] On what William of Auvergne and Thomas Aquinas thought about this matter see above, pp. 40, 43, 75-6, 120 n. 9; see further Mowbray, *Pain and*

situates herself within the doctrinal mainstream. But she avoids the issue of precisely *how*, in what sense, that material fire can be said to 'burn' the spiritual soul. A similar point can be made about her frequent assertion that the sight of devils exacerbates the pains of hell, as, for example, 'synful wrecchis ben encreessid in turmentis by þe horrible siȝt of feendis…'; 'þe conscience repreueþ hem wiþ wiþyn þe siȝt of fendis þat also rebukiþ hem…'; 'þi conscience vndirnymeth þee þere in þe siȝt of feendis'.[33] Again, we are dealing with a view that had frequently been considered by the theologians, as noted above. But in Catherine's case we have assertion rather than explanation of how the process works, and in particular how the sense of sight can function in the world to come; sometimes, but not always, Catherine specifies that she is talking about the hell that will come into existence following the General Resurrection, leaving unclear the issue of what happens in hell as presently constituted. Perhaps she felt it was best to leave such details to the *magistri*.[34]

The relationship between academics and *mulieres sanctae* could be fraught. The Benedictine nun Elisabeth of Schönau (1129-65) got into trouble when some of her prophecies were carelessly preached by her abbot, Hildelin, thereby exposing her to criticism.[35] Elisabeth was

Suffering, pp. 112, 114, 140, 154, 155, 156, and Wei, *Intellectual Culture in Medieval Paris*, pp. 208, 214.

[33] *The Orcherd of Syon*, ed. Hodgson and Liegey, pp. 89, 312, 313. Cf. *Dialogo*, 38 (ed. Fiorilli, p. 70; trans. Noffke, p. 80); and *Dialogo*, 132 (ed. Fiorilli, p 292; trans. Noffke, pp. 268-9).

[34] While this is true in respect of the specific matters here discussed, it should be noted that Catherine was well versed in many of the theological issues of the day. For example, she is knowledgeable concerning certain technical aspects of Resurrection Theology, including the belief that 'the body's happiness after the resurrection' will not 'add anything to the soul's happiness' (for otherwise the soul would not enjoy complete happiness in heaven at present). Yet the blessed shall 'be rewarded with endless glory and good in their glorified bodies … in body as well as in soul' (while the wicked shall 'be eternally punished in their bodies'). *Dialogo*, 41 and 42 (ed. Fiorilli, p. 75, 77; trans. Noffke, pp. 84, 86). On these arcane matters see Minnis, *From Eden to Eternity*, pp. 202, 207, 209-11, 225-6.

[35] *Visiones*, iii, 19, in *Die Visionen der hl. Elisabeth und die Schriften der Aebte Ekbert und Emecho von Schönau*, ed. F. W. E. Roth (Brno, 1884), p. 72;

sometimes put under pressure to come up with dangerously over-precise answers to knotty theological questions concerning the fates of souls in the afterlife. For instance, what happened to the soul of Origen, that great but heretical thinker; was he saved? In this case, Elisabeth wisely refused to be enlisted as a mediator between the conflicting views.[36] 'A certain friar' put the very same question to Mechthild of Hackeborn, Origen's soul being placed in the company of those of other problematic figures, Samson, Solomon, and the virtuous pagan emperor Trajan (believed to have been saved by the prayer of St Gregory). Origen's fate should remain hidden, God reportedly tells Mechthild, 'so no one who trusts in his own knowledge will dare to exalt himself' (the charge of intellectual pride being frequently levelled against Origen).[37] In similar vein, God tells her that he does not want people to know what, in his mercy, he has done with Solomon's soul, 'so they will be more careful to avoid carnal sins' – personably the divine concern here is that, if it becomes known that Solomon's many sexual sins were pardoned this would weaken the divine injunction against such deeds. Likewise, what the divine goodness has done with Samson's soul should 'remain unknown, so people will be terrified to take vengeance on their enemies'. As far as Trajan's soul is concerned, God wants no-one to know what his generosity has decreed in that case either, 'so the Catholic faith will be more highly valued'; apparently, the example of a man who 'lacked Christian faith and baptism', however virtuous he may have been, should not be publicized. Holy women were frequently credited with the gift of prophecy, as a means of their valorisation; in these cases, however, what they did *not* say is of greater significance than what they did say. Selective silence could

---

trans. Anne L. Clark, *Elisabeth of Schönau: The Complete Works* (New York and Mahwah, NJ, 2000), p. 140. See also *Visiones*, i.1, ed. Roth, p. 2; trans. Clark, p. 42.

[36] Anne L. Clark, *Elisabeth of Schönau: A Twelfth-Century Visionary* (Philadelphia, 1992), pp. 57, 59.

[37] *Liber specialis gratiae*, v.16, ed. Paquelin, II, 344; trans. Barbara Newman, *Mechthild of Hackeborn: The Book of Special Grace* (New York and Mahwah, NJ, 2017), pp. 195-6.

be a means of navigating the distance between their source of knowledge and the one maintained by the clerics.[38]

Holy women excelled in the praxis of suffering rather than its theorization; they became authorities on, and in, pain.[39] But not just pain. In an extraordinary passage in her *Liber specialis gratiae* Mechthild of Hackeborn describes how, following her request that God might give her some gift by which she would always remember Him, He gave to her soul His own senses to use.

'Ecce do tibi oculos meos, ut cum ipsis omnia videas, et aures meas, ut per eas omnia quæ audis intelligas; os etiam meum tibi do, ut

---

[38] For other instances of clerics trying to get quick answers to controversial theological questions by consulting holy women see Minnis, 'Religious roles: public and private', pp. 68-70.

[39] In her *Das fließende Licht der Gottheit*, iv, 12, Mechthild of Magdeburg declares that during his time on earth Christ loved 'Lady Pain' inasmuch as He suffered for humankind, and, although evil herself, she has led many holy people to heaven. Mechthild von Magdeburg, *Das fließende Licht der Gottheit*, ed. Hans Neumann, 2 vols., Münchener Texte und Untersuchungen zur deutschen Literatur des Mittelalters 100-1 (Munich, 1990-9), I, 123-7; trans. Frank Tobin, *The Flowing Light of the Godhead* (New York and Mahwah, NJ, 1998), pp. 152-6. However, Lady Pain is barred from entry into heaven – unsurprisingly, since pain has no place there. Bynum has remarked that Mechthild is 'no advocate of pain' – which may be true in ultimate terms, but she certainly esteems redemptive pain. *Resurrection*, p. 337. Esther Cohen has written provocatively about what she calls the 'philopassianism' of the later Middle Ages, whereby pain, far from avoided, is actually sought as an avenue to knowledge ('knowledge of the body, of the soul, of truth, of reality, and of God'). See her article, 'Towards a history of European physical sensibility: pain in the Later Middle Ages', *Science in Context*, 8 (1995), 47-74. See further, Mowbray on 'pain as a restorative power' (*Pain and Suffering*, pp. 61-80) and the cogent treatment of 'productive pain' in Gragnolati, *Experiencing the Afterlife*, pp. 89-137. An invigorating yet sometimes frustrating book on the general issues involved here has been written by Piero Camporesi, *The Incorruptible Flesh: Bodily Mutation and Mortification in Religion and Folklore*, trans. Tania Croft-Murray with the Latin texts trans. Helen Elsom (Cambridge, 2009). See also Giles Constable's pamphlet, *Attitudes toward Self-Inflicted Suffering in the Middle Ages* (Brookline, MA, 1982).

omnia quæ loquendo, orando, sive cantando proferre debes, per illud facias. Doque tibi Cor meum, ut per illud omnia cogites, et meipsum et omnia propter me diligas'.

['Loo, I gyffe þe myne eyene, þat þowe [m]owe see alle þynges with þame; also myn eren þat with thame þowe maye vnderstonde alle thynges þat þou hyeres. And I gyffe the my mowth þat þorowe þat þow maye schewe forth alle thynges in spekynge or prayenge or [syng]ynge. My herte I gyffe þe also þat with that þou thence alle goodnesse ande þat þowe luffe me ande alle goodnesse for me'.]⁴⁰

So saying, God drew the Soul 'totally into himself and united himself with her'; it seems to Mechthild that 'she saw with God's eyes, heard with his ears, and spoke with his mouth; and she felt that she had no other heart but his', an experience which subsequently occurred on frequent occasions.⁴¹ Mechthild's God goes on to tell her that the more she distances herself from all creatures 'the higher' she 'will be lifted toward the unattainable height of my majesty' – which is not only paradoxical but also somewhat ironic, given the creaturely sensations attributed to the divinity here, in contrast with the petitioning woman's presentation as Soul. In this text God is imaginatively embodied in order to possess and pass on his superlatively well-functioning nervous system to a woman who has been rendered disembodied – here, one might say, is a mystic union of transferred materiality. Mechthild wraps herself in the senses, celebrating them even as she professes her desire to rise above them, a desire itself expressed in sensory language.⁴² A magnificent iteration of 'vernacular theology'.

---

⁴⁰ *The Booke of Gostlye Grace*, ed. Halligan, p. 389.
⁴¹ In hoc verbo Deus animam illam sibi totaliter intraxit et secum ita univit, ut videretur sibi quod Dei oculis videret, et auribus ejus audiret, et ore ejusloqueretur, nullumque aliud cor quam Dei Cor se habere sentiret. Quod et sæpius postmodum illi datum est sentire. *Liber specialis gratiae*, ii, 34 (ed. Paquelin, II, 179; trans. Newman, *Mechthild of Hackeborn: The Book of Special Grace*, p. 139).
⁴² This striking episode illustrates what Barbara Newman has elegantly described as Mechthild's self-adopted role as 'an ambassador of joy, the apostle of a God so generous with his gifts that the whole purport of her

It is no coincidence that she has a tacit awareness of the drama of metaphor. In the prose of the *Liber specialis gratiae* abstractions take on forceful material form as they 'breathe in the lush atmosphere of the imagination'; 'poetry comes in' where 'philosophy no longer finds expression' (to adapt and apply statements by Johan Huizinga).[43] Could this Mechthild be the mysterious *bella donna* 'Matelda' of *Purgatorio* XXVIII (cf. XXXIII, 118-23)?[44] The possibility is tantalizing. Here poetry certainly 'comes in', as Dante has Matelda embody the beauty and innocence of the Earthly Paradise.

> A solitary woman! and she went
> Singing and gathering flower after flower,
> With which her way was painted and besprent.
>
> 'Bright lady, who, if looks had ever power
> To bear true witness of the heart within,
> Dost bask under the beams of love ...'[45]

Thus Shelley renders this epiphanic moment, with moving simplicity. Whoever Dante might have been referring to here (and, indeed, some

---

revelations is to awaken longing for heaven'. Introduction to *Mechthild of Hackeborn: The Book of Special Grace*, trans. Newman, p. 16.

[43] *The Waning of the Middle Ages*, trans. Hopman, p. 214.

[44] An enthusiastic argument for this identification has recently been made by Barbara Newman, 'The Seven-Storey Mountain: Mechthild of Hackeborn and Dante's Matelda', *Dante Studies*, 136 (2018), 62-92. But Jo Ann H. Moran Cruz has made a strong case for Queen and Saint Matilda of Saxony: 'Dante's Matelda: queen, saint, and mother of emperors', *Viator*, 47/3 (2016), 209-42. Newman critiques Cruz's argument as follows: 'A powerful matriarch rather than an innocent virgin, [Queen Matilda] does not obviously fit the lyrical mood of the Earthly Paradise. Further, it is hard to prove that Dante knew of this rather distant figure, whose *vitae* date from the late tenth and early eleventh centuries' (p. 64).

[45] *Shelley: Poetical Works*, ed. Thomas Hutchinson (London, 1965), p. 729. See further William Keach, 'The Shelleys and Dante's Matilda', in *Dante's Modern Afterlife: Reception and Response from Blake to Heaney*, ed. Nick Havely (Basingstoke and London, 1998), pp. 60-70.

critical opinion holds that he had no specific historical figure in mind), it is pleasing to think of Mechthild of Hackeborn basking under the beams of divine love ('...che a' raggi d'amore / ti scaldi', 43-4).[46] Here, as on so many other occasions in Dante's poem, metaphor and materiality become inseparable.

---

[46] As Newman eloquently puts it, Dante's Matelda and Mechthild of Hackeborn 'are versions of one another: liminal ladies on the threshold of heaven, joyfully chanting psalms on the mountaintop as they wait to usher purified souls into beatitude'. 'The Seven-Storey Mountain', p. 87.

CHAPTER 16

The death of purgatory and Protestant debate on hell-fire – metaphorical or material?

Admittedly, metaphor has sometimes been regarded as a kind of 'added extra' to plain and direct language, a 'seasoning of the meat', to adapt a phrase of Aristotle's.[1] But sometimes what looked like metaphor (and could function as metaphor) was actual meat. As we have seen, that was believed to be true of hell-fire, which remains material whether here or in hell, and resists being reduced to a metaphorical vehicle. Change came with the Protestant Reformation, when purgatory – that enormous source and vast place of pain – was abolished. As Peter Marshall has said, 'The outright proscription of purgatory, and of the whole gamut of traditional means of assisting the repose of the souls of the dead, must rank as one of the most audacious attempts at the restructuring of beliefs and values ever attempted in England, a kind of collective cultural de-programming'.[2]

---

[1] *Rhetoric*, 3 (1406a); trans. W. Rhys Roberts in *The Complete Works of Aristotle*, ed. Barnes, II. 2242-4. Here we encounter an opinion which Mark Johnson sees as characteristic of some narrow versions of the 'comparison theory' of metaphor, which tend to treat the phenomenon as 'either a deviant form of expression or a nonessential literary figure of speech'. *The Body in the Mind*, pp. 66, 68. Elsewhere, of course, Aristotle offers a more elevated view, as expressed in other citations in this essay. It should be noted that, in the present day, early cognitive science discussion tended to take a somewhat trivializing 'substitution view' of Aristotle's metaphor theory (a merely decorative or more pleasant word or phrase being substituted for another), but a more nuanced approach has been taken in some of the more recent analyses.

[2] *Beliefs and the Dead in Reformation England* (Cambridge, 2002), p.100. Marshall goes on to say (p. 108) that the 'campaign against purgatory' conducted during the reign of King Edward VI 'represents a moment of rupture, perhaps the most abrupt and traumatic of all the cultural apertures opened up in sixteenth-century England'.

An obvious concomitant of that tectonic religious shift was a reawakening of interest in the theory that hell-fire is a metaphor, a figurative way of expressing the horror of spending eternity separated from God. Hence, when faced with the references to fire and brimstone at Isaiah xxx.33, the French reformer John Calvin (1509-64) said that here corporeal language is working to assist us 'to conceive the miserable doom of the reprobate, so the consideration on which we ought chiefly to dwell is the fearful consequence of being estranged from all fellowship with God'.[3]

Martin Luther (1483-1546) has surprisingly little to say about hell,[4] though on one occasion, whilst commenting on Jonah, he ventures the opinion that 'Everybody carries his hell with him wherever he may be so long as he feels the final anguish of death and God's anger'.[5] This seems

[3] *Institutes of the Christian Religion* (1559), iii, 25.12; trans. Henry Beveridge, 2 vols. in one (Edinburgh, 1845-6), p. 275.

[4] Indeed, one of his biographers, Richard Marius, has opined that his 'greatest terror, one that came on him periodically as a horror of darkness, was the fear of death – death in itself, not the terror of a burning and eternal hell awaiting the sinner in an afterlife. It is startling to see how seldom he speaks of hell as a place of eternal torment, and indeed he finally rejected the notion of hell as any sort of place'. *Martin Luther: The Christian between God and Death* (Cambridge, MA, 1999), pp. xiii-xiv. I myself would query that final statement in particular – and, indeed, this book has been criticized for the extent to which it reflects its author's own preoccupations. Heiko Oberman has been its fiercest critic; for a (relatively temperate, in this case) statement of his reaction see his review in *The Historian*, 62/4 (2000), 926-7. 'Throughout the study, passages by Martin Luther are cited not to highlight the reformer's ideas but merely to illustrate the strong views of the author... Basically, Luther is presented – and condemned – as a late-medieval fundamentalist, but then as one who was no longer certain of his cause. The reformer is driven by a "fury," which is traced to a deep-seated doubt about the existence of God coupled with the growing awareness that death spells the end – the future is empty and the Resurrection a false hope' (p. 926). Unfortunately, Oberman's own masterful biography, *Luther: Man between God and the Devil* (New Haven, 1989), offers no substantive comment on Luther's views on hell.

[5] *Luther's Works*, vol. 19: *Lectures on the Minor Prophets, II: Jonah, Habakkuk*, ed. Jaroslav Pelikan (St Louis, MO, 1974), p. 74. The German version of the Jonah commentary was published in 1526.

to prioritize hellish fears and feelings in people's minds, in the present life. Luther goes on to admit uncertainty about 'what hell is like before the Day of Judgment. The notion that hell is a specific place, now tenanted by the souls of the damned, as artists portray it and the belly servers preach it, I consider of no value'. However, he continues, things will be very different following the Last Judgment, for 'Then hell will be a particular place and the abode of those consigned to it and the eternal wrath of God'. This entire discussion seems to indicate a belief that, until that major historical event occurs, hell will neither function as popularly expected – indeed, the devils are not yet in position! – nor occupy a specific position until the end of the present world. But what of the scriptural statements that 'many saints went down to hell', as Jonah does here?[6] Also, at Genesis xxxvii.35 Jacob laments, 'I shall go down to Sheol to my son, mourning'. Luther states that 'Scripture uses the word "Sheol" graphically to describe the anxiety and the agony of the dying. It adapts itself to their mood and feelings'. In other words, we are not dealing with literal statement in such passages, but rather with metaphorical expression of moods and feelings.

Calvin was more explicit.[7] In his *Institutes* he asserts that, since ordinary language 'cannot describe the severity of the divine vengeance on the reprobate, their pains and torments are figured to us by corporeal things, such as darkness, wailing and gnashing of teeth, inextinguishable fire, the ever-gnawing worm'.[8] He is 'certain that by such modes of expression the Holy Spirit designed to impress all our senses with dread' – in short, we are faced with figurative discourse which enlists material likenesses rather than with literal discourse which denotes material things.[9] Elsewhere, in his commentary on a Gospel harmony, Calvin addresses the same issue as follows:

---

[6] 'Out of the belly of hell cried I'; Jonah ii.2 in the Geneva and King James Bibles.

[7] The most thorough discussion of his relevant views remains Heinrich Quistorp, *Calvin's Doctrine of the Last Things*, trans. Harold Knight (London, 1955).

[8] Matthew viii.12; xxii.13; Mark ix.43; Isaiah lxvi.24.

[9] *Institutes of the Christian Religion* (1559), iii, 25.12, trans. Beveridge, p. 275.

> Many persons, I am aware, have entered into ingenious debates about the eternal fire, by which the wicked will be tormented after the judgment. But we may conclude from many passages of Scripture, that it is a metaphorical expression. For, if we must believe that it is real, or what they call material fire, we must also believe that the *brimstone* and the *fan* are material, both of them being mentioned by Isaiah. 'For Tophet[10] is ordained of old; the pile thereof is fire and much wood; the breath of the Lord, like a stream of brimstone, doth kindle it' (Isa[aih] xxx. 33). We must explain the *fire* in the same manner as the *worm* (Mark viii.44, 46, 48): and if it is universally agreed that the worm is a metaphorical term, we must form the same opinion as to the *fire*. Let us lay aside the speculations, by which foolish men weary themselves to no purpose, and satisfy ourselves with believing that these forms of speech denote, in a manner suited to our feeble capacity, a dreadful torment, which no man can now comprehend, and no language can express.[11]

Here the metaphorical nature of references to the 'worm' becomes the basis of an argument in favour of the metaphorical nature of references to 'fire' – 'we must form the same opinion'. The late-medieval consensus that the worm was metaphorical while the fire was material, is here dissolved. When the vast dogmatic structure of purgatorial pain and purgation, along with its elaborate encrustations of suffrages, indulgences, and the prayers and proxy sufferings of holy women, etc., was dismantled, scriptural discourse concerning hell itself was exposed to rigorous scrutiny.[12] That protective carapace having been shattered, the

---

[10] This was the place in Jerusalem where the gods Moloch and Baal were worshipped through the human sacrifice of children by burning them alive. With good reason, then, in Christianity 'Tophet' became a synonym for hell.

[11] *Commentary on a Harmony of the Evangelists, Matthew, Mark, and Luke*, trans. William Pringle, 3 vols (Edinburgh, 1845), I, 200-1. The italics are in the original; I have modernized the punctuation.

[12] Tarald Rasmussen has expressed a similar thought by asking if hell was in fact 'disarmed' in Reformation theology. His answer is that it was certainly 'not an important theme', and 'supposed to be a reality to be feared less than before', due to confidence in the 'external powers' of the Gospel and the sacraments, and the conviction that 'God alone makes the decision about

ontological domain was threatened with total occupation by metaphor.[13]

But not everyone agreed with this new 'metaphorical turn'[14] in scriptural exegesis relating to the next world.

> who will go there, and human beings should not try to find out too much about such things'. 'Hell disarmed? The function of hell in Reformation spirituality', *Numen*, 56, no. 2/3 (2009), 366-84 (pp. 366-7, 375). Peter Marshall has noted the reduced importance of hell in early Protestantism. While entering the caveat that it is 'certainly premature to speak of a "decline of hell"' in the Jacobean period, he emphasizes the fact that 'orthodox Protestantism clearly struggled to reconcile its conception of God's mercy with its insistence on God's justice'. *Beliefs and the Dead in Reformation England*, p. 202. Among the discussions of relevant doctrinal developments in the seventeenth century and beyond I have found particularly helpful John Casey's chapter on 'The decline of hell' in his *After Lives*, pp. 193-222, and Walker's *The Decline of Hell*, which includes evidence of the concern of seventeenth-century moralists that decline in the fear of hell was responsible for an increase in impiety and immorality (pp. 3, 5f.). 'It was a standard reproach to suggest that debauchees eagerly welcomed' any scheme to diminish 'the deterrent force of the orthodox hell' (p. 69).

[13] Cf. Peter Marshall's remark that some Jacobean 'authors insisted that the scriptural language of retribution – fire, brimstone, darkness, the worm that never dies – was to be understood figuratively'. However, he goes on to say that while 'in the Jacobean Church opinions differed over whether hellfire was best understood as a spiritual, corporal, or material fire', there was 'a general agreement that it was no mere allegory. Orthodox opinion held that it was the loss of the Beatific Vision that was the greatest punishment of hell, but it was the intensity, and particularly the eternity, of hellish pains that brought forth the most arresting images...'. *Beliefs and the Dead in Reformation England*, p. 191. Whatever Luther and Calvin may have said in their cerebral speculations, such perceptions persisted. This is brought out well in Tessa Watt's account of atavistic descriptions of hell in ballads and chapbooks; *Cheap Print and Popular Piety 1550-1640* (Cambridge, 1991), pp. 110-12, 171, 238-9, 312.

[14] This 'turn' manifests itself in many other areas of reformist theology, particularly within the controversy concerning whether the language used by Christ at his institution of the sacrament of the Eucharist should be understood literally or metaphorically. The Swiss Reformer Ulrich Zwingli (d. 1531) argued that Christ's words 'This is my body' should be taken metaphorically, with the sacramental rite being performed simply in memory of the Last Supper shared by Christ and his disciples. Here he parted company with Luther who, while rejecting the Catholic doctrine of

I must freely confess that I cannot see any manner of reason, why we should not suppose that the fire of Hell will not be a real and material, but only a metaphorical and figurative, fire.[15]

Thus the Anglican divine Sir William Dawes (1671-1724), a great favourite of Queen Anne's, who appointed him as Archbishop of York in 1714 – a passage which illustrates the fact that, in some instances and places, belief in the materiality of hell-fire survived the Reformation, and decades of doctrinal dispute within and outside Protestantism. Dawes proceeds to highlight what he identifies as metaphorical biblical references to the worm of conscience, as representing another terrible type of torment. Elsewhere, in a sermon on Proverbs xviii.14 ('A wounded Conscience who can bear?'), he affirms that no affliction is comparable to 'the sting and smart' of a 'wounded Conscience', the

---

transubstantiation, continued to believe that Christ was in some way physically present in the bread and wine; thus Christ's words 'this is my body' are understood in their literal sense (this being the doctrine sometimes designated – quite controversially – as consubstantiation). For Calvin, with Zwingli and against Luther, the real presence of Christ comes through the Holy Spirit and is no material matter. These issues are far beyond the scope of the present essay. A good way into them is provided by Richard C. Gamble, 'Calvin's controversies', in *The Cambridge Companion to John Calvin*, ed. Donald K. McKim (Cambridge, 2004), pp. 188-204 (pp. 193-6).

[15] William Dawes, *Sermons preach'd upon several occasions before King William and Queen Anne* (London, 1709), pp. 58-9. Dawes was, to be sure, not alone in his resistance to metaphorical interpretation. Many low-churchmen held similar views, excellent examples being found in statements by the Presbyterian minister Christopher Love (1618-51) and (to move ahead in time) the Baptist preacher Charles Haddon Spurgeon (1834-92). See Casey, *After Lives*, 201-4, 208-11. The Italian preachers and polemicists quoted by Piero Camporesi were also heavily invested in the material horrors of hell-fire – indeed, from the perspective of his Counter-Reformation sources, he claims that 'over no other age did hell exert such an attraction and repulsion, and in so spasmodic and obsessive a fashion as the seventeenth century'. *The Fear of Hell: Images of Damnation and Salvation in Early Modern Europe*, trans. Lucinda Byatt (Cambridge and Melford, MA, 1990, rpt. 2020), p. 28.

'Pains and Terrors of which are 'insupportable'.[16] Here Dawes has, as Scott Bruce puts it, 'demoted' the material torments of hell in order 'to emphasize the interior Hell of the wounded conscience',[17] a move in accord with the statements of Luther and Calvin quoted above. However, in the process Dawes has not 'demoted' the material torments of hell-fire. Quite the contrary.

Dawes' older contemporary, Tobias Swinden (1659-1719), rector of Cuxton, Kent, wrote a much longer defence of the materiality of the infernal fire, maintaining that the torments of hell are eternal and it has an actual location. Which is: the sun! In his *Enquiry into the Nature and Place of Hell* (1714, second edition 1727)[18] Swinden confronts, with some vigour, the notion that the 'unquenchable fire' alluded to at Mark ix.43-4 (cf. Vulgate ix.42-3) is 'only *metaphorically* spoken, to denote that grievous Burning and Anxiety of Mind, which doth torment the Souls of the Wicked, for the Sins they have committed in this Life, and because they are excluded from *God's* Presence'.[19] (The reference to exclusion from God's presence is, of course, reminiscent of Luther and Calvin.) 'To multiply Figures in the divine Writings, and to allegorize away the Text when there is no necessity for it, is unreasonable', he declares. We should take the repeated description of hell in Mark's gospel 'out of the Metaphor in which they are pleased to clothe it, and put it into plain Language'.[20] Plain language which, he believes, denotes the flames of hell as flourishing on the sun. We are invited to consider Christ's words on

---

[16] Dawes, *Sermons preach'd upon several occasions*, p. 14; cf. the table of contents.
[17] *The Penguin Book of Hell*, ed. Bruce, p. 171.
[18] This book enjoyed considerable success, French and German translations being published, perhaps in some measure due to the way it melded biblical testimony concerning the afterlife with the Copernican theory of the universe.
[19] *An Enquiry into the Nature and Place of Hell*, 2nd edn (London, 1727), pp. 43-4. The italics and capitalization are in the original; I have lightly modernized the punctuation.
[20] Ibid., p. 44.

Judgment Day, when he passes sentence on the wicked, telling them to depart into everlasting fire (Matt. xxv.41).[21]

> ... the sentence of a Judge cannot well be supposed to be wrapt up and delivered in Figures and Parables, especially at that time when Allegories must cease, and all dark and obscure, both Things and Words too, must be laid open to Light. ... The Use then of Parables or Allegories (for they are both one) is to hide the Meaning of the Speaker, and to darken the Understanding of the Hearer: But the last Judgment of Christ is to a quite contrary End, *viz.* That the whole World may not only hear it with their Ears, but understand it too with their Hearts, and see it executed with their Eyes. It is evident therefore, that the general and final Sentence, by which the Wicked shall be adjudged to *everlasting Fire*, must have in it no Figures or Allegories, but plain and proper Speech only....[22]

So, then, there is no place for figures, parables, allegories, and hence metaphor, on that momentous occasion – as the old world ends, plain language shall rule and hell-fire shall be revealed in all its horrific materiality. Which, he argues, we are able to deduce even now, led by reason and the literal testimony of Scripture.

> Why ... must these Truths be exploded as gross Imaginations, since they are delivered in the Scriptures, and received by the Church of God? ... Let us not spiritualize away the substantial Flames of *Hell*, and refine them into nothing. ... Will we confine the infinite Power of *God* to the scanty Laws of Nature, or to the more scanty Measures of our shallow Understandings?[23]

---

[21] Ibid., p. 48.
[22] Ibid., pp. 48-50.
[23] Ibid., pp. 70-1.

Swinden offers an ingenious (if quite verbose) demonstration of the improbability of hell-fire's being in 'the Bowels of the Earth' (as per the late-medieval doctrine), drawing on contemporary Copernican science, theologians ancient and modern, and the classical poets. Corporeal fire requires a lot of fuel to feed upon, likewise air to sustain and preserve it, and since 'a sufficient Quantity of either of these cannot reasonably be supposed to be about the Center of the Earth', he concludes that 'Hell cannot rationally be thought to be placed there'.[24] The earth's mightiest volcanoes, 'the Ætnas and Vesuvios', are 'mere Glow-worms' as compared to the sun![25] The body of which is fire, that being as evident as the fact that it shines; 'It is as demonstratively the Fountain of Heat as of Light'.[26] If those

> who suppose only a Metaphorical Hell, do it for this Reason, that they cannot conceive where such a material Fire should be, as is sufficient for so great a Work; let them but look on this, and they will see an Object adequate at least to, if not exceeding, the very utmost Stretch of their Imagination.[27]

Working against the tendency of Luther and Calvin to deny hell its location and full operation until the end of the world,[28] Swinden

---

[24] Ibid., p. 81.
[25] Ibid., p. 137.
[26] Ibid., pp. 133-4.
[27] Ibid., p. 137.
[28] Luther seems to have believed that, after death, the soul entered a deep sleep, from which it awakened at the Resurrection, to be judged. Calvin's view was similar, but he seems to have rejected the idea of total sleep, in the sense of unconsciousness. Fellowship with Christ cannot be suspended, however temporarily: 'To have fallen asleep with Christ means to remain in communion with Christ in death ...'. Quistorp, *Calvin's Doctrine of the Last Things*, p. 74. As Quistorp neatly sums up the idea, 'man's soul ... does not perish nor sleep in death but in so far as it is born again in Christ already enjoys heavenly peace in the expectation of the resurrection of the body, which will bring it consummate blessedness; but the souls of the impious will be held imprisoned in terrible expectation of their final condemnation' (p. 81). The 'rest' of the soul in the interval between death and Final Judgment

identifies the sun as a *local* hell, ready to receive damned souls right now. 'Men are in a suffering Condition presently after their Souls quit this mortal Station', he affirms, as 'our Saviour plainly telleth us in the 16th Chapter of St. *Luke*'s Gospel', where he 'representeth the State of the Dead, in Dives giving us an Instance of the wicked Man's Punishment in the Flames of Hell, and that immediately after his Death, whilst his Kinsfolk were alive, and might be warned from coming into that *Place of Torment*'.

> 'Tis true, this is a Parable, but certainly our Saviour would never deliver his Doctrine of the State of the Dead (which he purposely there doth) quite different from, if not contrary to that which in truth and reality it is.[29]

Furthermore, the sun is here for all eternity, enduring when 'the glorious Frame of this visible World shall be destroyed, and all the intermediate Orbs and Bodies in them shall be annihilated, so that Heaven and Hell

> 'consists in peace of conscience'. Its 'blessedness' is 'the awareness of reconciliation with God through faith, bringing peace to the conscience here and now', but only after death – when the flesh is slain and the spirit fully vivified – can the conscience rest and its security be completed. The soul is progressively transformed into the image of Christ, with consummation achieved at the Resurrection. Conversely, 'the souls of the reprobate ... are held prisoner and fearfully await the torments of eternal damnation' (pp. 79-84, 92). There is no rest, so to speak, for the wicked. In sum, Calvin's statements – masterfully pieced together by Quistorp – seem to intimate a doctrine of provisional blessedness and damnation respectively. See further the summary statement by Bruce Gordon, *Calvin* (New Haven, CT, 2009), p. 336.

[29] *An Enquiry*, p. 253. Earlier (p. 153) Swinden had cited Luke xvi.26 in support of the argument that an immense distance exists between the earth and hell, and this criterion is well met by the distance between the earth and the sun: 'For in the Parable the rich Man being tormented in Hell, lifted up his Eyes, and saw Abraham afar off. And Abraham afterwards told Dives, that between the two Places where they were, there was a mighty Gulph fixed, so that they who would pass from the one to the other could not'. Here, as elsewhere, 'the firm and stedfast Foundation of Scripture itself' allegedly accords with his views.

shall only remain'.[30] Then, and now, this fiery body will provide ample accommodation for all the devils and the 'prodigious Numbers of the damned' who must reside on it[31] – there is no risk of overcrowding, as would be an issue were hell to be located in the centre of the earth.[32] (Heaven does not have this problem, since the number of the blessed is far smaller.)[33] Although they may disagree on the numerical details, philosophers concur that the sun is 'many hundred thousand times ... bigger than the whole Earth' (let alone the earth's bowels), and therefore 'must be acknowledged by all to be capacious enough for that Purpose'.[34] Yet, despite all this evidence, and 'although the Holy Scriptures have plainly enough declared for such a Place', some men have 'chosen rather to expound away the Text, and make Hell a mere putative and phantastick Being, than to acknowledge the Reality of it'![35]

What, then, of that merely 'putative and phantastick Being', the worm? Here its metaphorical nature is assumed to be uncontroversial, and used to assert that, when Scripture talks of fire, it must be speaking in a way *different* from metaphorical expression:

[30] Ibid., p. 168.
[31] Given that the sun is obviously the provider of so many good things for earth-dwellers, Swinden has to engage in elaborate casuistry to explain why it can be the locus of so much evil.
[32] Piero Camporesi, whose overheated rhetoric often rivals that of his Counter-Reformation sources, notes that overcrowding is a regular feature of Baroque hells – and Jesuits, in particular, were zealous in drawing attention to it. *Fear of Hell*, pp. 8-9, 12-13, 30-32, 62, 70, 77, 122.
[33] That said, Bonaventure was able to cite the risk of overcrowding as a reason why animals cannot be resurrected; there simply would be no room for them in the *patria*, given their vast numbers. See Minnis, *From Eden to Eternity*, p. 147.
[34] *An Enquiry*, p. 141. Cf. pp. 89-93.
[35] Ibid., pp. 103-4.

If that late Repentance and Dolor of Mind be sufficiently express'd by the *Worm that dieth not*, to what End is the Addition of *Fire unquenchable*, and *Hell Fire* made, if not to denote something different from the other?[36]

Apparently the worm has fulfilled the metaphor quota, leaving fire to indicate something material. Swinden enlists Prosper of Aquitaine, St Gregory, St Bernard, Isidore and Bede in support of his contention that there is a double punishment in hell, of both body and soul, with the fire being 'a Torment outwardly raging, and the Worm a Grief inwardly accusing'.[37] (At one point he even manages to get Thomas Aquinas onside.)[38] In effect, Swinden is reprising the medieval distinction between

---

[36] Ibid., pp. 43-4.

[37] Ibid., pp. 69-70. Augustine (*De civitate Dei*, xxi, 9) is selectively quoted on the aptitude of certain animals to burn without being consumed and to be in pain without dissolution, 'by the miraculous Appointment of our Almighty Creator'. Swinden's interest in scientific updating does not extend to the issue of precisely how material fire can harm the separated soul; here he is content to fall back upon the wonders of nature and the miraculous powers of God.

[38] This occurs when he remarks that Aquinas, 'although he would be thought not to gainsay it, yet at the same Time shewed himself sufficiently dissatisfied' with the belief that hell is situated beneath the earth, owning himself 'at a Loss' – and, moreover, saying 'He thought no Man in the World would be ever able to tell where it is, excepting by express Revelation from the Spirit of *God*'. *An Enquiry*, pp. 190-1. Actually, here Aquinas was following Augustine, *De civitate Dei*, xv, 16. Cf. *In IV Sent.*, dist. 44, qu. 3, art. 2, qc. 3, co. (which doubtless Swinden read in the version of this *quaestio* included in the *supplementum* to Aquinas's *Summa theologiae*). The twist Swinden's argument takes here is quite ironic, given the fact that Protestant polemic often ridiculed Catholic inability to be precise about the location of hell. For example, Thomas Cranmer exclaims: 'where or what it is, they confess themselves they cannot tell. And of God's word they have nothing to shew, neither where it is, nor what it is, nor that it is. But all is feigned of their own brains, with out authority of scripture'. *Miscellaneous Writings and Letters of Thomas Cranmer, Archbishop of Canterbury, martyr, 1556*, ed. John Edmund Cox, The Parker Society (Cambridge, 1896), p. 181. See further Marshall, *Beliefs and the Dead in Reformation England*, p. 192.

two kinds of torment in hell, the pain of sense and the pain of loss (here seen as a form of 'desire'). Damned souls will be 'gnaw'd upon by the Worm of bitter Remorse, and horrid Despair'.[39] Since they shall be continually 'dying' (so to speak), both in 'sense' and in 'desire',

> it is evident that the Flame must be distinct from the Worm; the Flame by which the Body shall be tortured, and be continually dying in Sense, from the Worm by which the Soul is gnaw'd upon, and continually dying in Desire.

'Unless', Swinden provocatively trumpets, 'we will confound Sense and Desire, and make the Soul and the Body one and the same thing'.

So, then, even the ardent Swinden, passionately committed to ensuring that the substantial flames of hell are not to be 'spiritualized' away, finds a place of value for the metaphorical worm, although in the heat of the moment he can make extraordinarily hyperbolic assertions about not reading Scripture figuratively 'when there is no necessity for it'. Whereas for Calvin metaphorical references to the worm had served to support an argument in favour of fire sharing that linguistic status, for Swinden (as for his fellow high-churchman Sir William Dawes) they served the opposite argument, a sharp difference being declared between two modes of expression, and the materiality of hell-fire maintained.

In summarizing Dawes's beliefs, Scott Bruce has remarked that 'The undying worm of Christian scriptures is no longer a creature that gnaws painfully on the soul but a metaphor for the sinner's eternal remorse';[40] a similar statement could be made about Swinden. It should be acknowledged, however, that within medieval Christianity the worm had long been established as 'a metaphor for the sinner's eternal remorse', and its ability to 'gnaw painfully on the soul' had, as a literal statement, long been rejected by the schoolmen, as we have seen. The force of these ideas may become even clearer if we consider the doctrinal underpinning of many of the statements quoted above concerning the remorse of

---

[39] *An Enquiry*, p. 54.
[40] *The Penguin Book of Hell*, p. 171.

conscience, conscience being the worm-metaphor's most successful tenor and conceptual import in medieval thought (and far beyond). What exactly does it mean in theological parlance, and why should its characteristic activities be seen as resembling those of a worm, particularly the creature infernalized at Isaiah lxvi.24, Judith xvi.21, etc.?

CHAPTER 17

Conscience: the worm-metaphor's greatest tenor

Academic investigation of conscience often focused on its relationship with *synderesis* – a term likely to have been a corruption, perhaps originating with Jerome, of *syneidesis*, the Greek word for conscience;[1] sometimes *conscientia* was identified with *synderesis*, sometimes seen as functioning under its general direction. The term has a complicated history within scholastic philosophy, having a place in discussions of both moral psychology and mystical theology. In the latter context, it designates a spark (*scintilla*), a leap upwards, by which the human soul (as a recipient of special divine grace) travels from this world to unite with God.[2] In medieval moral psychologies, however, it is understood as

---

[1] Cf. Robert Glenn Davis, *The Weight of Love: Affect, Ecstasy, and Union in the Theology of Bonaventure* (New York, 2017), pp. 46-7, and Tobias Hoffmann, 'Conscience and *Synderesis*', in *The Oxford Handbook of Aquinas*, ed. Brian Davies (Oxford, 2012), pp. 255-63 (p. 255). Whereas Bonaventure understands *synderesis* in terms of affect, desire for the moral good, in sharp contrast Aquinas (like Albert the Great before him) assigns a primarily cognitive role to it. Timothy C. Potts has provided a useful introduction to scholastic discussion of the matter, in his *Conscience in Medieval Philosophy* (Cambridge, 1980), which addresses crucial statements by Bonaventure, Albert the Great, and Aquinas, providing useful translations of key passages. The most extensive overview remains Odon Lottin, 'Syndérèse et conscience aux XII et XIII siècles', in *Psychologie et morale aux XIIe et XIIIe siècles*, 6 vols in 8 (Leuven and Gembloux, 1942-60), II/1, 103-349.

[2] As Davis's monograph *The Weight of Love* brings out well, Bonaventure's version of this doctrine is heavily indebted to the Victorine theologian Thomas Gallus. In his *Explanatio* on Pseudo-Dionysius's *Mystical Theology* Gallus identifies the capacity in the human soul for affective union with God as the 'spark of *synderesis*' or *principalis affectio*, this being the highest part of the soul, by which means – and by this means alone – it can achieve union with the divine spirit. On Gallus's apophatic discourse see especially the articles by Declan Lawell: 'Affective Excess', and '*Ne de ineffabili penitus taceamus*: Aspects of the Specialized Vocabulary of the Writings of Thomas Gallus', *Viator*, 40/1 (2009), 151-84. On the influence of Gallus's doctrine

humankind's fundamental grasp of right and wrong, as bestowed upon Adam and Eve at their creation and damaged though not destroyed by the Fall. Aquinas explains the matter as follows:

> Unde et in operibus humanis, ad hoc quod aliqua rectitudo in eis esse possit, oportet esse aliquod principium permanens, quod rectitudinem immutabilem habeat, ad quod omnia humana opera examinentur; ita quod illud principium permanens omni malo resistat, et omni bono assentiat. Et haec est synderesis, cuius officium est remurmurare malo, et inclinare ad bonum ...
> [For probity to be possible in human actions, there must be some permanent principle which has unwavering integrity, in reference to which all human works are examined, so that that permanent principle will resist all evil and assent to all good. This is *synderesis*, whose task it is to warn against evil and incline to good...][3]

Having identified this permanent principle as *synderesis*, Aquinas proceeds to affirm that it is indestructible, with reference to Isaiah lxvi.24, 'Their worm shall not die'. Augustine is (not quite accurately)[4] cited as saying that this refers to the worm of conscience, i.e. remorse of conscience, which 'is caused by *synderesis* protesting against evil'. Conscience can be mistaken, but synderesis is infallible. In certain specific applications of conscience a person's reason may 'not follow the light of *synderesis* in making its choice',[5] but as a habitual light (*lumen habituale*) which belongs to the very nature of the soul 'it is impossible

---

of the penetrating, transcending spark on the Middle English mystical treatise *The Cloud of Unknowing* see Minnis, 'Affection and Imagination'.

[3] *Quaestiones disputatae de veritate*, qu.16, art. 2; *Questiones disputatae de veritate, quaestiones 10-20*, trans. James V. McGlynn (Chicago, 1953), consulted online at https://isidore.co/aquinas/QDdeVer.htm. Cf. Hoffmann, 'Conscience and *synderesis*', pp. 256-7, who notes that Aquinas 'conceives of *synderesis* as habitual knowledge', understanding conscience as 'the act of applying ethical knowledge to a specific case'.

[4] Presumably Aquinas has in mind *De civitate Dei*, xxi, 9, although there the term *conscientia* is not actually used.

[5] *Quaestiones disputatae de veritate*, qu.16, art. 2.

for *synderesis* to be extinguished'. Little wonder, then, that this inextinguishable light could be brought into a symbiotic relationship with the indestructible worm of Isaiah. The transition from *scintilla* to *vermis* was effected with little ado, one metaphor easily being substituted for another.[6] As an abundance of early-medieval treatises and sermons make clear: the metaphor of conscience as a gnawing worm seems to have been consolidated and popularized in the twelfth century, around the same time as purgatory, its hour come at last, was slouching towards Armageddon to be 'born'.[7]

Consequently, the worm was seen not only as an agent of torture in the afterlife but also as a goad to people living in the present life. It was, to use yet another metaphor, bilocated, given residence both in hell (along with purgatory) and in the human heart. This situation is writ large in the testimony of many of the abovementioned *mulieres sanctae*, even as they worked to blur the differences between the two states. A particularly effective dramatization of the worm's role as persistent truth-teller to the soul while it remains in the body is found in Guillaume de

---

[6] This could occur whether the conscience was identified as a faculty or as a habit, deemed cognitive or affective.

[7] To note a few examples: in addition to Hugh of St Victor's *De sacramentis* (quoted in Chapter 3 above), see Pseudo-St Patrick of Ireland, *De tribus habitaculis animae*, 2 (*PL*, LIII, col. 832B-C); Haymo of Halberstadt, *De varietate librorum sive de amore coelestis patriae*, iii, 46 (*PL*, CXVIII, col. 957C-D); Hildebert of Tours, *Sermones de tempore, XX. in quadragesima sermo primus: de poenitentia* (*PL*, CLXXI, col. 430D); Bernard of Clairvaux, *De conversione ad clericos sermo seu liber*, 5 (*PL*, CLXXXII, cols 838C-3B); Adam of Dryburgh, *Sermo xlii: item in die circumcisionis domini* (*PL*, CXCVIII, cols 382D, 387D); Peter Comestor, *Sermo xvi. in hebdomada poenosa* (*PL*, CXCVIII, col. 1766D); Thomas of Perseigne, *In Cantica Canticorum commentarii*, v and 8 (*PL*, CCVI, cols 320B and 561D); Alan of Lille, *De arte praedicatoria*, capi v and xiv (*PL*, CCX, cols 122A and 139C); Sicardus of Cremona, *Mitrale seu de officiis ecclesiasticis summa*, iv, 6 (*PL*, CCXIII, cols 213, 177C); and Pope Innocent III, *De miseria condicionis humane*, iii, 2, ed. Robert E. Lewis (Athens, GA, and London, 1978), pp. 206-9.

Deguileville's *Le Pèlerinage de l'âme* (c. 1355).⁸ At the court of heaven, where the soul of the pilgrim (the poem's protagonist) is being judged, an old and ugly figure appears to accuse him – promptly identified as 'Synderesis' (line 1193) and 'the Worme of Conscience' (following the Middle English translation of 1413 – a fascinating text in its own right, which takes many creative liberties with the original).⁹ This grisly

---

8   *Le Pèlerinage de l'âme*, ed. J. J. Stürzinger, Roxburghe Club (London, 1895). All references are to this edition. Modern research on the Deguileville corpus has been surprisingly sparse, particularly given the popularity it enjoyed in fourteenth-century Europe. For exceptions, and a very recent resurgence of interest, see Susan K. Hagen, *Allegorical Remembrance: A Study of 'The Pilgrimage of the Life of Man' as a Medieval Treatise on Seeing and Remembering* (Athens, GA, and London, 1990); Kinsley Alexander, 'Beauty and the Pilgrim Soul: a study of *Le Pèlerinage de vie humaine* as an allegory of Cistercian aesthetics' (unpub. Ph.D. diss., Boston College, 2007); Sarah Kay, *The Place of Thought*, pp. 70-94; Marco Nievergelt's essays 'Can thought experiments backfire?' and 'From *disputatio* to *predicatio*' together with his monograph *Allegorical Quests from Deguileville to Spenser* (Cambridge, 2012), pp. 23-44; *The Pèlerinage Allegories of Guillaume de Deguileville: Tradition, Authority and Influence*, ed. Marco Nievergelt and Stephanie A. Viereck Gibbs Kamath (Cambridge, 2013); and *Mittelalterliche Literatur als Retextualisierung*, ed. Kablitz and Peters.
9   *The Pilgrimage of the Soul: A Critical Edition of the Middle English Dream Vision*, vol. 1, ed. Rosemarie Potz McGerr (New York, 1990), p. 26. Attributions of this translation to John Lydgate (usually credited with a Middle English verse translation of *Le Pèlerinage de vie humaine*) and Thomas Hoccleve are implausible. In the *Verba translatoris* with which the English work concludes, the anonymous translator complains about his badly-written French exemplar and modestly professes his lack of expertise in that language, then (even more interestingly) remarks that also because 'of somme thinges þat were diffuse and in som place ouerderk' he has 'in dyuers places added and with drawe litel what as me semed needful, no thing chaunging of the processe ne substaunce of the matier, but as it myght be most lusti to the reder or herer of the matier'. He apologizes to that audience for the fact that, in some places, the matter is 'ouer fantastyk, nought grounded nor foundable in holy scripture, ne in doctoures wordes' – but he could not depart from what his author said, 'I myght not go fro myn auctor'. 'The Middle English Pilgrimage of the Soul. An edition of MS. Egerton 615', ed. Merrel D. Clubb (unpub. Ph.D. diss., University of Michigan,

amalgam has a human head, with a mouthful of broken teeth, and a serpent's tail.

> 'Quant je l'apercu et la vi,
> Tresgrandement fu esbai,
> Mesmement car sens corps estoit
> Et sous sa teste rien n'avoit
> Fors une queue seulement
> Qui sembloit estre proprement
> De ver, mes grosse moult estoit
> Et bien grant longueur ell' avoit'. (lines 1209-16)
> ['When I looked at her I was astonished, because she had no body beneath her head but a tail like a worm, long and thick'.][10]

Specifically called a *vielle* (line 1200), the creature has more than a passing resemblance to the Old Woman who features so conspicuously and loudly in Jean de Meun's part of *Le Roman de la Rose*; both figures offer long accounts of past deeds, and the latter manages to include some relatively straightforward moral doctrine amidst her dubious amatory advice.[11] However, of the probity of Deguileville's Synderesis there is no

---

1953), pp. 338-9. I have switched editions because McGerr has not published beyond the first volume of hers.

[10] Trans. Eugene Clasby, *Guillaume de Deguileville, Le Pèlerinage de l'âme / The Pilgrimage of the Soul* (Tempe, AZ, 2017), p. 13. The Middle English translation is more vivid: 'And whanne I hadde aspied h[er], I was ful sore abasshed, for he hadde vpon h[ir]self no flesh at al; ne no body hadde he vndir [t]his hede, but only a tayl, which s[e]mede the tayl of a worme and was despitous of leng[th] and gretnesse'. *Pilgrimage of the Soul*, ed. McGerr, p. 26.

[11] It is generally accepted that the influence of *Le Roman de la Rose* permeates Deguileville's *œuvre*; indeed, at the very beginning of the *Pèlerinage de vie humaine* he says that the beautiful *Rose* set his own vision in motion (9-11). Deguileville scholarship has tended to read that 'biau' ironically, with Deguileville setting out to provide a moral counterblast to a deeply suspect poem which celebrates carnal love. The matter is more complicated than that, however, because some of the *Rose*'s most sophisticated medieval readers praised it as a rigorous satire and commended Jean de Meun as a lofty

doubt. I am not accustomed to tell lies or fables, it declares, for 'in alle places I am byleued of trouthe' (to draw on the dynamic Middle English). Having accompanied the pilgrim since he was old enough to make moral choices ('from the firste tyme þat euere þu haddest discrecioun and verrey vnderstondyng'), it has intimate knowledge of his words and deeds.

> 'Jë ai bonne renommee
> Et moult t'ai este privee,
> De tes fautes t'ai avisie
> Souvent par tresgrant charite,
> Pour ce que ton bien vouloie
> Et ton salut pourchacoie.
> Pour tes mefiais et tes mesdis
> T'ai si souvent mors et repris
> Que tous mes dens en sont uses
> Et tous rompus et tous quasses'. (lines 1225-34)
> ['I am well-known and I know all your secrets. I have warned you often, in charity, about your faults because I wished you well and I wanted you to be saved, I have bitten and gnawed you for your misdeeds and sinful words so often that my teeth are all broken and worn down'.][12]

That explains the creature's dental crisis – incessant biting of the pilgrim's hard and obstinate wicked heart has ruined its teeth.

---

philosopher. (In face of strident attacks on the poem by Christine de Pizan and Jean Gerson). An excellent introduction to the fifteenth-century controversy may be found in the texts collected and translated by David F. Hult in *The Debate of the 'Romance of the Rose'* (Chicago, 2010).

[12] Trans. Clasby, p. 13. The Middle English runs: 'And ful priue haue I warned the of thy misgouernaunce as thilke that loueth the, awaytinge thy profite and procurynge thyn hele. I haue ful oftentimes, for thy misdedes and thy misgouernaunce of words and of thoughtes, vndertake the and ful sore biten the, so ferforth þat alle my teeth ben wasted and broken'. *Pilgrimage of the Soul*, ed. McGerr, p. 26.

> Si dur as en tous temps este,
> Et si rebours et obstine
> Que pour mordre ne remordre
> Ne t'ai peu [de] mal destordre,
> Si que drois est que m'en plaigne
> Et quë em portes la paine ... (lines 1235-40)
> ['You have always been so obstinate and contrary and stubborn that I have not hesitated to bite you again and again to turn you away from evil. And it is right that I complain about it and you suffer for it'.]

One might recall the remark which Shakespeare puts into the mouth of his King Richard III, 'My conscience has a thousand several tongues, / And every tongue brings in a several tale'...,[13] tongues having been preferred to teeth as the vehicle to convey incessant morally-justified nagging here.

Synderesis then accuses the pilgrim of having made a misshapen monster of his own soul. Whereupon the two proceed to engage in an exercise in competitive monstrosity, Deguileville's quirky sense of humour here being deployed to good effect. How dare you presume to accuse me, the aggrieved pilgrim exclaims, for I am made in God's image (cf. Genesis i.27, also v.1 and ix.6) while you are a deformed worm! (lines 1295-304).[14] The 'tailed worme' responds, if you had guarded the nobility that God bestowed upon you then, or if, when it became deformed, you had restored it through repentance, then you might well object in that manner. But because you are all deformed and disfigured with many sins and excesses, by the 'shameful thoughts' and 'corrupt desires' that are fully known to me, you are more vile than I. 'Plus vil es que moi!' (lines 1305-29).

---

[13] *Richard III*, act V, scene 3. See further Daniel E. Hughes, 'The "Worm of Conscience" in "Richard III" and "Macbeth"', *The English Journal*, 55/7 (1966), 845-85.

[14] *Pilgrimage of the Soul*, ed. McGerr, p. 28.

'En moi n'a nuls maux amasses,
Nulle repruche de mefi"ait.
Se laide sui, ce m'as tu fait ...' (lines 1330-2)
['There are no evil deeds piled up in me, no guilt for wickedness. If I am ugly, you have made me so...'][15]

One may recall Aquinas's statement, in answer to the question, can synderesis err (*peccare*)?, that this is impossible: it 'never consents to evil, and so never sins'.[16] Of course, men can sin, when they fail to 'follow the light of synderesis' in making their specific moral choices. And Deguileville's pilgrim has made many bad moral choices, much to the distress of Synderesis. By your own wretched misdeeds you have many times troubled and distressed me, it declares, bringing me great heaviness and pain more than a hundred times a week! I have 'used up all my strength and spent all my time on you, with no thanks at all from you' (lines 1332-40). At this point Synderesis, a personification of a 'permanent principle which has unwavering integrity', reveals 'her' intimate knowledge of the pilgrim's behaviour, working hard to 'warn against evil and incline to good'.[17]

Here I have brought together material from two sections of Deguileville's psychomachia, lines 1191-266 and 1295-344, because they form a coherent and consistent presentation of Synderesis as the intimate and private moral arbiter of the soul of this representative human, a long-

---

[15] Trans, Clasby, p. 14. Cf. the Middle English: 'For in me is ther no maner euel but that thyself hast caused. 3if I am foule, that hast thou made thyself ...'. *Pilgrimage of the Soul*, ed. McGerr, p. 28,
[16] *Quaestiones disputatae de veritate*, qu. 16, art. 2, resp.
[17] This view of conscience has obvious similarities with the way in which the principle features in *Piers Plowman*, a poem generally believed to be indebted to the Deguileville corpus – though Langland's writing is (notoriously) good at covering the tracks of its sources. However, Langland's personified Conscience (a creation imagistically quite different from Deguileville's gummy crone) goes far beyond its origins in faculty psychology to become an invariably wise yet dynamic and evolving character in its own right, as has been brought out by Sarah Wood, *Conscience and the Composition of 'Piers Plowman'* (Oxford, 2012).

term function which puts it in pole position for its present task, as the pilgrim's accuser at the court of heaven.[18] (Romans ii.15-16 may be recalled here, where St Paul speaks of conscience 'bearing witness ... In the day when God shall judge the secrets of men by Jesus Christ'.) The devil eagerly records this testimony, though the poem tells us only part of it, explaining that the full account is far too long to repeat. This transition from the one role to the other is (fairly) seamless, marking the fact that Synderesis's ultimate loyalty is to God rather than the pilgrim; if yet another role is assumed, as tormentor of the sinful soul in (at best) purgatory or (at worst) hell, Deguileville does not develop that idea later in this poem.

However, in lines 1267-94 a strikingly different image of the vocal *ver* is enclosed; the consequences of the creature's theological bilocation are manifest as its iteration grows in complexity. In a dramatic moment, Synderesis specifically identifies 'herself' as the worm of conscience, bred and nourished within the pilgrim's heart, which must be beaten with the mallet of contrition. Here Deguileville refers to a point far back in his series of pilgrimage poems (requiring quite a feat of recollection or reading-back on the reader's part), to the scene in *Le Pèlerinage de vie humaine* when Lady Penance advocates breaking with the hammer of contrition the vessel which contains all the sins within one's conscience. In this vessel a worm – the worm of conscience – is engendered, which can do great damage if it is not slain with that hammer (lines 2123-86).[19] Here we encounter a creature which preys on rather than serves its master, violently biting him unless Penance unsparingly strikes and breaks the receptacle of sin in which conscience itself resides. Returning to the *Le Pèlerinage de l'âme*: here that worm is given a voice, and we hear it advocating its own demise, complaining that the pilgrim has not beaten its 'venymous tayle' as he should. Now it is that tail which is to be hammered, rather than the worm's dwelling-place, the receptacle of sin.

---

[18] Synderesis's role as accuser in *Le Pèlerinage de l'âme* is emphasized by Gustav Zamore in the final chapter of his thesis, 'The term "synderesis" and its transformations: a conceptual history of *synderesis, ca.* 1150-1450' (unpub. D.Phil. diss., University of Oxford, 2016).

[19] Here I return to Stürzinger's edition of *Le Pèlerinage de vie humaine*.

Here Deguileville may have had in mind the idiom of Genesis iii.15, where God says to the serpent who has led Eve to eat the forbidden fruit, 'I will put enmities between thee and the woman, and thy seed and her seed: she shall crush thy head, and thou shalt lie in wait for her heel'. As traditionally interpreted, 'her seed' refers to Christ, the descendant of Eve in respect of His human nature, who shall crush the head of the serpent, the devil – a fate which he can assuredly expect. Deguileville's pilgrim has sinned in failing to take part in this bruising and beating of the serpent. What is different here, of course, is the fact that Synderesis actually *wants* to be beaten violently, in a seemingly masochistic twist: 'I never complain if I am struck and killed with the mallet' (lines 1281-6).

Put into context, this seems a poor reward for a creature which, as a descendant of Augustine's worm of anguish (*verme moeroris*) and Hugh of St Victor's 'accuser within' (*intus accusatrix*), has done its best to bring the pilgrim to repentance and salvation. Indeed, the grotesque ugliness visited upon 'her' seems far more appropriate in the cases of the many vices who get similar treatment – Deguileville's personification policy appears rather indiscriminate.[20] The venom which Synderesis emits issues

---

[20] Deguileville's unrelenting insistence on old age as a marker of spiritual deformity is remarkable. C. S. Lewis, who was repelled by this and other aspects of the poet's 'nightmare shapes', critiqued his treatment of the Seven Deadly Sins as a 'chorus of witches – aged, obscene shape, all female and all monstrous'. For Lewis the *Pèlerinage de vie humaine* (as translated by John Lydgate) is an 'unrelieved picture of evil, of bewildered degradation, of nausea', 'unpleasant to read, not only because of its monstrous length and imperfect art, but because of the repellent and suffocating nature of its content'. *The Allegory of Love: A Study in Medieval Tradition* (Oxford, rpt. 1968), pp. 270-1. The 'monstrosities' created by this 'fierce and gloomy' man give allegory a bad name – little wonder, Lewis declares, that in the 'past century of criticism' the form could be denigrated as a 'mere disease of literature' (pp. 268-70). Kinsley Alexander has pushed back against this, arguing persuasively that Deguileville is vigorously pursuing a Cistercian aesthetic; far from being 'a dark and monstrous mistake', the poem 'abounds in references to art and beauty, and the dialogue continually returns to a discussion of their complex nature and design'. 'Beauty and the Pilgrim Soul', pp. 2-3. She sees *Le Pèlerinage de l'âme* as Deguileville's effort 'to counter the materialism' of the *Roman de la Rose* and of 'the new scientific

from the pilgrim's sins and is not of its own making: *in ea peccatum esse non potest*, to echo Aquinas.[21] But this transition is explicable in terms of the associational procedure which characterizes monkish meditational technique, sudden leaps from one application of a capacious image to another being commonplace. And perhaps the ubiquitous notion of the worm as a denizen of hell[22] *has*, in some measure, influenced the imagery here — for later in *Le Pèlerinage de l'âme* Deguileville describes how the lecherous are surrounded by 'toads and snakes and other noxious vermin' that bite them (lines 5416-20). Besides, it is hard to envisage a benevolent worm or serpent; Mechthild of Hackeborn's loyal doggy worm is quite the exception.

At any rate, Deguileville does effectively drive home his crucial point: the size of the worm's tail is the direct consequence of the pilgrim's actions (or rather, the lack of decisive remedial action). As his sins have grown hugely, become gross, so has the worm's tail; had he controlled his behaviour, such monstrous increase could not have occurred, for by nature nothing can grow beyond measure in a confined space.

> 'Grant queue et grosse ai maintenant,
> Bien le saras, et bien poingnant.
> Ta conscience large et grant
> L'a fait et laissie(e) croistre tant;
> Se plus estroicte ell' eust este,
> Tel grandeur n'eust pas aequeste.
> En lien estroit par nature
> Ne croist rien sus la mesure'. (lines 1287-95)

---

scholasticism' by 'turning their principles upside down and exposing their weaknesses and fallacies' (p. 367).

[21] *Quaestiones disputatae de veritate*, qu. 16, art. 2, resp.
[22] Or, to be more precise in this case, a creature which, because of its incessant gnawing in this present life, anticipates its role as a tormentor in the next life.

['I have a great fat tail now, you know, and it is sharply pointed. Your conscience made it grow and increase. If your conscience had been stricter it would not have grown so large, for in a confined space nothing may, by nature, increase beyond measure'.][23]

That 'sharp point' seems to indicate that the tail itself has become an agent of torment within the human body which has unwittingly become its host, as it grows like some gross tapeworm, thus adding to the pain caused by the head's teeth – seemingly as hard as iron in *Le Pèlerinage de vie humaine* (lines 2161-5), now worn down and broken in *Le Pèlerinage de l'âme*.

For a moment, Deguileville's interest in elaborating the significance of the worm's tail seems to rival Mechthild of Hackeborn's. But only for a moment. Soon he returns to the narrative of Synderesis as the pilgrim's inner remorse, speaking truth to power and ultimately answering to the highest power of all. Subsequently the poet's heavily Augustinian theory of the powers of the soul becomes apparent, as he follows the saint's Trinitarian division of memory, intellect and will (see especially lines 6948-64), the same division which was deployed at *Purgatorio* XXV, 83-4.[24] It seems that the pilgrim's (temporarily but representatively) disembodied soul retains the powers of imagination, reason, and

---

[23] Trans. Clasby, p. 13. Cf. once again the Middle English: 'And that shalt thou knowe hereafter, for sykyrly thou hast made thy conscience to large þat nedes muste this worme woxe therafter. And ȝif thy conscience hadde be more streite, þis tayle ne shulde not have ben so ouerwoxen. For in a place streite, of nature may nothing ouerpasse mesure in wexing'. *Pilgrimage of the Soul*, ed. McGerr, p. 27.

[24] Particularly interesting is the fact that, when the anonymous Middle English translator sought to clarify 'somme thinges þat were diffuse and in som place ouerderk' in *Le Pèlerinage de l'âme*, one of the sources he turned to was *De spiritu et anima*. At the same point he also names an authentic work by Augustine, *De duabus animabus*, wherein the unity of the human soul is defended against the Manichaeans, who had argued that it consisted of two co-eternal parts, one part being of God, the other of the flesh and from the race of darkness. 'The Middle English Pilgrimage of the Soul', ed. Clubb, pp. 235, 339.

memory. Deguileville has rightly been called 'an Augustinian and Cistercian warrior in an Aristotelian universe'.[25]

Le Pèlerinage de l'âme vividly illustrates, in the case of the worm of conscience, the potency of the alliance between vehicle or pictorial envelope and tenor or conceptual import. In the Protestant Reformation that import came to enjoy a more central position within both academic theology and popular devotion. Inner remorse became a dominant feature of religious interiority; the gnawing worm was firmly located within the human heart, mind, and/or soul. Without the protective carapace of saintly intervention and prayerful intercession, conscience took on a new significance as the mental means through which God worked his will in men. In his *The Whole Treatise of the Cases of Conscience*, William Perkins (1558–1602), 'the prince of puritan theologians and the most eagerly read',[26] complains about how papists teach that their priests are appointed by Christ as judges of cases of conscience, 'hauing in their owne hands a iudicarie power and authoritie, truly and properly to binde or to loose,[27] to remitte or to retaine sinnes, to open or to shut the kingdome of heauen'. This, Perkins argues, is quite opposed to what the Scriptures actually say: 'Christ onely hath the keyes of Dauid, which properly and truly openeth, and no man shutteth, and properly and truly shutteth, and no man openeth'.[28] The individual faces God alone, whose power is singular and total. Only when the conscience is brought into full conformity with the divine word, can true spiritual understanding, genuine godliness, occur. As Calvin put it when expounding Romans xiv.23, 'every work, however splendid and excellent in appearance, is counted as sin, except it be founded on a right

---

[25] Alexander, 'Beauty and the Pilgrim Soul', p. 33. Referring especially to *De trinitate*, Sarah Kay discusses Deguileville's debt to Augustinian thought in *Le Pèlerinage de vie humaine* in her *The Place of Thought*, pp. 73-4, 83, 87, 88, 90-4.

[26] According to Patrick Collinson, *The Elizabethan Puritan Movement* (Berkeley, CA, 1967), p. 125.

[27] Cf. Matthew xvi.19.

[28] *The Whole Treatise of the Cases of Conscience* (Cambridge, 1606), unpag.

conscience; for God regards not the outward display, but the inward obedience of the heart, by this alone is an estimate made of our works'.[29]

So complex and multifarious were the actions of conscience that it became difficult, if not impossible, to pin down literally. Abraham Stoll has drawn attention to the 'seemingly endless recourse to metaphor' which marks 'early modern discussions of conscience'; theologians frequently turned to 'the dynamic and imaginative realms of figurative language', reached 'for the tools of poetry'.[30] The worm metaphor was a tool continually reached for, as the iterations by Sir William Dawes and Tobias Swinden have already made clear. William Perkins, affirming that 'conscience is appointed of God to declare and put in execution his just judgment against sinners', goes on to describe persons who act against conscience as having, following the Last Judgment, 'not onely their bodies in torment, but the worme in the soule and conscience shall neuer die: and what will it profit a man to gain the whole world by doing things against his owne conscience, and loose his own soule'.[31] When men's bodies lie dead in the earth,

> there breed certaine wormes in them whereby they are consumed. For of the flesh come the wormes which consume the fleshe: but vnles we take great heed, out of the sins & corruptions of our hearts, there wil breed a worme a thousand folde more terrible, euen the *worme of*

---

[29] John Calvin, *Commentaries on the Epistle of Paul the Apostle to the Romans*, trans. John Owen (Edinburgh, 1849), p. 512. See further Quistorp, *Calvin's Doctrine of the Last Things*, pp. 71, 93, 105; and Meg Lota Brown, 'The politics of conscience in Reformation England', *Renaissance and Reformation / Renaissance et réforme*, n.s. 15/2 (1991), 101-14.

[30] Abraham Stoll, *Conscience in Early Modern English Literature* (Cambridge, 2017), pp. 1-2.

[31] *A discovrse of conscience: wherein is set downe the nature, properties, and differences thereof: as also the way to get and keepe good conscience* (Cambridge, 1596), The Epistle, pages unnumbered. Cf. Mark viii.36.

> *conscience* that neuer dieth, which wil in a lingering maner wast the conscience, the soule, & the whole man, because he shal be always dying & neuer dead.[32]

Conscience is perpetual, bearing witness forever, in this life and continuously through into the next.

> How long conscience beares witnes, it doth it continually; not for a minut, or a day, or a moneth, or a yeare, but for euer: when a man dies, conscience dieth not; when the bodie is rotting in the graue, conscience liueth and is safe and sound: and when we shall rise againe, conscience shall come with vs to the barre of Gods iudgement, either to accuse or excuse vs before God, Rom. 2.15,16. *Their conscience bearing witness at the day when God shall iudge the secrets of men by Iesus Christ.*[33]

Guillaume de Deguileville, creator of a trenchantly witness-bearing Synderesis, would have found nothing to protest against there. But of course, the overall context within which Perkins places his 'worme of conscience' could hardly be more different. For, in *Le Pèlerinage de l'âme*, after the pilgrim's soul is condemned at the court presided over by the archangel St Michael, it is whisked off to sample the pains of purgatory, where its sins must be purged away to render it fit to enter heaven.

No matter what uses that 'phantastick Being', the worm of Old Testament prophecy, was made to serve, or what configurations and shapes its protean body assumed, or whatever thought-system it was obliged to support, it may be recognized and valued as one of the most perpetual of Christian metaphors. And, moreover, one of the most widely-recognized uses of a metaphor. That width of recognition is one obvious reason for its plasticity; perhaps writers felt relatively free in shaping and re-shaping its semantic contours with an imaginative freedom they could not feel in the case of hell-fire, in all its irreducible and uncompromising materiality (setting aside for a moment the

---

[32] Ibid., p. 167.
[33] Ibid., p. 8.

occasional attempts to 'allegorize away the Text when there is no necessity for it', to recall Swinden's thunderous rhetoric).

Perhaps at least one of the secrets of the worm-metaphor's success can be discovered by bringing to bear Conceptual Metaphor Theory (CMT), as defined in contemporary Cognitive Linguistics. Cognitive linguists have taught us to understand 'the term metaphor' as referring 'to a pattern of conceptual association' rather than to a one-off, individual, metaphorical usage or linguistic convention.[34] According to this approach, the specific 'similarity' between the source and target ideas need not be immediately obvious, indeed may be somewhat obscure, but when the underlying conceptual patterns are investigated the associations between the respective conceptual domains can become clearer. In CMT the crucially important object of study is not simply or specifically a 'figurative application of a single term to a new referent' but rather the 'underlying pattern of thought which allows the phrase to have the meaning it does', its place within the 'important elements of conceptual structure and reflections of ways in which humans experience the world'.[35]

The underlying pattern of conceptual association which allows the worm of conscience to have its meaning is a particularly complicated one, featuring a rich array of cross-domain correspondences. In the relevant discourses of medieval theology and devotion, the activities of an actual worm – a creature which bites, gnaws, and causes pain – are 'mapped'[36] onto the domains of: incessant awareness of personal sin, and remorse (what is usually understood by the term 'conscience'); the infliction of pain as justly-deserved punishment by a higher authority (within which lies the associated, or perhaps even parallel, domain of redemptive pain); the body as food for worms (worm-filled cadavers being a common feature of the plastic arts, including tomb sculpture) and hence of little

---

[34] Joseph E. Grady, 'Metaphor', in *The Oxford Handbook of Cognitive Linguistics*, ed. Dirk Geeraerts and Hubert Cuyckens (Oxford, 2007), pp. 188-213.
[35] Grady, 'Metaphor', pp. 189, 191, 192.
[36] Cf. the terminology used by Grady, 'Metaphor', pp. 190-2.

worth as compared to the soul;[37] that same gnawing as mordant yet not consuming, since it must continue for a specific period of time in purgatory and forever in hell, so destruction cannot occur. Then there is the thought that our conceptual worm belongs in two domains in terms of possession, responsibility, and ownership: on the one hand, it relates to the sinner, on whom it inflicts mental pain and seeks to counsel here on earth, while on the other it relates to God, serving as his authorized torturer in this life and in the next. Rich pickings for cognitive linguists; loud resonances for anyone involved in the theory and praxis of theology and morality (whether the latter is centred on religious belief or has a secular basis). This legacy from Old Testament prophets, at once time-worn and time-tested, has proved a gift that has gone on giving.

Here is a compelling example of how the total inadequacy of any attempt to relegate metaphor to the role of gratuitous 'linguistic extra' is revealed by the longevity of so many metaphors, the power they have maintained over the centuries, and their persistence in the face of major cultural and ideological changes.

But what, then, of hell itself in the present age? Piero Camporesi has confidently declared that its drama is over.

> A powerful instrument of conditioning which was continuously perfected and updated over the centuries, the inexhaustible source of anguish and nightmares, is now quietly dissolving in man's conscious and unconscious mind. ... We can now affirm with some justification that hell is finished, that the great theatre of torments is closed for an indeterminate period, and that after almost 2,000 years of horrifying performances the play will not be repeated. The long, triumphal season has come to an end. ... There is no room in the post-modern and post-industrial world for the howling criminal warehouses of hell. They existed for a long time, almost for an

---

[37] Plus, the worm itself was regarded as a product of putrefaction (cf. p. 79 above). While no animal (or plant) life will remain in existence following the end of the present world, the worm's chances of survival were particularly slim, given that no decay can occur in the impassible new heaven and earth.

eternity, while men worked the earth and wondered with anxious curiosity what lurked in the ground beneath their feet. Today the vertical depths of cosmic space have ousted those of the abyss.[38]

In a gentler, and somewhat bemused, manner, the English novelist David Lodge has written,

> At some point in the nineteen-sixties, Hell disappeared. No one could say for certain when this happened. First it was there, then it wasn't. ... Some realized that they had been living for years as though Hell did not exist, without having consciously registered its disappearance. Others realized that they had been behaving, out of habit, as though Hell was still there, though in fact they had ceased to believe in its existence ....[39]

The most influential theologians have continued to believe in its existence whilst redefining its meaning, as when, in 1999, Pope John Paul II said that hell is 'the state of those who definitively reject the Father's mercy'.[40] Holy Scripture used 'a symbolical language' to describe this

---

[38] Camporesi, *Fear of Hell*, pp. vi-vii.

[39] *Souls and Bodies* (London, 1980), p. 113. Lodge, who was raised as a Catholic, goes on to say, 'On the whole, the disappearance of Hell was a great relief, though it brought new problems'. Comparably, Camporesi declares that 'We need to realize once and for all that we have entered a post-infernal age, with all the problems that this change will certainly bring' (*Fear of Hell*, p. vii). See also the remarks in Casey, *After Lives*, pp. 1-10, 403-4.

[40] John Paul II, General Audience, Wednesday 28 July, 1999; consulted at http://www.vatican.va/content/john-paul-ii/en/audiences/1999/documents/hf_jp-ii_aud_28071999.html. Some conservative Catholics, together with some evangelical Protestants, have been unmoved. See the excellent discussion by R. Albert Mohler, 'Modern theology: the disappearance of hell', in *Hell under Fire: Modern Scholarship Reinvents Eternal Punishment*, ed. Christopher W. Morgan and Robert A. Peterson (Grand Rapids, MI, 2004), pp. 15-41. However, Sister Elizabeth Johnson, a professor of theology at Fordham University, responded to the pope's words by saying that for her students it makes more sense to understand that hell 'isn't literal, but that it's a powerful metaphor – and I would say a needed one – to indicate the

'reality', he continues. Imagery presenting it as 'a fiery furnace' must be 'correctly interpreted', as showing 'the complete frustration and emptiness of life without God. Rather than a place, hell indicates the state of those who freely and definitively separate themselves from God, the source of all life and joy'. Reading those words, it is hard not to reach the conclusion that, in the struggle for the rationalization of hellish imaginations, metaphor has proved the clear victor, triumphing over the appeal to materiality.

But hellish reality is ever with us, and during the twentieth century took on an essentially this-worldly rather than other-worldly character. 'If the atrocities of the Holocaust and genocide represented hell on earth, what fear did secular moderns have of a hell to come?'[41] For the devil had been outdone.

seriousness of moral choices, that what we do has consequences and eternal ones'. As quoted by Gustav Niebuhr, 'Hell is getting a makeover from Catholics; Jesuits call it a painful state but not a sulfurous place', *The Guardian* (18 September, 1999), Section B, p. 9. Putting the opposing viewpoint, Camporesi has cited 'some people' as speaking of hell 'unwillingly, somewhat embarrassed, as a worn-out metaphor' (*Fear of Hell*, p. vi).

[41] Mohler, 'Modern theology: the disappearance of Hell', p. 26. 'What World War I did not destroy, World War II took by assault and atrocity. The battlefields of Verdun and Ypres gave way to the ovens of Dachau and Auschwitz as symbols of the century'. Thus the monstrous, insistent problem of evil thrust aside the belief of liberal Victorian theologians in the universal benevolence of God.

Coda: final judgments

This study has offered abundant evidence for the claim that, at the cutting-edge of late-medieval thought, 'Ideas about suffering were used to explain what corporeality could mean'; that it was in pain that 'a theory of explanation for corporeality' was found, a theory which 'changed the way in which the composite [of body and soul] was perceived'.[1] And yet: it could equally well be argued that it was in the investigation of pleasure, as experienced by the blessed both in the present heaven and in the post-resurrection *patria*, that 'a theory of explanation for corporeality' was found, one that was far more crucial in changing the way in which the body-soul composite was perceived. My own recent research on medieval creations of paradise offers much by way of support for that latter argument. But I would contend that the way forward is to investigate the above formulations as being not in competition with each other but rather as constituting a single and unified 'grand narrative' about how the soul can be rewarded and punished both within and without the body. A narrative which, inter alia, generates a symbiotic relationship between metaphor and materiality.

'Despite its suspicion of flesh and lust', Caroline Walker Bynum has claimed, 'Western Christianity did not hate or discount the body. Indeed, person was not person without body, and body was the carrier or the expression ... of what we today call individuality'.[2] This, I believe, is totally and profoundly true.[3] But a major caveat must be entered. To

---

[1] Mowbray, *Pain and Suffering*, p. 144.
[2] Bynum, *Resurrection*, p. 11. The discussion has been advanced by Antonia Fitzpatrick's work; see especially her article 'Mendicant Order politics and the status of Christ's Shed Blood', *Historical Research*, 85, no. 228 (May 2012), 210-27, which contributes significantly to a viable 'bigger picture'.
[3] I fully endorse Bynum's statement, in the new introduction to her 2017 reprint of *Resurrection*, that 'Christian concepts of person before the early modern period were not fundamentally dualist nor did they stereotype body only as negative – that is, as a carapace to be gotten rid of' (p. xvi). Sometimes, however, medieval thought, or at least rhetoric, does pull

push the argument to its ultimate conclusion, the only true and full beneficiaries of this apotheosis of the material are a very select and exclusive group, the community of the blessed. It gets difficult if not impossible to isolate and unqualifiedly celebrate a positive medieval valuation of body (as Bynum tends to do) when faced with the fact that, as far as those excluded from that community are concerned, the body needs to be in good shape specifically so that bad things can happen to it.[4] The wondrous *renovatio* of the human body achieved when the dead arise is a mixed blessing indeed. Here the body is rendered perfect in its physical abilities and sensory capacities, so that the saved may enjoy

alarmingly in that direction, with negative stereotypes of the body taking centre stage. It may be noted that Augustine, that eloquent advocate of the existence of a *similitudo corporis* within the soul, declared that 'the body, simply in virtue of being a body, will always be inferior to the soul'. 'Any soul, however abject, is more excellent than the most excellent body'; 'even a disreputable, sinful soul is nobler than a fine, outstandingly beautiful body'. This, he declares, will be true even when the body is clothed in immortality after the General Resurrection – 'when it has become a spiritual, heavenly body, an angelic body fit for companionship with angels, even then it will not be giving advice to the soul'. Reaching for metaphors based on metals, Augustine explains that even tarnished gold, is better than the purest lead. For tarnished gold is capable of being purified, and therefore is of higher worth, whereas the purest lead is already 'so well purified it is not capable of further improvement'. In sum, 'the soul is better not by its merits but by its nature, and this is true even of a sinful soul'. *In psalmum cxlv enarratio*, 3-4 (n *PL*, XXXVII, cols 1885-6; *Saint Augustine of Hippo, Expositions of the Psalms*, trans. Maria Boulding, 5 vols (New York, 2000-4), V: Psalms 121-50, pp. 402-3). The genre of the medieval body-soul debate affords a particularly fruitful area for investigation of intimations of dualism and reactions against it. For two recent discussions of that genre, which are distinguished by the attention they pay to the issue of the gendering of the soul, see Emily Jean Richards, 'Body-soul debates in English, French and German manuscripts *c.* 1200 - *c.* 1500' (unpub. Ph.d diss., University of York, Centre for Medieval Studies, 2009), and Masha Raskolnikov, *Body against Soul: Gender and Sowlehele in Middle English Allegory* (Columbus, OH, 2009).

4 See Bynum, *Resurrection*, pp. 265-6, and especially the account of Aquinas's views (which here differ from Bonaventure's) provided by Mowbray, *Pain and Suffering*, pp. 148-9.

extremes of pleasure while the damned suffer extremes of pain. Hence Mowbray's dour declaration that, as far as Albert the Great and Thomas Aquinas are concerned, 'a perfectly formed body was required in order for it to suffer the punishments of hell'; 'the body required perfection in order to suffer'.[5] Medieval Western Christianity may not (at an abstract level) have hated the body; rather the contrary seems to be true. But (at a viscerally individual level) the damned hated what their bodies were enabling them to experience; in their situation, person was not person without pain.[6]

That pain, its nature, operation and function, was adumbrated in a rich corpus of scriptural imagery which was interpreted as prophecy of punitive suffering in the afterlife. 'To be a master of metaphor', Aristotle wrote in his *Poetics*, 'is the greatest thing by far', a 'sign of genius'.[7] When thirteenth-century *magistri* sought to master the ingenious metaphors of holy Scripture, they encountered a major hermeneutic challenge in the

[5] Mowbray, *Pain and Suffering*, pp. 147, 149. It should be noted that, while the blessed have certain gifts (*dotes*) or 'dowers' granted to them, the damned have the hellish opposites imposed on them. For discussion see Bynum, *Resurrection*, pp. 131-2, 232, 235-6; Minnis, *From Eden to Eternity*, p. 157-60, 300 note 91. There were different schema. The fullest, seven-fold, one (which is deployed in *The Prick of Conscience*, lines 7873-8643) goes back to Anselm of Canterbury and his circle; see Anselm, *Proslogion*, ch. 25, in *Anselmi opera omnia*, ed. F. S. Schmitt, 6 vols (Edinburgh, 1940-61), I, 118-20, and the *Dicta Anselmi*, ch. 5, ed. R. W. Southern and F. S. Schmitt, *Memorials of St Anselm*, Auctores Britannici Medii Ævi 1 (London, 1969), pp. 127-41.

[6] Hence I have much sympathy with Joseph Canning's remark, included in his review of Donald Mowbray's book, that 'a reader with ordinary human feelings' could well be revolted by 'the inhumanity of the ideas of medieval theologians'; *The English Historical Review*, 126, issue 521 (2011), 911-12. On the other hand, medieval scholasticism did contribute to 'an ideological accommodation of the body in pleasure – or, more accurately, of the full person as experiencing pleasure in which the somatic is honored'; Minnis, *From Eden to Eternity*, p. 241. But what Canning (here professedly stepping outside his professional sphere) calls 'the inhumanity and insensitivity of ecclesiastics' has, on innumerable occasions, been obvious for all to see.

[7] *Poetics*, 22 (1459a5-7); trans. Bywater, in *The Complete Works of* Aristotle, ed. Barnes, II, 2334-5.

shape (or shapes) of hellish imaginations. Their responses offer a quite extraordinary prism through which the scholastic contribution to metaphor-theory may be discerned. This was not a matter of aloof and chilling abstraction (though that did occur in abundance), an unemotional consideration of language use; what was at issue was the nature of punishment in the afterlife, and how it related to pain in the present life. That meant decoding the apparent metaphors in the Bible, and in the final analysis (so to speak) determining how they referred to the End of Days and existence beyond. The stakes could hardly have been higher, and the theory and praxis of metaphor remained persistently and pressingly at the very centre of the hermeneutic enterprise.

Which prompts the speculation, what is the final destiny of metaphor? (Not unduly whimsical, I hope. And in part promoted by Tobias Swinden's animadversion that, at the Final Judgment, Christ will have no use for metaphor.) Resurrected bodies will get back their 'tonge and teeth' (to echo Langland's phrasing), the corporeal instruments which enable speech. The blessed will engage in singing praises of the Lord (or so it was widely believed), and presumably they will enjoy holy conversation concerning matters divine.[8] But will they use metaphorical speech? If God believes in the likes of Vico, Nietzsche, Derrida, Ricoeur, de Man, Lakoff, and Johnson, who hold that language is fundamentally metaphorical, then they will have little choice; that will be their habitual form of discourse. If, on the other hand, Plato,[9] Hobbes, Descartes, Locke and Wittgenstein have the divine ear, then one might envisage blessed conversation resembling the speech of Jonathan Swift's

[8] Given human nature, including glorified human nature, that seems a reasonable expectation. And angels are there to talk to, though they themselves have no need for anything like human language (cf. above, pp. 142-3, particularly note 26), their duty of divine service will ensure that they talk to the blessed, presumably though the assumption of facsimile bodily organs which are necessary for speech.

[9] Plato's position is especially complicated. For, as Mark Johnson points out, his 'critique of imitative poetry has often been read as applying to metaphor generally, despite his supreme use of metaphor to convey most of his philosophical convictions'. 'Introduction' to *Philosophical Perspectives on Metaphor*, ed. Johnson, p. 5.

Houyhnhnms, who are incapable of saying 'the thing which was not'; an Orwellian 'Newspeak' in which 'all ambiguities and shades of meaning' are purged from language, metaphor being rendered obsolete and forbidden.[10]

But it is difficult to believe that God would wish to reduce all the beautiful figurative language in his Book of Life and his liturgy to extreme literalism.[11] To do so would be to withhold a source of pleasure in a place

---

[10] George Orwell, *Nineteen Eighty-Four* (New York, 1949), p. 304.

[11] Of course, the blessed would have no *need* to use metaphorical language, or indeed any spoken language at all, because everything they need to know will be conveyed by divine infusion, thanks to their participation in the Beatific Vision, the ultimate and total source of happiness. But some delight in imaginative and figurative expression may well persist. Further, the body will have returned, with its inner and outer senses functioning to a level far in excess of what is possible in the present world, and engaging in its own epistemological processes – among which one may expect a return to the pleasures of metaphorical and figurative language as experienced nowadays by the embodied soul, though then they will be enjoyed in a more intense form. That much may be speculated. The enigma remains of the extent to which metaphorical discourse – indeed, language at all – might be involved in the soul's participation in the Beatific Vision. As does the question of how angels and demons might regard metaphor: is it an aspect of, or indeed essential to, their mental 'language'? Another strand of the question relating to the relationship between divine power and human creativity has been explored by Rondo Keele, 'Can God make a Picasso? William Ockham and Walter Chatton on divine power and real relations', *Journal of the History of Philosophy*, 45/3(2007), 395–411. Can God make a Picasso painting directly, or can this not be brought about with Picasso himself as an intermediary, a secondary cause? William of Ockham would argue that an omnipotent being can dispense with the agency of any given painter; to argue otherwise would be to impose limits on his power. However, Walter Chatton, a relentless critic of Ockham, would argue in favour of Picasso's indispensability; even God cannot do the impossible. Here Chatton carefully negotiates the 1277 Parisian condemnation of the denial that God can make any thing whatsoever without the aid of another thing. What, then, might the resurrected Picasso get up to? (Here I move beyond Keele's article.) Nothing material, one may well speculate, since paints, canvas etc. will be unavailable in the brave new world. Maybe he will have to be content with mental painting, communicating his masterpieces to other blessed souls (the angels being loftily uninterested) by mental processes.

where all the bodily senses are expected to have their reward.[12] Conversely, anything remotely pleasurable will be denied to the damned, who will suffer 'in þair wyttes fyve' (as *The Prick of Conscience* puts it, line 8152). Normally, seeing is a most pleasant experience, the schoolmen note (citing Aristotle), before going on to declare that this is certainly not the case in hell, where vision induces pain.[13] So, then, evidently any pleasure in language would also be ruled out. Only exclamations of agony and expressions of despair seem appropriate, and since amicability and friendship are impossible in that place,[14] so (it may be inferred) is any verbal exchange of a kind which might promote companionship and solidarity.[15] On this reasoning, metaphor will become the prerogative of the spiritual elite. I have not come across an actual scholastic discussion which treats the issue in so many words. But some *quaestiones* I do know about come close, so here I am extrapolating rather than inventing. Engaging, one might say, in an act of that associative and compositive imagination which in the later Middle Ages was treated with both respect and caution.

---

[12] At least, according to Aquinas. Bonaventure was less confident. See Minnis, *From Eden to Eternity*, pp. 201-2, 207.

[13] Thomas Aquinas, among others, cites Aristotle as saying that the sense of sight is most highly valued, because by it many things are known ('sensus oculorum est maxime diligibilis, eo quod per ipsum plura cognoscimus'), before going on to declare that what is seen in hell is conducive to sorrow rather than happiness. *In IV Sent.*, dist. 50, qu. 2, art. 3, qc. 4, co. The reference is to the *Metaphysics*, i.1 (980a25), where the Philosopher remarks that 'even apart from their usefulness', the senses 'are loved for themselves; above all others is the sense of sight. For not only with a view to action, but even when we are not going to do anything, we prefer sight to almost everything else. The reason is that this, most of all the senses, makes us know and brings to light many differences between things'. Trans. W. D. Ross in *The Complete Works of Aristotle*, ed. Barnes, II, 1553.

[14] For instance, *The Prick of Conscience* is quite clear that shared suffering does not offer a basis for bonding. See especially lines 8400-43 and 8466-81.

[15] Purgatory is different, of course; there some measure of companionship and solidarity is allowed, as already noted.

Coming back to earth: there is talk nowadays of an 'explosion of research on metaphor'[16] which, since the latter part of the twentieth century, has involved linguists, psychologists, cognitive scientists, anthropologists, sociologists and political scientists, along with philosophers. A recently published mass-market book about how metaphor has shaped the way we see the world enthusiastically declares, as if this were a new discovery, that 'metaphorical thinking ... is essential to how we communicate, learn, discover, and invent', and even of crucial importance for stock-market traders, business people, and politicians'.[17] 'New research in the social and cognitive sciences' is making this 'increasingly plain', goes the pitch. However, in the later Middle Ages it was the theologians who were best placed (indeed, exclusively well placed) to make the matter as plain as humanly possible, and to plumb the inquiry to its depths. Even to the very depths of hell.

---

[16] To quote Raymond W. Gibbs, in the introduction to his *Cambridge Handbook of Metaphor and Thought*. 'The incredible rise in the sheer number of scholarly works on metaphor in different academic fields illustrates a heightened sensitivity to metaphor. This increased attention demonstrates how scholars in virtually every discipline (e.g., mathematics, law, music, art) can contribute to understanding the functions and meanings of metaphor. Thus, research on metaphor is now as multidisciplinary, and interdisciplinary, as perhaps any topic being studied in contemporary academia'. 'The state of the art in metaphor studies is a rich, colorful mosaic of ideas and research activities' ('Metaphor and thought: the state of the art', pp. 4, 12). However, as a sign of the times, no chapter in this handbook is devoted to theology, and 'Bible' does not appear in the index. Yet contemporary metaphor theory and Christian mystical expression have many shared underpinnings, some of which are brought out by Rachael Victoria Matthews, 'The mystical utterance and the metaphorical mode in the writings of Marguerite d'Oingt and Marguerite Porete' (unpub. Ph.D. diss., School of Modern Languages and Cultures and the Department of English Studies, Durham University, 2014). Much more remains to be done.

[17] James Geary, *I Is an Other: The Secret Life of Metaphor and How It Shapes the Way We See the World* (New York, 2011); cf. the review by Carlin Romano, 'What's a metaphor for?', *The Chronicle of Higher Education*, 3 July, 2011, at https://www.chronicle.com/article/Whats-a-Metaphor-For-/128079.

BIBLIOGRAPHY

PRIMARY SOURCES

Adam of Dryburgh, *Sermo xlii: item in die circumcisionis domini*, in *PL*, CXCVIII, cols 382-93

Alan of Lille, *Contra hereticos*, in *PL*, CCX, cols 305-430

- , *De arte praedicatoria*, in *PL*, CCX, cols 109-98

Angelic Spirituality: Medieval Perspectives on the Ways of Angels, ed. and trans. Steven Chase (New York and Mahwah, NJ, 2002)

Anonymus Lombardus, *Chiose di Dante le quali fece el figliuolo co le sue mani*, ed. F. P. Luiso, vol. II (Florence, 1904)

Anselm of Canterbury, *Dicta Anselmi*, in *Memorials of St Anselm*, ed. R. W. Southern and F. S. Schmitt, Auctores Britannici Medii Ævi, 1 (London, 1969), pp. 105-95

- , *Opera omnia*, ed. F. S. Schmitt, 6 vols (Edinburgh, 1940-61)

Aquinas, Thomas, *Commentary on the Nicomachean Ethics*, trans. C. I. Litzinger, 2 vols (Chicago, 1964)

- , *Compendium theologiae*, trans. Cyril Vollert (St Louis, MO and London, 1952). At https://www.corpusthomisticum.org/ott101.html

- , *In librum de Anima commentarium*, ed. Angelo M. Pirotta, 2nd edn (Turin, 1936). Trans. Kenelm Foster and Silvester Humphries (New Haven, CT, 1951)

- , *De malo*, ed. and trans. Richard Regan and Brian Davies (Oxford, 2001)

- , *Quaestiones disputatae de anima*, trans. John Patrick Rowan (St Louis, MO and London, 1949); html edition by Joseph Kenny at https://dhspriory.org/thomas/QDdeAnima.htm

– , *Quaestiones disputatae de potentia dei*, ed. and trans. by the English Dominican Fathers (Westminster, MD, 1932, rpt 1952), html edition by Joseph Kenny at https://isidore.co/aquinas/QDdePotentia.htm

– , *Questiones disputatae de veritate, quaestiones 10-20*, trans. James V. McGlynn (Chicago, 1953), at https://dhspriory.org/thomas/ QDdeVer.htm

– , *Summa contra gentiles* (Parma edn), at http://www.corpusthomisticum.org/scg4079.html. Trans. Anton C. Pegis, James F. Anderson, Vernon J. Bourke, and Charles J. O'Neil, at https://isidore.co/aquinas/english/ContraGentiles.htm

Aristotle, *The Complete Works: The Revised Oxford Translation*, ed. Jonathan Barnes, 2 vols (Princeton, NJ, 1995)

Augustine, *De cura pro mortuis*, in *PL*, XL, cols 591-610

– , *De diversis quaestionibus lxxxiii*, in *PL*, XL, cols 11-100

– , *De doctrina christiana*, trans. D. W. Robertson (Indianapolis, IN, 1958; repr. 1980)

– , *Epistola cxviii, ad Dioscurum*, in *PL*, XXXIII, cols 432-49

– , *In psalmum cxlv enarratio*, in *PL*, XXXVII, cols 1884-98. Trans. Maria Boulding, in *Saint Augustine of Hippo, Expositions of the Psalms*, 5 vols (New York, 2000-4), V: Psalms 121-50, pp. 402-3

– , *De trinitate*, in *PL*, cols 819-1098

Bacon, Roger, *Opus maius*, ed. J. H. Bridges, 3 vols (London, 1900)

Bartholomew the Englishman, *De proprietatibus rerum* (Nuremberg, 1519)

Bonaventure, *Breviloquium*, trans. Dominic Monti, Works of St Bonaventure, IX (St Bonaventure, NY, 2005)

The Book of the Knight of La Tour-Landry, ed. Thomas Wright, EETS os 33, rev. edn (London, 1906)

Calvin, John, *Commentaries on the Epistle of Paul the Apostle to the Romans*, tr. John Owen (Edinburgh, 1849)

- , *Commentary on a Harmony of the Evangelists, Matthew, Mark, and Luke*, trans. William Pringle, 3 vols (Edinburgh, 1845)

- , *Institutes of the Christian Religion*, trans. Henry Beveridge, 2 vols in one (Edinburgh, 1845-6)

Catherine of Genoa, *Dialogo spirituale tra anima e corpo; Trattato del purgatorio*, ed. Palmina Trovato (Casale Monferrato, 1999)

Catherine of Siena, *Dialogo*, ed. Matilde Fiorilli, *Libro della divina dottrina: volgarmente detto Dialogo della divina Provvidenza* (Bari, 1912). Trans. Suzanne Noffke, *Catherine of Siena: The Dialogue* (New York and Mahwah, NJ, 2017)

Chartularium Universitatis Parisiensis, ed. Henricus Denifle and Aemilio Chatelain, 4 vols (Paris, 1889-97)

Il codice cassinese della Divina Commedia ... per cura dei monaci benedettini della badia di Monte Cassino (Monte Cassino, 1865)

Comestor, Peter, *Sermo xvi. in hebdomada poenosa*, in *PL*, CXCVIII, cols 1764-8

Cranmer, Thomas, *Miscellaneous Writings and Letters*, ed. John Edmund Cox, The Parker Society (Cambridge, 1896)

Dante Alighieri, *La Commedia secondo l'antica vulgata*, ed. Giorgio Petrocchi, 4 vols, rev. repr. edn (Florence, 1994)

- , *The Divine Comedy*, ed. and trans. Charles S. Singleton, 3 vols, rev. repr. edn (Princeton, NJ, 1977)

- , *The Divine Comedy, vol. 2: Purgatorio*, ed. and trans. Robert M. Durling, with Ronald L. Martinez (Oxford, 2003)

- , *The Divine Comedy, vol. 3: Paradise*, trans. Mark Musa (Harmondsworth, 1986)

Dawes, William, *Sermons preach'd upon several occasions before King William and Queen Anne* (London, 1709)

The Debate of the 'Romance of the Rose', ed. and trans. David F. Hult (Chicago, 2010)

Deguileville, Guillaume de, 'The Middle English *Pilgrimage of the Soul*. An edition of MS. Egerton 615', ed. Merrel D. Clubb (unpub. Ph.D. diss., University of Michigan, 1953)

- , *Le Pèlerinage de l'âme*, ed. J. J. Stürzinger, Roxburghe Club (London, 1895). Trans. Eugene Clasby (Tempe, AZ, 2017)

- , *Le Pèlerinage de vie humaine*, ed. J. J. Stürzinger, Roxburghe Club (London, 1893)

- , *The Pilgrimage of the Soul: A Critical Edition of the Middle English Dream Vision*, vol. 1, ed. Rosemarie Potz McGerr (New York, 1990)

Dionysiaca: recueil donnant l'ensemble des traductions latines des ouvrages attribués au Denys de l'aréopage, ed. P. Chavellier, 2 vols (Paris, 1937)

Dionysius, Pseudo-, *The Complete Works*, trans. Colm Luibheid (New York and Mahwah, NJ, 1987)

Donne, John, *Songs and Sonets*, ed. Theodore Redpath (London, 1967)

Early Dominicans: Selected Writings, trans. Simon Tugwell (New York and Mahwah, NJ, 1982)

Elisabeth of Schönau, *Visiones*, in *Die Visionen der hl. Elisabeth und die Schriften der Aebte Ekbert und Emecho von Schönau*, ed. F. W. E. Roth (Brno, 1884). Trans. Anne L. Clark, *Elisabeth of Schönau: The Complete Works* (New York and Mahwah, NJ, 2000)

Gallus, Thomas, *Explanatio in libros Dionysii*, CCCM 223 (Turnhout, 2011)

Giles of Rome, *Errores philosophorum*, ed. Joseph Koch and English trans. by John O. Riedl (Milwaukee, WI, 1944)

-, *In secundum librum sententiarum quaestiones* (Venice, 1581)

Giovanni da Serravalle, *Translatio et comentum totius libri Dantis Aldigherii*, ed. Marcellino da Civezza and Teofilo Domenichelli (Prati, 1891)

Grammatici latini, ed. Henry Keil, 8 vols (Hildesheim, 1961)

Gregory the Great, *Dialogi*, in *PL*, LXXVII, cols 149-430. Trans. Odo John Zimmerman (Washington, DC, 2002)

-, *Homiliae in Evangelia*, *PL*, LXXVI, cols 1075-312

Grosseteste, Robert, 'Robert Grosseteste's Commentary on the "Celestial Hierarchy" of Pseudo-Dionysius the Areopagite: an edition, translation, and introduction to his text and commentary', by J. S. McQuade (unpub. Ph.D. diss., The Queen's University of Belfast, 1961)

Guido da Pisa, *Expositiones et glose super Comediam Dantis, or Commentary on Dante's 'Inferno'*, ed. Vincenzo Cioffari (Albany, NY, 1974)

Haymo of Halberstadt, *De varietate librorum sive de amore coelestis patriae*, in *PL*, CXVIII, cols 875-958

Hildebert of Tours, *Sermones de tempore, XX. in quadragesima sermo primus: de poenitentia*, in *PL*, CLXXI, cols 428-32

Hobbes, Thomas, *Leviathan*, ed. Mark C. Rooks (Charlottesville, NC, 2000)

Hugh of St Victor, *De sacramentis christiane fidei*, in *PL*, CLXXVI, cols 173-618. Trans. Roy J. Deferrari (Cambridge, MA, 1951)

Hugh Ripelin of Strasburg, *Compendium theologicae veritatis*, in *Alberti Magni opera omnia*, 21 vols, ed. Pierre Jammy (Lyon, 1651), XIII, text C

Innocent III, Pope, *De miseria condicionis humane*, ed. Robert E. Lewis (Athens, GA, and London, 1978)

Isaac of Stella, *Epistola de anima*, in *PL*, CXCIV, cols 1875-90. Trans. Bernard McGinn, *Three Treatises on Man*, pp. 155-77

Isidore of Seville, *Etymologiae*, ed. W. M. Lindsay, 2 vols (Oxford, 1911). Trans. Stephen A. Barney *et al.*, *The Etymologies of Isidore of Seville* (Cambridge, 2006)

Julian of Toledo, *Prognosticon futuri saeculi*, in *PL*, XCVI, cols 453-524

Kyteler, Alice, trial of; *A Contemporary Narrative of the Proceedings against Dame Alice Kyteler, Prosecuted for Sorcery in 1324 by Richard de Ledrede*, ed. Thomas Wright, Camden Society (London, 1843)

Langland, William, *The Vision of Piers Plowman*, 2nd edn, ed. A. V. C. Schmidt (London, 1995)

The Life of Saint Thomas Aquinas: Biographical Documents, ed. and trans. Kenelm Foster (London and Baltimore, 1959)

Le Livre du Chevalier de la Tour Landry pour l'enseignement de ses filles, ed. M. A. de Montaiglon (Paris, 1854)

Lodge, David, *Souls and Bodies* (London, 1980)

Luther, Martin, *Luther's Works*, vol. 19: *Lectures on the Minor Prophets, II: Jonah, Habakkuk*, ed. and trans. Jaroslav Pelikan (St Louis, MO, 1974)

Mechthild of Hackeborn, *The Booke of Gostlye Grace*, ed. Theresa A. Halligan (Toronto, 1979)

- , *Liber specialis gratiae*, in *Revelationes Gertrudianae ac Mechtildianae*, ed. Louis Paquelin and the monks of Solesmes, 2 vols (Poitiers and Paris), II. Trans. Barbara Newman (New York and Mahwah, NJ, 2017)

Mechthild of Magdeburg, *Das fließende Licht der Gottheit*, ed. Hans Neumann, 2 vols, Münchener Texte und Untersuchungen zur deutschen Literatur des Mittelalters 100-1 (Munich, 1990-9). Trans. Frank Tobin (New York and Mahwah, NJ, 1998)

Milton, John, *The Poetical Works*, ed. Helen Darbishire (London, 1963)

Nemerov, Howard, *A Howard Nemerov Reader* (Columbia, MI, 1991)

The Orcherd of Syon, ed. Phyllis Hodgson and Gabriel M. Liegey, EETS os 258 (London, 1966)

Oresme, Nicole, *De causis mirabilium*, ed. Bert Hansen (Toronto, 1985)

Orwell, George, *Nineteen Eighty-Four* (New York, 1949)

Patrick of Ireland, Pseudo-, *De tribus habitaculis animae*, in *PL*, LIII, cols 831-8

Les Peines de purgatorie, ed. Robert J. Relihan (unpub. Ph.D. diss., University of Iowa, 1978)

The Penguin Book of Hell, ed. Scott G. Bruce (New York, 2018)

Perkins, William, *A discovrse of conscience: wherein is set downe the nature, properties, and differences thereof: as also the way to get and keepe good conscience* (Cambridge, 1596)

- , *The Whole Treatise of the Cases of Conscience* (Cambridge, 1606)

Peter of Tarantasia (Pope Innocent V), *in IV libros sententiarum*, 3 vols (Toulouse, 1649-52).

Pietro Alighieri, *Comentum super poema Comedie Dantis: A Critical Edition of the Third and Final Draft of Pietro Alighieri's Commentary on Dante's 'Divine Comedy'*, ed. Massimiliano Chiamenti (Tempe, AZ, 2002)

- , *Petri Allegherii super Dantis ipsius genitoris Comoediam commentarium*, ed. Vincenzo Nannucci (Florence, 1845)

The Prick of Conscience, Richard Morris's text, prepared by Ralph Hanna and Sarah Wood, EETS os 342 (Oxford, 2013)

A Revelation of Purgatory, ed. and trans. Liz Herbert McAvoy (Cambridge, 2017)

The Revelation of the Monk of Eynsham, ed. Robert Easting, EETS os 318 (Oxford, 2008)

Richard of Middleton, *Questions disputées, tome IV, 23-32: Les démons*, ed. with French trans. by Alain Boureau (Paris, 2011)

- , *Super quatuor sententiarum*, 4 vols (Brescia, 1591)

Sawles Warde, in *The Katherine Group: MS Bodley 34*, ed. Emily Rebekah Huber and Elizabeth Robertson (Kalamazoo, MI, 2016), at https://d.lib.rochester.edu/teams/text/sawles-warde

Shelley, Percy Bysshe, *Poetical Works*, ed. Thomas Hutchinson (London, 1965)

Sicardus of Cremona, *Mitrale seu de officiis ecclesiasticis summa*, in *PL*, CCXIII, cols 13-434

De spiritu et anima, in *PL*, XL, cols 779-832. Trans. Bernard McGinn, *Three Treatises on Man*, pp. 181-288

St. Patrick's Purgatory: Two Versions of 'Owayne Miles' and the 'Vision of William of Stranton', together with the long text of the *'Tractatus de purgatorio sancti Patricii'*, ed. Robert Easting, EETS os 298 (Oxford, 1991)

Swinden, Tobias, *An Enquiry into the Nature and Place of Hell*, 2nd edn (London, 1727)

Thomas of Cantimpré, *The Collected Saints' Lives: Christina the Astonishing, Lutgard of Aywières, Margaret of Ypres and Abbot John of Cantimpre ́*, ed. Barbara Newman and trans. Margot H. King and Barbara Newman (Turnhout, 2008)

Thomas of Perseigne, *In Cantica Canticorum commentarii*, in *PL*, CCVI, cols 15-861

Three Medieval Rhetorical Arts, ed. James J. Murphy (Berkeley, CA, 1971)

Three Purgatory Poems: 'The Gast of Gy', 'Sir Owain', 'The Vision of Tundale', ed. Edward E. Foster (Kalamazoo, MI, 2004), at https://d.lib.rochester.edu/teams/publication/foster-three-purgatory-poems

Three Treatises on Man: A Cistercian Anthropology, trans. Bernard McGinn (Kalamazoo, MI, 1977). Translations of William of St Thierry, *De natura corporis et animae*, Isaac of Stella, *Epistola de anima*, and the anon. *De spiritu et anima*

Three Women of Liège: A Critical Edition of and Commentary on the Middle English Lives of Elizabeth of Spalbeek, Christina Mirabilis and Marie d'Oignies, ed. Jennifer N. Brown (Turnhout, 2008)

Trevisa, John, *On the Properties of Things: John Trevisa's Translation of Bartholomaeus Anglicus De proprietatibus rerum*, ed. M. C. Seymour *et al.*, 3 vols (Oxford, 1975-88)

Venturi, P. Pompeo, *La Divina Commedia di Dante Alighieri ... col comento del P. Pompeo Venturi* (Florence, 1821)

De vera et falsa poenitentia, in *PL*, XL, cols 1113-30

Vincent of Beauvais, *Speculum maius*, 4 vols (Douai, 1624)

Die Visio Pauli: Wege und Wandlungen einer orientalischen Apokryphe im lateinischen Mittelalter unter Einschluss der alttschechischen und deutschsprachigen Textzeugen, ed. L. Jiroušková, Mittellateinische Studien und Texte 34 (Leiden, 2006)

Visio Thurkilli relatore, ut videtur, Radulpho de Coggeshall, ed. P. G. Schmidt (Leipzig, 1978)

Visio Tnugdali: Lateinisch und Altdeutsch, ed. Albrecht Wagner (Erlangen, 1882)

Visions of Heaven and Hell before Dante, trans. Edith Gardner (New York, 1989)

William of Auvergne, *Opera omnia*, 2 vols (Paris, 1674; repr. Frankfurt, 1963)

William of St Thierry, *De natura corporis et animae*, in *PL*, CLXXX, cols 695-726. Trans. Bernard McGinn, *Three Treatises on Man*, pp. 103-52

Yeats, W. B., *The Collected Poems*, ed. Richard J. Finneran, rev. 2nd edn (New York, 1996)

SECONDARY LITERATURE

Alexander, Kinsley, 'Beauty and the Pilgrim Soul: a study of *Le pèlerinage de vie humaine* as an allegory of Cistercian aesthetics' (unpub. Ph.D. diss., Boston College, 2007)

Angels in Medieval Philosophical Inquiry, ed. Isabel Iribarren and Martin Lenz (London, 2008)

Barański, Zygmunt, 'Canto XXV', in *Lectura Dantis Turicensis*, ed. Georges Güntert and Michelangelo Picone, vol. 2: *Purgatorio* (Florence, 2001), pp. 389-406

- , 'On Dante's trail', *Italian Studies*, 72/1 (2017), 1-15

Barbezat, M. D., 'In a corporeal flame: the materiality of hellfire before the Resurrection in six Latin authors', *Viator*, 44 (2013), 1-20

Barsella, Susanna, *In the Light of the Angels: Angelology and Cosmology in Dante's 'Divina commedia'* (Florence, 2010)

Bartlett, Robert, *The Natural and the Supernatural in the Middle Ages* (Cambridge, 2008)

- , *Why Can the Dead Do Such Great Things? Saints and Worshippers from the Martyrs to the Reformation* (Princeton, NJ, 2013)

Beckwith, Sarah, 'A very material mysticism: the medieval mysticism of Margery Kempe', in *Gender and Text in the Later Middle Ages*, ed. Jane Chance (Gainesville, FL, 1996), pp. 195-215

Berk, Philip R., 'Shadows on the Mount of Purgatory', *Dante Studies*, 97 (1979), 47-63

Bernstein, Alan E., 'Esoteric theology: William of Auvergne on the fires of hell and purgatory', *Speculum*, 57/3 (1982), 509-31

- , *The Formation of Hell: Death and Retribution in the Ancient and Early Christian Worlds* (Ithaca, NY, 1993)

- , *Hell and its Rivals: Death and Retribution among Christians, Jews and Muslims in the Early Middle Ages* (Ithaca, NY, 2017)

- , 'The invocation of hell in thirteenth-century Paris', *Supplementum festivum: Studies in Honor of Paul Oskar Kristeller*, ed. James Hankins, John Monfasani, and Frederick Purnell, Jr. (Binghamton, NY, 1987), pp. 13-54

Bianchi, Luca, '1277: a turning point in medieval philosophy?', in *Was ist Philosophie im Mittelalter? = Qu'est-ce que la philosophie au Moyen Âge? = What is philosophy in the Middle Ages?: Akten des X. Internationalen Kongresses für mittelalterliche Philosophie der Sociéte ́ Internationale pour l'Étude de la Philosophie Médiévale, 25. bis 30. August 1997 im Erfurt*, ed. Jan A. Aertsen and Andreas Speer (Berlin and New York, 1998), pp. 90-110

Bieniak, Magdalena, and Raffaella Roncarati, *The Soul-Body Problem at Paris ca. 1200-1250: Hugh of St-Cher and his Contemporaries* (Leuven, 2010)

Black, Deborah L., 'Imagination and estimation: Arabic paradigms and Western transformations', *Topoi*, 19 (2000), 59-60

Boitani, Piero, '"Trattando l'ombre come cosa salda": Fisiologia, metafisica e poetica dell'ombra', in *Elogio dell'ombra*, ed. Stefano Colmagro (Venice, 1995), pp. 33-47

Botterill, Steven, *Dante and the Mystical Tradition: Bernard of Clairvaux in the Commedia* (Cambridge, 1994)

Boyde, Patrick, *Dante, Philomythes and Philosopher: Man in the Cosmos* (Cambridge, 1983)

Brooke, O, 'The trinitarian aspect of the ascent of the soul to God in the theology of William of St. Thierry', *Recherches de théologie ancienne et médiévale*, 26 (1959), 85-127

Brower, Jeffrey, *Aquinas's Ontology of the Material World: Change, Hylomorphism, and Material Objects* (Oxford, 2014)

Brown, Meg Lota, 'The politics of conscience in Reformation England', *Renaissance and Reformation / Renaissance et réforme*, n.s. 15/2 (1991), 101-14.

Brown, Peter, *Augustine of Hippo: A Biography*, new edn with an Epilogue (London, 2000)

Burrell, Margaret, 'Hell as a geological construct', *Florilegium*, 24 (2007), 37-54

Buttigieg, Emanuel C., 'The definition of the human soul in the *Commentary on the Sentences of Peter Lombard* by Peter of Tarantasia, O. P.' (unpub. Ph.D. diss., Marquette University, 1984)

Bynum, Caroline Walker, *Holy Feast and Holy Fast: The Religious Significance of Food to Medieval Women* (Berkeley, CA, 1987)

- , 'Mendicant Order politics and the status of Christ's shed blood', *Historical Research*, 85, no. 228 (May 2012), 210-27

- , *The Resurrection of the Body in Western Christianity, 200-1336*, expanded edition (New York, 2017)

Callan, Maeve Brigid, *The Templars, the Witch, and the Wild Irish: Vengeance and Heresy in Medieval Ireland* (Ithaca, NY, 2014)

The Cambridge Companion to Augustine, 2nd edn, ed. David Vincent Meconi and Eleonore Stump (Cambridge, 2014)

The Cambridge Companion to John Calvin, ed. Donald K. McKim (Cambridge, 2004)

The Cambridge Handbook of Metaphor and Thought, ed. Raymond W. Gibbs (Cambridge, 2008)

The Cambridge History of Later Medieval Philosophy: From the Rediscovery of Aristotle to the Disintegration of Scholasticism, 1100-1600, ed. Norman Kretzmann, Anthony Kenny, Jan Pinborg, and Eleonore Stump (Cambridge, 1982)

The Cambridge History of Medieval Philosophy, ed. Robert Pasnau, 2 vols (Cambridge, 2009-10)

Cameron, Averil, *Christianity and the Rhetoric of Empire: The Development of Christian Discourse* (Berkeley, CA, 1991)

Camporesi, Piero, *The Fear of Hell: Images of Damnation and Salvation in Early Modern Europe*, trans. Lucinda Byatt (Cambridge and Melford, MA, 1990, rpt. 2020)

- , *The Incorruptible Flesh: Bodily Mutation and Mortification in Religion and Folklore*, trans. Tania Croft-Murray with the Latin texts trans. Helen Elsom (Cambridge, 2009)

Canning, Joseph, review of David Mowbray, *Pain and Suffering in Medieval Theology: Academic Debates at the University of Paris in the Thirteenth Century* (Woodbridge, 2009), in *The English Historical Review*, 126, issue 521 (2011), 911-12

Carruthers, Mary, *The Book of Memory: A Study of Memory in Medieval Culture* (Cambridge, 1990)

Casey, John, *After Lives: A Guide to Heaven, Hell, and Purgatory* (Oxford, 2009)

Cerbo, Anna, *Poesia e scienza del corpo nella 'Divina Commedia':'dicer del sangue e de le piaghe...'* (Naples, 2001)

Chenu, Marie-Dominique, *La Théologie comme science au XIIIe siècle*, 3rd edn, Bibliothèque Thomiste 33 (Paris, 1969)

- , *Toward Understanding Saint Thomas*, trans. A. M. Landry and D. Hughes (Chicago, 1964)

Clark, Anne L., *Elisabeth of Schönau: A Twelfth-Century Visionary* (Philadelphia, 1992)

Clark, Elizabeth A., 'The celibate bridegroom and his virginal brides: metaphor and the marriage of Jesus in Early Christian ascetic exegesis', *Church History*, 77/1 (2008), 1-25

Cogan, Marc, *The Design in the Wax: The Structure of the 'Divine Comedy' and its Meaning* (Notre Dame, IN, 1999)

The Cognitive Linguistics Reader, ed. Vyvyan Evans, Benjamin K. Bergen and Jörg Zinken (London and Oakville, CT, 2007)

Cohen, Esther, 'The animated pain of the body', *The American Historical Review*, 105/1 (2000), 36-68

- , *The Modulated Scream: Pain in Late Medieval Culture* (Chicago, 2010)

- , 'Towards a history of European physical sensibility: pain in the Later Middle Ages', *Science in Context*, 8 (1995), 47-74

Collinson, Patrick, *The Elizabethan Puritan Movement* (Berkeley, CA, 1967)

A Companion to Angels in Medieval Philosophy, ed. Tobias Hoffmann (Leiden, 2012)

Constable, Giles, *Attitudes toward Self-Inflicted Suffering in the Middle Ages* (Brookline, MA, 1982)

Coolman, Boyd Taylor, 'The medieval affective Dionysian tradition', in *Modern Theology*, 24/4 (2008), 615-32

Cortezo, Carlos López, '*Amor, da che convien pur ch'io mi doglia*. Alcune precisazioni', in *Le Rime di Dante*, ed. Claudia Berra and Paolo Borsa (Milan, 2010), pp. 213-9

Cruz, Jo Ann H. Moran, 'Dante's Matelda: queen, saint, and mother of emperors', *Viator*, 47/3 (2016), 209-42

Dales, Richard C., 'The de-animation of the heavens in the Middle Ages', *Journal of the History of Ideas*, 41/4 (1980), 531-50

—, *The Problem of the Rational Soul in the Thirteenth Century* (Leiden, 1995)

Davidson, Herbert A., *Alfarabi, Avicenna, and Averroes, on Intellect: Their Cosmologies, Theories of the Active Intellect, and Theories of Human Intellect* (Oxford, 1992)

Davis, Robert Glenn, *The Weight of Love: Affect, Ecstasy, and Union in the Theology of Bonaventure* (New York, 2017)

Davis, Thomas X., 'The trinity's glorifying embrace: *concientia* in William of Saint-Thierry', in *A Companion to William of Saint-Thierry*, ed. F. Tyler Sergent (Leiden, 2019), pp. 131-59

de Boer, Sander W., *The Science of the Soul: The Commentary Tradition on Aristotle's 'De anima', c. 1260 - c. 1360* (Leuven, 2012)

Dell'Oso, Lorenzo, 'Per la formazione intellettuale di Dante: i cataloghi librari, le tracce testuali, *il Trattatello* di Boccaccio', *Le Tre Corone: Rivista internazionale di studi su Dante, Petrarca, Boccaccio*, 4 (2017), 129-61

de Man, Paul, 'The epistemology of metaphor', in *On Metaphor*, ed. Sacks, pp. 11-28

Denery, Dallas, *Seeing and Being Seen in the Later Medieval World: Optics, Theology and Religious Life* (Cambridge, 2005)

Dragulinescu, Stefan, 'Thomas of Hereford's miracles – between Aquinas and Augustine', *Journal of Medieval History*, 44/5 (2018), 543-68

Dronke, Peter, *Fabula: Explorations into the Uses of Myth in Medieval Platonism* (Leiden, 1974)

Druart, Thérèse-Anne, 'The human soul's individuation and its survival after the body's death: Avicenna on the causal relation between body and soul', *Arabic Sciences and Philosophy*, 10 (2000), 259-73

Dudden, Holmes, *Gregory the Great: His Place in History and Thought*, 2 vols (London, 1905)

Duffy, Eamon, *The Stripping of the Altars: Traditional Religion in England, c. 1400-c. 1580*, 2nd edn (New Haven, Conn., 2005)

Dumsday, Travis, 'Alexander of Hales on angelic corporeality', *The Heythrop Journal*, 54/3 (2013), 360-70.

Easting, Robert, 'Owein at St. Patrick's Purgatory', *Medium Ævum*, 55/2 (1986), 159-75

— , 'Purgatory and the Earthly Paradise in the *Purgatorio sancti Patricii*', *Cîteaux: commentarii cistercienses*, 37 (1986), 23-48

Eitenmiller, Melissa, 'On the separated soul according to St. Thomas Aquinas', *Nova et Vetera*, 17/1 (2019), 57-91

Elder, Marcus Paul, '*Eruditio sacri eloquii*: the integration of scriptural hermeneutics and theological system in Hugh of St Victor' (unpub. D. Phil. diss., Yale University, 2010)

Elliott, Dyan, *The Bride of Christ Goes to Hell: Metaphor and Embodiment in the Lives of Pious Women, 200-1500* (Philadelphia, 2012)

— , *Fallen Bodies: Pollution, Sexuality, and Demonology in the Middle Ages* (Philadelphia, 1999)

Fitzpatrick, Antonia, *Thomas Aquinas on Bodily Identity* (Oxford, 2017)

Gardner, Patrick Meredith, 'Dante and the suffering soul' (unpub. Ph.D. diss., University of Notre Dame, 2009)

Geary, James, *I Is an Other: The Secret Life of Metaphor and How it Shapes the Way We See the World* (New York, 2011)

Gillespie, Vincent, 'Vernacular theology', in *Oxford Twenty-First Century Approaches to Literature: Middle English*, ed. Paul Strohm (Oxford, 2007), pp. 401-20

Gilson, Étienne, 'Dante's notion of a shade: *Purgatorio* xxv', *Mediaeval Studies*, 29 (1967), 124-42

Gilson, Simon, 'The anatomy and physiology of the human body in the *Commedia*', in *Dante and the Human Body: Eight Essays*, ed. John C. Barnes and Jennifer Petrie (Dublin, 2007), pp. 11-42

Goodich, M., *Miracles and Wonders. The Development of the Concept of Miracle, 1150-1350* (Aldershot, 2007)

Gordon, Bruce, *Calvin* (New Haven, CT, 2009)

Goris, Harm, 'The Angelic Doctor and angelic speech: the development of Thomas Aquinas's thought on how angels communicate', *Medieval Philosophy and Theology*, 11 (2003), 87-105

- , 'Angelic knowledge in Aquinas and Bonaventure', in *A Companion to Angels in Medieval Philosophy*, ed. Hoffmann, pp. 149-85

Grady, Joseph E., 'Metaphor', in *The Oxford Handbook of Cognitive Linguistics*, ed. Dirk Geeraerts and Hubert Cuyckens (Oxford, 2007), pp. 188-213

Gragnolati, Manuele, *Experiencing the Afterlife: Soul and Body in Dante and Medieval Culture* (Notre Dame, IN, 2005)

Gray, Douglas, 'Notes of some medieval mystical, magical and moral cats', in *Langland, the Mystics and the Medieval English Religious Tradition: Essays in Honour of S. S. Hussey*, ed. Helen Philipps (Cambridge, 1990), pp. 185-202

Green, Richard Firth, *Elf Queens and Holy Friars: Fairy Beliefs and the Medieval Church* (Philadelphia, 2016)

Gurevich, Aron, 'Popular and scholarly medieval cultural traditions: notes in the margin of Jacques Le Goff's book', *Journal of Medieval History*, 9/2 (1983), 71-90

Hagen, Susan K., *Allegorical Remembrance: A Study of 'The Pilgrimage of the Life of Man' as a Medieval Treatise on Seeing and Remembering* (Athens, GA, and London, 1990)

Haldane, John, 'Body and soul', in *The Cambridge History of Medieval Philosophy*, ed. Pasnau, I, 293-304

Harley, Marta Powell, 'Last things first in Chaucer's *Physician's Tale*: final judgment and the worm of conscience', *Journal of English and Germanic Philology*, 91/1 (1992), 1-16

Harrison, Peter, 'Angels on pinheads and needles' points', *Notes and Queries*, 63 (2016), 45-7

Hawkins, Peter S., review of Steven Botterill, *Dante and the Mystical Tradition: Bernard of Clairvaux in the Commedia* (Cambridge, 1994), in *Speculum* 71/ 1 (1996), 127-9

Heath, Peter, *Allegory and Philosophy in Avicenna (Ibn Sina): With a Translation of the Book of the Prophet Muhammad's Ascent to Heaven* (Philadelphia, 1992)

Hillgarth, J. N., 'St. Julian of Toledo in the Middle Ages', *Journal of the Warburg and Courtauld Institutes*, 21, no. 1/2 (1958), 7-26

Hoffmann, Tobias, 'Conscience and *synderesis*', in *The Oxford Handbook of Aquinas*, ed. Brian Davies (Oxford, 2012), pp. 255-63

Hughes, Daniel E., 'The "Worm of Conscience" in "Richard III" and "Macbeth"', *The English Journal*, 55/7 (1966), 845-85.

Hui, Andrew, 'Dante's book of shadows: *ombra* in the *Divine Comedy*', *Dante Studies*, 134 (2016), 195-224

Huizinga, Johan, *The Waning of the Middle Ages*, trans. F. Hopman (Harmondsworth, rpt. 1965)

Imbach, Ruedi, *Dante, la filosofie et les laïcs* (Fribourg, Suisse, and Paris, 1996)

Intellect et imagination dans la philosophie médiévale, ed. M. C. Pacheco and J. F. Meirinhos, 3 vols (Turnhout, 2006)

Irvine, Martin, 'Medieval grammatical theory and Chaucer's *House of Fame*', *Speculum*, 60/4 (1985), 850-76

Jacoff, Rachel, 'Our bodies, our selves: the body in the *Commedia*', in *Sparks and Seeds: Medieval Literature and its Afterlife. Essays in Honor of John Freccero*, ed. Dana E. Stewart and Alison Cornish (Turnhout, 2000), pp. 119-38

Johnson, Ian, *The Middle English Life of Christ: Academic Discourse, Translation and Vernacular Theology* (Turnhout, 2013)

Johnson, Mark, *The Body in the Mind: The Bodily Basis of Meaning, Imagination, and Reason* (Chicago, 1987)

Kaeuper, Richard, *Holy Warriors: The Religious Ideology of Chivalry* (Philadelphia, 2009)

Kamath, Stephanie A. Viereck Gibbs, 'Rewriting ancient *auctores* in the *Pèlerinage de la vie humaine*', in *Mittelalterliche Literatur als Retextualisierung*, ed. Kablitz and Peters, pp. 321-41

Karnes, Michelle, *Imagination, Meditation, and Cognition in the Middle Ages* (Chicago, 2011)

- , 'Marvels in the medieval imagination', *Speculum*, 90/2 (2015), 327-65

- , 'Nicholas Love and medieval meditations on Christ', *Speculum*, 82/2 (2007), 380-408

Kay, Sarah, *The Place of Thought: The Complexity of One in Late Medieval French Didactic Poetry* (Philadelphia, 2007)

Keach, William, 'The Shelleys and Dante's Matilda', in *Dante's Modern Afterlife: Reception and Response from Blake to Heaney*, ed. Nick Havely (Basingstoke and London, 1998), pp. 60-70

Keck, David, *Angels and Angelology in the Middle Ages* (Oxford, 1998)

Keele, Rondo, 'Can God make a Picasso? William Ockham and Walter Chatton on divine power and real relations', *Journal of the History of Philosophy*, 45/3(2007), 395-411

Keenan, Joseph M., 'The Cistercian pilgrimage to Jerusalem in Guillaume de Deguileville's *Pèlerinage de vie humaine*', in *Studies in Medieval Cistercian History, II*, ed. John R. Sommerfeldt (Kalamazoo, MI, 1976), pp. 166-85

King, Peter, 'Augustine on knowledge', in *The Cambridge Companion to Augustine*, 2nd edn, ed. Meconi and Stump, pp. 142-65

Kitzler, Petr, 'Tertullian's concept of the soul and his corporealistic ontology', in *Tertullianus Afer. Tertullien et la littérature chrétienne d'Afrique*, ed. J. Lagouanere and S. Fialon, Instrumenta patristica et mediaevalia 70 (Turnhout, 2015), pp. 43-62

Kleinberg, Aviad, 'Proving sanctity: selection and authentication of saints in the Later Middle Ages, *Viator*, 20 (1989), 183-205

Knowledge, Mental Language, and Free Will, ed. Gyula Kilma and Alexander W. Hall (Newcastle upon Tyne, 2011)

Kobusch, Theo, 'The language of angels: on the subjectivity and intersubjectivity of pure spirits', in *Angels in Medieval Philosophical Inquiry*, ed. Iribarren and Lenz, pp. 131-42

Köpf, Ulrich, *Die Anfänge der theologischen Wissenschaftstheorie im 13. Jahrhundert*, Beiträge zur historischen Theologie 49 (Tubingen, 1974)

Kruger, Steven F., *Dreaming in the Middle Ages* (Cambridge, 1992)

Kuksewicz, Z., 'Criticisms of Aristotelian psychology and the Augustinian-Aristotelian synthesis', in *The Cambridge History of Later Medieval Philosophy*, ed. Kretzmann, Kenny, Pinborg and Stump, pp. 623-28

- , 'The potential and the agent intellect', in *The Cambridge History of Later Medieval Philosophy*, ed. Kretzmann, Kenny, Pinborg, and Stump, pp. 593-601

Lakoff, George, *Women, Fire, and Dangerous Things: What Categories Reveal about the Mind* (Chicago, 1987)

- , and Mark Johnson, *Metaphors we live by* (Chicago, 1980)

- , *Philosophy in the Flesh: The Embodied Mind and its Challenge to Western Thought* (New York, 1999)

Le langage mental du moyen âge à l'âge classique, ed. Joël Biard (Leuven, 2009)

Lanza, Adriano, *Dante eterodosso: una lettura diversa della Commedia* (Bergamo, 2004)

Lawell, Declan, 'Affective excess: ontology and knowledge in the thought of Thomas Gallus', *Dionysius*, 26 (2008), 139-74

- , '*Ne de ineffabili penitus taceamus*: aspects of the specialized vocabulary of the writings of Thomas Gallus', *Viator*, 40/1 (2009), 151-84

Le Goff, Jacques, *The Birth of Purgatory*, trans. Arthur Goldhammer (Chicago, 1984)

- , *L'imaginaire médiéval: Essais* (Paris, 1985). Trans. Arthur Goldhammer as *Medieval Imagination* (Chicago, 1988)

Lenz, Martin, 'Why can't angels think properly? Ockham against Chatton and Aquinas', in *Angels in Medieval Philosophical Inquiry*, ed. Iribarren and Lenz, pp. 155-67

Lewis, C. S., *The Allegory of Love: A Study in Medieval Tradition* (Oxford, rpt. 1968)

Lindhelm, Nancy, 'Body, soul, and immortality: some readings in Dante's *Commedia*', *Modern Language Notes*, 10/1, Italian Issue (1990), 1-32

Lipton, Sara, 'Jews, heretics and the sign of the cat in the *Bible moralisée*', *Word & Image*, 8/4 (1992), 362-77

Living Saints of the Thirteenth Century: The Lives of Yvette, anchoress of Huy; Juliana of Cornillon, author of the Corpus Christi feast; and Margaret the Lame, anchoress of Magdeburg, ed. Anneke B. Mulder-Bakker and trans. Jo Ann McNamara (Turnhout, 2011)

Lottin, Odon, *Psychologie et morale aux XIIe et XIIIe siècles*, 6 vols in 8 (Leuven and Gembloux, 1942-60)

Marius, Richard, *Martin Luther: The Christian between God and Death* (Cambridge, MA, 1999)

Marshall, Peter, *Beliefs and the Dead in Reformation England* (Cambridge, 2002)

Masseron, Alexandre, *Dante et Saint Bernard* (Paris, 1953)

Matsuda, Takami, *Death and Purgatory in Middle English Didactic Poetry* (Cambridge, 1997)

Matthews, Gareth B., 'Augustinianism', in *The Cambridge History of Medieval Philosophy*, ed. Pasnau, I, 86-98

- , 'Death in Socrates, Plato and Aristotle', in *The Oxford Handbook of Philosophy of Death*, ed. Ben Bradley and Fred Feldman (Oxford, 2015), pp. 186-8

Matthews, Rachael Victoria, 'The mystical utterance and the metaphorical mode in the writings of Marguerite d'Oingt and Marguerite Porete' (unpub. Ph.D. diss., School of Modern Languages and Cultures and the Department of English Studies, Durham University, 2014)

Maurer, Armand, *The Philosophy of William of Ockham in the Light of its Principles* (Toronto, 1999)

Mazzotta, Giuseppe, *Dante, Poet of the Desert: History and Allegory in the 'Divine Comedy'* (Princeton, NJ, 1979)

McCann, Daniel, *Soul-Health: Therapeutic Reading in Later Medieval England* (Cardiff, 2018)

—, 'Dreadful health: fear and "sowle-hele" in *The Prickynge of Love*', in *Fear in the Medical and Literary Imagination, Medieval to Modern: Dreadful Passions*, ed. Daniel McCann and Claire McKechnie-Mason (Basingstoke and London, 2018), pp. 17-36

McCluskey, Stephen, 'Boethius's astronomy and cosmology', in *A Companion to Boethius in the Middle Ages*, ed. Noel Harold Kaylor and Philip Edward Phillips (Leiden, 2012), pp. 47-73

McCready, William, *Signs of Sanctity: Miracles in the Thought of Gregory the Great*, Studies and Texts 91 (Toronto, 1984)

McGinn, Bernard, 'Thomas Gallus and Dionysian Mysticism', *Studies in Spirituality*, 8, (1998), 81-96

McGuire, Brian Patrick, 'Purgatory, the communion of saints, and medieval change', *Viator*, 20 (1989), 61-84

Medieval Thought Experiments: Poetry, Hypothesis, and Experience in the European Middle Ages, ed. Philip Knox, Jonathan Morton, and Daniel Reeve (Turnhout, 2018)

Mental Language: from Plato to William of Ockham, ed. Claude Panaccio, trans. Joshua P. Hochschild and Meredith K. Ziebart (New York, 2017)

Mews, Constant, 'Debating the authority of Pseudo-Augustine's *De spiritu et anima*', *Przegląd Tomistyczny*, 24 (2018), 321-48

Michot, Jean R., *La destinée de l'homme selon Avicenne* (Louvain, 1986)

Minnis, Alastair, 'Affection and imagination in *The Cloud of Unknowing* and Walter Hilton's *Scale of Perfection*', *Traditio*, 39 (1983), 323-66

—, 'Fifteenth Century versions of literalism: Girolamo Savonarola and Alfonso de Madrigal', in *Neue Richtungen in der hoch- und spätmittelalterlichen Bibelexegese*, Schriften des Historischen Kollegs Kolloquien 32, ed. Robert Lerner (Munich, 1996), pp. 163-80

—, *From Eden to Eternity: Creations of Paradise in the Later Middle Ages* (Philadelphia, 2016)

- , 'Literary imagination and memory', in *The Cambridge History of Literary Criticism, vol. 2: The Middle Ages*, ed. Alastair Minnis and Ian Johnson (Cambridge, 2005), pp. 239-74

- , *Medieval Theory of Authorship: Scholastic Literary Attitudes in the Later Middle Ages*, reissued second edn with a new preface (Philadelphia, 2009)

- , 'Medium and message: Henry of Ghent on scriptural style', in *Literature and Religion in the Later Middle Ages: Philological Studies in Honor of Siegfried Wenzel*, ed. R. Newhauser and John Alford (Binghamton, NY, 1994), pp. 209-35

- , 'Religious roles: public and private', in *Medieval Holy Women in the Christian Tradition, c.1100-c.1500*, ed. Alastair Minnis and Rosalynn Voaden (Turnhout, 2010), pp. 47-81

- , '*Respondet Walterus Bryth* ...Walter Brut in debate on women priests', in *Text and Controversy from Wyclif to Bale: Essays in Honour of Anne Hudson*, ed. Helen Barr and Ann M. Hutchinson, Medieval Church Studies 4 (Turnhout, 2005), pp. 229-49

- , *Translations of Authority in Medieval English Literature: Valuing the Vernacular* (Cambridge, 2009)

- , 'The trouble with theology: ethical poetics and the ends of Scripture', in *Author, Reader, Book: Medieval Authorship in Theory and Practice*, ed. Stephen Partridge and Erik Kwakkel (Toronto, 2011), pp. 21-37

- , and A. B. Scott with David Wallace, eds., *Medieval Literary Theory and Criticism c. 1100-c. 1375: The Commentary Tradition*, rev. edn (Oxford, 1991)

Mittelalerliche Literatur als Retextualisierung: Das 'Pelerinage'-Corpus des Guillaume de Deguileville im europaischen Mittelalter, ed. Andreas Kablitz and Ursula Peters (Heidelberg, 2014)

Moevs, Christian, *The Metaphysics of Dante's 'Comedy'* (Oxford, 2005)

Mohler, R. Albert, 'Modern theology: the disappearance of Hell', in *Hell under Fire: Modern Scholarship reinvents Eternal Punishment*, ed. Christopher W. Morgan and Robert A. Peterson (Grand Rapids, MI, 2004), pp. 15-41

Mowbray, Donald, *Pain and Suffering in Medieval Theology: Academic Debates at the University of Paris in the Thirteenth Century* (Woodbridge, 2009)

Murray, Alexander, 'Demons as psychological abstractions', in *Angels in Medieval Philosophical Inquiry*, ed. Iribarren and Lenz, pp. 171-84

Nardi, Bruno, 'Il Canto XXV del Purgatorio', in *Lecturae et altri studi danteschi*, ed. Rudy Abardo (Florence, 1990), pp. 139-50

- , *Studi di filosofia medievale* (Rome, 1960)

Nauta, Lodi, 'The *Consolation*: the Latin commentary tradition, 800-1700', in *The Cambridge Companion to Boethius*, ed. John Marenbon (Cambridge, 2009), pp. 255-78

Newman, Barbara, *From Virile Woman to WomanChrist: Studies in Medieval Religion and Literature* (Philadelphia, 1995)

- , 'The Seven-Storey Mountain: Mechthild of Hackeborn and Dante's Matelda', *Dante Studies*, 136 (2018), 62-92

- , 'What did it mean to say "I saw"? The clash between theory and practice in medieval visionary culture', *Speculum*, 80/1 (2005), 1-43

Niederbacher, Bruno, 'The human soul: Augustine's case for soul-body dualism', in *The Cambridge Companion to Augustine*, ed. Meconi and Stump, pp. 125-41

Niebuhr, Gustav, 'Hell is getting a makeover from Catholics; Jesuits call it a painful state but not a sulfurous place', *The Guardian* (18 September, 1999), Section B, p. 9

Nievergelt, Marco, *Allegorical Quests from Deguileville to Spenser* (Cambridge, 2012)

- , 'Can thought experiments backfire? Avicenna's flying man, self-knowledge, and the experience of allegory in Deguileville's *Pèlerinage de vie humaine*', in *Medieval Thought Experiments*, ed. Knox, Morton and Reeve, pp. 41-69

- , 'From *disputatio* to *predicatio* – and back again: dialectic, authority, and epistemology between the *Roman de la Rose* and the *Pèlerinage de vie humaine*', *New Medieval Literatures*, 16 (2015), 135-71

Norpoth, L., 'Der pseudo-augustinische Traktat "De spiritu et anima"'(unpub. Ph.D. diss., Cologne, Institut für Geschichte der Medizin, 1971)

Oberman, Heiko, *Luther: Man between God and the Devil* (New Haven, CT, 1989)

- , review of Richard Marius, *Martin Luther: The Christian between God and Death* (Cambridge, MA, 1999), in *The Historian*, 62/4 (2000), 926-7

Olson, Linda S., 'Visions of the other world (heaven, hell, purgatory) in Medieval French saint's lives and other didactic literature' (unpub. Ph.D. diss., University of Wisconsin-Madison, 1996)

O'Neill, Seamus, 'The demonic body: demonic ontology and the domicile of the demons in Apuleius and Augustine', in *Philosophical Approaches to Demonology*, ed. Benjamin W. McCraw and Robert Arp (New York, 2017), pp. 39-58

On Metaphor, ed. Sheldon Sacks (Chicago, 1970)

Ortony, Andrew, 'The role of similarity in similes and metaphors', in *Metaphor and Thought*, ed. Andrew Ortony (Cambridge, 1993), pp. 186-201

Owens, Joseph, 'Faith, ideas, illumination, and experience', in *The Cambridge History of Later Medieval Philosophy*, ed. Kretzmann, Kenny, Pinborg and Stump, pp. 440-59

Owst, G. R., *Literature and Pulpit in Medieval England* (Cambridge, 1933)

—, *Preaching in Medieval England: An Introduction to Sermon Manuscripts of the Period c. 1350-1450* (Cambridge, 1926)

The Oxford Latin Dictionary, ed. P. G. W. Glare, 2nd edn, 2 vols (Oxford, 2012)

Palmer, Nigel F., *'Visio Tnugdali': The German and Dutch Translations and Circulation in the Later Middle Ages*, Münchener Texte und Untersuchungen zur deutschen Literatur des Mittelalters 76 (Munich, 1982)

Pasnau, Robert, 'The mind-soul problem', in *Mind, Cognition and Representation: The Tradition of Commentaries on Aristotle's 'De anima'*, ed. Paul J. J. M. Bakker and Johannes M. M. H. Thijssen (Aldershot, 2007), pp. 3-19

—, *Theories of Cognition in the Later Middle Ages* (Cambridge, 1997)

Pasulka, Diana Walsh, *Heaven Can Wait: Purgatory in Catholic Devotional and Popular Culture* (Oxford, 2014)

Pegis, A. C., 'Between immortality and death: some further reflections on the *Summa Contra Gentiles*', *The Monist*, 58/1 (1974), 1-15

—, 'The separated soul and its nature in St. Thomas', in *St. Thomas Aquinas, 1274-1974: Commemorative Studies*, ed. É. Gilson (Toronto, 1974), pp. 131-58

—, *St. Thomas and the Problem of the Soul in the Thirteenth Century* (Toronto, 1934)

The Pèlerinage Allegories of Guillaume de Deguileville: Tradition, Authority and Influence, ed. Marco Nievergelt and Stephanie A. Viereck Gibbs Kamath (Cambridge, 2013)

Perler, Dominik, 'Thought experiments: the methodological function of angels in Late Medieval epistemology', in *Angels in Medieval Philosophical Inquiry*, ed. Iribarren and Lenz, pp. 143-53

Philosophical Perspectives on Metaphor, ed. Mark Johnson (Minneapolis, MN, 1981)

Pincikowski, Scott E., *Bodies of Pain: Suffering in the Works of Hartmann von Aue* (New York, 2002)

Piron, Sylvain, '*Ut philosophia poesis*', in *Questions philosophiques dans l'oeuvre de Dante, Pétrarque et Boccacce*, ed. Joël Biard and Fosca Mariani Zini (Paris, 2008), pp. 73-112

Porcell, Joan Martínez, 'Introducción y traducción del *De Spiritu et Anima*, un opúsculo inédito atribuido a Alcher de Clairvaux', *Espíritu*, 67, issue 155 (2018), 265-90

Potts, Timothy C., *Conscience in Medieval Philosophy* (Cambridge, 1980)

Quistorp, Heinrich, *Calvin's Doctrine of the Last Things*, trans. Harold Knight (London, 1955)

Ramachandran, V. S., and William Hirstein, 'The perception of phantom limbs: the D. O. Hebb Lecture', *Brain*, 121 (1998), 1603-30

Raskolnikov, Masha, *Body against Soul: Gender and Sowlehele in Middle English Allegory* (Columbus, OH, 2009)

Rasmussen, Tarald, 'Hell disarmed? the function of hell in Reformation spirituality', *Numen*, 56, no. 2/3 (2009), 366-84

Regan, Teresa (Sister Frances Carmel), 'A study of The *Liber de spiritu et anima*: its doctrine, sources and historical significance' (unpub. Ph.D. diss., University of Toronto, 1948)

Reynolds, P. L., *Food and the Body: Some Peculiar Questions in High Medieval Theology* (Leiden, 1999)

Richards, Emily Jean, 'Body-soul debates in English, French and German manuscripts *c.* 1200 -*c.* 1500' (unpub. Ph.D. diss., University of York, Centre for Medieval Studies, 2009)

Richards, I. A., *The Philosophy of Rhetoric* (London and New York, 1936)

Ricoeur, Paul, 'The metaphorical process as cognition, imagination, and feeling', in *On Metaphor*, ed. Sacks, pp. 141-57

— , *Rule of Metaphor: Multi-disciplinary Studies of the Creation of Meaning in Language*, trans. Robert Czerny, with Kathleen McLaughlin and John Costello (Toronto, 1977)

Roling, Bernd, 'Angelic language and communication', in *A Companion to Angels in Medieval Philosophy*, ed. Hoffmann, pp. 223-60

Romano, Carlin, review of James Geary, *I Is an Other: The Secret Life of Metaphor and How It Shapes the Way We See the World* (New York, 2011), in *The Chronicle of Higher Education*, 3rd July, 2011, at https://www.chronicle.com/article/Whats-a-Metaphor-For-/128079

Roper, Lyndal, *The Witch in the Western Imagination* (Charlottesville, 2012)

Russo, Vittorio, 'A proposito del canto xxv del *Purgatorio*', in idem, *Esperienze e/di letture dantesche* (Naples, 1971), pp. 101-58

Schmidt, A. V. C., 'Langland and scholastic philosophy', *Medium Ævum*, 38/2 (1969), 134-56

— , 'A note on Langland's conception of "Anima" and "Inwit"', *Notes and Queries*, n.s.15 (1968), 363-4

Seligman, Adam B. and Robert P. Weller, *How Things Count as the Same: Memory, Mimesis, and Metaphor* (New York and Oxford, 2019)

Silva, José Filipe, and Juhana Toivanen, 'The active nature of the soul in sense perception: Robert Kilwardby and Peter Olivi', *Vivarium*, 48/3-4 (2010), 245-78

Simpson, James, *Piers Plowman: An Introduction to the B-Text* (London and New York, 1990)

Smalley, Beryl, *The Study of the Bible in the Middle Ages*, 3rd edn (Oxford, 1984)

Smith, A. Mark, 'Perception', in *The Cambridge History of Medieval Philosophy*, ed. Pasnau, I, 334-45

Smith, Gregory A., 'How thin is a demon?', *Journal of Early Christian Studies*, 16/4 (2008), 479-512

Spencer, Mark K., 'The personhood of the separated soul', *Nova et Vetera*, 12/3 (2014), 863-912

Stewart, Charles, 'Dreams and desires in ancient and early Christian thought', in *Dreams and History: The Interpretation of Dreams from Ancient Greece to Modern Psychoanalysis*, ed. Daniel Pick and Lyndal Roper (Hove, East Sussex, 2004), pp. 37-56

Stoll, Abraham, *Conscience in Early Modern English Literature* (Cambridge, 2017)

Stone, Martin, 'The soul's relation to the body: Thomas Aquinas, Siger of Brabant and the Parisian Debate on monopsychism', ed. Tim Crane and Sarah Patterson, *History of the Mind-Body Problem* (London, 2000), pp. 34-69

Suarez-Nani, Tiziana, *Connaissance et langage des anges selon Thomas d'Aquin et Gilles de Rome* (Paris, 2002)

- , 'Space and movement in medieval thought: the angelological shift', in *Space, Imagination and the Cosmos from Antiquity to the Early Modern Period*, ed. Frederik A. Bakker, Delphine Bellis and Carla Rita Palmerino (Cham, Switzerland, 2018; corrected publication, 2019), pp. 69-89

Tachau, Katherine, *Vision and Certitude in the Age of Ockham: Optics, Epistemology and the Foundations of Semantics 1250-1340* (Leiden, 1988)

Teske, Roland J., 'Augustine's philosophy of memory', in *The Cambridge Companion to Augustine*, 1st edn, ed. Eleonore Stump and Norman Kretzmann (Cambridge, 2001), pp. 148-58

- , *Studies in the Philosophy of William of Auvergne, Bishop of Paris (1228-1249)* (Milwaukee, WI, 2006)

Théry, G., 'L'Authenticité du *De spiritu et anima* dans Saint Thomas et Albert le Grand', *Revue des sciences philosophiques et théologiques*, 10/3 (1921), 373-7

Toner, Patrick, 'St. Thomas Aquinas on death and the separated soul', *Pacific Philosophical Quarterly*, 91/4 (2010), 587-99

Turner, Denys, *Thomas Aquinas: A Portrait* (New Haven and London, 2013)

Walker, D. P., *The Decline of Hell: Seventeenth-Century Discussions of Eternal Torment* (London, 1964)

Walker-Meikle, Kathleen, 'Late Medieval pet keeping: gender, status and emotions' (unpub. Ph.D. diss., University College London, 2008)

- , *Medieval Pets* (Woodbridge, 2012)

Watson, Nicholas, 'Censorship and cultural change in Late-Medieval England: Vernacular Theology, the Oxford translation debate, and Arundel's Constitutions of 1409', *Speculum*, 70 (1995), 822-64

- , 'The *Gawain* Poet as a vernacular theologian', in *A Companion to the Gawain Poet*, ed. Derek Brewer and Jonathan Gibson (Cambridge, 1997), 293-314.

- , The phantasmal past: time, history, and the recombinative imagination', *Studies in the Age of Chaucer*, 32 (2010), 1-37

- , 'Visions of inclusion: universal salvation and vernacular theology in Pre-Reformation England', *Journal of Medieval and Early Modern Studies*, 27 (1997), 145-87

Watt, Tessa, *Cheap Print and Popular Piety 1550-1640* (Cambridge, 1991)

Webb, Heather, *Dante's Persons: An Ethics of the Transhuman* (Oxford, 2016)

Wei, Ian P., *Intellectual Culture in Medieval Paris: Theologians and the University, c.1100-1330* (Cambridge, 2012)

Wenzel, Siegfried, *Latin Sermon Collections from Later Medieval England: Orthodox Preaching in the Age of Wyclif* (Cambridge, 2005)

Wippel, John F., 'The Condemnations of 1270 and 1277 at Paris', *Journal of Medieval and Renaissance Studies*, 7 (1977), 169-201

— , 'Metaphysical composition of angels in Bonaventure, Aquinas, and Godfrey of Fontaines', in *A Companion to Angels in Medieval Philosophy*, ed. Hoffmann, pp. 45-78

Wittig, Joseph S. '*Piers Plowman* B, Passus IX - XII: elements in the design of the inward journey', *Traditio*, 28 (1972), 211-80

Wolfson, Harry, 'The internal senses in Latin, Arabic and Hebrew philosophic texts', *Harvard Theological Review*, 28/2 (1935), 70-133

Wood, Sarah, *Conscience and the Composition of 'Piers Plowman'* (Oxford, 2012)

Woods, B. Allen, 'The devil in dog form', *Western Folklore*, 13/4 (1954), 229-35

Yates, Frances A., *The Art of Memory* (1966, rpt. Harmondsworth, 1969)

Zaleski, Carol, *Otherworld Journeys: Accounts of Near-Death Experience in Medieval and Modern Times* (Oxford, 1988)

— , ' St. Patrick's Purgatory: pilgrimage motifs in a medieval otherworld vision', *Journal of the History of Ideas*, 46/4 (1985), 467-85

Zamore, Gustav, 'The term "synderesis" and its transformations: a conceptual history of *synderesis, ca.* 1150-1450' (unpub. D.Phil. diss., University of Oxford, 2016)

General Index

Adam, 102, 129, 203
Adam of Dryburgh, 204 n. 7
aerial bodies, 15-16, 96-9, 117-21, 124, 130, 132-3, 136-42 passim, 144-8, 151-2, 154-5, 166
Alan of Lille, 176 n. 17, 204 n. 7
Albert the Great, 49, 54-8, 65, 89, 125, 129, 149-50, 151, 162, 202 n. 1, 223
Alexander of Hales, 95 n. 5, 97 n. 12 & n. 14, 125 n. 18, 141 n. 22
Alexander, Kinsley, 205 n. 8, 211-12 n. 20, 214
Algazel (Al-Ghazālī), 35-6
Alkerton, Richard, 91
angels, 13, 16 n. 22, 28, 42 n. 10, 55, 67 n. 18, 94, 101, 107 n. 13, 108 n. 15, 113, 121, 153 n. 51, 222 n. 3
   cognition, 70-3, 115, 123, 142, 148, 158-9
   communication, 142-2, 147, 224 n. 8, 225-6 n. 11
   localisation, 55, 64, 85 n. 2
   materialisation, 95-9, 118-19, 133, 137-42, 144, 145-6, 155, 157, 160
   seraphim (fire-makers), 84-5 n. 1, 135
Anne, Queen of England, 194

apprehensio (apprehension, initial seizing upon), 67, 78 n. 15, 89
Aquinas, Thomas, 122-3
   Commentary on Aristotle's *De anima*, 30 n. 11, 31 n. 15, 34, 64
   Commentary on Peter Lombard's *Sentences*, 1, 54 n. 17, 60-8, 69-71, 74-6, 78, 80, 81, 121, 123-4, 127-9, 130
   Compendium theologiae ad fratrem Raynaldum, 76-8, 86-7 n. 7
   De malo, 31 n. 15, 69 n. 21, 114-5, 142 n. 24, 145, 161
   Quaestiones disputatae de anima, 69, 75-6, 127 n. 24
   Quaestiones disputatae de potentia dei, 98, 142 n. 24
   Questiones disputatae de veritate, 203-4, 209, 212
   Summa contra gentiles, 70 n. 28, 86-8, 121, 123, 163 n. 26
   Summa theologiae, 1, 28-9, 33, 34, 71, 81, 96, 99, 115 n. 40 & n. 41, 127, 129, 130, 135, 141, 145, 150, 161, 199 n. 38
Aristotle, 28, 29-30, 31 n. 15, 33, 35, 37, 66, 70 n. 28, 105-6, 129, 132 n. 32, 150 n. 42, 162, 226
   on metaphor, xvi, 7, 157, 188
   De anima, 30 n. 11, 31 n. 15, 34, 64

GENERAL INDEX 261

Metaphysics, 162, 226 n. 13
Nicomachean Ethics, 31 n. 55, 66 n. 15
Poetics, xvi, 7, 156, 223
Rhetoric, 188
Augustine, 4 n. 9, 9 n. 5, 14 n. 20, 15-16 n. 22, 19, 22, 25, 26, 32, 35, 42 n. 9, 44 n. 14, 46, 50, 53, 56, 96-7, 109, 113 n. 32, 139, 148-9
  De civitate Dei, xviii n. 12, 8-19 passim, 23, 48, 74 n. 3, 75-80 passim, 82 n. 33, 85, 95, 109, 114, 115 n. 42, 199 n. 27 & n. 38, 203, 211
  De cura pro mortuis, 153 n. 51
  De diversis quaestionibus lxxxiii, 32-3
  De doctrina christiana, 45
  De duabus animabus, 213 n. 24
  Epistola 118, ad Dioscursum, 81
  Epistola 159, ad Evodium, 153-4, n. 51
  De Genesi ad litteram, 2-7, 25, 16, 19 n. 1, 30-1, 33, 39, 41, 54, 56, 58, 62, 64-6, 67-73 passim, 78, 89, 97, 112 n. 28, 123, 125-8, 136, 154 n. 51, 159, 222 n. 3
  In psalmum cxlv enarratio, 222 n. 3
  Retractationes, 54 n. 17
  De trinitate, 112 n. 13, 132
Avicenna (Ibn-Sīnā), 36, 50-3, 60-4, 127

Bacon, Roger, 28
Barbezat, M. D., 2 n. 4, 13 n. 17, 17 n. 25, 31 n. 14, 74 n. 3
Barsella, Susanna, 157 n. 5
Bartholomew the Englishman, 84-5, 139-41
Bartlett, Robert, 36 n. 27, 112 n. 28, 113 n. 32
Beatific Vision, 71 n. 29, 192 n. 13, 225 n. 11
Beatrice (in Dante's *Comedy*), 135, 150-1 n. 43
Beckwith, Sarah, 168
Bede, 199
Benedict XII, Pope, 71 n. 29
Bernard of Clairvaux, 104, 131-2, 150-1, 199, 204 n. 7
Bernstein, Alan E., 7 n. 16, 10 n. 8, 38 n. 1, 41 n. 6, 43-4, 45-6, 50-1, 53, 59, 100 n. 25
Bible
  Gen. i.27, 208
  Gen. iii.15, 211
  Gen. v.1, 208
  Gen. ix.6, 208
  Gen. xxxvii.35, 190
  Gen. xli.1-32, 3
  Deut. xxxii.24, 92
  Judith xvi.21, 10, 80-2 passim, 92, 201
  Job xxiv.19, 24
  Prov. ix.2, 4-5, 86
  Prov. xvii.22, 82
  Prov. xviii.14, 196
  Prov. xix.29, 95 n. 4
  Prov. xxv.20, 10

Wisdom xi.17, 178
Sirach vii.19, 10, 11, 23, 80, 81
Sirach xv.3, 86
Isaiah xiv.9, 54
Isaiah xiv.11, 79, 92
Isaiah xxx.33, 189, 191
Isaiah lvi.10, 179
Isaiah lxvi.24, 10, 78, 79, 87, 88, 92, 173, 190 n. 8, 201, 203, 204
Jonah ii.2, 190
Matt. viii.12, 24, 87, 88, 190 n. 8
Matt. xv.21-8, 178 n. 24
Matt. xvi.19, 214 n. 27
Matt. xxii.13, 190 n. 8
Matt. xxv.41, 13, 67
Mark viii.36, 215 n. 31
Mark viii.44-8, 191
Mark ix.42-3, 194
Mark ix.43, 190 n. 8
Luke xvi.24, 13, 14. 17, 57, 58, 72, 75
Luke xvi.26, 197 n. 29
Luke xxiv.43, 86
Acts x.40-1, 86
Romans i.20, 86 n. 6
Romans ii.15-16, 210
Romans viii.13, 11 n, 11
Romans xiv.23, 214
I Cor. xiii.9, 12
I Cor. xv.52, xviii n. 12
II Cor. xii.2-3, 3
Apoc. xx.9 13
Apoc. xx.14, 58

Apoc. xxi.1, xviii n. 14
Bieniak, Magdalena, 30, 52 n. 9
Boccaccio, Giovanni, 150
Bonaventure, 26, 27 n. 2, 35 n. 26, 54 n. 17, 67 n. 18, 75, 102, 124, 125 n. 18, 133, 148, 151, 154, 158 n. 8, 160, 162, 198 n. 33, 203 n. 1, 222 n. 2, 226 n. 22
Breviloquium, 78 n. 17
Sentences commentary, 1, 66 n. 16, 71-3, 76, 78-82 passim, 89 n. 12, 119, 140 n. 20, 141, 143 n. 26, 152
The Booke of Gostlye Grace, 172-3, 185
Botterill, Steven, 131-2 n. 32
Brown, Peter, 9 n. 5
Bruce, Scott G. xv, 194, 200
Brut, Walter, 45 n. 17
Bynum, Caroline Walker, 81 n. 31, 112, 155 n. 52, 156 n. 1, 162 n. 2, 170 n. 5, 171 n. 7, 184 n. 39, 221-2, 223 n. 5
Calvin, John, 189, 190-1, 192 n. 13, 193 n. 14, 194-7 passim, 200, 214, 215 n. 29
Cameron, Averil, xvii
Camporesi, Piero, xi, 184 n. 39, 193 n. 15, 198 n. 32, 218, 219 n. 39, 220 n. 40
Carruthers, Mary, xiv n. 2, 30 n. 13, 162 n. 23
Casey, John, xi, 27-8, 192 n. 12, 193 n. 15, 219 n. 39
Catherine of Genoa, 27-8, 168-9

Catherine of Siena, 178-82 passim
cats, 100 n. 23, 174-8
Chatton, Walter, 72 n. 31, 225-6 n. 11
Chaucer, Geoffrey, 142 n. 25, 176
Chenu, Marie-Dominique, 161-2, 164 n. 32
Christina of Sint-Truiden (Christina Mirabilis), 170-1
Christine de Pizan, 206-7 n. 11
Cistercian spirituality, 104-6, 118 n. 2, 124-5, 130, 131-3, 148-9, 151, 205 n. 8, 211-12 n. 20, 214
Clark, Elizabeth A., xvii n. 9
Clarke, K. P., 147 n. 32
The Cloud of Unknowing, 104 n. 6, 158 n. 8, 202-3 n. 12
Cogan, Marc, 147 n. 33
Cohen, Esther, 13 n. 16, 169 n. 3, 184 n. 39
Comestor, Peter, 204 n. 7
Conceptual Metaphor Theory, xix, 160 n.16, 166-7 n. 36, 217-18
conscience, 21, 23, 24, 79-80, 82-3, 87-8, 90-1, 95, 102, 171-4, 176 n. 18, 178-82, 194, 196-7 n. 28, 201, 202-18 passim
Cranmer, Thomas, 199 n. 33
Dante Alighieri, 26, 106, 117-24 passim, 127-39 passim, 144-8, 150-2, 154-5, 156-60 passim, 163, 166, 167, 186-7
Davidson, Herbert A., 51-3

Dawes, Sir William, 193-4, 200, 215
Deguileville, Guillaume de, 104-6, 205
  Le Pèlerinage de l'âme, 205-14 passim, 216
  Le Pèlerinage de vie humaine, 104, 106, 210
de Man, Paul, 163-4, 224
demons, 4 n. 8, 14-16, 26-7, 31 n. 15, 54-5 n. 18, 66-8, 74-6, 96-101 passim, 112, 131, 145, 180
  as fallen angels, 67 n. 18, 68, 73, 96, 139
  interaction with humans, 97, 98, 100 n. 23, 101, 113-15, 139-43, 152, 225-6 n. 11
  lacking imagination, 114-15, 159
Derrida, Jacques, xvi n. 5, 224
Descartes, René, 224
Dinzelbacher, Peter, 138 n. 9
Diomedes, 115
Dionysius, Pseudo-, 29, 35, 68, 84 n. 1, 99, 135, 142, 156, 157-60
Dives and Lazarus, 13, 15, 57-8, 72, 163, 197
dogs / hounds, 100 n. 23, 171-2, 174-80, 212
Dominic, St, 113 n. 31
Donne, John, 99
dreams and dreaming, 2-6, 13 n. 17, 16, 31 n. 14, 38-40, 41 n. 4, 42-3, 47, 50-2, 56, 61, 63,

67, 69, 70, 73, 106, 126, 133, 134, 146 n. 31, 149, 153-4, 174, 205 n. 9
Duffy, Eamon, 26-7, 137 n. 7
Durling, Robert M., 148 n. 35
Earthly Paradise, 137 n. 7, 177 n. 22, 186
Easting, Robert, 26 n. 1, 108 n. 14 & n. 17, 137 n. 7, 177 n. 22
Edward VI, King of England, 188 n. 2
Elisabeth of Schönau, 27 n. 3, 182-3
Empyrean Heaven, 9 n. 5, 55 n. 19, 84-5, 131, 143 n. 26
Eriugena, John Scotus, 157 n. 6
Eve, 100, 102, 129, 203, 211
Evodius, 153-4 n. 51
fascinatio (hostile enchantment), 36, 76 n. 9
fire, 9, 47-8, 57-8, 79, 80, 84, 85, 89, 90, 92, 93, 104, 107 n. 13, 108, 120 n. 9, 136, 156-7, 173, 180, 189
  body-fire composite, 14, 19, 76-7, 78, 84, 88, 89
  as element, 10, 85, 96, 98-9 n. 9
  entrapping fire, 76-8, 88, 169
  and the empyrean, 8, 84-5
  hell-fire, material or metaphorical, xii, 8, 10, 11, 13-24 passim, 32, 36-43 passim, 46-7, 54-70 passim,
73, 75-85 passim, 87-8, 90-1, 109, 163, 181-2, 188-9, 190-6 passim
Gallus, Thomas, 157 n. 6, 158, 162, 202-3 n. 2
Gardner, Patrick, 134, 137-9
Gauthier of Bruges, 82, 83 n. 34
Gennadius, 153 n. 51
Geoffroy IV de la Tour Landry, 175-6
Gerson, Jean, 207 n. 11
Gertrude the Great, 171
Gervase of Mont-Saint-Eloi, 82-3
Gibbs, Raymond W., xix n. 16, 227 n. 16
Giles of Rome, 35-6
Gillespie, Vincent, 111 n. 23
Gilson, Étienne, 146 n. 31, 147
Gilson, Simon, 135 n. 3
Giovanni da Serravalle, 119, 122 n. 12, 133
Green, Richard Firth, 178 n. 23
Gregory the Great, 18-19, 21-2, 25, 26, 38, 39, 46, 50, 53, 57, 66, 67, 74, 75, 77, 86 n. 6, 103 n. 4, 107, 107-12 passim, 126, 134, 153, 167, 171, 183, 199
Grosseteste, Robert, 156-8, 162
Gui, Bernard, 112-13
Guido da Pisa, 139 n. 17
Gurevich, Aron, 109-11
Hawkins, Peter S., 131-2 n. 32
Haymo of Halberstadt, 204 n. 7
Heath, Peter, 51, 52

hell
   creatures of, xiii-xv, 10, 79, 80, 85, 88, 90-6 passim, 99-101, 115, 163, 171-81, 200-1, 206-7, 210-14, 217
   darkness of, xii, 89-90, 175-6, 180 n. 28, 190, 192 n. 13
   location, 6, 7, 15, 54-8, 194, 196, 199 n. 38, 198
   post-resurrection, xiv, xv, xviii, 8, 14-15, 27, 65, 66, 78-82, 84-90 passim, 94, 109, 121, 123-4, 130, 182, 196-7 n. 28
Henry of Ghent, 29, 35 n. 26, 44-5, 143 n. 26, 162
Henry of Herford, 106-7
Hildebert of Tours, 204 n. 7
Hildelin of Schönau, 182-3
Hobbes, Thomas, 165, 224
Hoccleve, Thomas, 205 n. 9
Hugh of Balma, 158 n. 8
Hugh of St Victor, 1, 19-24 passim, 28, 39, 46, 53, 73, 77, 103, 107-9, 111, 126-7, 157 n. 6, 204 n. 7, 211
Hugh Ripelin of Strasbourg, 89 n. 12, 94-5
Huizinga, Johan, 165, 186
Humbert of Romans, 179 n. 25
imagination
   compositive imagination, 34-5, 47 n. 21, 49-50, 51, 52-3, 62-4, 68 n. 20, 114-16, 147, 166, 226
   l'imaginaire, 47

imaginative vision, 2-4, 64, 66, 69-70, 98-9, 108, 115, 126, 135, 153 n. 51
virtus / vis imaginativa, 39, 63, 64, 69, 115, 151-2, 159
impassibilitas (inability to change), 21, 88, 94, 121, 218 n. 37
Innocent III, Pope, 204 n. 7
Isaac of Stella, 105 n. 10, 131, 132 n. 33, 149
Isidore of Seville, 96, 97, 139-40, 199
Jacob, 190
Jean de Meun, 206-7
John XXII, Pope, 106-7
John Paul II, Pope, 219-20
John the Saracen, 157 n. 6
Johnson, Ian, 30 n. 13, 110 n. 23
Johnson, Mark, 161, 164-5, 166, 188 n. 1, 224
Jonah, 189-90
Julian of Toledo, 17, 18, 24, 75
Karnes, Michelle, 30 n. 13, 72 n. 32
Kitzler, Petr, 57
Kyteler, Alice, 177-8 n. 23
Lakoff, George, xviii-ix, 166, 224
Langland, William, 104, 150 n. 41, 204 n. 17, 224
Le Goff, Jacques, 26 n. 1, 26-7 n. 2, 27 n. 3, 40 n. 3, 45-8, 49, 54 n. 17, 59, 76 n. 9, 109-11, 137 n. 7
Lewis, C. S., 211-12 n. 20
Lindhelm, Nancy, 156 n. 1

literal / corporeal sense of Scripture, 10-12 passim, 19, 28-9, 57, 85, 86-8, 160-2, 164, 190, 134 n. 14, 195-6, 200
literal (*proprie*) language, 11, 12, 86, 164
Locke, John, 164, 224
Lodge, David, 219
Lombard, Peter, xviii n. 12, 1, 12, 16-19 passim, 24-5, 55 n. 19, 56, 60-6 passim, 75-6, 85 n. 2, 96-7, 128-9, 140
Luther, Martin, 189-90, 192-7 passim
Lydgate, John, 205 n. 19, 211 n. 20
Maimonides, 98
Malleus maleficarum, 178 n. 23
Marius, Richard, 189 n. 4
Marshall, Peter, 188, 192 n. 12 & n. 13, 199 n. 38
Mary, Blessed Virgin, xviii, 107, 177
Masseron, Alexandre, 131 n. 32
Matelda (in *Purgatorio* XXVIII), 186-7
Matsuda, Takami, 27 n. 4, 169 n. 3
Matthew of Aquasparta, 82
McAvoy, Liz Herbert, 177-8
McCann, Daniel, xiii-iv n. 12
McGinn, Bernard, 124-5 n. 18, 149
McGuire, Brian Patrick, 109 n. 21

Mechthild of Hackeborn, 167, 171-7, 183-7, 212-13
Mechthild of Magdeburg, 171, 184 n. 30
memory, xiii-iv n. 2, 2-3, 30 n. 13, 50, 52 n. 9, 69, 72, 122-4, 129, 132, 162, 193 n. 14, 213-14
mental language, 142-3, 224 n. 8, 225-6 n. 11.
Mews, Constant, 125 n. 18, 131 n. 30, 150 n. 42
Michot, Jean R., 51, 52
Milton, John, 100-1, 102
Minnis, Alastair, 28 n. 6, 30 n. 13, 44 n. 15, 45 n. 17, 71 n. 29, 110 n. 23, 137 n. 7, 143 n. 26, 158 n. 81, 161 n. 21, 163 n. 25, 165 n. 32, 182 n. 34, 184 n. 38, 198 n. 33, 203 n. 2, 223 n. 6, 226 n. 12.
Mohler, R. Albert, 219 n. 40, 222 n. 41
The Monk of Eynsham, xiv-xv, 49, 106
Mowbray, Donald, 53-4, 74, 89, 130, 183 n. 34, 222 n. 4, 223
Murray, Alexander, 58-9, 100 n. 23
Nardi, Bruno, 118 n. 2, 122 n. 13, 128 n. 25
Nemerov, Howard, 157 n. 1
Newman, Barbara, 2 n. 3, 27, 168, 179, 185-6 n. 42, 187 n. 46
Niederbacher, Bruno, 4

Nievergelt, Marco, 105, 106 n. 11, 205 n. 8
Norton, Thomas, 104 n. 6
Oberman, Heiko, 189 n. 4
The Orcherd of Syon, 179-82 passim
Oresme, Nicole, 36
Origen, 41 n. 8, 53, 183
Ortony, Andrew, 7 n. 15, 157
Orwell, George, 225
Ovid, 114
parable, 29, 111, 195, 197
paradise, creations of, 221
  Eden, 26, 102
  the *patria*, xv, 26, 144
Paris condemnations (1270 and 1277), 36-7, 80
Pasulka, Diana Walsh, 54-5 n. 18
Patrick of Ireland, Pseudo-, 204 n. 7
Paul, St, xiv, 3, 4, 210
Pegis, Anton C., 70 n. 28, 123-4
Les Peines de purgatorie, 94, 95
Perkins, William, 214-16
Peter of Tarantasia (Pope Innocent V), 128 n. 24
Peter of Trabibus, 151 n. 43
Pharaoh, 3, 6
Picasso, Pablo, 225-6 n. 11
Pietro Alighieri, 127-8, 130, 133, 136, 146 n. 31
Plato and Neoplatonism, 3-4, 29, 30, 32, 33, 35, 40, 50, 63, 81, 84 n. 1, 125 n. 18, 130, 150, 224

metaphoras platonicas, 40
Pliny, 9
The Prick of Conscience, 90 n. 13, 91 n. 15, 92-5, 99, 101, 137 n. 7, 139, 169 n. 3, 223 n. 5, 226
Prosper of Aquitaine, 199
purgatory, xiv, xv, 26-7, 46, 49, 54 n. 17, 54-5 n. 18, 55, 106, 109 n. 21, 110-11, 113, 117, 121, 134, 136-7, 153, 168-74 passim, 177, 188, 201, 210, 216, 218, 226 n. 15
Pythagoras, 64
Quistorp, Heinrich, 190 n. 7, 196-7 n. 28, 215 n. 29
Rasmussen, Tarald, 192 n. 12
redundantia (overflow), 81, 88, 89
Reparatus, 119
resurrected body, 8-9, 16, 86, 88, 104, 121, 129, 136, 148, 155, 198 n. 33, 224, 225 n. 11
Resurrection, General, xiv, xv, xvii n. 9, xviii, 8, 14, 15, 20, 21, 27, 54, 60, 65, 66, 78 n. 17, 79, 80, 81, 84-9 passim, 94, 109, 121-3 passim, 128 n. 24, 196-7 n. 28, 222 n. 3
A Revelation of Purgatory (fifteenth-century Middle English tract), 174-8
Reynolds, Philip L., 86 n. 5
Richard of Middleton, 82, 83 n. 34, 89-90 n. 12, 114, 128 n. 24
Richards, I. A., xvi

Ricoeur, Paul, xvi, xviii, 7 n. 15, 51, 224
Le Roman de la Rose, 206-7, 211-12 n. 20
Romanus (Dominican friar), 112-13
Roncarati, Raffaella, 30, 51 n. 9
salamander, 9, 47-8, 85
Samson, 183
Sawles Warde, xii-iv, 58, 89-90, 92
Schmidt, A. V. C., 104 n. 5, 150 n. 41
Shakespeare, William, xii, 208
Shelley, Percy Bysshe, 186-7
Sicardus of Cremona, 204 n. 7
similitudo corporis (mental image / likeness of human body), 2, 5-7, 15, 18 n. 1, 30-1, 39, 56, 65, 67-8, 78, 102, 105 n. 10, 125-7, 136, 154 n. 51, 222 n. 3
snakes and serpents, 90, 100, 106, 167, 211, 212
Solomon, 144, 183
soul
    disembodied / separated, xiv, 2-3 n. 4, 5-7, 10-32 passim, 36-7, 39-41, 46-7, 50-1, 53, 56, 63-74 passim, 134, 137, 143-9 passim, 152-3, 163, 165-6, 167, 169, 199 n. 37
    re-embodied (following Resurrection), xiv, 8, 16, 26, 84-9, 121, 144-5, 154, 225-6 n. 11
    soul-body composite / relationship, 14, 19, 30-2, 35, 39, 56, 64, 69-72 passim, 76, 77 n. 14, 88, 89, 127, 129, 145-6, 221
    transmigration of, 53 n. 13, 64, 130
Spencer, Mark K., 71 n. 29
Spinoza, Baruch, 59
De spiritu et anima, 42 n. 9, 105 n. 10, 124-33 passim, 149-50, 154, 213 n. 24
De spiritu Guidonis ('Gast of Gy'), xiv-xv, 106
spiritual
    deformity, 208-14 passim
    manifestation of, 134-67 passim
    sense of Scripture, 28, 58, 79, 86
    substance / entities, xvi, 5, 10, 14, 16 n. 22, 19, 20, 24, 28, 29, 38, 39, 55, 64, 65, 68, 76-8, 80, 84, 87, 88, 102-16 passim, 236, 139-43 passim, 222 n. 3
    vision, 2-3, 6
Spurgeon, Charles Haddon, 193 n. 14
Statius, 117, 120, 128-9, 145, 147, 151, 156 n. 1
Stephen of Bourbon, 43 n. 12
St Patrick's Purgatory, xiv-xv, 54-5 n. 18, 106, 108
Tractatus de purgatorio sancti Patricii, 107-9 passim, 167

Suarez-Nani, Tiziana, 54-5, 143 n. 26
Swift, Jonathan, 224-5
Swinden, Tobias, 194-20 passim, 215-17 passim, 224
synderesis, 202-11 passim, 213, 216
Teske, Roland J., 50 n. 3, 122 n. 13
Tertullian, 56-7
Thomas of Cantimpré, 100 n. 23, 170, 171 n. 6
Thomas of Perseigne, 204 n. 7
Tophet, 191
Trajan, 183
Trevisa, John, 140-1
Turner, Denys, 122-3
Venturi, P. Pompeo, 119-20
Vico, Giambattista, 224
Vincent of Beauvais, 85 n. 2, 127, 139 n. 18
Virgil, 114, 117, 132 n. 32, 146-7
Visio Pauli, xiv, xv n. 3
Visio Thurkilli, xiv, xv n. 3, 49, 106-7
Visio Tnugdali, xiv, xv n. 3, 49, 106-7
Visio Wettini, 108 n. 15
Walker, D. P., 43 n. 13, 44 n. 14, 59 n. 27, 192 n. 12
Watson, Nicholas, 47 n. 21
Webb, Heather, 136-7 n. 7
Wei, Ian P., 37 n. 31, 40 n. 4, 41 n. 6, 43-4 n. 14, 45 n. 18, 111 n. 24, 168 n. 3, 182 n. 32

William of Auvergne, 1-2, 37, 38-48 passim, 50, 54 n. 17, 61, 62, 70, 126-7, 181 n. 32
William of Ockham, 72 n. 31, 143 n. 26, 225 n. 11
William of St Thierry, 103 n. 10, 131, 132, 178 n. 24,
Wittgenstein, Ludwig, 164, 224
Wolfson, Harry, 34 n. 25
worm of conscience, 23, 24, 79, 80, 82, 87, 90, 92, 95, 171, 174, 176 n. 18, 177, 180, 181 n. 30, 194, 203, 205
see also conscience
worm(s) of hell, xii, xiv, 10-11, 12, 23, 32, 58, 78-83 passim, 85, 87-8, 91, 93, 100-1, 102, 109, 163, 167, 171-4, 177, 190-2, 198-9, 200-1, 203, 204-18 passim
Yeats, W. B., 133
Zaleski, Carol, 102-3, 108 n. 14 & n. 16, 166
Zwingli, Ulrich, 193 n. 14

www.ingramcontent.com/pod-product-compliance
Lightning Source LLC
Chambersburg PA
CBHW030529230426
43665CB00010B/814